CONTENTS

W0006242

PREFACE

Until now there has not been an Aris and Phillips edition of any part of Herodotus' *Histories*. I have made this start with book V, where after the varied preliminaries in books I–IV Herodotus begins (though still with digressions large and small) to provide a continuous narrative from the late sixth century BC to the end of the Persian Wars in 479. I thank Prof. A. H. Sommerstein for inviting me to embark on this project, and for reading and helping me to improve what I first produced; and Prof. A. J. Woodman for perceptively reading and commenting on this edition as he did on my editions of Thucydides. My thanks also to Prof. J. S. Rusten for helping me to an on-line Greek text which I was able to modify, and to all involved in the production of this book.

The division of Herodotus' work into nine books is not his own (cf. Introduction, pp. 1–2); and, whereas the other books end with a natural break in the subject-matter, book V ends (presumably in order to obtain books of approximately equal length) very unnaturally in the middle of the Ionian Revolt: I hope to follow this edition with an edition of book VI, which continues the narrative to the battle of Marathon in 490.

In this edition the Greek text is my own in so far as I have made up my own mind on all the substantial matters which seemed to call for a decision. However, as regards forms of words and names it is exceptionally difficult to decide what Herodotus' own usage will have been (cf. Introduction, p. 23), and this is not an area in which I can claim particular expertise, so here I have followed the new Oxford Text of N. G. Wilson. In the translation I have seen it as my primary task to express the meaning accurately in good English; sometimes that has led me to vary Herodotus' sentence structure; where I could reasonably use the same English word for the same Greek word and a different English word for a different Greek word I have done so, but that has not always been possible. In the introduction and commentary I

have been particularly but not exclusively concerned with the subject-matter: the history which Herodotus narrates, and how and why he narrates it as he does. My debt to previous editors, and particularly to Prof. S. Hornblower, is much greater than is indicated by my explicit citations of them.

University of Durham
Michaelmas Term 2018   *P. J. R.*

REFERENCES

Ancient authors and their works are in general abbreviated as in the fourth edition of the *Oxford Classical Dictionary*, but I occasionally use a fuller form of reference, and in particular I cite Athenian speeches both by number and by short title. References without indication of author are to Herodotus, and those without indication of book are to book V. A few standard modern works, such as *CAH*, are cited by the abbreviations of the fourth edition of the *Oxford Classical Dictionary*.

The following collections of texts of inscriptions are cited:

IChS	Masson, O., *Les Inscriptions chypriotes syllabiques.* Paris: De Boccard, 1961.
IG	*Inscriptiones Graecae.*
LSCG	Sokolowski, F. *Lois sacrées des cités grecques.* Paris: De Boccard, 1969.
M&L	Meiggs, R. and Lewis, D. M., *A Selection of Greek Historical Inscriptions to the End of the Fifth Century BC.* Oxford UP, 1969; reprinted with addenda 1988.
Milet I. iii	Kawerau, G. and Rehm, A. (eds), *Milet*, I. iii. *Das Delphinion in Milet.* Berlin: Reimer, 1914.
Nomima	van Effenterre, H. and Ruzé, F. (eds), *Nomima: Recueil d'inscriptions politiques et juridiques de l'archaïsme grec.* Rome: École Française de Rome, 1994–95.
O&R	Osborne, R. G. and Rhodes, P. J. *Greek Historical Inscriptions, 478–404 BC* Oxford UP, 2017.
R&O	Rhodes, P. J. and Osborne, R. G. *Greek Historical Inscriptions, 404–323 BC* Oxford UP, 2003; corrected reprint 2007.
SEG	*Supplementum Epigraphicum Graecum.*
*SIG*³	Dittenberger, W. (first ed.), *Sylloge Inscriptionum Graecarum.* Leipzig: Hirzel, ³1915–24.

The following collections of other texts are cited:

FGrH	Jacoby, F., *et al.*, *Die Fragmente der griechischen Historiker*. Berlin: Weidmann → Leiden: Brill, 1926–.
Fornara	Fornara, C. W. *Translated Documents of Greece and Rome*, i. *Archaic Times to the End of the Peloponnesian War*. Cambridge UP, ²1983. [cited here for some texts other than inscriptions]
GGM	Müller, C. W. L. *Geographi Graeci Minores*. Paris: Didot, 1855–61.
PLF	Lobel, E. and Page, D. L. *Poetarum Lesbiorum Fragmenta*. Oxford UP, 1955.
PMG	Page, D. L. *Poetae Melici Graeci*. Oxford UP, 1962.
POxy	*Oxyrhynchus Papyri.*
TrGF	Snell, B., *et al.*, *Tragicorum Graecorum Fragmenta*. Göttingen: Vandenhoeck and Ruprecht, 1971–2004.
Vorsokr.	Diels, H., rev. Kranz., W. *Die Fragmente der Vorsokratiker*. Berlin: Weidmann, ⁶1951.
West	West, M. L. *Iambi et Elegi Graeci ante Alexandrum Cantati*. Oxford UP, ²1989–92.

Otherwise, details are given in the Bibliography of modern books which are cited frequently (with abbreviations for some which are cited very frequently), and at the point of citation of modern books which are cited occasionally. Details of articles in periodicals are given at the point of citation. The titles of periodicals are given as follows: superior figures (e.g. CQ^2) denote the second and subsequent series.

Einz.	Einzelschriften
*GRB*Mon	*Greek, Roman and Byzantine* Monographs
Supp.	Supplement

Achaemenid History	*Achaemenid History*
AJA	*American Journal of Archaeology*
AJP	*American Journal of Philology*
AMI	*Archäologusche Mitteilingen aus Iran*
Archeologija	*Archeologija*
BICS	*Bulletin of the Institute of Classical Studies* (London)

BPW	*Berliner Philologische Wochenschrift*
BSA	*Annual of the British School at Athens*
Chiron	*Chiron*
CP	*Classical Philology*
CQ	*Classical Quarterly*
CR	*Classical Review*
Eranos	*Eranos*
G&R	*Greece and Rome*
GRBS	*Greek, Roman and Byzantine Studies*
Hesperia	*Hesperia*
Historia	*Historia*
HSCP	*Harvard Studies in Classical Philology*
Iran	*Iran*
JARCE	*Journal of the American Research Center in Egypt*
JHS	*Journal of Hellenic Studies*
JRS	*Journal of Roman Studies*
Kadmos	*Kadmos*
Mem. Acc. Naz. Linc.	*Memorie dell' Accademia nazionale dei Lincei, Classe di scienze morali, storiche e filologiche*
Mnemosyne	*Mnemosyne*
N. Clio	*La Nouvelle Clio*
PCPS	*Proceedings of the Cambridge Philological Society*
Phoenix	*Phoenix*
RDAC	*Report of the Department of Antiquities, Cyprus*
REA	*Revue des Études Anciennes*
REG	*Revue des Études Grecques*
Syll. Class.	*Syllecta Classica*
TAPA	*Transactions of the American Philological Association*
Tyche	*Tyche*
ZPE	*Zeitschrift für Papyrologie und Epigraphik*

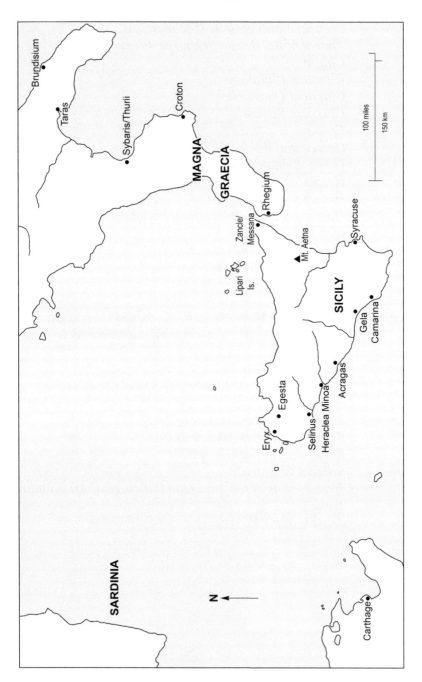

Map 1. Sicily and Southern Italy

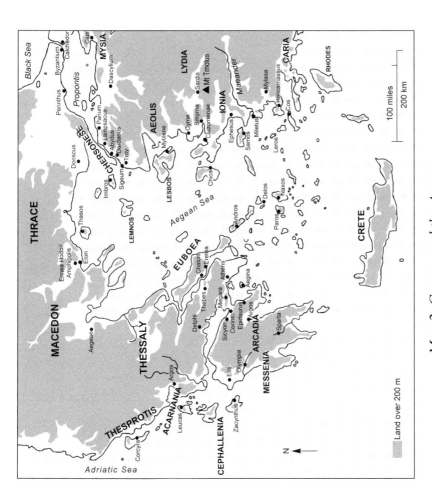

Map 2. Greece and the Aegean

Map 3. The Near East

INTRODUCTION

1. Herodotus and his History

Herodotus

The most detailed account of Herodotus' life is the entry in the tenth-century lexicon known as *Suda*:

> Λύξου καὶ Δρυοῦς, Ἁλικαρνασσεύς, τῶν ἐπιφανῶν, καὶ ἀδελφὸν ἐσχηκὼς Θεόδωρον. μετέστη δ᾽ ἐν Σάμῳ διὰ Λύγδαμιν τὸν ἀπὸ Ἀρτεμισίας τρίτον τύραννον γενόμενον Ἁλικαρνασσοῦ· Πισίνδηλις γὰρ ἦν υἱὸς Ἀρτεμισίας, τοῦ δὲ Πισινδήλιδος Λύγδαμις. ἐν οὖν τῇ Σάμῳ καὶ τὴν Ἰάδα ἠσκήθη διάλεκτον καὶ ἔγραψεν ἱστορίαν ἐν βιβλίοις θ´, ἀρξάμενος ἀπὸ Κύρου τοῦ Πέρσου καὶ Κανδαύλου τοῦ Λυδῶν βασιλέως. ἐλθὼν δὲ εἰς Ἁλικαρνασσὸν καὶ τὸν τύραννον ἐξελάσας, ἐπειδὴ ὕστερον εἶδεν ἑαυτὸν φθονούμενον ὑπὸ τῶν πολιτῶν, εἰς τὸ Θούριον ἀποικιζόμενον ὑπὸ Ἀθηναίων ἐθελοντὴς ἦλθε, κἀκεῖ τελευτήσας ἐπὶ τῆς ἀγορᾶς τέθαπται· τινὲς δ᾽ ἐν Πέλλαις αὐτὸν τελευτῆσαί φασιν. ἐπιγράφονται δὲ οἱ λόγοι αὐτοῦ Μοῦσαι.
> [*There follows a quotation about Herodotus from Julian the Apostate.*]

(*Suda* η 536 Adler Ἡρόδοτος)

Son of Lyxus and Dryo: a Halicarnassian, one of the distinguished men, and he had a brother Theodorus. He migrated to Samos on account of Lygdamis, the third tyrant of Halicarnassus after Artemisia: for Pisindelis was son of Artemisia and Lygdamis was son of Pisindelis. In Samos he practised the Ionian dialect, and he wrote a history in 9 books, beginning from Cyrus the Persian and Candaules the king of Lydia. He went to Halicarnassus and expelled the tyrant, but later when he saw that he was envied by the citizens he went as a volunteer to Thurium which was being colonised by the Athenians, and he died there and is buried in the agora; but some say that he died in Pella. His books bear the Muses as titles.

The division of his work into nine books seems to have been made in the hellenistic period (there is a citation by book number in the Lindian Chronicle of 99 BC, *FGrH* 532 C 29, and the nine books are mentioned by Diod. Sic. XI. 37. 6). The use of the nine Muses to denote the nine books is first explicitly attested in the second century AD by Lucian, *Her.* 1 and *De Hist. Conscrib.* 42 (cf. *Anth. Pal.* IX. 160); book V is *Terpsichore*. Whereas the other books end at a natural break in the subject-matter, the end of book V has been placed unnaturally, presumably in order to obtain books of approximately equal length: in the middle of the Ionian Revolt, but at the point where its originator Aristagoras has departed to Myrcinus in Thrace, and immediately before Histiaeus reappears in Asia Minor. The division of the books into chapters was first made by G. Jungermann in his edition of 1608, with long speeches assigned to a single chapter which was divided into sections labelled with Greek letters (in book V, see 92). The division of the chapters into numbered sections seems to have been first made by K. Hude in his Oxford Text of 1908 (and not all subsequent editions have used that division).

A birth date of fifty-three years before the beginning of the Peloponnesian War, i.e. *c.* 484, is given by Gell. *N.A.* XV. 23, and should be at least approximately correct, since the latest events mentioned by Herodotus occurred in 431–430 (cf. below).[1] *Suda* π 248 Adler Πανύασις states that Herodotus was related to the poet Panyassis, who lived in the 78th Olympiad (468–464) and was put to death by the tyrant Lygdamis. Lygdamis is presumably the same man as the Lygdamis of a 'meeting of the Halicarnassians and Salmacians and Lygdamis' which enacted a law about disputed property about the middle of the fifth century (O&R 132: one of the men named in it is a son of a Panyassis). Evidently Herodotus belonged to a prominent family in Halicarnassus. That he spent some time in Samos is credible, in view of his interest in and knowledge of the island (see esp. III. 60), but inscriptions including the one cited above show

---

1   However, it may well be based simply on the assumption that his *akme* was at the age of forty and coincided with the foundation of Thurii (cf next note): e.g. Gould, *Herodotus*, 17; D. Asheri, in Asheri *et al.*, 5.

that Dorian Halicarnassus (whose inhabitants display a mixture of Greek, Carian and occasionally Persian names) used the eastern Ionic dialect, so Samos does not need to be invoked to explain his use of that. That he went to and died at Thurii[2] is supported by a quotation of I. *praef.* in Arist. *Rh.* III. 1409 A 28 which calls him Herodotus not of Halicarnassus but of Thurii, and by an epitaph from there quoted by Steph. Byz. θ 55 Billerbeck and Zubler Θούριοι.

Whether or not he went to live in Thurii, at its foundation or later, he travelled widely. He claims to have been to Thebes (59), Sparta (III. 55. 2) and Zacynthus (IV. 195. 2), and probably visited Dodona (II. 55); he went to the north of the Black Sea (IV. 81); in the south and east he went to Egypt (e.g. II. 29. 1, 143, III. 12. 4), from there to Tyre in Phoenicia (II. 44. 1), to Palestine (II. 106. 1) and perhaps to Babylon (I. 193–4); from his attribution of information to sources (on which cf. pp. 9–13, below), in the west he went perhaps to Cyrene (IV. 154. 1); and in Italy to Metapontium (IV. 15), and not only to Sybaris → Thurii but also to its rival Croton (V. 43–6).

There are references to his giving recitals of his work in various places, and it is inherently likely that he did give such recitals, even if the particular stories are problematic; Thucydides' claim to have omitted a fabulous element, and to have written 'a possession for all time rather than a prize composition for a single hearing' (Thuc. I. 22. 4), may well be aimed at Herodotus. *Suda* θ 414 Adler Θουκυδίδης alleges that the young Thucydides heard Herodotus giving a recitation at Olympia and was moved to tears, and that Herodotus congratulated Thucydides' father on a son with a passion for learning; and Lucian, *Her.* 1–2 claims that he judged it more effective to give recitations at Olympia than in individual cities. Honour from the council for a recitation in Athens was dated 446/5 or 445/4 by Eusebius (Euseb. *Chron.* Armenian version p. 193 Karst / Jer. *Chron.* p. 113 Helm[2]), cf. reports of an award of (the incredibly large sum of) 10 talents according to Diyllus, *FGrH* 73 F 3 *ap.* Plut. *De Her. Mal.* 862 B, of his

---

2   The Athenians refounded what had been Sybaris, in southern Italy, under that name, perhaps *c.* 444/3 (cf. Rhodes, *A History of the Classical Greek World, 478–323 BC*[2], 74).

failure to obtain money or permission to talk to young men in Thebes, Plut. *De Her. Mal.* 864 D, and of his writing unfavourably of the Corinthians in the Persian Wars because they refused to pay him, Dio Chrys. *Or.* XXXVII. *Corinthian* 7. Resemblances between passages in Herodotus and passages in the tragedies of the Athenian Sophocles (particularly III. 119. 6 with *Ant.* 905–12, perhaps late 440s,[3] and II. 35. 2 with *O.C.* 337–41, produced posthumously in 401[4]) suggest that the two knew each other, and Plut. *An Seni* 785 B cites an epigram said to have been written for Herodotus by Sophocles.

While Herodotus' main narrative ends in 479, he refers on various occasions to later events,[5] the latest of which are the Theban attack on Plataea in 431 (VII. 233. 2 with Thuc. II. 2–6), the Spartans' sparing of Decelea when they invaded Attica in and after 431 (IX. 73. 3), the Athenians' expulsion of the Aeginetans in 431 (VI. 91. 1 with Thuc. II. 27), Athens' killing of Peloponnesian envoys sent to the Persians in 430 (VII. 137. 3, with Thuc. II. 67), and, not precisely datable, the death of Xerxes' widow Amestris (VII. 114. 2). The fact that Herodotus does not mention at VI. 91. 1 that the Aeginetans who after their expulsion settled in Thyrea were attacked and killed by the Athenians in 424 (Thuc. IV. 56. 2–57. 4) has suggested to most scholars that he was dead or had ceased writing by then.[6] A minority of scholars have argued that he remained alive and active later: How and Wells wrote of this as a view which 'is now generally given up', but it has had more recent champions,[7] though I remain unconvinced. However, it

---

3 Sometimes considered a later interpolation, but it was in the text known to Arist. *Rh.* III. 1417 A 29–33.

4 For other possibilities see How and Wells, i. 7 n. 3.

5 See Macan, *Herodotus, The Seventh, Eighth and Ninth Books*, I. i, pp. li–liii; How and Wells, i. 51.

6 E.g. How and Wells, i. 9.

7 E.g. Fornara, *Herodotus*, 43 n. 13, 'Evidence for the Date of Herodotus' Publication', *JHS* 91 (1971), 25–34, 'Herodotus' Knowledge of the Archidamian War', *Hermes* 109 (1981), 149–56 (*c.* 414); most recently, E. K. Irwin, 'The Hybris of Theseus and the Date of the Histories', in K. Ruffing and B. Dunsch (eds), *Source References in Herodotus – Herodotus' Sources: Conference in Memoriam Detlev Fehling* (Wiesbaden: Harrassowitz, 2013), 7–93, and 'The End of the *Histories* and the End of the Atheno-Peloponnesian Wars', in Harrison and Irwin (eds),

must be granted, in view of the nature of ancient 'publication', that the parody of I. 1. 1–5. 3 in Ar. *Ach.* 524–9 does not suffice to prove that the work had been finished and definitively published when that play was performed in 425.

His History

Herodotus has given us a lengthy work with a wide-ranging theme:

Ἡροδότου Ἁλικαρνησσέος ἱστορίης ἀπόδειξις ἥδε, ὡς μήτε τὰ γενόμενα ἐξ ἀνθρώπων τῷ χρόνῳ ἐξίτηλα γένηται, μήτε ἔργα μεγάλα τε καὶ θωμαστά, τὰ μὲν Ἕλλησι, τὰ δὲ βαρβάροισι ἀποδεχθέντα, ἀκλεᾶ γένηται, τά τε ἄλλα καὶ δι' ἣν αἰτίην ἐπολέμησαν ἀλλήλοισι.

(I. *praef.*)

This is the presentation of the enquiry of Herodotus of Halicarnassus, so that the happenings of men should not be obliterated by time, and that great and wonderful deeds, some presented by the Greeks and some by the barbarians, should not lose their renown, in general and in particular the reason for which they went to war against each other.

As a result of this preface *historia*, and its plural *historiai*, came to mean 'history', but to Herodotus himself it was not yet a technical term but will have meant simply an 'enquiry' – into the wonderful deeds of the past, and in particular into the great conflict between the Greeks and the Persians which reached its climax in the wars of 490 and 480–479, which occurred about the time when he was born (cf. above). But his interest was not limited to wonderful deeds, but also embraced places, peoples and customs. In book V we have an account of the Thracians and the people to the north of them (3–10), the Paeonian woman viewed by Darius (12–13) and those who live on Lake Prasias (16); Aristagoras' attempt to win the support of Sparta includes an account of the various peoples between the Aegean and Susa (49. 4–7).

In his history he regards the conflict as being between Europe and Asia (cf. on 106. 1); and he makes a false beginning in the Greeks' legendary past, with stories of conflicts between Greeks and various

---

Interpreting Herodotus, 279–334 (even later: Herodotus responding to Thucydides).

Asiatics involving the seizure of women (I. 1. 1–5. 3); but he then dismisses that and makes a fresh start in the comparatively recent past:

> ἐγὼ δὲ περὶ μὲν τούτων οὐκ ἔρχομαι ἐρέων ὡς οὕτως ἢ ἄλλως κως ταῦτα ἐγένετο· τὸν δὲ οἶδα αὐτὸς πρῶτον ὑπάρξαντα ἀδίκων ἔργων ἐς τοὺς Ἕλληνας, τοῦτον σημήνας προβήσομαι ἐς τὸ πρόσω τοῦ λόγου, ὁμοίως σμικρὰ καὶ μεγάλα ἄστεα ἀνθρώπων ἐπεξιών.

(I. 5. 3)

But concerning these matters I shall not go on to say that these things happened in this way or in some other way. But as for the man who is the first whom I know to have begun unjust deeds against the Greeks, I shall indicate him and then proceed forwards with my account, ranging over small and great cities of men alike.

'The first whom I know' is a favourite expression of Herodotus, and tends to be used to separate from what went before a historical period beginning about the middle of the sixth century, as far back as the oldest men whom he met will have been able to remember.[8] In this case, 'the first whom I know to have begun unjust deeds against the Greeks' was the last Lydian king, Croesus, who is further characterised as 'the first whom we know to have overcome some of the Greeks to the point of paying tribute and to have made others his friends' (I. 6. 1–2) – but Herodotus then backtracks to the replacement of the Heraclid dynasty by the Mermnad dynasty to which Creosus belonged (I. 7–13), and gives an account of each of the Mermnad kings, all of whom campaigned against the Greeks of Asia Minor (I. 14–94 with digressions).

That digression ends with the conquest of the Lydian kingdom by the Persians under Cyrus; and thereafter the main thread of Herodotus' narrative is devoted to the Greeks and the Persians (in what follows, digressions from the main thread of the narrative are indented):

I. 95–140   The Medes and the rise of the Persians
I. 141–76   Persia's conquest of the Asiatic Greeks
I. 177–216   Cyrus' reign after the conquest of Lydia

---

8   See B. Shimron, 'πρῶτος τῶν ἡμεῖς ἴδμεν', *Eranos* 71 (1973), 45–51.

---

9 For a more detailed analysis of the contents of book V see p. 44.

How Herodotus went about writing this complex work we do not
know. It is possible that passages with allusions to the events of 431–
430 represent revisions of material originally written earlier. The work

is incomplete, in so far as there are unfulfilled promises, of a *logos* which would deal with the history of Assyria (I. 106. 2, 184) and of later *logoi* which would deal with the death of Ephialtes the traitor (VII. 213. 3), and mention of a Median revolt against Darius (I. 130. 2), which might have been dealt with in book III but is not. However, the ending of the work with the campaign of Mycale and its aftermath (IX. 90–121), and finally a harking back to Cyrus (IX. 122), looks like a planned ending, and there is no reason to think that Herodotus ever intended to continue his narrative beyond that.[10]

Sources

Herodotus obtained his material primarily by visiting places in which he was interested, talking to people and seeing things. His informants will largely have been men of similar social standing to himself, telling him sometimes folk tales, sometimes things preserved in the traditions of their own families. As noted above, he seems to draw a line about the middle of the sixth century, as far back as the oldest people he met will themselves have remembered. He frequently gives divergent accounts from different sources, sometimes expressing an opinion but at other times leaving a matter open (Thucydides later was far more inclined to give only the version which he believed and to expect readers to accept that on his authority). Thus in V. 10 he reports the claim that it is impossible to venture north of the Danube because of bees, but he thinks that bees are intolerant of cold and it is the cold which makes it impossible to venture further north. On the war between Sybaris and Croton (44–5) he cites the accounts of each side and the evidence with which they support their accounts, and concludes, 'That is the evidence cited by each of them, and it is possible to go along with whichever one finds persuasive' (45. 2).

He distinguishes what he has verified for himself from what is mere hearsay (II. 99. 1). He says that he must report what he is told, but does not have to believe it (II. 123. 1, IV. 195. 2, VII. 152. 3). On the claim that a Phoenician expedition circumnavigated Africa he expresses disbelief but gives as his reason a point which we may think

---

10　But Asheri, in Asheri *et al.*, 10–11, thought that 'at least an epilogue is missing'.

justifies belief, that in part of the voyage the sun was to the north of the sailors (IV. 42–3).

He mentions practices and objects from the past which still survived for him to see, such as 'Land ... in Crotoniate territory, which the descendants of Callias were continuing to cultivate to my time' (45. 2). 'Since long ago the Ionians have called scrolls skins, ... and still in my time many of the barbarians write on skins of that kind' (58. 3). 'I myself saw Cadmean letters in the sanctuary of Apollo Ismenias at Thebes in Boeotia, which in general are like those of the Ionians, carved on three tripods' – and Herodotus proceeds to quote the three texts and to associate each with individuals of the legendary period (59–61). The fetters used to bind Chalcidians captured by the Athenians *c.* 506 'they hung up on the acropolis, and they still survived to my time, hanging from the walls which had been scorched by fire by the Medes, opposite the building which faces west. From the ransom they dedicated a tithe, making a bronze four-horse chariot: that stands on the left as soon as you enter the propylaea on the acropolis' – and he then quotes the epigram inscribed on it (77. 3–4).[11] On account of an episode in the past 'Argive and Aeginetan women, since that time, in contention against the Athenian women have continued to my time to wear brooches with longer pins than before then' (88. 3). On account of an episode in the Cyprian part of the Ionian Revolt an oracle advised the people of Amathus to 'sacrifice to Onesilus as a hero every year. ... The Amathusians continued to do that to my time' (114. 2–115. 1).

However, problems have been found in Herodotus' citations. With regular neatness, as with Sybaris and Croton in 44–5, stories to the credit of the different parties are attributed to people from those parties (not further identified): are these authentic attributions or are they pure invention, a literary device to give an impression of authoritativeness?[12] There are cases in which what Herodotus claims

11   Herodotus' location of the chariot is hard to reconicle with Paus. I. 28. 2, but it may have been moved.

12   This view was expressed sometimes in the nineteenth century, and in the twentieth century by Fehling, *Die Quellenangaben bei Herodot*, trans. J. G. Howie as *Herodotus and His 'Sources'*.

to have seen cannot in reality have existed. At Exampaeus, to the north of the Black Sea, Herodotus claims to have been shown a bronze bowl with a capacity of 600 amphorae, six fingers thick (IV. 81. 2–4): in modern terms the capacity would be up to 4,400 imp. gallons (20,000 litres), and the thickness 4½–5 inches (110–30 mm.), and it has been estimated that the height would have been 4–9.5 m (13–30 ft) and the weight more than 7 tonnes (or tons).[13] Are we here too dealing with pure invention?[14]

We should avoid both extreme scepticism and extreme credulity.[15] Probably Herodotus wrote what he honestly thought he remembered, but his memory may on occasions have been exaggerated or otherwise distorted, and he may have assumed that a piece of information had come to him from the obvious source. There is no indication that, while he noticed the odd word (e.g. 'The Ligyes who live beyond Massalia call salesmen *sigynnai*, but the Cyprians give the name to spears', 9. 3), he knew any language other than Greek; but he had access to information about the Persians as well as about the Greeks, and there were bilingual secretaries in Persian service.[16] It has often been remarked that, of the six Persian fellow-conspirators of Darius after the death of Cambyses, Darius' Behistun Inscription shows that Herodotus had five right and his sixth was an important man at

---

13   Height and weight K. K. Marčenko and O. M. Ščeglov, *Archeologija* 67 (1989), 117–21 (not accessible to me: cited by A. Corcella, in Asheri *et al.*, 640–41).

14   O. K. Armayor, 'Did Herodotus Ever Go to the Black Sea?', *HSCP* 82 (1978), 45–62; cf. his 'Herodotus' Catalogues of the Persian Empire in the Light of the Monuments and the Greek Literary Tradition', *TAPA* 108 (1978), 1–9; 'Sesostris and Herodotus' Autopsy of Thrace, Colchis, Inland Asia Minor and the Levant', *HSCP* 84 (1980), 51–74; 'Did Herodotus Ever Go to Egypt?', *JARCE* 15 (1980), 59–71; *Herodotus' Autopsy of the Fayoum: Lake Moeris and the Labyrinth of Egypt* (Amsterdam: Gieben, 1985).

15   The most vigorous defence of Herodotus' veracity is W. K. Pritchett, *The Liar School of Herodotos* (Amsterdam: Gieben, 1993). For a more nuanced response see G. S. Shrimpton with K. M. Gillis, *History and Memory in Ancient Greece* (McGill–Queen's UP, 1997), 229–65.

16   See D. M. Lewis, *Sparta and Persia* (Leiden: Brill for U. of Cincinnati, 1977), 14. Herodotus mentions interpreters in several places, including I. 86. 4, III. 38. 4, 140. 3.

the time, whereas Ctesias, who denigrated Herodotus, had only one right.[17] Yet in connection with the same episode Herodotus insists on the authenticity of a debate among the conspirators over democracy, oligarchy and monarchy, when the only question which will have arisen among the Persians in 522 was who the next King should be, and his debate is clearly a product of Greece in his own time.[18] D. Asheri has suggested, 'Herodotus knew very well that the empire had undergone a radical change after a severe crisis; he therefore tried to understand the phenomenon within the limits of his own frame of reference: the constitutional changes of the Greek *poleis*'.[19]

As in some of the examples given above, Herodotus sometimes cites inscriptions; but he did not use them as documents in the sense in which a modern historian might do so, and he by no means always cites an inscription where he usefully could have done. Commonly, reference to an inscription has come to Herodotus with a story, as something mentioned by an informant to support the story, and he has tended to accept the inscription and its interpretation fairly uncritically.[20] There will also have been documents of some kind behind other material, such as the account of the Royal Road from Ephesus and Sardis to Susa (52–4), but that does not necessarily mean that Herodotus derived his information directly from the documents. The tripods at Thebes in 'Cadmean letters', if they in any way resembled Ionian inscriptions, must have been inscribed in alphabetic Greek, and must therefore be not earlier than the eighth century, but

---

17   Hdt. III. 70 (Aspathines was Darius' bow-bearer – for that position see on 105. 1 – but was not one of the seven); Ctesias *FGrH* 688 F 13. 16 (Hydarnes was one of the seven), his disagreements with Herodotus, 688 T 8; Behistun Inscription, e.g. A. Kuhrt, *The Persian Empire*, i. 141–58, §68.

18   III. 80–3; authenticity III. 80. 1, VI. 43. 3. Among recent discussions see C. B. R. Pelling, 'Speech and Action: Herodotus' Debate on the Constitutions', *PCPS* [2]48 (2002), 123–58.

19   Asheri, in Asheri *et al.*, 471–73.

20   On Herodotus and inscriptions see S. R. West, 'Herodotus' Epigraphical Interests' CQ^2 35 (1985), 278–305 (more sceptical than I am); R. G. Osborne, 'Archaic Greek History', in *Brill's Companion*, 497–520 at 510–13; Rhodes, 'Documents and the Greek Historians', in J. Marincola (ed.), *A Companion to Greek and Roman Historiography* (Malden, Mass.: Blackwell, 2007), i. 56–66 at 56–58.

these may have been genuine archaic inscriptions, bearing the names of men of that period. Two versions, an earlier and a later, survive of the inscription which accompanied the chariot on the Athenian acropolis (77. 4).

As for literary sources, Herodotus refers to his predecessor Hecataeus, as a 'prose-writer' (36. 2, 125, also II. 143. 1); but only in book II and in VI. 137. 1 is he concerned with the content of Hecataeus' writing. However, it has been suspected that Hecataeus lies behind various other passages, as a source or as somebody to be controverted.[21] Herodotus often doubts geographical and ethnographical reports, if they are not supported by eye-witnesses (e.g. III. 115).[22] He mentions Homer, Hesiod and a range of archaic poets, in 67. 1 using what Homer says to explain why Cleisthenes of Sicyon banned recitations of Homer, but there is no sign that he quarried the poets for material which he could use in his history, to add to what his informants told him or to resolve a disagreement, and indeed he was sceptical of information supplied by the poets (e.g. II. 23).[23] In 113. 2 Solon is mentioned, incidentally, as having praised Philocyprus of Soli in Cyprus: in Herodotus' history Solon is a wise man, a poet, a lawgiver and a traveller, but there is no mention of the crisis in Athens and his part in trying to resolve it, such as could have been added to the account of the rise of Pisistratus in I. 59.

Narrative
Homer, and epic poetry generally, provided Herodotus with his main precedent for telling a long story which could switch from one place to another, and that is one way in which [Longinus]' description of him as 'most Homeric' seems apposite.[24] He is external to the narrative, not playing a direct part in it, but he intrudes his own personality, by remarking on his sources of information, places he has visited and things he has seen, opinions on the likelihood of what he has been

---

21   See Lateiner, *The Historical Method of Herodotus*, 93–95.
22   Cf. Lateiner, *op. cit.* 96–97.
23   Cf. Lateiner, *op. cit.* 99–100, Osborne, *op. cit.* 510; and on the story of Helen and the Trojan War cf. below, p. 18.
24   Cf. below, pp. 18, 22.

told, and so on. He does not tell his story uniformly from an external viewpoint, but often 'focalises' on the viewpoint of one of the actors. In 12 we see the Paeonian woman through Darius' eyes before he asks about her. The account of Hippias' expulsion from Athens begins with an Athenian focus, on the Alcmaeonids and Delphi (62. 2–3); but then the focus switches to the Spartans, persuaded by Delphi, sending the unsuccessful expedition of Anchimolus (63, cf. 90. 1) and the successful expedition of Cleomenes (64); while for the conclusion of the affair the focus is on the Pisistratids (65).

Within the overall line of the narrative there are passages which look back to an earlier occurrence (*analepsis*: e.g. the invocation in 67–8 of Cleisthenes of Sicyon as a precedent for the tribal manoeuvres of Cleisthenes of Athens, and the digression in 82–8 on the ancient enmity between Aegina and Athens to explain Aegina's willingness to support Thebes against Athens *c.* 506), and passages which look ahead to something relevant which was to happen later (*prolepsis*: e.g. 32, mentioning in connection with the Persian Megabates the story that the Spartan Pausanias was to marry his daughter).

The pace of the narrative can vary: in 110–2 a dialogue between Onesilus and his armour-bearer slows down the encounter between Onesilus and the mounted Persian commander Artybius; but 117 deals briskly with Daurises' capture of a number of Greek cities, one on each day (cf. 26). The long digressions on Sparta and Athens, with their own sub-digressions, provide a substantial retardation between Aristagoras' first contemplating the Ionian Revolt (28–38) and the beginning of military action in the Revolt (98–126), making the culmination of the preparations the more effective when at last it arrives. Details are sometimes mentioned not at the first point where they could be mentioned but at a later point where they are more apposite: for instance, we are told in 37. 2–38. 2 that tyrants in the Ionian cities were deposed but in most cases not executed; we learn only in VI. 9. 2–10 that they fled to the Persians, and before the battle of Lade were used in an unsuccessful attempt to win back their cities to Persian allegiance, and only in VI. 13 that one of them was Aeaces the tyrant of Samos, and his advice to desert was eventually accepted

– and here a question arises: is this simply the natural practice of a writer who mentions details where he considers them relevant, or did he consciously not supply the details at the earlier point because he was aware then that he would be able to mention them more effectively later?

The narrative includes speeches by various participants (ranging from long speeches such as that of Socles the Corinthian in 92 to dialogues such as that between Aristagoras and Artaphernes in 31), as epic poetry included speeches, and drama alternated between speeches by and dialogues between the actors and reflections on what was happening by the chorus. Thucydides notoriously was to claim some degree of authenticity for his speeches (Thuc. I. 22. 1), while what degree of authenticity he was claiming and how far the claim was justified have been endlessly debated.[25] Herodotus makes no such claim, apart from his insistence on the authenticity of the Persian constitutional debate (III. 80. 1, VI. 43. 3). In some cases there may be a factual basis (presumably Aristagoras did successfully incite Artaphernes to undertake a campaign against Naxos; there may have been a Corinthian called Socles who did cite Corinth's experience of tyranny to argue against Sparta's plan to reinstate Hippias in Athens); but the conversation between Darius and the Paeonians Pigres and Mastyes (13) belongs to a floating story, told of different people in different contexts, and may have no basis in reality at all. Beyond the minimal factual basis in some cases, scholars have been happy to accept Herodotus' speeches as his own compositions, a vivid feature of his story-telling manner.[26]

A particular category of speech found often in Herodotus and elsewhere is the warning which should have been heeded but was not: Hecataeus warned against embarking on the Ionian Revolt (36); and later, when Aristagoras was considering withdrawal either to Sardinia or to Myrcinus (and in fact went to Myrcinus and was killed when

---

25   For my view see e.g. Rhodes, *Thucydides, History, I* (Aris and Phillips Classical Texts. Oxford: Oxbow, 2014), 7–9 and commentary on I. 22. 1.

26   But C. W. Fornara, *The Nature of History in Ancient Greece and Rome* (U. of California P., 1983), 162–66, argues that in many cases the speeches are based on reports which Herodotus himself believed.

undertaking an expedition from there), Hecataeus advised him instead to occupy Leros as a base from which he might later be able to return to Miletus (124–6). In book V there are also some warnings which were heeded: Megabazus succeeded in persuading Darius not to leave Histiaeus in Myrcinus (23–4); Socles' long speech succeeded in preventing the Spartans from going ahead with their plan to reinstate Hippias in Athens (while Hippias countered with his own unheeded warning, that Corinth would pine for the Pisistratids when it was troubled by Athens: 93. 1).

The characters of some prominent individuals are strongly indicated. Cleomenes of Sparta was king 'in accordance not with personal merit but with descent' (39. 1), and 'was not of sound mind but was slightly mad. But Dorieus was first among all his contemporaries, and was confident that in accordance with personal merit he would have the kingship' (42. 1). Indeed 'Cleomenes did not rule for a long time' (48) – which appears to be untrue. Although at first he resisted the cajolery of Aristagoras, in the end he might have yielded if he had not been stiffened by his daughter Gorgo (49–51), and he behaved improperly to the priestess of Athena in Athens (72. 3). Though the Alcmaeonids of Athens had improperly influenced the Delphic oracle to urge Sparta to expel the Pisistratids (63. 1), as the Spartans no doubt including Cleomenes later discovered (90. 1), subsequently he was to influence the oracle improperly in order to get rid of his fellow king Demaratus (VI. 65–6); he again misbehaved at the temple of Hera in Argos (VI. 81), yet he successfully provided a religious reason for not following up his victory over the Argives at Sepeia (VI. 76–82). When his machinations against Demaratus were found out he withdrew into exile, but he was induced to return, went mad and cut himself to death, and of the various explanations offered Herodotus favoured divine retribution (VI. 74–5, 84).

Aristagoras at his first mention is merely deputy of Histiaeus in Miletus (30. 2; but see commentary). He misled Artaphernes on how easy it would be to conquer Naxos and other islands (31); by quarrelling with Megabates he wrecked the campaign against Naxos (33. 2–4); and it was partly because of this that he changed tack and decided

to revolt against the Persians (35. 1–2) . He suggested to Cleomenes that the Persians would be easy to defeat (49. 3), and when argument failed he tried to bribe Cleomenes (51. 2). Through the Ionian Revolt 'evil began to come to the Ionians for a second time, from Naxos and Miletus' (28); the invitation to the deported Paeonians to return home was 'a plan from which no advantage was to come to the Ionians' (98. 1). It is probably to be seen as a sign of cowardice that when the fighting began, with the attack on Sardis, Aristagoras 'did not go on the campaign himself, but he stayed in Miletus' (99. 2); and so, once the Persians were striking back successfully, 'Aristagoras of Miletus was as he demonstrated not keen in spirit: after throwing Ionia into confusion and stirring up great trouble, on seeing this he planned to run away' (124. 1). His death in the campaign from Myrcinus seems to be due to misjudgment, since he was 'besieging a city when the Thracians were willing to evacuate it under truce' (126. 2).

Opinions and beliefs

Scholars are nowadays strongly conscious that an authorial *persona* can be assumed and can differ from the actual personality of the author; but we have no evidence from elsewhere for the actual opinions of Herodotus the man, so I use 'Herodotus thinks' as shorthand for 'Herodotus the author gives the impression of thinking'.

Inevitably Herodotus was formed by and engaged with his background, as an upper-class Greek writing in the third quarter of the fifth century. Up to a point, the anthropomorphic gods familiar from Homer onwards were still accepted, and throughout Greece they were worshipped; but already in the sixth century some thinkers had expressed doubts about gods of that kind,[27] and literature shows us that within the basic outline stories about the gods and mortals of the legendary period could be subjected to considerable variation as they were told and retold on different occasions.[28]

27   E.g. Thales, *Vorsokr.* 11 A 22 (Arist. *Anim.* 411 A 9); Pythagoras, Diog. Laert. VIII. 21; Xenophanes, *Vorsokr.* 21 B 11–12, 14–16, 23–6; Heraclitus, *Vorsokr.* 22 B 1, 42 (Diog. Laert. IX. 1), 128.

28   On Herodotus' attitude to religion see G. E. M. de Ste. Croix, 'Herodotus', *G&R*[2] 24 (1977), 130–48 at 138–47; Gould, *Herodotus*, 67–76; T. E. H. Harrison,

In Herodotus' narrative, although human purposes and reasoning are never excluded, things sometimes happen because they are fated to happen, and the gods (often 'the god', not further specified) are jealous of great human success and punish great human offences. Gould remarks that

> The distinctive quality of Herodotus' perception of human experience is the tragic perception that it is always and everywhere vulnerable to time and chance and to the grim inevitabilities of existence. Of all the qualities that bear out Longinus' passing description of Herodotus as 'the most Homeric' of historians (13. 3), it is perhaps this quality of sympathetic engagement with human suffering that is the most fundamental.[29]

Strikingly, Herodotus refuses to believe that Helen was taken to Troy, because the Trojans would have returned her to the Greeks rather than endure ten years of war to retain her – but the Greeks' refusal to believe that she was not there was due to a divine purpose that the Trojans should meet with utter destruction in order to demonstrate that great offences are met with great punishments (II. 112–20). Croesus was rebuked by Solon for considering himself the happiest of men; eventually *nemesis* overtook him; Croesus misinterpreted a Delphic oracle and destroyed his own great empire; he thus paid the penalty in the fifth generation for Gyges' killing of the Heraclid king Candaules, since even the god cannot evade the fate which is laid down (Apollo tried to delay it to the next generation but could not even do that) (I. 6–91). The grisly end of Cleomenes of Sparta was a divine punishment for one of his offences rather than the result of drinking undiluted wine (VI. 75, 84). Xerxes invaded Greece in 480 in spite of the warnings of Artabanus, because he was convinced that the god wanted him to invade Greece, and eventually Artabanus was convinced too, though at first he argued that dreams are merely a reflection of what men have been thinking about (VII. 8–18). When

---

Divinity and History: The Religion of Herodotus (Oxford UP, 2000); J. D. Mikalson, *Herodotus and Religion in the Persian Wars* (U. of North Carolina P., 2003); S. Scullion, 'Herodotus and Greek Religion', in *Cambridge Companion*, 192–208.
29   Gould, *Herodotus*, 132.

the Persians besieging Potidaea were overwhelmed by a tidal wave, Herodotus accepts the view of the Potidaeans that this was punishment for desecrating their shrine of Poseidon (VIII. 129). A more sceptical note is sounded by the remark that the gorge of Tempe, through which the Peneus flows from the interior of Thessaly to the sea, is attributed by the Thessalians to Poseidon, and that is fair enough if one accepts that earthquakes are the work of Poseidon, since the gorge is certainly the result of an earthquake (VII. 129. 3).

In addition to the major gods and goddesses there were lesser divinities, such as Damia and Auxesia (82–6). Heroes, often legendary or historical mortals who had died, could receive lesser devotions (*enagismata*), as in some strains of Christianity God is worshipped but saints are venerated (47. 2, 66. 2, 67, 114).

As a part of his interest in places and peoples, Herodotus was interested in the gods worshipped in different places, and as Greeks often did he tended to identify foreign divinities with the closest Greek equivalents.. The Ethiopians of Meroë worship Zeus and Dionysus (II. 29. 7); various Egyptian gods are identified with Greek gods (II. 42–3); Herodotus went from Egypt to Tyre to see a temple of Heracles there, and when he also found there a temple of Thasian Heracles he went to Thasos, where he saw a Phoenician temple of Heracles (II. 44). He rejects a Greek story that Heracles was taken by the Egyptians to be sacrificed to Zeus, since the Egyptians refuse to sacrifice most animals so it is highly unlikely that they would have sacrificed a human being – 'and I pray to receive the kindness of the gods and heroes after saying such things about them' (II. 45). Egypt had snakes sacred to Zeus (II. 74); and there were oracles of various gods (II. 83). In book V the Thracians worship only Ares, Dionysus and Artemis, except that their kings worship Hermes also and claim to be descended from him (7); Darius prays to Zeus, as the Greek equivalent of Ahuramazda (105. 2).

As in the case of Xerxes and Artabanus, gods speak to sleeping mortals through dreams (in book V, 56); less often, they manifest themselves through epiphanies to mortals who are awake (no straightforward instance in book V, but in 56 Hipparchus dreams of

an epiphany, and in 86. 3 the images of Damia and Auxesia are said
to have fallen on their knees ('what they say is incredible to me, but
somebody else may believe it'); for epiphanies during the Persian
Wars see e.g. VI. 105, 117. 3). Gods make their will known also
through oracles (43, 90. 2 with 93. 2, 114. 2), though it is up to human
beings to interpret them, and as in the case of Croesus they sometimes
misinterpret them. Herodotus' uncle Panyassis was a *teratoskopos*, an
observer of omens (*Suda* π 248 Adler Πανύασις).

Dorieus of Sparta failed to consult the Delphic oracle before
leading a colonising expedition to Libya, and that was unsuccessful;
he did then consult Delphi before going to Sicily, and was killed when
he took part in a war in Italy instead of concentrating on his mission
(42. 2–45. 1). Delphi would not allow Cleisthenes of Sicyon to expel
the hero Adrastus, so he had to find a way round the ban (67). When
the Thebans wanted to take revenge for their defeat by Athens *c.* 506,
Delphi told them 'to bring the matter forward to the many-voiced,
and to ask those nearest': they convened an assembly (the 'many-
voiced'), but were puzzled by the reference to 'those nearest', since
those topographically nearest to them were loyal allies anyway, but
it occurred to somebody that Thebe and Aegina were sisters and that
Aegina was meant (79–80). It was when the Epidaurians were suffering
from famine and consulted Delphi that they were commanded to set
up statues of Damia and Auxesia, which must be of olive wood (to
be obtained from Athens) (82). Eëtion consulted Delphi when he was
unable to obtain children (92. β. 2). But oracles could be corrupted,
and the Alcmaeonids of Athens improperly induced Delphi to tell
Spartans who consulted the oracle that they must liberate Athens (63.
1, cf. 66. 1, 90. 1).

As Hornblower remarks,[30] Herodotus' account of the Ionian Revolt
is remarkable for its lack of a religious dimension. Although through
the Revolt 'there was a reveual of evil, and evil began to come to the
Ionians for a second time' (28), there is no suggestion that the Revolt
and its failure were fated; there is no mention of the consultation of

---

30   Hornblower, 32–35, 41, citing C. B. R. Pelling, 'Aristagoras (45, 49–55, 97)',
in Irwin and Greenwood (eds), *Reading Herodotus*, 179–201 at 197–98.

oracles, and the Milesians' oracle at Branchidae is referred to only as a possible source of funds to support the Revolt, not in fact drawn on and therefore looted by the Persians after the suppresion of the Revolt (36. 3–4 with VI. 18–20). We do learn, however, when Miletus and Branchidae were sacked at the end of the Revolt, that Argos had obtained a Delphic oracle which predicted disaster for Miletus and Branchidae and something puzzling for itself (VI. 18–19 with 77. 2).

Politically, Herodotus was writing at a time when much of the Greek world was polarised between Athens with its Delian League, associated with democracy, and Sparta with its Peloponnesian League, associated with oligarchy (e.g. Thuc. III. 82. 1); and that present will inevitably have affected his view of the past. Athens was certainly one of the places visited by Herodotus (cf. above, pp. 3–4), and there was a time when scholars commonly regarded him as particularly associated with Athens, and specifically with the Alcmaeonid family, and, while overall remarkably dispassionate, as supporting Athens and its democracy though not uncritically.[31] Some have reacted by arguing that Herodotus was more sympathetic to Sparta than to Athens;[32] but that I think takes the reaction too far, and I do not think he can be categorised as either pro-Athenian or pro-Spartan.[33] On political régimes, I agree with those who have stressed that the most important distinction for Herodotus was between monarchy, whether that of a Greek tyrant or that of an oriental despot, and the freedom of constitutional government, and he undoubtedly preferred the latter.[34] He sometimes applied the categories of his own time to

31   This was the view of F. Jacoby, 'Herodotos', *RE* Supp. ii (1913), 205–520 at 237–42; cf. e.g. How and Wells, i. 6–9, 37–42. Notice particularly VII. 139 (Athens the saviour of Greece), 161. 2–3 (Athens' right to command at sea if Sparta does not), IX. 27 (Athens' right to take second place after Sparta at Plataea); and VI. 121–4 (the Alcmaeonids could not have been traitors at Marathon). Doubts were expressed by H. Strasburger, 'Herodot und das perikleische Athen', *Historia* 4 (1955), 1–25.

32   E.g. Fornara, *Herodotus*, 41–58; but on p. 90 'With his sympathy for Athens and for Sparta he could see neither side as the villain of his day'.

33   Rhodes, 'Herodotus and Democracy', in Harrison and Irwin, *Interpreting Herodotus*, 265–77 at 276–77.

34   Wells, *Studies in Herodotus*, 153; Fornara, *Herodotus*, 48–50; J. L. Moles,

earlier phenomena which may have been somewhat different, and he thus blurred the difference between democracy as it was when he was writing and forms of constitutional government up to a century earlier, but I do not think he expressed an opinion on democracy as it was understood in his own day.[35]

Was he, as has sometimes been argued recently, not merely affected by his own time but, under the cover of writing about the past, to a serious extent writing about and conveying a message to his own time?[36] Does his sole mention of Pericles, in VI. 131. 2, point to Pericles the 'lion' as a tyrannical leader? When he writes that 'Cities which in the past were great, the majority of them have become small, and those which in my time were great were previously small; I know that human prosperity never remains in the same man' (I. 5. 4), when he makes Solon warn Croesus that the god is jealous of human prosperity and nobody can be judged happy until he has ended his life well (I. 30–3), is this a warning to the prosperous Athens of his own time? I think the answer must be, up to a point: he will certainly have realised that the rise and fall of individuals and states was not just a feature of the past but would continue, and to that extent he will not have expected Athens to remain powerful and prosperous for ever; but I think his primary objective was what he said it was, to write about great and wonderful deeds of the past – this was one of the respects in which Herodotus was 'most Homeric' (cf. above) – and not to convey a warning to his contemporaries, and it is by no means certain that

'Herodotus and Athens', in *Brill's Companion*, 33–52 at 50–51, and ' "Saving" Greece from the "Ignominy" of Tyranny? The "Famous" and "Wonderful" Speech of Socles (5. 92)', in Irwin and Greenwood, *Reading Herodotus*, 245–68 at 264.

35   Rhodes, 'Herodotus and Democracy'; cf. Asheri, in Asheri *et al.*, 45–47.

36   In general, Fornara, *Herodotus*, 75–91, cf. 60. More specifically, J. L. Moles, e.g. 'Herodotus Warns the Athenians', in *Leeds International Latin Seminar* 9 (1996), 259–84, and in *Brill's Companion*, 33–52; W. Blösel, 'The Herodotean Picture of Themistocles: A Mirror of Fifth-Century Athens', in N. Luraghi (ed.), *The Historian's Craft in the Age of Herodotus* (Oxford U.P., 2001), 179–97 (based on his *Themistokles bei Herodot* [*Historia* Einz.183, 2004]). For a more nuanced view see R. F. Buxton, 'Instructive Irony in Herodotus: The Socles Scene', *GRBS* 52 (2012), 559–86 (for Moles's treatment of that episode see n. 34, above). Against this approach in principle see Gould, *Herodotus*, 116–19.

the reference to Pericles is intended to represent him as a tyrant (for lion imagery in book V see 56. 1, 92. β. 3).[37] Thucydides, by contrast, avowedly wrote a history which he hoped would be 'judged useful by those who want to study the clear truth of what has happened, the like of which in accordance with the human condition will at some time happen again' (Thuc. I. 22. 4).

Text[38]

Attic and Ionic are two sub-branches of one of the main branches of the Greek language. Herodotus was an eastern Greek who wrote in the eastern Ionic dialect,[39] and it is exceptionally hard to establish letter by letter what he will have written. The manuscripts vary between themselves at the same point, and even within themselves at different occurrences of the same word or comparable words. We do not know how consistent he himself will have been in the course of a long work probably written over a long period, and copyists would have been capable either of changing the form in their exemplar to a more familiar standard form or of 'correcting' the form in their exemplar to what they considered the proper Ionic form. This is not an area in which I can claim any particular expertise, and in this respect I have followed the 2015 Oxford Text of N. G. Wilson (though I do not use the lunate *sigma*, c, as he does). Sometimes the manuscripts give us what certainly is, or what seems to some editors to be, impossible Greek. Editors have also emended the text on factual grounds, where the transmitted text is known or is believed to be erroneous.

We need to achieve a realistic balance: texts do become corrupted in

---

37   V. J. Gray, 'Herodotus and Images of Tyranny: The Tyrants of Corinth', *AJP* 117 (1996), 361–89 at 386–87, argues that the image invokes Athenian imperialism, not Pericles' position within Athens. Brock, *Greek Political Imagery*, 89–90, sees lion images as ambiguous.

38   On the transmission of Herodotus' text see particularly S. R. West, in Bowie (ed.), *Herodotus, Histories, Book VIII*, 30–34, and the Preface of N. G. Wilson's Oxford Text; and, in more detail, Wilson, *Herodotea*, xi–xxvi (whose dates for the manuscripts I give here).

39   He was from Dorian Halicarnassus, but inscriptions from there likewise use eastern Ionic (cf. pp. 2–3).

transmission, and some kinds of corruption (such as contamination from a nearby word: e.g. in 69. 2, where the demes are known to have numbered more than 100, but the transmitted text repeats δέκα from immediately before in place of the rarer δέχακα which the sense requires) are well-known phenomena; on the other hand, ancient writers did not always obey the rules which have been inferred by modern grammarians, what have been regarded as factual errors have sometimes been judged not to be errors after all, and some which we do have to accept as errors may have been perpetrated by the author rather than introduced by a copyist.[40] Current fashion, in which I share, is more willing to try to defend the transmitted text and less enthusiastic in emending it than the fashion of earlier generations of editors (and Wilson's 2015 Oxford Text is in fact more willing to doubt the transmitted text than might have been expected of an edition published in today's climate).

I give some examples from book V (in each case see critical apparatus and commentary). In 28 the manuscripts' ἄνεος or ἄνεως κακῶν makes no sense, and the context requires a statement that evils did occur rather than that they did not, so I adopt the emendation ἀνανέωσις rather than ἄνεσις. In 30. 6 the likelihood that τῶν Κυκλάδων is to be deleted as an interpolated gloss is increased by τὰς Κυκλάδας καλευμένας in 31. 2, which we should not expect if the Cyclades had been mentioned very shortly before. In 41. 3 καὶ τὸ δεύτερον ἐπελθοῦσα γυνή, ἐοῦσα θυγάτηρ Πρινητάδεω τοῦ Δημαρμένου is stated at what might seem to us not to be the best point, but I am not convinced that Herodotus did not write that here, and I retain that text. In 62. 2 the manuscripts' Παιονίης seems to result from a confusion between the demes Paeonidae (where Leipsydrium was) and Paeania, but I suspect that the error is Herodotus' own and I do not emend. In 63. 2, 4, it seems that the correct form of the name of

---

40　The Teubner edition of H. B. Rosén tried to purge the text of emendations introduced unnecessarily on linguistic grounds (cf. vol. i, pp. v–xxiv); D. Gilula, 'Who was Actually Buried in the First of the Three Spartan Tombs (Hdt. 9. 85. 1)? Textual and Historical Problems', in *Herodotus and His World*, 73–87, discusses some factual emendations in books VIII–IX which have long been generally but unnecessarily accepted.

the Spartan commander is Ἀγχίμολος, though the manuscripts agree on Ἀγχιμόλιος, and in this case there are grounds for believing that Ἀγχίμολος is what Herodotus wrote, so I do emend.

There are short passages of Herodotus preserved in papyri, many centuries earlier than the mediaeval manuscripts: they exhibit the same kind of linguistic variability as the mediaeval manuscripts (but not yet the division into two 'families' noted below); I have not had occasion to cite any in this volume. The mediaeval manuscripts which I cite in the critical apparatus are the following:

from the 'Florentine family'
A   Laurentianus 70.3, Florence, early C10
B   Romanus Angelicus gr. 83, Rome, C11

from the 'Roman family'
D   Vaticanus gr. 2369, Vatican, C10
S   Cantabrigiensis Sancroftianus coll. Emmanuelis gr. 30, Cambridge, mid C15
V   Vindobonensis gr. 85, Vienna, early C15

wavering between the two traditions
C   Laurentianus Conv. Suppr. gr. 207, Florence, C11

Language[41]
On the difficulty of establishing what forms of words Herodotus used see above; but I note here some of the main differences between what seems to be Herodotus' Greek and standard Attic Greek:

many uncontracted forms, e.g. Περσέων, 1. 1, ἐποίεον, 1. 2.

γιν for γιγν, e.g. γινομένων, 2. 1.

ει for ε, normally where a consonant has been lost, e.g. ξεῖνε (from earlier *ξένϝε), 18. 2; similarly ου for ο, e.g. μουνομαχίη (from *μονϝο-), 1. 2.

ευ for ου when contracted from εο or εου, e.g. ποιεῦσι, 4. 1.

η for long α: e.g. τρηχέως, 1. 1.

---

41   See especially Bowie (ed.), *Herodotus, Histories, Book VIII*, 22–27, reprinted in Hornblower, 41–47, and Hornblower and Pelling (eds), *Herodotus, Histories, Book VI*; 30–36; Flower and Marincola (eds), *Herodotus, Histories, Book IX*, 44–48.

κ for π in interrogative and indefinite adjectives / adverbs, e.g. κου, 1. 3.

σσ for ττ, e.g. φυλάσσουσι, 6.[42]

ω and in crasis ωυ for αυ, e.g. θῶμα, 92. 5; τὠυτό, 3. 1.

aspirate omitted, e.g. ἀντικατιζόμενοι, 1. 2; κατ' ἑωυτούς, 15. 3.[43]

aspirate transposed, e.g. ἐνθαῦτα for ἐνταῦθα, 1. 2.

1st declension masculine genitive singular -εω for -ου, e.g. Κώεω, 11.

1st and 2nd declension long dative plurals with -σι, e.g. αὐτοῖσι, 1. 3.

ἐμέο etc. or ἐμεῦ etc. for ἐμοῦ etc., e.g. ὅτεῳ, 87. 3; σεῦ, 24. 1.

μιν for αὐτόν, αὐτήν = 'him', 'her', e.g. 4. 2.

σφεας etc. for αὐτούς etc. (not only when referring to subject of main verb), e.g. σφεων, 1. 3.

τὰ etc. for relative ἃ etc., e.g. τῶν ὁ Μεγάβαζος ἦρχε, 1. 1.

-αται and -ατο for -νται and -ντο, e.g. ἐξανιστέαται, 61. 2; συναπισταίατο, 37. 2.

verbs in -μι conjugated like contracted verbs, e.g. διδοῖ, 14. 2.

δέκομαι etc. for δέχομαι etc., e.g. ἀναδεκομένους, 91. 2.

εἶπα etc. for εἶπον etc., e.g. εἶπάν, 1. 3.

ὦν for οὖν, e.g. 1. 2.

As for other matters, Herodotus is probably the earliest Greek prose writer whose work survives intact. His sentences are simpler in structure than the sentences of Thucydides (particularly, than the sentences of Thucydides' speeches). They do however represent a considerable advance in fluency on Herodotus' predecessor Hecataeus, if the first fragment of his work is typical of him:

Ἑκαταῖος Μιλήσιος ὧδε μυθεῖται· τάδε γράφω, ὥς μοι δοκεῖ ἀληθέα εἶναι· οἱ γὰρ Ἑλλήνων λόγοι πολλοί τε καὶ γελοῖοι, ὡς ἐμοὶ φαίνονται, εἰσίν.

(Hecataeus, *FGrH* 1 F 1)

---

42   These forms are also used by some Attic writers (e.g. the tragedians and Thucydides), and become standard in the later *koine*.

43   It is customary in texts of Herodotus to print the rough breathing in words that would have had initial [h] in Attic, but this is purely a graphic convention; in the Ionic dialect initial aspirates had long been lost.

Hecataeus of Miletus tells thus: I write these things, as I judge them to be true: for the accounts of the Greeks are many and ridiculous, as they seem to me.

[Longinus], *Subl.* 13. 3–4, asked whether Herodotus was *Homerikotatos* ('most Homeric'), and then mentioned Stesichorus, Archilochus and particularly Plato as other imitators. He seemed to be thinking primarily of language, and we can see resemblances both on the level of particular expressions and in the structuring of the narrative. Homeric expressions in book V, noted in the commentary, are ἀναπλῆσαι κακά ('endure misfortunes', 4. 2), ἤρχετο ... γίνεσθαι κακά ('evil began to come', 28), τῷ Διὶ ... ἐρίζετε ('rival ... Zeus', 49. 7), ἔρξαν ἢ ἔπαθον ('did or had done to them', 65. 5), πολύφημον of an assembly ('many-voiced', 79. 1), ὑπὸ γούνατα λύσει ('loosen the knees', in an oracle, 92. β. 3), ἴστε ὑμῖν Κορινθίους γε οὐ συναινέοντας ('know that the Corinthians do not approve of your doing that', 92. η. 5), κοῖον ἐφθέγξαο ἔπος ('what a saying you have uttered', 106. 3). In 105. 2 the infinitive ἐκγενέσθαι in Darius' prayer ὦ Ζεῦ, ἐκγενέσθαι μοι Ἀθηναίους τίσασθαι ('Zeus, may it fall to me to be avenged on the Athenians') is a feature of Homeric prayers.

Homer can be seen also as a predecessor of Herodotus in narrative: not only the *Iliad*, with its narrative of (part of) the Trojan War, but also the *Odyssey*, where Odysseus engages in travels and enquiries, and there is an interest in the rise and fall of cities and individuals, in cunning men and in tall stories.[44]

In the organisation of his material Herodotus can seem to ramble. Most striking on a small scale in book V is 99. 1, where the sentence is in fact symmetrically constructed, and (grammatically superfluously) Aristagoras is named again at a^2 to help readers who may have lost the thread:

a^1 Ἀρισταγόρης δέ,
b^1 ἐπειδὴ οἵ τε Ἀθηναῖοι ἀπίκοντο εἴκοσι νηυσί, ἅμα ἀγόμενοι Ἐρετριέων πέντε τριήρεας,

---

44 See J. Marincola, 'Odysseus and the Historians', *Syll. Class.* 18 (2007), 1–79, esp. 14–15 (Herodotus and the cities of men), 30–31 (Themistocles as an Odyssean figure), 36–37, 52–66 (book II, on Egypt), 38–39 (reversals of fortune), 49 (tall stories).

c^1 οἳ οὐ τὴν Ἀθηναίων χάριν ἐστρατεύοντο ἀλλὰ τὴν αὐτῶν Μιλησίων, ὀφειλόμενά σφι ἀποδιδόντες

c^2 (οἱ γὰρ δὴ Μιλήσιοι πρότερον τοῖσι Ἐρετριεῦσι τὸν πρὸς Χαλκιδέας πόλεμον συνδιήνεικαν, ὅτε περ καὶ Χαλκιδεῦσι ἀντία Ἐρετριέων καὶ Μιλησίων Σάμιοι ἐβοήθεον).

b^2 οὗτοι ὦν ἐπείτε σφι ἀπίκοντο καὶ οἱ ἄλλοι σύμμαχοι παρῆσαν,

a^2 ἐποιέετο στρατηίην ὁ Ἀρισταγόρης ἐς Σάρδις.

a^1 As for Aristagoras,

b^1 the Athenians arrived in their twenty ships, bringing also five triremes of the Eretrians,

c^1 who came on the campaign to gratify not the Athenians but the Milesians themselves, to repay a debt to them

c^2 (for earlier the Milesians had helped them in waging their war against the Chalcidians, when the Samians were giving support to the Chalcidians against the Eretrians and Milesians).

b^2 When these had arrived and the other allies were present,

a^2 Aristagoras made a campaign against Sardis.

Herodotus' manner of presentation is one in which one thing leads to another, and that in turn leads to yet another; but, as in 99. 1, he remains in control and does in due course return to the points from which he launched into his digressions. In 25. 1 we are given the appointment of Otanes as 'general of the men by the sea'; in the remainder of 25 a story about Otanes' background is told; and at the beginning of 26 Herodotus returns to the point with 'This Otanes, who had sat on that throne, then became successor to Megabazus in his command'. On a large scale, Aristagoras' visits to win the support of Sparta and Athens are first mentioned in 38. 2. The section on Sparta covers 39–53: 39–41, how Cleomenes had become king; 42–8, what became of Cleomenes' half-brother Dorieus; 49–51, Aristagoras and Cleomenes; 52–4, Persia's Royal Road (which Aristagoras had mentioned to Cleomenes, 50. 2). Similarly the section on Athens covers 55–97: 55–6, the killing of Hipparchus; 57–61, the Gephyraei (the family of Hipparchus' killers); 62–5, the expulsion of Hippias (with a reminder of Aristagoras' mission in 65. 5); 66, Cleisthenes; 67–8, Cleisthenes of Sicyon (ancestor and forerunner of Cleisthenes);

69–81, Cleisthenes and after; 82–8, origin of enmity between Athens and Aegina; 89–96, after Cleisthenes (with Socles' account of the Corinthian tyranny in 92); 97, Aristagoras and Athens. To help readers to follow Herodotus' thread, there are passages such as 62. 1, where he writes δεῖ δὲ πρὸς τούτοισι ἔτι ἀναλαβεῖν τὸν κατ' ἀρχὰς ἤια λέξων λόγον, ὡς τυράννων ἐλευθερώθησαν Ἀθηναῖοι ('I still need to take up the account on which I embarked at the beginning, of how the Athenians were freed from tyrants').

One device which suits that manner of presentation, and which probably originated as an aid to the hearers of an oral performance, is used a great deal by Herodotus, as it was used before him by Homer (it is used also, though less frequently, by Thucydides): this is ring composition, where the end of a short or long section of text is marked by the repetition of words (or sometimes ideas but without verbal repetition) which began it. At the beginning of book V, a substantial though not verbal ring opens in 2. 2 with ὁ Μεγάβαζος … ἡμερούμενος βασιλέϊ ('Megabazus … taming to the King'), and closes at the end of 10 with Μεγάβαζος Περσέων κατήκοα ἐποίεε ('Megabazus was making subject to the Persians'). In 12. 1 a ring is opened with ἐντείλασθαι Μεγαβάζῳ Παίονας ἑλόντα ἀνασπάστους ποιῆσαι ἐκ τῆς Εὐρώπης ἐς τὴν Ἀσίην ('instruct Megabazus to take the Paeonians and uproot them from Europe to Asia') which has a first closure in 14. 1 with ἐντελλόμενος ἐξαναστῆσαι ἐξ ἠθέων Παίονας καὶ παρ' ἑωυτὸν ἀγαγεῖν ('instructing him to remove the Paeonians from their habitat and bring them to him') and a second in 17. 1 with Παιόνων μὲν δὴ οἱ χειρωθέντες ἤγοντο ἐς τὴν Ἀσίην ('Those of the Paeonians who had been subjected were taken to Asia').

More elaborately, a large ring (R1) opens in 55 with τὰς Ἀθήνας, γενομένας τυράννων ὧδε ἐλευθέρας ('Athens … had become free from tyrants in this way'), is reopened in 62. 1 (quoted above), and is closed in 65. 5 with οὕτω μὲν Ἀθηναῖοι τυράννων ἀπαλλάχθησαν ('In this way the Athenians were rid of tyrants'). Within that, in 55 immediately after the opening of ring R1 a smaller ring (R2) opens with ἐπεὶ Ἵππαρχον τὸν Πεισιστράτου, Ἱππίεω δὲ τοῦ τυράννου ἀδελφεόν, ἰδόντα ὄψιν ἐνυπνίου τῷ ἑωυτοῦ πάθεϊ ἐναργεστάτην

κτείνουσι Ἀριστογείτων καὶ Ἁρμόδιος, γένος ἐόντες τὰ ἀνέκαθεν Γεφυραῖοι ('Hipparchus son of Pisistratus, brother of Hippias the tyrant, though he had seen in his sleep a vision very similar to his disaster, was killed by Harmodius and Aristogeiton, whose family was descended from the Gephyraei'). A still smaller ring (R3) is anticipated by the mention of the Gephyraei there and opens in 57. 1 with οἱ δὲ Γεφυραῖοι, τῶν ἦσαν οἱ φονέες οἱ Ἱππάρχου ὡς μὲν αὐτοὶ λέγουσι, ἐγεγόνεσαν ἐξ Ἐρετρίης τὴν ἀρχήν ('The Gephyraei, to whom the killers of Hipparchus belonged, as they themselves say were originally from Eretria'). Rings R2 and R3 close in 62. 1, before ring R1 is reopened, with ἡ μὲν δὴ ὄψις τοῦ Ἱππάρχου ἐνυπνίου καὶ οἱ Γεφυραῖοι ὅθεν ἐγεγόνεσαν, τῶν ἦσαν οἱ Ἱππάρχου φονέες, ἀπήγηταί μοι ('Hipparchus' vision in his sleep, and the origin of the Gephyraei, to whom the killers of Hipparchus belonged, I have set out').

After Herodotus[45]
Herodotus visited Athens and is said to have given recitations from his work (cf. pp. 3–4, above); certainly in the second half of the fifth century his work was known there. As noted above, Sophocles' *Ant.* 905–12 and *O.C.* 337–41, and perhaps some other passages, show knowledge of Herodotus (cf. p. 4). Aristophanes' *Ach.* 524–9 (425) is a parody of I. 1. 1–5. 3 (cf. p. 5); and in his two plays surviving from 411 Aristophanes alludes to the exploits of Artemisia of Halicarnassus in the battle of Salamis (*Lys.* 674–5, *Thesm.* 1200–1: cf. VIII. 87–8).

And Thucydides, though he never names him, certainly knew and engaged with the work of his great predecessor. When Thuc. I. 20. 3 complains of 'many other things, even in the present and not forgotten in the course of time, about which the Greeks in general do not think correctly', his two examples are both from Herodotus: 'that Spartan kings do not cast one vote each [in the *gerousia*] but two' (see VI. 57. 5), 'and that Sparta [in its army] has a *lochos* of Pitana, which has never

---

45 See J. Priestley and V. Zali (eds), *Brill's Companion to the Reception of Herodotus in Antiquity and Beyond* (Leiden: Brill, 2016); also S. Hornblower, 'Herodotus' Influence in Antiquity', in *Cambridge Companion*, 306–18, and on Herodotus and Thucydides his *A Commentary on Thucydides* (Oxford UP, 1991–2008), ii. 19–38, 122–45.

existed at all' (see IX. 53. 2: it may be that there was a change between the Persian Wars and the Peloponnesian War of which Thucydides was unaware, or that '*lochos* of Pitana' was not the official title of the unit which Herodotus identifies thus). When Thuc. I. 22. 4 writes of 'the absence of a fabulous element' in his history, and claims to have written 'a possession for all time rather than a prize composition for a single hearing', he is likely to have had Herodotus in mind (cf. p. 3). Thucydides' war was greater than the Persian War, which was 'the greatest of the previous actions' but 'nevertheless had a quick decision in two naval battles and two land battles' (Thuc. I. 23. 1).

Various other allusions to Herodotus can be found, and Hornblower has argued that Thucydides assumed knowledge of Herodotus in his readers, and that he was particularly dependent on Herodotus for facts about the past mentioned in his speeches. As in the examples I have given above, Thucydides distanced himself from Herodotus, and in most of his history he focused far more narrowly than Herodotus on the military history of his war and on the political background when that was immediately relevant to it – but not quite in all of his history: there are some passages which are Herodotean both in content and in manner (such as the account of the Odrysian kingdom in Thrace, with distances in terms of time taken by a man travelling light, Thuc. II. 97; or the Spartan who complained at Mantinea that Agis was intending 'to cure evil with evil', after which Agis changed tack whether because of the shout or not, Thuc. V. 65. 2–3 cf. Hdt. III. 53. 4). Thucydides 'was not above showing off how well he could "do a Herodotus" when he felt like it.'[46]

In the fourth century Ctesias, a Greek doctor at the Persian court, wrote an account of Persia and criticised Herodotus as a liar, but what we know of his own work does not command confidence (cf. above, pp. 11–12); Aristotle criticised Herodotus as a story-teller (*mythologos*: *Gen. An.* III. 756 A 32–B 13), but the *Athenian Constitution* used him as a source where he provided suitable material (*Ath. Pol.* 14–15, 19).[47]

---

46 Hornblower, in *Cambridge Companion*, 308.
47 See Rhodes, *The Athenian Constitution Written in the School of Aristotle* (Aris and Phillips Classical Texts. Liverpool UP, 2017), 222.

Xenophon was said by Dionysius of Halicarnassus to have modelled himself on Herodotus in both subject-matter and language (*Ep. Pomp.* 4 / Loeb *Critical Essays*, ii. 384–89), and Hornblower singles out his emphasis on moral and praiseworthy behaviour.[48] Though later writers who aimed to outdo Herodotus in any area would criticise him, they made extensive use of him. Callisthenes followed him on the Athenians' fining Phrynichus for his tragedy on the Persians' *Capture of Miletus* at the end of the Ionian Revolt (*FGrH* 124 F 30: cf. VI. 21. 2); and the eastward expansion of the Greek world by Alexander provided opportunities for the use of Herodotean approaches and Herodotean material.

    Cicero called Herodotus the 'father of history', while adding that he and Theopompus have many tall stories (*pater historiae, fabulae*: Cic. *Leg.* I. 5), and in various places he praised his fluent style (e.g. 'like a peaceful stream', *sedatus amnis*, *Orat.* 39). Dionysius of Halicarnassus remarked on the scope of his work (*Thuc.* 5 / Loeb i. 474–75) and like [Longinus] compared him with Homer (his successful combinations of words, *Comp.* 3 / Loeb ii. 24–33; his 'well mixed' style, 24 / Loeb ii. 204–207); and echoes of Herodotean formulations have been found in Dionysius' *Antiquitates Romanae*.[49] For Quintilian Herodotus' Roman parallel was Livy (Quint. *Inst.* X. 1. 101), and he was characterised as 'pleasant, unaffected and flowing' (*dulcis et candidus et fusus*: X. 1. 73). There are some traces of Herodotus remembered or misremembered in Latin writers.[50] The Boeotian Plutarch, upset by Herodotus' treatment of the Boeotians who had gone over to the Persian side in 480–479, wrote his essay *On The Malice of Herodotus* (see his introduction, *De Her. Mal.* 854 E–F). But Pausanias, who wrote a guidebook to Greece and its monuments, frequently used and imitated Herodotus, sometimes naming him (e.g. Paus. I. 5. 1, citing V. 69. 2) but more often not. The

---

48   Hornblower, in *Cambridge Companion*, 311–12.
49   See S. Ek, *Herodotismen in der Archäologie des Dionys von Halikarnass* (Lund: Ohlsson, 1942). Cf. for Josephus Ek, *Herodotismen in der jüdischen Archäologie des Josephos und ihre textkritische Bedeutung* (Lund: Gleerup, 1946).
50   See F. Racine, 'Herodotus' Reputation in Latin Literature from Cicero to the 12th Century', in *Brill's Companion to the Reception of Herodotus*, 193–212 at 194–99.

Indike which Arrian wrote in addition to his *Anabasis of Alexander* was written in Ionic Greek, and begins with an account of India in the Herodotean manner before proceeding to the voyage of Alexander's admiral Nearchus (see Arr. *Ind.* 17. 6–7). Another exercise in the Herodotean manner was the *De Deo Syria* of Lucian, on the sanctuary of Atargatis at Hierapolis.

Herodotus was translated into Latin by Lorenzo Valla (in the 1450s, after he had translated Thucydides); a Greek text was printed in the Aldine series in 1502 (and Thucydides in the same year). In 1531 the Spanish Juan Luis Vives called Herodotus 'father of lies' (*mendaciorum patrem: De Disciplinis*, ii = *De Causis Corruptarum Artium*, ii[51]), while in 1566 Henri Estienne (Henricus Stephanus) published an edition of Valla's translation of Herodotus (after his Thucydides in 1564), with an *Apologia pro Herodoto* as preface. Comparison between Herodotus the entertainer and Thucydides the instructor was commonplace, and in the nineteenth and early twentieth centuries, as concepts of professional, 'scientific' history were developed, Thucydides was seen as the ideal and Herodotus was disparaged by comparison with him.[52] But beginnng with F. M. Cornford's *Thucydides Mythistoricus* of 1907, and gathering pace since the middle of the twentieth century, there have been studies of Thucydides seeing him as more than or other than a dispassionate purveyor of truth, which have dethroned him from his pedestal and made it easier to study in a balanced way what each writer aimed to do, and how and how successfully he did it.

---

51   *Quem uerius mendaciorum patrem quam (quomodo illum uocant nonnulli) patrem historiae* (p. 114 in T. Vigiliano (ed.), Vives, *De Disciplinis* = *Savoir et enseigner* [Paris: Les Belles Lettres, 2013]). He was more indulgent in *De Disciplinis*, xii = *De Tradendis Disciplinis*, v (p. 442), where Herodotus is called the father of history, and 'has much that is fabulous', but licence can be allowed to a work which takes the Muses as its title (*habet fabulosa permulta, sed operis titulo excusatur*).

52   The first translation of Herodotus published by Penguin Books was A. J. Evans (ed.; not the archaeologist), *The Penguin Herodotus* (Harmondsworth: Penguin, 1941), a selection from Rawlinson's translation of books I–IV – in orange covers, with the label 'Fiction'; a reprint retained the orange covers but omitted the label.

2. The Conflicts between the Greeks and the Persians

Beginnings

In the dark age which followed the fall of the Mycenaean kingdoms of the second millennium, Greeks migrated eastwards from the mainland to the islands of the Aegean and to the west coast of Asia Minor; Athens was regarded as the mother city of the Greeks of the Ionian strand who had taken part in this (cf. 97. 2 and commentary on 65. 3).[53] This brought them into contact with the Lydians, whose kingdom predominated in western Asia Minor: we have seen above that Herodotus sets his history in the context of conflict between Europe and Asia, and begins his account of the historical period with Croesus, 'the first whom I know to have begun unjust deeds against the Greeks', but then gives an account of each of the Mermnad kings of Lydia, all of whom campaigned against the Greeks of Asia Minor (I. 6–94 with digressions).

The Persian kingdom began in Anshan, to the east of the Persian Gulf, perhaps dependent on the Elamites of Susa, near the head of the Gulf. In 550/49 Cyrus II, possibly as in Herodotus the son of a Median mother, was victorious in a war against the Medes of Ecbatana, between the Persian Gulf and the Caspian (I. 95–140, an account which other evidence suggests is in various respects distorted). Croesus of Lydia saw the downfall of the Medes as an opportunity to expand eastwards into the vacuum, and so undertook the campaign which resulted in his own overthrow by the Persians *c.* 546 and led to the Persians' succeeding the Lydians as overlords of the Greeks of Asia Minor (I. 46–94, 141–76). The Lydians had not extended their power from the mainland even to the islands nearest to Asia Minor (I. 27), but in due course the Persians did go that far: for the conquest of Samos *c.* 522–517 see III. 120–8, 139–49, cf. IV. 138. 2; by the time of the Scythian expedition of *c.* 514 the Persians had also gained Chios (IV. 138. 2) and Lesbos (IV. 97, V. 11, cf. 26), and on the European side of the straits between the Black Sea and the Aegean Byzantium (IV. 138. 1) and the

---

53 Miletus, at least, received Minoan and Mycenaean settlers in the second millennium: see *C.A.H.* II. ii.[3] 184, 340, 362, 370.

Chersonese (IV. 137–8). The conquest of Lydia was followed by that of Babylon, in 539/8 (I. 178–200), and Cyrus' successor Cambyses in 525–523 conquered Egypt and made expeditions beyond it (II. 1, III. 1–29). Persia was now secure as the unrivalled power in western Asia, and was soon to become the first power to rule in Asia, Europe and Africa.

Cambyses died in 522 in circumstances of unrest, and Darius I succeeded him and reinvented the Achaemenid dynasty (III. 30–8, 61–97). The Persians' first expedition into Europe beyond the straits was that of Darius *c.* 514, which went into Thrace and then north of the Danube to fight against the Scythians; it was a failure, to the extent that Darius was lucky to return alive (IV. 83–144). Book V begins with Darius' leaving Megabazus as commander in Thrace: he deported the Paeonians to Asia, conquered the other coastal Thracians, and had some kind of contact with the Macedonians, which may have involved (as Herodotus believed) their making formal submission to the Persians; Histiaeus of Miletus had persuaded Darius to let him establish a base at Myrcinus in Thrace, but Megabazus persuaded Darius to take him to Susa instead (1–24). Otanes, appointed to succeed Megabazus, captured Byzantium, Calchedon and other places near the straits (which must have revolted after the failure of the Scythian campaign), and also in the north-east Aegean the islands of Imbros and Lemnos (25–7). Presumably soon after Darius' withdrawal, the Scythians in retaliation had made a raiding expedition as far as the Hellespont, which led the Athenian Miltiades to flee from the Chersonese (VI. 40, but the text and interpretation of that chapter are problematic).

From Thrace the Persians had gone north against the Scythians, not west towards Greece. Herodotus has a story of an Italian Greek doctor, Democedes, who had gained a position at the Persian court but in order to return home induced Darius' wife Atossa to incite him to attack Greece rather than Scythia: Darius persisted with his Scythian plan, but sent a reconnaissance party with Democedes which reached southern Italy (III. 125. 1, 129–38; cf. on 31. 3). Whatever truth there may be behind that story, after *c.* 506 the Persians received the ex-

tyrant Hippias from Athens, and the Athenians refused Artaphernes' order to take him back (65. 3, 91, 94. 1, 96); but otherwise there is no further sign of Persian interest in the Aegean and Greece until the foray against Naxos in 499 (28–34),[54] and then after the Ionian Revolt, which Athens and Eretria had supported (99. 1).

The Ionian Revolt

As Herodotus tells the story, the origin of the Ionian Revolt is to be seen first in the appeal to Aristagoras of Miletus from Naxian exiles, his decision to urge the Persian satrap Artaphernes to undertake an expedition to reinstate them, and then the wrecking of the expedition by his quarrel with its Persian commander Megabates and his consequent decision to revolt (28–35. 2). Secondly Herodotus mentions a secret message from Histiaeus in Susa: he says Histiaeus hoped that if a revolt broke out he would himself be sent to deal with it (35. 2–4), but possibly Histiaeus' actual intention was to warn Aristagoras of a plan to move the Ionians to Phoenicia and *vice versa* (VI. 3). There are later mentions of deliberation by the Ionians in connection with the Revolt, and Aristagoras would hardly have been able to bring about the Revolt unless there were at any rate feelings of dissatisfaction with Persian rule, and perhaps also feelings that the Persians were not invincible, to which he could appeal (see on 35. 2, 108. 2). Aristagoras then resigned his tyranny in Miletus (while still retaining some kind of commanding position), encouraged the other Ionian cities to depose their tyrants (36–8), and in 499/8 set off to win support from Sparta (where he was unsuccessful) and Athens (where he was successful) (38. 2–97. 3). Support was sent also by Eretria, which had an ancient connection with Miletus (99. 1).

In 498 Aristagoras invited the deported Paeonians to return home (98), and military action began with a raid on Sardis, formerly the Lydian capital and now the chief city of a Persian province. This began successfully, but the Ionians were unable to capture the citadel and were forced to withdraw, and were defeated in battle as they did

---

54   For dates in the 490s see Rhodes, in *Herodotus and His World*, 58–72 at 60–62, 71.

so (99–102, 116). The Athenians then returned home (103. 1: various reasons are possible and none is certain), but if there is truth behind a garbled account of Plutarch the Eretrians may have stayed longer (Plut. *De Her. Mal.* 861 B–C: see on 103. 1).

The Revolt spread, northwards to the Hellespont and Bosporus, southwards to Caria (103), and south-eastwards to Cyprus, which was always poised between the Greek and the Asiatic world. Probably the campaigning in Cyprus, which ended in defeat for the rebels (104, 108–15), and the Persian recovery of control in western Asia Minor (116–23: the Persians did not keep large forces in their provinces, but given time they could bring in irresistibly large forces) occurred in parallel in 497 and 496. Meanwhile Histiaeus persuaded Darius to send him back to western Asia Minor (105–7). Aristagoras did not take part in the campaign against Sardis (99. 2), and is next heard of contemplating flight, going to Myrcinus in Thrace (where Histiaeus had been earlier) and being defeated and killed in 496/5 in a campaign from there (124–6).

In 495 the Persians prepared for a major assault on Miletus; the Ionians decided to abandon the city and fight a naval battle from a base on the island of Lade; but there was disunity and resistance to serious training among the forces of the various cities. In the battle, in the autumn, most of the Samians and all the Lesbians deserted, and the Persians were victorious (VI. 6–17). Miletus was besieged, and was captured and looted in the spring of 494; captives were deported from there and from Branchidae (VI. 18–21).

Histiaeus, as a loyal servant of Darius ought, when he arrived in western Asia Minor went first to Sardis, but Artaphernes did not trust him. He then went to Chios, was distrusted there at first, persuaded the Chians to restore him to Miletus, but the attempt failed. After that he seems to have turned to simple opportunism, obtaining ships from Mytilene, establishing himself in Byzantium and attacking ships travelling to the Aegean from the Black Sea (VI. 1–5). On hearing of the battle of Lade he left a deputy in Byzantium, returned to the Aegean, attacked Chios and then attacked Thasos. As the Persians' Phoenician fleet moved northwards he went to Lesbos, perhaps

hoping to do a deal with the Persians, but when he ventured on to the mainland he was captured, taken to Sardis and killed, and his head sent to Darius; Herodotus thought that Darius still believed in Histiaeus and was angry at his death (VI. 26–30).

The Persians in the remainder of 494 and the first half of 493 regained control generally, on the mainland, the nearby islands and the European side of the straits; but Samos because of its desertion at Lade was spared damage to its city and sanctuaries (VI. 25, 31–3). However, in 493/2 Artaphernes imposed a settlement which was anything but savage, arranging for arbitration in disputes between cities, and making an assessment of their obligations to pay tribute, at roughly the previous rate, 'and they have continued to pay this always to my time' (VI. 42). In 493/2 Mardonius was sent with a large force, and he 'put an end to all the tyrants and established democracies in the cities' (VI. 43. 1–3). 'Democracy' here will be constitutional government, not necessarily democracy as it was understood in the second half of the fifth century; either tyrannies had been briefly reimposed or (as Hornblower suggests: see on 38. 1) Mardonius accepted what had already come into being.

The Greeks' Persian Wars

Athens had fallen out with Persia over Hippias, the Persian attempt to capture Naxos had failed, and both Athens and Eretria had supported the Ionian Revolt, at any rate at first: this was a sufficient incentive for the Persians to advance on the Aegean islands and the Greek mainland. It was perhaps in 493/2 that Darius sent heralds to demand the submssion of the Greeks (mentioned in a context of 491/0, VI. 48. 1–49. 1, but I believe it to be a flashback: see on 31. 3). Athens and Sparta both refused, but Aegina was one of the cities which complied, and this led to a series of events involving in Sparta the deposition of king Demaratus and his replacement by a relative, Leotychidas II, and the exile, return and death of Cleomenes and his replacement by Leonidas, a younger brother of Cleomenes' half-brother Dorieus (VI. 49–93). Mardonius in 492 campaigned into Thrace: according to Herodotus he was aiming to punish Athens and Eretria for supporting

the Ionians, and to conquer as many Greek cities as he could, and that is plausible if Darius' heralds had already been sent. However, while Thasos submitted and Macedon (re)submitted, after his fleet was wrecked off Athos and his army suffered badly in a night attack by a Thracian force, he returned to Asia, and some have thought that he had never intended to go beyond Thrace and Macedon.[55] In 491/0 there were rumours that Thasos was having second thoughts, but when Darius ordered it to demolish its walls and dismiss its fleet it obeyed (VI. 46. 1–48. 1).

In spring 490 the command was given to Datis (a Mede who had been involved in the suppression of the Ionian Revolt) and Artaphernes (son of Artaphernes the satrap of Sardis); Hippias travelled with them, hoping to be reinstated in Athens. Rather than follow Mardonius' route they crossed the Aegean, capturing and sacking Naxos but sparing the sacred island of Delos. In Euboea they besieged Carystus until it surrendered. Eretria after hesitating resisted until some men betrayed the city to the Persians: the temples were burned and the citizens enslaved (VI. 94–101).

The Persians then crossed to Attica, landing at Marathon (near Euboea, and in the east of Attica where the Pisistratids were influential). The Athenians sent their full army with all ten generals to confront them: the Spartans said they would come but not immediately; only Plataea sent a force at once. The Persians waited for Athens to be betrayed to them, and the Athenians waited for reinforcements to arrive from Sparta, but in the end the battle was fought before either of those things had happened: the Athenians thinned their centre to match the Persian line, and were victorious (Greek hoplites were superior to Persian infantry); and, when the Athenians returned to the city by land before the Persians had been able to sail round, the Persians withdrew (VI. 102–24). For the Athenians this was a great achievement; for the Persians it was one further slight to be avenged.

Persia had many other concerns, in particular a revolt in Egypt in 486–485. Darius died in November 486 and was succeeded by Xerxes

---

55   E.g. J. F. Lazenby, *The Defence of Greece, 490–479 BC* (Warminster: Aris and Phillips, 1993), 45.

(a son, not the eldest but for some time the designated heir). He made lengthy preparations for invading by Mardonius' route, round the north of the Aegean, again demanding the submission of the Greeks, bridging the Hellespont and the Strymon, and cutting a canal through the neck of Athos; he probably travelled from Susa to Sardis in 481 and set out from Sardis in the spring of 480 (VII. 1–36). Herodotus' figures for the Persian forces are incredible, perhaps based on an estimate of the total manpower of the Persian Empire: more than 2,500,000 warriors plus an equal number of camp followers; 1,207 ships (VII. 184–6 cf. 61–88). In 483/2 Athens had been persuaded by Themistocles to spend a surplus from its silver mines on a new fleet of 200 triremes, ostensibly and perhaps in fact for use against Aegina (VII. 144. 1–2). Otherwise there is no sign of Greek anxiety until the autumn of 481, when a congress of Greeks willing to resist under Spartan leadership (by no means all were willing) settled local disputes, sent spies to Sardis and tried without success to recruit more resisting states (VII. 132–71).

The Persians advanced (VII. 37–131); and, whatever the actual figures, they will have outnumbered the resisting Greeks so the Greeks needed to pick points where a smaller force would stand a chance against a larger; each side needed to keep its land forces and its sea forces reasonably close to each other. The Greeks' first attempt was in Thessaly, but they went there too soon, and they found that the Thessalians were not solidly in favour of resistance and there were alternatives to the Persians' obvious route through the gorge of Tempe to the interior, so they withdrew (VII. 172–4). Their next attempt, probably in August, involved sending an army to Thermopylae, a narrow coastal stretch on the gulf opposite the north of Euboea, and their navy to Artemisium at the north of Euboea; the Persian army needed to force its way through Thermopylae, and the navy faced the Greeks and needed to defeat them. The Greek army was small (Sparta intended to send larger forces after a festival), but it succeeded in holding the Persians for two days; then the Persians were shown a mountain route which enabled a force to descend in the Greeks' rear; some Greeks got away, while others including Leonidas and

the Spartans covered their retreat and were killed. After skirmishing between the navies the news of what had happened at Thermopylae arrived, so there was no point in the Greek navy's staying and it withdrew (VII. 175–VIII. 39).

There was nowhere else north of the Isthmus of Corinth where a smaller army might stop a larger one: Attica was abandoned to the Persians, and Herodotus has stories in which Themistocles had to try again and again to keep the Greek fleet at Salamis rather than let it retire to the Peloponnese and disperse. To bring about a naval battle which the Greeks could win he sent a misleading message to Xerxes, and the upshot was a battle fought in September, in the narrow waters between Salamis and the mainland where the Persians could not benefit from their superior numbers and skill (VIII. 40–96). Xerxes returned to Sardis with most of his army, and his fleet retired across the Aegean, but Mardonius stayed in Greece with part of the army and tried without success to win over the Athenians (VIII. 97–IX. 5).

In 479 Athens eventually persuaded Sparta to send an army north of the Isthmus, and the two armies faced each other on the north side of the mountains separating Boeotia from Attica. A first confrontation failed to tempt either side to fight a battle; a more risky Greek position in front of Plataea was made untenable by the Persians; by some combination of design and luck the Greek withdrawal from that position lured the Persians into a battle in which they were defeated (IX. 6–89). At sea the year began with the Persians based on Samos and the Greeks on Aegina; when the Greeks finally advanced to Samos the Persians withdrew to the mainland, and were defeated in a land battle on the south side of the Mycale promontory opposite Samos (IX. 90–106). The Greeks sailed north to the Hellespont, where they found Xerxes' bridges already destroyed by storms; the Peloponnesians sailed home, but, anticipating later developments, the Athenians with others stayed on to capture Sestos (IX. 114–21).

After the Persian Wars
We know that the Persians were never to invade Europe again, but it must have seemed to the Greeks after 479 that as after 490 they would

bide their time and then make another attack. Although they did not do
that, they continued to be involved with the Greeks in various ways.

In 478 the Greeks returned to the Aegean under Spartan leadership,
but the Spartan Pausanias made himself unpopular; after he was
recalled the Athenians became leaders of the Delian League (a league
based on the island of Delos), of those Greeks who wished to continue
fighting against the Persians, while Sparta concentrated its focus on
the Greek mainland. Athens became increasingly domineering in the
League; and, while at first Sparta acquiesced in Athens' new position,
Athens also became ambitious on the mainland. About the middle
of the century regular warfare against the Persians came to an end
(whether or not there was an actual treaty, as texts from the fourth
century onwards claim). The First Peloponnesian War (*c.* 460–446)
ended with Athens' losing its mainland gains, but Athens remained
too ambitious for Sparta to coexist with it, and they clashed again in
the Peloponnesian War of 431–404. Both sides tried to obtain Persian
support: Sparta needed Persian money if it was to have any chance
of defeating Athens at sea, and Athens needed at least to ensure that
Sparta did not obtain Persian money. An Athenian treaty with Persia in
or after 423 was perhaps a non-aggression pact; but later the Athenians
supported a Persian dissident in Asia Minor, and in 412–411 the
Spartans did succeed in gaining Persian support, which enabled them
to continue fighting until Athens could not. The price for that was the
return of the Greeks of mainland Asia Minor to Persian control.

When the war ended the Spartans did not hand over the Asiatic
Greeks to Persia (they had perhaps negotiated a revision of their
agreement) but tried to take over Athens' position, and soon Athens
found itself not only joining former allies of Sparta in a war against
Sparta on the Greek mainland but also cooperating with the Persians
against Sparta in the Aegean. Failing to make progress, Sparta turned
to diplomacy, and in 387/6 obtained the King's Peace, a 'common
peace' treaty by which the Asiatic Greeks were at last returned to
Persia and Persia gave its backing to a Greek settlement which Sparta
would interpret to suit its own interests. That provoked the foundation
in 378 of the Second Athenian League, to uphold the King's Peace and

resist Spartan domination. Sparta was defeated, on land, irreversibly, by Thebes in 371, and in the years which followed Thebes hoped to weaken Athens too and to obtain Persian backing for a common peace which would suit Theban interests.

But Philip II of Macedon (359–336) gained supremacy over the mainland Greeks, and his son Alexander III ('the Great': 336–323) acted on Philip's plan of attacking Persia, conquered the whole of the Persian empire, and represented this to the Greeks as retaliation for the Persians' fifth-century wars against the Greeks. A period of instability after his death ended with the emergence of three major kingdoms, based in Macedon, Egypt and Syria; but by the end of the first century BC all the regions around the Mediterranean had been incorporated in the Roman empire. To the east of that empire, beyond Syria, the dominant powers were the Parthians from the third century BC to the third century AD and the Sasanian Persians after that. The Roman empire came to be divided into western and eastern halves, and while the western half broke up in the fifth century the eastern persisted until the fifteenth.

Christianity developed out of Judaism, spread throughout the Roman empire and became the official religion of the empire in the fourth century AD. Islam originated in Arabia in the seventh century; it was soon spread through north Africa and for a time into Spain by the Arabs, and from the fourteenth century until the twentieth it was taken into south-eastern Europe by the Ottoman Turks. Crusades by western Christians from the end of the eleventh century to the end of the thirteenth, to reclaim the Biblical lands for Christianity, were ultimately unsuccessful. Still today the successor to Herodotus' division between the Greeks of Europe and the Persians of Asia is a division between a western, Christian or post-Christian world and an eastern, Muslim world, and topographically the main part of the Muslim world comes close to matching the territories of the Achaemenid Persian empire.

3. Summary of Book V

4. Abbreviations Used in Critical Apparatus (cf. p. 25)

from the 'Florentine family'

 A Laurentianus 70.3, Florence, early C10

 B Romanus Angelicus gr. 83, Rome, C11

from the 'Roman family'

 D Vaticanus gr. 2369, Vatican, C10

 S Cantabrigiensis Sancroftianus coll. Emmanuelis gr. 30, Cambridge, mid C15

 V Vindobonensis gr. 85, Vienna, early C15

wavering between the two traditions

 C Laurentianus Conv. Suppr. gr. 207, Florence, C11

BIBLIOGRAPHY

Here I give details of modern books which are cited frequently [with abbreviations, in square brackets, for some which are cited very frequently], and a few other fundamental books; I give details at the point of citation of modern books which are cited occasionally, and of articles in periodicals.

Herodotus: Greek text (cited by editor's name)
ed. Hude, K. (Oxford Classical Text.) Oxford UP, 1908; ^{2}1913–20; ^{3}1927.
ed. Rosén, H. B. (Teubner Text.) Leipzig: Teubner, 1987–97.
ed. Wilson, N. G. (Oxford Classical Text.) Oxford UP, 2015.

Herodotus: commentaries (cited by commentator's name)
Asheri, D., *et al.*, eds Murray, O., and Moreno, A. *A Commentary on Herodotus, Books I–IV.* Oxford UP, 2007. [citations of 'Asheri *et al.*' are of this work]
How, W. W., and Wells, J. *A Commentary on Herodotus* [vol. i = I–IV by Wells, vol. ii = V–IX by How]. Oxford UP, 1912; corrected 1928.
Lloyd, A. B. *Herodotus, Book II.* Leiden: Brill, 1975–88.
Macan, R. W. *Herodotus, The Fourth, Fifth and Sixth Books.* London: Macmillan, 1895.
Macan, R. W. *Herodotus, The Seventh, Eighth and Ninth Books.* London: Macmillan, 1908.
Scott, L. *Historical Commentary on Herodotus, Book 6. Mnemosyne* Supp. 268, 2005.
ERODOTO, *LE STORIE*
(MILAN: MONDADORI FOR FONDAZIONE LORENZO VALLA):
— vol. i, ed. Asheri, D. 1988. [includes general introduction]
— vol. ii, ed. Lloyd, A. B. 1989.
— vol. iii, ed. Asheri, D. 1990.
— vol. iv, ed. Corcella, A. *et al.*, 1993.
— vol. v, ed. Nenci, G. 1994.
— vol. vi, ed. Nenci, G. 1998.
— vol. vii, ed. Vannicelli, P., *et al.*, 2017.
— vol. viii, ed. Asheri, D., *et al.*, 2003.
— vol. ix, ed. Asheri, D., *et al.*, 2006.

HERODOTUS, *HISTORIES*
(CAMBRIDGE GREEK AND LATIN CLASSICS. CAMBRIDGE UP):
— Book V, ed. Hornblower, S. 2013.
— Book VI, eds Hornblower, S., and Pelling, C. 2017.
— Book VIII, ed. Bowie, A. M. 2007.
— Book IX, eds Flower, M. A. and Marincola, J. 2002.

Herodotus: English translations
de Sélincourt, A. *Herodotus, The Histories* (Penguin Classics). Harmondsworth: Penguin, 1954; most recently revised by Marincola, J., 2003.
Greene, D. *Herodotus, The History.* U. of Chicago P., 1987.
Rawlinson, G. *The History of Herodotus.* London: Murray, 1858–60; revised editions later, and subsequently reissued in various formats with reduced and updated annotation.
Waterfield, R., with introduction and notes by Dewald, C. (Oxford World's Classics). Oxford UP, 1998.

Herodotus: works of reference
Bakker, E. J., *et al.* (eds), *Brill's Companion to Herodotus.* Leiden: Brill, 2002. [*Brill's Companion*]
Dewald, C., and Marincola, J. (eds), *The Cambridge Companion to Herodotus.* Cambridge UP, 2006. [*Cambridge Companion*]
Jacoby, F. 'Herodotos von Halikarnassos', *RE* Supp. ii (1913), 205–520 (reprinted in his *Griechische Historiker.* Stuttgart: Druckenmüller, 1956, 7–164).
Legrand, P.-E. *Hérodote: Introduction* (Collection Budé). Paris: Les Belles Lettres, 1932.
Priestley, J., and Zali, V. (eds), *Brill's Companion to the Reception of Herodotus in Antiquity and Beyond.* Leiden: Brill, 2016.
Powell, J. E. *A Lexicon to Herodotus* [in fact not simply a lexicon but a full concordance]. Cambridge UP, 1938.

Other books frequently cited
Barrington Atlas. See Talbert.
Briant, P., trans. Daniels, P. T. *From Cyrus to Alexander: A History of the Persian Empire.* Winona Lake: Eisenbrauns, 2002.

Brock, R. W. *Greek Political Imagery from Homer to Aristotle*. London: Bloomsbury, 2013.

Burn, A. R. *Persia and the Greeks: The Defence of the West, c. 546–478 BC.* London: Arnold, 1962.

Davies, J. K. *Athenian Propertied Families, 600–300 BC.* Oxford UP, 1971. [Davies, *A.P.F.*]

Fehling, D. *Die Quellenangaben bei Herodot: Studien zur Erzählkunst Herodots*. Berlin: De Gruyter, 1971.

Fehling, D. trans. Howie, J. G. *Herodotus and His 'Sources': Citation, Invention and Narrative Art.* Leeds: Cairns, 1989.

Figueira, T. J. *Excursions in Epichoric History: Aiginetan Essays.* Lanham, Md: Rowman and Littlefield, 1993.

Fornara, C. W. *Herodotus: An Interpretative Essay*. Oxford UP, 1971.

Forrest, W. G. *Herodotus and His World: Essays from a Conference in Memory of G. Forrest*, eds Derow, P. S., and Parker, R. C. T. Oxford UP, 2003. [*Herodotus and His World*]

Fraser, P. M., Matthews, E., *et al. Lexicon of Greek Personal Names.* Oxford UP, 1987– . [*L.G.P.N.*]

Gould, J. P. A. *Herodotus*. London: Weidenfeld and Nicolson, 1989.

Hammond, N. G. L. *A History of Macedonia*, i. Oxford UP, 1972.

Hansen, M. H., and Nielsen, T. H. (eds), *An Inventory of Archaic and Classical Poleis.* Oxford UP, 2004. [*Inventory*]

Harrison, T. E. H., and Irwin, E. K. (eds), *Interpreting Herodotus*. Oxford UP, 2018.

Herodotus and His World. See Forrest.

Hornblower, S. (ed.), *Greek Historiography*. Oxford UP, 1994.

Inventory. See Hansen and Nielsen.

Irwin, E. K., and Greenwood, E. (eds), *Reading Herodotus: A Study of the Logoi in Book 5 of Herodotus' Histories*. Cambridge UP, 2007.

Kuhrt, A. *The Persian Empire: A Corpus of Sources from the Achaemenid Period.* London: Routledge, 2007.

Lateiner, D. *The Historical Method of Herodotus. Phoenix* Supp. 23, 1989.

L.G.P.N. See Fraser, Matthews *et al.*

Mee, C., and Spawforth, A. *Greece: An Oxford Archaeological Guide.* Oxford UP, 2001. [Mee and Spawforth]

Morrison, J. S., Coates, J. F., and Rankov, N. B. *The Athenian Trireme.* Cambridge UP, ²2000.

Parker, R. C. T. *Athenian Religion: A History*. Oxford UP, 1996.

Parker, R. C. T. *On Greek Religion*. Cornell UP, 2011.

Rhodes, P. J. *A History of the Classical Greek World, 478–323 BC* Chichester: Wiley–Blackwell, ²2010.

Talbert, R. J. A. (ed.), *Barrington Atlas of the Greek and Roman World*. Princeton UP, 2000. [*Barrington Atlas*]

Wells, J. *Studies in Herodotus*. Oxford: Blackwell, 1923.

ἩΡΟΔΌΤΟΥ ἹΣΤΟΡΙΩΝ Ε

HERODOTUS: HISTORIES V

ΗΡΟΔΟΤΟΥ

Ἱστοριῶν Ε

(1) οἱ δὲ ἐν τῇ Εὐρώπῃ τῶν Περσέων καταλειφθέντες ὑπὸ Δαρείου, τῶν ὁ Μεγάβαζος ἦρχε, πρώτους μὲν Περινθίους Ἑλλησποντίων οὐ βουλομένους ὑπηκόους εἶναι Δαρείου κατεστρέψαντο, περιεφθέντας πρότερον καὶ ὑπὸ Παιόνων τρηχέως. (2) οἱ γὰρ ὧν ἀπὸ Στρύμονος Παίονες χρήσαντος τοῦ θεοῦ στρατεύεσθαι ἐπὶ Περινθίους, καὶ ἢν μὲν ἀντικατιζόμενοι ἐπικαλέσωνταί σφεας οἱ Περίνθιοι ὀνομαστὶ βώσαντες, τοὺς δὲ ἐπιχειρέειν, ἢν δὲ μὴ ἐπιβώσωνται, μὴ ἐπιχειρέειν, ἐποίεον οἱ Παίονες ταῦτα. ἀντικατιζομένων δὲ τῶν Περινθίων ἐν τῷ προαστίῳ, ἐνθαῦτα μουνομαχίη τριφασίη ἐκ προκλήσιός σφι ἐγένετο· καὶ γὰρ ἄνδρα ἀνδρὶ καὶ ἵππον ἵππῳ συνέβαλον καὶ κύνα κυνί. (3) νικώντων δὲ τὰ δύο τῶν Περινθίων, ὡς ἐπαιώνιζον κεχαρηκότες, συνεβάλοντο οἱ Παίονες τὸ χρηστήριον αὐτὸ τοῦτο εἶναι, καὶ εἶπάν κου παρὰ σφίσι αὐτοῖσι· "νῦν ἂν εἴη ὁ χρησμὸς ἐπιτελεόμενος ἡμῖν, νῦν ἡμέτερον τὸ ἔργον". οὕτω τοῖσι Περινθίοισι παιωνίσασι ἐπιχειρέουσι οἱ Παίονες, καὶ πολλόν τε ἐκράτησαν καὶ ἔλιπόν σφεων ὀλίγους. (2) τὰ μὲν δὴ ἀπὸ Παιόνων πρότερον γενόμενα ὧδε ἐγένετο· τότε δὲ ἀνδρῶν ἀγαθῶν περὶ τῆς ἐλευθερίης γινομένων τῶν Περινθίων οἱ Πέρσαι τε καὶ ὁ Μεγάβαζος ἐπεκράτησαν πλήθεϊ. (2) ὡς δὲ ἐχειρώθη ἡ Πέρινθος, ἤλαυνε τὸν στρατὸν ὁ Μεγάβαζος διὰ τῆς Θρηίκης, πᾶσαν πόλιν καὶ πᾶν ἔθνος τῶν ταύτῃ οἰκημένων ἡμερούμενος βασιλέϊ· ταῦτα γὰρ οἱ ἐνετέταλτο ἐκ Δαρείου, Θρηίκην καταστρέφεσθαι.

(3) Θρηίκων δὲ ἔθνος μέγιστόν ἐστι μετά γε Ἰνδοὺς πάντων ἀνθρώπων. εἰ δὲ ὑπ᾽ ἑνὸς ἄρχοιτο ἢ φρονέοι κατὰ τὠυτό, ἄμαχόν τ᾽ ἂν εἴη καὶ πολλῷ κράτιστον πάντων ἐθνέων κατὰ γνώμην τὴν ἐμήν. ἀλλὰ γὰρ τοῦτο ἄπορόν σφι καὶ ἀμήχανον μή κοτε ἐγγένηται· εἰσὶ

---

2. 2.   Θρηίκην καταστρέφεσθαι deleted Cobet.
3. 1.   comma and <οὐδὲ> inserted after ἀμήχανον Richards.

HERODOTUS

Histories V

(**1**) Those of the Persians who were left in Europe by Darius, under the command of Megabazus, first subdued the Perinthians, a Hellespontine community, who were not willing to be subject to Darius. They had previously been treated harshly by the Paeonians also. (*2*) For the Paeonians from the Strymon received an oracle from the God to campaign against the Perinthians, and to attack the Perinthians if they took up position against them and called out, shouting at them by name, but not to attack them if they did not shout at them; and the Paeonians did this. The Perinthians took up position against them in the outer city, and then after a challenge a triple duel took place: they set man against man, horse against horse and dog against dog. (*3*) When the Perinthians won two of the contests, and began to sing a paean in joy, the Paeonians reckoned that this was the point of the oracle, and will have said to one another, 'Now the oracle is fulfilled for us; now it is up to us'. So when the Perinthians sang the paean the Paeonians attacked them; and they were by far superior, and left few of them alive. (**2**) That was the outcome of what was done by the Paeonians previously. On this occasion the Perinthians were valiant in the cause of their freedom, but the Persians and Megabazus gained superiority over them by their numbers. (*2*) When Perinthus had been subdued, Megabazus drove his force through Thrace, taming for the King every city and every people of those living there: for that was the instruction he had been given by Darius, to subdue Thrace.

(**3**) The Thracian people are the greatest of all mankind, at any rate after the Indians. If they were ruled by a single man or had an agreed policy, they would be impossible to fight against and would be by far the supremest of all peoples, in my judgment. But this is impossible for them, and it could not be contrived that it would ever happen: for

δὴ κατὰ τοῦτο ἀσθενέες. (*2*) οὐνόματα δ᾽ ἔχουσι πολλὰ κατὰ χώρας ἕκαστοι, νόμοισι δὲ οὗτοι παραπλησίοισι πάντες χρέωνται κατὰ πάντα, πλὴν Γετέων καὶ Τραυσῶν καὶ τῶν κατύπερθε Κρηστωναίων οἰκεόντων. (**4**) τούτων δὲ τὰ μὲν Γέται οἱ ἀθανατίζοντες ποιεῦσι, εἴρηταί μοι. Τραυσοὶ δὲ τὰ μὲν ἄλλα πάντα κατὰ ταὐτὰ τοῖσι ἄλλοισι Θρήιξι ἐπιτελέουσι, κατὰ δὲ τὸν γινόμενον σφίσι καὶ ἀπογινόμενον ποιεῦσι τοιάδε· (*2*) τὸν μὲν γενόμενον περιιζόμενοι οἱ προσήκοντες ὀλοφύρονται, ὅσα μιν δεῖ ἐπείτε ἐγένετο ἀναπλῆσαι κακά, ἀνηγεόμενοι τὰ ἀνθρωπήια πάντα πάθεα, τὸν δ᾽ ἀπογενόμενον παίζοντές τε καὶ ἡδόμενοι γῇ κρύπτουσι, ἐπιλέγοντες ὅσων κακῶν ἐξαπαλλαχθεὶς ἔστι ἐν πάσῃ εὐδαιμονίῃ. (**5**) οἱ δὲ κατύπερθε Κρηστωναίων ποιεῦσι τοιάδε· ἔχει γυναῖκας ἕκαστος πολλάς· ἐπεὰν ὦν τις αὐτῶν ἀποθάνῃ, κρίσις γίνεται μεγάλη τῶν γυναικῶν καὶ φίλων σπουδαὶ ἰσχυραὶ περὶ τοῦδε, ἥτις αὐτέων ἐφιλέετο μάλιστα ὑπὸ τοῦ ἀνδρός· ἣ δ᾽ ἂν κριθῇ καὶ τιμηθῇ, ἐγκωμιασθεῖσα ὑπό τε ἀνδρῶν καὶ γυναικῶν σφάζεται ἐς τὸν τάφον ὑπὸ τοῦ οἰκηιοτάτου ἑωυτῆς, σφαχθεῖσα δὲ συνθάπτεται τῷ ἀνδρί. αἱ δὲ ἄλλαι συμφορὴν μεγάλην ποιεῦνται· ὄνειδος γάρ σφι τοῦτο μέγιστον γίνεται. (**6**) τῶν δὲ δὴ ἄλλων Θρηίκων ἐστὶ ὅδε νόμος· πωλεῦσι τὰ τέκνα ἐπ᾽ ἐξαγωγῇ. τὰς παρθένους οὐ φυλάσσουσι, ἀλλ᾽ ἐῶσι τοῖσι αὐταὶ βούλονται ἀνδράσι μίσγεσθαι. τὰς γυναῖκας ἰσχυρῶς φυλάσσουσι· ὠνέονται τὰς γυναῖκας παρὰ τῶν γονέων χρημάτων μεγάλων. (*2*) τὸ μὲν ἐστίχθαι εὐγενὲς κέκριται, τὸ δὲ ἄστικτον ἀγεννές. ἀργὸν εἶναι κάλλιστον, γῆς δὲ ἐργάτην ἀτιμότατον. τὸ ζῆν ἀπὸ πολέμου καὶ ληιστύος κάλλιστον. οὗτοι μέν σφεων οἱ ἐπιφανέστατοι νόμοι εἰσί. (**7**) θεοὺς δὲ σέβονται μούνους τούσδε, Ἄρεα καὶ Διόνυσον καὶ Ἄρτεμιν· οἱ δὲ βασιλέες αὐτῶν, πάρεξ τῶν ἄλλων πολιητέων, σέβονται Ἑρμέην μάλιστα θεῶν, καὶ ὀμνύουσι μοῦνον τοῦτον καὶ

---

3. 2.   ἕκαστοι retained Wilson text: ἑκάστου Nenci; ἑκάστων, perhaps
    <διαιρεθέντες> Wilson *apparatus* (cf. *Herodotea*, 93).
    Τετέων misprint in Wilson.
4. 2.   ἀνηγεόμενοι: ἀπηγεόμενοι Bekker.
6. 1.   ἐστὶ ὅδε νόμος: εἰσὶ οἵδε νόμοι Powell.

this reason they are weak. *(2)* The tribes have many names according to the locations of each; but they all follow more or less the same institutions in all respects, apart from the Getae, the Trausi and those living beyond the Crestonaeans. (**4**) Of these, what the Getae who consider themselves immortal do I have already said. The Trausi in all other respects perform the same rites as the other Thracians, but for those who are born and who die among them they do this: *(2)* when one is born the relatives sit around him and bewail how many misfortunes he will have to endure since he has been born, recounting all the sufferings of mankind, but when one has died they bury him in the earth with merriment and rejoicing, saying what misfortunes he has been freed from and that he is in total bliss. (**5**) Those above the Crestonaeans behave as follows. Each man has many wives; so when one of the men dies there is a great judgment among the women and mighty enthusiasm among his friends over the question which of them was loved most by the man. Whichever one the judgment falls on and is honoured, she is lauded by the men and women and slaughtered at the tomb by the man most closely related to her; and having been slaughtered she is buried with the man. The others take this as a great disaster, for this rejection is the greatest disgrace for them.

(**6**) The other Thracians have this institution: they sell their children for export. They do not guard their virgins, but allow them to have intercourse with whatever men they wish. But they do mightily guard their wives: they buy their wives from their parents for large sums of money. *(2)* Being tattooed is judged noble, and not being tattooed ignoble. To have leisure is judged finest, and to be a worker of the land most dishonourable. Living from war and plundering is judged finest. These are their most conspicuous institutions. (**7**) They worship only these gods: Ares, Dionysus and Artemis. But their kings, unlike the other citizens, worship Hermes most of the gods; and they swear only

λέγουσι γεγονέναι ἀπὸ Ἑρμέω ἑωυτούς. (**8**) ταφαὶ δὲ τοῖσι εὐδαίμοσι αὐτῶν εἰσὶ αἵδε· τρεῖς μὲν ἡμέρας προτιθεῖσι τὸν νεκρὸν καὶ παντοῖα σφάξαντες ἱρήια εὐωχέονται, προκλαύσαντες πρῶτον· ἔπειτα δὲ θάπτουσι κατακαύσαντες ἢ ἄλλως γῇ κρύψαντες, χῶμα δὲ χέαντες ἀγῶνα τιθεῖσι παντοῖον, ἐν τῷ τὰ μέγιστα ἄεθλα τίθεται κατὰ λόγον μουνομαχίης. ταφαὶ μὲν δὴ Θρηίκων εἰσὶ αὗται.

(**9**) τὸ δὲ πρὸς βορέω ἔτι τῆς χώρης ταύτης οὐδεὶς ἔχει φράσαι τὸ ἀτρεκές οἵτινές εἰσι ἄνθρωποι οἰκέοντες αὐτήν, ἀλλὰ τὰ πέρην ἤδη τοῦ Ἴστρου ἔρημος χώρη φαίνεται ἐοῦσα καὶ ἄπειρος. μούνους δὲ δύναμαι πυθέσθαι οἰκέοντας πέρην τοῦ Ἴστρου ἀνθρώπους τοῖσι οὔνομα εἶναι Σιγύννας, ἐσθῆτι δὲ χρεωμένους Μηδικῇ. (**2**) τοὺς δὲ ἵππους αὐτῶν εἶναι λασίους ἅπαν τὸ σῶμα, καὶ ἐπὶ πέντε δακτύλους τὸ βάθος τῶν τριχῶν, σμικροὺς δὲ καὶ σιμοὺς καὶ ἀδυνάτους ἄνδρας φέρειν, ζευγνυμένους δὲ ὑπ’ ἅρματα εἶναι ὀξυτάτους· ἁρματηλατέειν [δὲ] πρὸς ταῦτα τοὺς ἐπιχωρίους, κατήκειν δὲ τούτων τοὺς οὔρους ἀγχοῦ Ἐνετῶν τῶν ἐν τῷ Ἀδρίῃ. (**3**) εἶναι δὲ Μήδων σφέας ἀποίκους λέγουσι· ὅκως δὲ οὗτοι Μήδων ἄποικοι γεγόνασι, ἐγὼ μὲν οὐκ ἔχω ἐπιφράσασθαι, γένοιτο δ’ ἂν πᾶν ἐν τῷ μακρῷ χρόνῳ. σιγύννας δ’ ὦν καλέουσι Λίγυες οἱ ἄνω ὑπὲρ Μασσαλίης οἰκέοντες τοὺς καπήλους, Κύπριοι δὲ τὰ δόρατα. (**10**) ὡς δὲ Θρήικες λέγουσι, μέλισσαι κατέχουσι τὰ πέρην τοῦ Ἴστρου, καὶ ὑπὸ τουτέων οὐκ εἶναι διελθεῖν τὸ προσωτέρω. ἐμοὶ μέν νυν ταῦτα λέγοντες δοκέουσι λέγειν οὐκ οἰκότα· τὰ γὰρ ζῷα ταῦτα φαίνεται εἶναι δύσριγα· ἀλλά μοι τὰ ὑπὸ τὴν ἄρκτον ἀοίκητα δοκέει εἶναι διὰ τὰ ψύχεα. ταῦτα μέν νυν τῆς χώρης ταύτης πέρι λέγεται· τὰ παραθαλάσσια δ’ ὦν αὐτῆς Μεγάβαζος Περσέων κατήκοα ἐποίεε.

(**11**) Δαρεῖος δὲ ὡς διαβὰς τάχιστα τὸν Ἑλλήσποντον ἀπίκετο ἐς Σάρδις, ἐμνήσθη τῆς ἐξ Ἱστιαίου τε τοῦ Μιλησίου εὐεργεσίης καὶ τῆς

---

8.   κατὰ λόγον obelised Powell, perhaps κατὰ νόμον Wilson *apparatus* (cf. *Herodotea*, 94).
      perhaps lacuna before μουνομαχίης, or read εὐδαιμονίης, Wilson *apparatus*;
      perhaps κατὰ λόγον <εὐδαιμονίης διὰ> μουνομαχίης, Wilson, *Herodotea*, 94.
9. 2.   δὲ A: τε D, omitted other MSS, δὴ Richards.
9. 3.   σιγύννας ... δόρατα deleted Reiske.

by him, and say that they themselves are descended from Hermes. (**8**) For the prosperous among them burials are like this: for three days they lay out the body and sacrifice victims of all kinds, having first wept. Then they hold the funeral, cremating them or otherwise burying them in the earth, and they heap up a mound and hold contests of every kind, in which the greatest prizes are awarded for single combat. That is the Thracians' form of funeral.

(**9**) Farther to the north beyond this land, nobody can tell for certain who are the men who live there, but beyond the Ister the land appears to be uninhabited and boundless. The only men I can learn of who live beyond the Ister are those named Sigynnae, who wear Median clothing. (*2*) Their horses are shaggy all over their bodies, with hairs five fingers long; they are small, snub-nosed and unable to carry men, but very fast when harnessed to chariots. Because of this the men of the region drive chariots. Their boundaries extend near to the Enetae in the Adriatic. (*3*) They say that they are colonists of the Medes: how they came to be colonists of the Medes I cannot tell, but anything might happen in the course of a long time. The Ligyes who live beyond Massalia call salesmen *sigynnai*, but the Cyprians give the name to spears. (**10**) As the Thracians say, bees occupy the region beyond the Ister, and because of these it is impossible to penetrate farther. But when they say that they seem to me to be saying what is not reasonable, for these creatures seem to me to be intolerant of cold; and my opinion is that the regions under the Bear are uninhabited because of the cold. That is what is said about this land, and it was the coastal stretch of it that Megabazus was making subject to the Persians.

(**11**) Darius when he had crossed the Hellespont went as quickly as he could to Sardis. Remembering Histiaeus the Milesian's good

παραινέσιος τοῦ Μυτιληναίου Κώεω, μεταπεμψάμενος δέ σφεας ἐς
Σάρδις ἐδίδου αὐτοῖσι αἵρεσιν. ὁ μὲν δὴ Ἱστιαῖος, ἅτε τυραννεύων τῆς
Μιλήτου, τυραννίδος μὲν οὐδεμιῆς προσεχρήιζε, αἰτέει δὲ Μύρκινον
τὴν Ἠδωνῶν, βουλόμενος ἐν αὐτῇ πόλιν κτίσαι. οὗτος μὲν δὴ ταύτην
αἱρέεται, ὁ δὲ Κώης, οἷά τε οὐ τύραννος δημότης δὲ ἐών, αἰτέει
Μυτιλήνης τυραννεῦσαι.

(12) τελεωθέντων δὲ ἀμφοτέροισι, οὗτοι μὲν κατὰ τὰ εἵλοντο
ἐτράποντο, Δαρεῖον δὲ συνήνεικε πρῆγμα τοιόνδε ἰδόμενον
ἐπιθυμῆσαι ἐντείλασθαι Μεγαβάζῳ Παίονας ἑλόντα ἀνασπάστους
ποιῆσαι ἐκ τῆς Εὐρώπης ἐς τὴν Ἀσίην. ἦν Πίγρης καὶ Μαντύης
ἄνδρες Παίονες, οἳ ἐπείτε Δαρεῖος διέβη ἐς τὴν Ἀσίην αὐτοὶ ἐθέλοντες
Παιόνων τυραννεύειν ἀπικνέονται ἐς Σάρδις, ἅμα ἀγόμενοι ἀδελφεὴν
μεγάλην τε καὶ εὐειδέα. (2) φυλάξαντες δὲ Δαρεῖον προκατιζόμενον
ἐς τὸ προάστιον τὸ τῶν Λυδῶν ἐποίησαν τοιόνδε· σκευάσαντες τὴν
ἀδελφεὴν ὡς εἶχον ἄριστα, ἐπ' ὕδωρ ἔπεμπον ἄγγος ἐπὶ τῇ κεφαλῇ
ἔχουσαν καὶ ἐκ τοῦ βραχίονος ἵππον ἐπέλκουσαν καὶ κλώθουσαν
λίνον. (3) ὡς δὲ παρεξήιε ἡ γυνή, ἐπιμελὲς τῷ Δαρείῳ ἐγένετο· οὔτε
γὰρ Περσικὰ ἦν οὔτε Λύδια τὰ ποιεύμενα ἐκ τῆς γυναικός, οὔτε πρὸς
τῶν ἐκ τῆς Ἀσίης οὐδαμῶν. ἐπιμελὲς δὲ ὥς οἱ ἐγένετο, τῶν δορυφόρων
τινὰς πέμπει κελεύων φυλάξαι ὅ τι χρήσεται τῷ ἵππῳ ἡ γυνή. (4) οἱ
μὲν δὴ ὄπισθε εἵποντο, ἡ δὲ ἐπείτε ἀπίκετο ἐπὶ τὸν ποταμὸν ἦρσε τὸν
ἵππον, ἄρσασα δὲ καὶ τὸ ἄγγος τοῦ ὕδατος ἐμπλησαμένη τὴν αὐτὴν
ὁδὸν παρεξήιε, φέρουσα τὸ ὕδωρ ἐπὶ τῆς κεφαλῆς καὶ ἐπέλκουσα ἐκ
τοῦ βραχίονος τὸν ἵππον καὶ στρέφουσα τὸν ἄτρακτον. (13) θωμάζων
δὲ ὁ Δαρεῖος τά τε ἤκουσε ἐκ τῶν κατασκόπων καὶ τὰ αὐτὸς ὥρα,
ἄγειν αὐτὴν ἐκέλευε ἑωυτῷ ἐς ὄψιν. ὡς δὲ ἄχθη, παρῆσαν καὶ οἱ
ἀδελφεοὶ αὐτῆς οὔ κῃ πρόσω σκοπιὴν ἔχοντες τούτων. εἰρωτῶντος
δὲ τοῦ Δαρείου ὁποδαπὴ εἴη, ἔφασαν οἱ νεηνίσκοι εἶναι Παίονες καὶ
ἐκείνην εἶναι σφέων ἀδελφεήν. (2) ὁ δ' ἀμείβετο, τίνες δὲ οἱ Παίονες
ἄνθρωποι εἰσὶ καὶ κοῦ γῆς οἰκημένοι, καὶ τί κεῖνοι ἐθέλοντες ἔλθοιεν
ἐς Σάρδις. οἱ δέ οἱ ἔφραζον ὡς ἔλθοιεν μὲν ἐκείνῳ δώσοντες σφέας

---

11.   δὲ ἐών Bekker: τε ἐών MSS.

12. 1.   κατὰ τὰ: τὰ omitted A.

   ἐκ τῆς Εὐρώπης ἐς τὴν Ἀσίην: ἐς τὴν Ἀσίην ἐκ τῆς Εὐρώπης A.

   ἦν Πίγρης καὶ Μαντύης doubtful: perhaps <ἐς τ>ἦν ... [οἳ] Wilson.

service and the advice of the Mytilenaean Coes, he summoned them to Sardis and gave them a choice. (*2*) Histiaeus, being tyrant of Miletus, had no further wish for any tyranny, but asked for Myrcinus of the Edones, wanting to found a city there. That was his choice. Coes, being not a tyrant but one of the people, asked to become tyrant of Mytilene. (**12**) This was accomplished for both of them, and they departed in accordance with their choices. Then it happened that Darius saw something which made him desire to instruct Megabazus to take the Paeonians and uproot them from Europe to Asia. There were two Paeonian men, Pigres and Mastyes, who after Darius had crossed to Asia wanted to be tyrants of the Paeonians and arrived at Sardis, bringing with them their tall and handsome sister. (*2*) After waiting for Darius to take his seat in front of the Lydian capital, they acted as follows. Dressing their sister as well as they could, they sent her to fetch water, with a jar on her head, leading a horse from her arm and spinning flax. (*3*) As the woman passed, Darius noticed her; for what the woman was doing was not characteristic of Persia or Lydia, or indeed of any of the peoples of Asia. Since he noticed it, he sent some of his spear-bearers, telling them to watch what the woman did with the horse. (*4*) They followed behind her; and when she arrived at the river she watered the horse, and having done that and filled the jar with water she went back the same way, carrying the water on her head, leading the horse from her arm and turning the spindle. (**13**) Darius was amazed at what he heard from the observers and what he saw himself, and he ordered her to be brought into his presence. When she was brought, there came also her brothers, who had been watching this from not far away. Darius asked where she was from, and the young men said that they were Paeonians and she was their sister. (*2*) He asked in response what people the Paeonians were, what territory they lived in and what was their own wish in coming to Sardis. They told him that they had come to give themselves up to

αὐτούς, εἴη δὲ ἡ Παιονίη ἐπὶ τῷ Στρυμόνι ποταμῷ πεπολισμένη, ὁ δὲ Στρυμὼν οὐ πρόσω τοῦ Ἑλλησπόντου, εἴησαν δὲ Τευκρῶν τῶν ἐκ Τροίης ἄποικοι. (3) οἱ μὲν δὴ ταῦτα ἕκαστα ἔλεγον, ὁ δὲ εἰρώτα εἰ καὶ πᾶσαι αὐτόθι αἱ γυναῖκες εἴησαν οὕτω ἐργάτιδες. οἱ δὲ καὶ τοῦτο ἔφασαν προθύμως οὕτω ἔχειν· αὐτοῦ γὰρ ὦν τούτου εἵνεκα καὶ ἐποιέετο.

(14) ἐνθαῦτα Δαρεῖος γράφει γράμματα Μεγαβάζῳ, τὸν ἔλιπε ἐν τῇ Θρηίκῃ στρατηγόν, ἐντελλόμενος ἐξαναστῆσαι ἐξ ἠθέων Παίονας καὶ παρ' ἑωυτὸν ἀγαγεῖν καὶ αὐτοὺς καὶ τὰ τέκνα τε καὶ τὰς γυναῖκας αὐτῶν. (2) αὐτίκα δὲ ἱππεὺς ἔθεε φέρων τὴν ἀγγελίην ἐπὶ τὸν Ἑλλήσποντον, περαιωθεὶς δὲ διδοῖ τὸ βυβλίον τῷ Μεγαβάζῳ. ὁ δὲ ἐπιλεξάμενος καὶ λαβὼν ἡγεμόνας ἐκ τῆς Θρηίκης ἐστρατεύετο ἐπὶ τὴν Παιονίην. (15) πυθόμενοι δὲ οἱ Παίονες τοὺς Πέρσας ἐπὶ σφέας ἰέναι, ἀλισθέντες ἐξεστρατεύσαντο πρὸς θαλάσσης, δοκέοντες ταύτῃ ἐπιχειρήσειν τοὺς Πέρσας ἐμβάλλοντας. (2) οἱ μὲν δὴ Παίονες ἦσαν ἕτοιμοι τὸν Μεγαβάζου στρατὸν ἐπιόντα ἐρύκειν, οἱ δὲ Πέρσαι πυθόμενοι συναλίσθαι τοὺς Παίονας καὶ τὴν πρὸς θαλάσσης ἐσβολὴν φυλάσσοντας, ἔχοντες ἡγεμόνας τὴν ἄνω ὁδὸν τράπονται, λαθόντες δὲ τοὺς Παίονας ἐσπίπτουσι ἐς τὰς πόλιας αὐτῶν ἐούσας ἀνδρῶν ἐρήμους· οἷα δὲ κεινῇσι ἐπιπεσόντες εὐπετέως κατέσχον. (3) οἱ δὲ Παίονες ὡς ἐπύθοντο ἐχομένας τὰς πόλιας, αὐτίκα διασκεδασθέντες κατ' ἑωυτοὺς ἕκαστοι ἐτράποντο καὶ παρεδίδοσαν σφέας αὐτοὺς τοῖσι Πέρσῃσι. οὕτω δὴ Παιόνων Σιριοπαίονές τε καὶ Παιόπλαι καὶ οἱ μέχρι τῆς Πρασιάδος λίμνης ἐξ ἠθέων ἐξαναστάντες ἤγοντο ἐς τὴν Ἀσίην.

(16) οἱ δὲ περί τε Πάγγαιον ὄρος καὶ αὐτὴν τὴν λίμνην τὴν Πρασιάδα οὐκ ἐχειρώθησαν ἀρχὴν ὑπὸ Μεγαβάζου· ἐπειρήθη δὲ καὶ Δόβηρας καὶ Ἀγριᾶνας καὶ Ὀδομάντους καὶ τοὺς ἐν τῇ λίμνῃ κατοικημένους ἐξαιρέειν ὧδε. ἴκρια ἐπὶ σταυρῶν ὑψηλῶν ἐζευγμένα ἐν μέσῃ ἕστηκε τῇ λίμνῃ, ἔσοδον ἐκ τῆς ἠπείρου στεινὴν ἔχοντα μιῇ γεφύρῃ. (2) τοὺς

---

13. 3. αὐτοῦ γὰρ ὦν: πάντα γὰρ ὦν Richards.
16. 1.   καὶ Δόβηρας καὶ Ἀγριᾶνας καὶ Ὀδυμάντους transposed to here Weber: after τὸ Πάγγαιον ὄρος MSS, deleted Stein, obelised Wilson (who follows Powell in marking lacunae before ἐπειρήθη δὲ and after ἐξαιρέειν).

him, that Paeonia was settled on the River Strymon and the Strymon was not far from the Hellespont, and that they were colonists of the Teucrians from Troy. (*3*) They said each of these things, and he asked them if all the women there were workers as she was. They answered emphatically that that was indeed so – for that indeed was precisely why they had done this.

(**14**) Then Darius wrote a message to Megabazus, whom he had left as general in Thrace, instructing him to remove the Paeonians from their habitat and bring them to him, themselves and their children and wives. (*2*) Immediately a horseman hurried and took the message to the Hellespont, and after crossing it he gave the scroll to Megabazus. He read it, took guides from Thrace and began a campaign against Paeonia. (**15**) When the Paeonians learned that the Persians were moving against them, they came together and advanced on campaign towards the sea, expecting the Persians to attempt their invasion that way. (*2*) The Paeonians were ready to resist Megabazus' force when it attacked; but, when the Persians learned that the Paeonians had come together and were guarding against an invasion from the sea, with the help of their guides they turned to the inland route. Undetected by the Paeonians, they fell on their cities, which were bereft of men; and by attacking when they were empty they easily got control of them. (*3*) When the Paeonians learned that their cities had been taken, they immediately broke up, went each to their own homes and gave themselves up to the Persians. In this way the Paeonian Siriopaeones and Paeoplae and those as far as Lake Prasias were removed from their habitat and taken to Asia.

(**16**) But those around Mount Pangaeum and Lake Prasias itself were not at first subjected by Megabazus. He did attempt to obliterate the Doberes, Agrianes and Odomantians, and those living on the lake, in this way. In the middle of the lake there are planks joined together, on tall posts, with a narrow entrance from the land by a single bridge.

δὲ σταυροὺς τοὺς ὑπεστεῶτας τοῖσι ἰκρίοισι τὸ μέν κου ἀρχαῖον ἔστησαν κοινῇ πάντες οἱ πολιῆται, μετὰ δὲ νόμῳ χρεώμενοι ἱστᾶσι τοιῷδε· κομίζοντες ἐξ ὄρεος τῷ οὔνομα ἐστὶ Ὄρβηλος, κατὰ γυναῖκα ἑκάστην ὁ γαμέων τρεῖς σταυροὺς ὑπίστησι· ἄγεται δὲ ἕκαστος συχνὰς γυναῖκας. (*3*) οἰκέουσι δὲ τοιοῦτον τρόπον, κρατέων ἕκαστος ἐπὶ τῶν ἰκρίων καλύβης τε ἐν τῇ διαιτᾶται καὶ θύρης καταρρακτῆς διὰ τῶν ἰκρίων κάτω φερούσης ἐς τὴν λίμνην. τὰ δὲ νήπια παιδία δέουσι τοῦ ποδὸς σπάρτῳ, μὴ κατακυλισθῇ δειμαίνοντες. (*4*) τοῖσι δὲ ἵπποισι καὶ τοῖσι ὑποζυγίοισι παρέχουσι χόρτον ἰχθῦς· τῶν δὲ πλῆθός ἐστι τοσοῦτο ὥστε, ὅταν τὴν θύρην τὴν καταρρακτὴν ἀνακλίνῃ, κατιεῖ σχοίνῳ σπυρίδα κεινὴν ἐς τὴν λίμνην, καὶ οὐ πολλόν τινα χρόνον ἐπισχὼν ἀνασπᾷ πλήρεα ἰχθύων. τῶν δὲ ἰχθύων ἐστὶ γένεα δύο, τοὺς καλέουσι πάπρακάς τε καὶ τίλωνας.

(**17**) Παιόνων μὲν δὴ οἱ χειρωθέντες ἤγοντο ἐς τὴν Ἀσίην. Μεγάβαζος δέ, ὡς ἐχειρώσατο τοὺς Παίονας, πέμπει ἀγγέλους ἐς Μακεδονίην ἄνδρας ἑπτὰ Πέρσας, οἳ μετ᾽ αὐτὸν ἐκεῖνον ἦσαν δοκιμώτατοι ἐν τῷ στρατοπέδῳ· ἐπέμποντο δὲ οὗτοι παρὰ Ἀμύντην αἰτήσοντες γῆν τε καὶ ὕδωρ Δαρείῳ βασιλέϊ. (*2*) ἔστι δὲ ἐκ τῆς Πρασιάδος λίμνης σύντομος κάρτα ἐς τὴν Μακεδονίην· πρῶτον μὲν γὰρ ἔχεται τῆς λίμνης τὸ μέταλλον ἐξ οὗ ὕστερον τούτων τάλαντον ἀργυρίου Ἀλεξάνδρῳ ἡμέρης ἑκάστης ἐφοίτα, μετὰ δὲ τὸ μέταλλον Δύσωρον καλεόμενον ὄρος ὑπερβάντι εἶναι ἐν Μακεδονίῃ. (**18**) οἱ ὦν Πέρσαι οἱ πεμφθέντες οὗτοι παρὰ τὸν Ἀμύντην ὡς ἀπίκοντο, αἴτεον ἐλθόντες ἐς ὄψιν τὴν Ἀμύντεω Δαρείῳ βασιλέϊ γῆν τε καὶ ὕδωρ. ὁ δὲ ταῦτά τε ἐδίδου καί σφεας ἐπὶ ξείνια καλέει, παρασκευασάμενος δὲ δεῖπνον μεγαλοπρεπὲς ἐδέκετο τοὺς Πέρσας φιλοφρόνως.

(*2*) ὡς δὲ ἀπὸ δείπνου ἐγένοντο, διαπίνοντες εἶπαν οἱ Πέρσαι τάδε· "ξεῖνε Μακεδών, ἡμῖν νόμος ἐστὶ τοῖσι Πέρσῃσι, ἐπεὰν δεῖπνον προτιθώμεθα μέγα, τότε καὶ τὰς παλλακὰς καὶ τὰς κουριδίας γυναῖκας ἐσάγεσθαι παρέδρους. σύ νυν, ἐπεί περ προθύμως μὲν ἐδέξαο μεγάλως δὲ ξεινίζεις, διδοῖς δὲ βασιλέϊ Δαρείῳ γῆν τε καὶ ὕδωρ, ἕπεο νόμῳ

---

16. 3–4. καταρρακτῆς, καταρρακτὴν Reiske: καταπακτῆς, καταπακτὴν MSS.
17. 2. ὑπερβάντι Abicht, Bernhardy, perhaps ὑπερβάντι <ἔξεστι> Wilson: ὑπερβάντα MSS.

(*2*) The poles which support the planks were at some time in the past set up by common action of all the citizens; but since then they have set them up by using the following rule: bringing them from a mountain whose name is Orbelus, a man sets up three poles for each wife whom he marries – and each man marries many wives. (*3*) They live in this sort of way, each man possessing on the planks a hut in which he lives, and a trapdoor through the planks giving access to the lake below. Their young children they fasten with a cord from their feet, in fear that they will fall down. (*4*) Their horses and beasts of burden they feed on fish: these are so abundant that, whenever they open the trapdoor, they let down an empty basket on a rope into the lake, and after waiting no long time they pull it up full of fish. There are two kinds of fish, which they call *paprakes* and *tilones*.

(**17**) Those of the Paeonians who had been subjected were taken to Asia; and when Megabazus had subjected the Paeonians he sent as messengers to Macedon seven Persian men who after himself were the most high-ranking in the force. These were sent to Amyntas to ask him to give earth and water to King Darius. (*2*) There is a very short route from Lake Prasias to Macedon. First adjoining the lake is the mine from which later there came to Alexander a talent of silver every day, and after the mine when one crosses the mountain called Dysorum one is in Macedon. (**18**) When these Persians who had been sent reached Amyntas, they went into the presence of Amyntas and asked him for earth and water for King Darius. He gave these and invited them to hospitality, and after preparing an impressive dinner he received the Persians generously.

(*2*) When they had finished their dinner, during their drinking the Persians said this: 'Macedonian foreigner, it is an institution among us Persians, when we lay on a great dinner, then to bring in the concubines and the wedded wives to sit with us; so now you, since you have received us enthusiastically and entertained us grandly, and are giving earth and water to King Darius, follow our custom.'

τῷ ἡμετέρῳ." (*3*) εἶπε πρὸς ταῦτα Ἀμύντης· "ὦ Πέρσαι, νόμος μὲν ἡμῖν γέ ἐστι οὐκ οὗτος, ἀλλὰ κεχωρίσθαι ἄνδρας γυναικῶν· ἐπείτε δὲ ὑμεῖς ἐόντες δεσπόται προσχρηίζετε τούτων, παρέσται ὑμῖν καὶ ταῦτα." εἴπας τοσαῦτα ὁ Ἀμύντης μετεπέμπετο τὰς γυναῖκας· αἱ δ᾽ ἐπείτε καλεόμεναι ἦλθον, ἐπεξῆς ἀντίαι ἵζοντο τοῖσι Πέρσῃσι. (*4*) ἐνθαῦτα οἱ Πέρσαι ἰδόμενοι γυναῖκας εὐμόρφους ἔλεγον πρὸς Ἀμύντην φάμενοι τὸ ποιηθὲν τοῦτο οὐδὲν εἶναι σοφόν· κρέσσον γὰρ εἶναι ἀρχῆθεν μὴ ἐλθεῖν τὰς γυναῖκας ἢ ἐλθούσας καὶ μὴ παριζομένας ἀντίας ἵζεσθαι ἀλγηδόνας σφίσι ὀφθαλμῶν. (*5*) ἀναγκαζόμενος δὲ ὁ Ἀμύντης ἐκέλευε παρίζειν· πειθομένων δὲ τῶν γυναικῶν αὐτίκα οἱ Πέρσαι μαστῶν τε ἅπτοντο οἷα πλεόνως οἰνωμένοι, καί κού τις καὶ φιλέειν ἐπειρᾶτο. (**19**) Ἀμύντης μὲν δὴ ταῦτα ὀρέων ἀτρέμας εἶχε, καίπερ δυσφορέων, οἷα ὑπερδειμαίνων τοὺς Πέρσας· Ἀλέξανδρος δὲ ὁ Ἀμύντεω παρεών τε καὶ ὀρέων ταῦτα, ἅτε νέος τε ἐὼν καὶ κακῶν ἀπαθής, οὐδαμῶς ἔτι κατέχειν οἷός τε ἦν, ὥστε δὲ βαρέως φέρων εἶπε πρὸς Ἀμύντην τάδε· "σὺ μέν, ὦ πάτερ, εἶκε τῇ ἡλικίῃ ἀπιών τε ἀναπαύεο, μηδὲ λιπάρεε τῇ πόσι· ἐγὼ δὲ προσμένων αὐτοῦ τῇδε πάντα τὰ ἐπιτήδεα παρέξω τοῖσι ξείνοισι." (*2*) πρὸς ταῦτα συνιεὶς Ἀμύντης ὅτι νεώτερα πρήγματα πρήσσειν μέλλοι ὁ Ἀλέξανδρος, λέγει· "ὦ παῖ, σχεδὸν γάρ σευ ἀνακαιομένου συνίημι τοὺς λόγους, ὅτι ἐθέλεις ἐμὲ ἐκπέμψας ποιέειν τι νεώτερον· ἐγὼ ὦν σευ χρηίζω μηδὲν νεοχμῶσαι κατ᾽ ἄνδρας τούτους, ἵνα μὴ ἐξεργάσῃ ἡμέας, ἀλλὰ ἀνέχευ ὀρέων τὰ ποιεύμενα· ἀμφὶ δὲ ἀπόδῳ τῇ ἐμῇ πείσομαί τοι."

(**20**) ὡς δὲ ὁ Ἀμύντης χρήσας τούτων οἰχώκεε, λέγει ὁ Ἀλέξανδρος πρὸς τοὺς Πέρσας· "γυναικῶν τουτέων, ὦ ξεῖνοι, ἔστι ὑμῖν πολλὴ εὐπετείη, καὶ εἰ πάσῃσι βούλεσθε μίσγεσθαι καὶ ὁκόσῃσι ὦν αὐτέων. (*2*) τούτου μὲν πέρι αὐτοὶ ἀποσημανέετε· νῦν δέ, σχεδὸν γὰρ ἤδη τῆς κοίτης ὥρη προσέρχεται ὑμῖν καὶ καλῶς ἔχοντας ὑμέας ὁρῶ μέθης, γυναῖκας ταύτας, εἰ ὑμῖν φίλον ἐστί, ἄφετε λούσασθαι, λουσαμένας δὲ ὀπίσω προσδέκεσθε." (*3*) εἴπας ταῦτα, συνέπαινοι γὰρ ἦσαν οἱ Πέρσαι, γυναῖκας μὲν ἐξελθούσας ἀπέπεμπε ἐς τὴν γυναικηίην, αὐτὸς δὲ ὁ Ἀλέξανδρος ἴσους τῇσι γυναιξὶ ἀριθμὸν ἄνδρας λειογενείους τῇ

19. 1.   σὺ μέν, ὦ πάτερ: ὦ πάτερ, σὺ μὲν A.
19. 2.   ὁ before Ἀλέξανδρος AD: omitted other MSS.

(*3*) Amyntas said in response to that, 'Persians, the institution among us is not that, but that the men are separated from the women. But, since you are the masters and make this additional request, this too shall be provided for you.' After saying this Amyntas sent for the women. When they came in response to his call, they sat in a row opposite the Persians. (*4*) Then the Persians, seeing the attractive women, spoke to Amyntas and said that doing that was unwise: it would be better that the women had not come at all than that they should come and not sit beside the Persians but sit opposite them as a distressing sight for their eyes. (*5*) Under pressure, Amyntas told them to sit beside the Persians; and, when they obeyed, the Persians, who were badly drunk, immediately began to touch their breasts, and one or another even tried to kiss them. (**19**) Amyntas on seeing this remained calm, although he was displeased, because he was greatly afraid of the Persians. Alexander, Amyntas' son, was present and saw this, and as a young man without experience of evil he could not restrain himself but in his anger was driven to say this to Amyntas: 'You, father, give way to your age and go and rest, and don't persist in the drinking. I shall stay here for it and provide everything that is appropriate for the foreigners.' (*2*) Amyntas, realising that Alexander was planning to take drastic action, said in reply, 'My boy, I hardly understand what you are saying in your inflamed state, wanting to send me away and do something drastic. I beg you not to do anything wild against these men, in case it ruins us, but put up with the sight of what they are doing. But as for my own departure I shall take your advice.'

(**20**) When Amyntas had made that request and gone, Alexander said to the Persians, 'Foreigners, these women are very much at your disposal, even if you want to go to bed with all or any of them. (*2*) It is for you to indicate your wishes about this. But now, since your bed time is approaching and I see you are well primed with drink, send these women away to bath, if that is agreeable to you, and welcome them back after they have bathed.' (*3*) When he had said this and

τῶν γυναικῶν ἐσθῆτι σκευάσας καὶ ἐγχειρίδια δοὺς ἦγε ἔσω, παράγων δὲ τούτους ἔλεγε τοῖσι Πέρσῃσι τάδε· (4) "ὦ Πέρσαι, οἴκατε πανδαισίῃ τελέῃ ἱστιῆσθαι· τά τε γὰρ ἄλλα ὅσα εἴχομεν, καὶ πρὸς τὰ οἷά τε ἦν ἐξευρόντας παρέχειν, πάντα ὑμῖν πάρεστι, καὶ δὴ καὶ τόδε τὸ πάντων μέγιστον, τάς τε ἑωυτῶν μητέρας καὶ τὰς ἀδελφεὰς ἐπιδαψιλευόμεθα ὑμῖν, ὡς παντελέως μάθητε τιμώμενοι πρὸς ἡμέων τῶν πέρ ἐστε ἄξιοι, πρὸς δὲ καὶ βασιλέϊ τῷ πέμψαντι ἀπαγγείλητε ὡς ἀνὴρ Ἕλλην Μακεδόνων ὕπαρχος εὖ ὑμέας ἐδέξατο καὶ τραπέζῃ καὶ κοίτῃ." (5) ταῦτα εἴπας ὁ Ἀλέξανδρος παρίζει Πέρσῃ ἀνδρὶ ἄνδρα Μακεδόνα ὡς γυναῖκα τῷ λόγῳ· οἱ δέ, ἐπείτέ σφεων οἱ Πέρσαι ψαύειν ἐπειρῶντο, διεργάζοντο αὐτούς.

(21) καὶ οὗτοι μὲν τούτῳ τῷ μόρῳ διεφθάρησαν, καὶ αὐτοὶ καὶ ἡ θεραπηίη αὐτῶν· εἵπετο γὰρ δή σφι καὶ ὀχήματα καὶ θεράποντες καὶ ἡ πᾶσα πολλὴ παρασκευή· πάντα δὴ ταῦτα ἅμα πᾶσι ἐκείνοισι ἠφάνιστο. (2) μετὰ δὲ χρόνῳ οὐ πολλῷ ὕστερον ζήτησις τῶν ἀνδρῶν τούτων μεγάλη ἐκ τῶν Περσέων ἐγίνετο, καί σφεας Ἀλέξανδρος κατέλαβε σοφίῃ, χρήματά τε δοὺς πολλὰ καὶ τὴν ἑωυτοῦ ἀδελφεὴν τῇ οὔνομα ἦν Γυγαίη· δοὺς δὲ ταῦτα κατέλαβε ὁ Ἀλέξανδρος Βουβάρῃ ἀνδρὶ Πέρσῃ, τῶν διζημένων τοὺς ἀπολομένους τῷ στρατηγῷ. ὁ μέν νυν τῶν Περσέων τούτων θάνατος οὕτω καταλαμφθεὶς ἐσιγήθη.

(22) Ἕλληνας δὲ εἶναι τούτους τοὺς ἀπὸ Περδίκκεω γεγονότας, κατά περ αὐτοὶ λέγουσι, αὐτός τε οὕτω τυγχάνω ἐπιστάμενος καὶ δὴ καὶ ἐν τοῖσι ὄπισθε λόγοισι ἀποδέξω ὡς εἰσὶ Ἕλληνες, πρὸς δὲ καὶ οἱ τὸν ἐν Ὀλυμπίῃ διέποντες ἀγῶνα Ἑλλήνων οὕτω ἔγνωσαν εἶναι. (2) βουλομένου γὰρ Ἀλεξάνδρου ἀεθλεύειν καὶ καταβάντος ἐπ' αὐτὸ τοῦτο, οἱ ἀντιθευσόμενοι Ἑλλήνων ἐξεῖργόν μιν, φάμενοι οὐ βαρβάρων ἀγωνιστέων εἶναι τὸν ἀγῶνα ἀλλὰ Ἑλλήνων· Ἀλέξανδρος δὲ ἐπειδὴ ἀπέδεξε ὡς εἴη Ἀργεῖος, ἐκρίθη τε εἶναι Ἕλλην καὶ ἀγωνιζόμενος στάδιον συνεξέπιπτε τῷ πρώτῳ. ταῦτα μέν νυν οὕτω κῃ ἐγένετο.

20. 5.   ὁ before Ἀλέξανδρος A: omitted other MSS.
22. 1.   Ἑλλήνων: Ἑλληνοδίκαι A.
22. 2.   βουλομένου γὰρ Ἀλεξάνδρου ἀεθλεύειν A: Ἀλεξάνδρου γὰρ ἀεθλεύειν ἑλομένου other MSS.

the Persians had approved, Alexander sent the women to go out to the women's quarters, and he himself dressed in the women's clothes smooth-cheeked men equal in number to the women, gave them daggers and brought them in. When he had brought them in he said this to the Persians: (*4*) 'Persians, you seem to have had your fill of a sumptuous feast. Everything else that we have, and that we could devise to provide for you, is at your disposal, and now we lavish on you this greatest thing of all, our mothers and sisters. In this way you will learn that you are fully honoured by us as you deserve, and you can report to the King who sent you that a Greek man, governor of the Macedonians, received you well both at table and in bed.' (*5*) After saying this Alexander placed beside each Persian man a Macedonian man as if he were a woman; and when the Persians tried to touch them they dispatched them.

(**21**) By this fate the Persians were destroyed, themselves and their attendants – for there followed them into oblivion their carriages and attendants and all their abundant paraphernalia; all of these disappeared along with them. (*2*) Not long afterwards there was a great search for these men on the part of the Persians, and Alexander dealt with them by his cleverness, in giving them a large sum of money and his own sister, whose name was Gygaea. Alexander dealt with them by giving these to Bubares, a Persian man who was commander of those searching for the men who had perished. In this way the death of these men was dealt with and hushed up.

(**22**) That these descendants of Perdiccas are Greeks, as they themselves say, is something of which I myself have gained knowledge, and indeed I shall demonstrate in my later account that they are Greeks. In addition, those who administer the Greeks' contest at Olympia have judged this to be the case. (*2*) For, when Alexander wanted to compete and went down for that purpose, those of the Greeks intending to run against him tried to exclude him, saying that the competition was not for barbarian competitors but for Greek. But Alexander, when he had demonstrated that he was Argive, was judged to be Greek, competed in the foot race and came first equal. That is how it turned out.

(**23**) Μεγάβαζος δὲ ἄγων τοὺς Παίονας ἀπίκετο ἐπὶ τὸν Ἑλλήσποντον· ἐνθεῦτεν διαπεραιωθεὶς ἀπίκετο ἐς τὰς Σάρδις. ἅτε δὲ τειχέοντος ἤδη Ἱστιαίου τοῦ Μιλησίου τὴν παρὰ Δαρείου αἰτήσας ἔτυχε μισθὸν δωρεὴν φυλακῆς τῆς σχεδίης, ἐόντος δὲ τοῦ χώρου τούτου παρὰ Στρυμόνα ποταμὸν τῷ οὔνομα ἐστὶ Μύρκινος, μαθὼν ὁ Μεγάβαζος τὸ ποιεύμενον ἐκ τοῦ Ἱστιαίου, ὡς ἦλθε τάχιστα ἐς τὰς Σάρδις ἄγων τοὺς Παίονας, ἔλεγε Δαρείῳ τάδε· (*2*) "ὦ βασιλεῦ, κοῖόν τι χρῆμα ἐποίησας, ἀνδρὶ Ἕλληνι δεινῷ τε καὶ σοφῷ δοὺς ἐγκτίσασθαι πόλιν ἐν Θρηίκῃ, ἵνα ἴδη τε ναυπηγήσιμος ἐστὶ ἄφθονος καὶ πολλοὶ κωπέες καὶ μέταλλα ἀργύρεα, ὅμιλός τε πολλὸς μὲν Ἕλλην περιοικέει, πολλὸς δὲ βάρβαρος, οἳ προστάτεω ἐπιλαβόμενοι ποιήσουσι τοῦτο τὸ ἂν κεῖνος ἐξηγέηται καὶ ἡμέρης καὶ νυκτός. (*3*) σύ νυν τοῦτον τὸν ἄνδρα παῦσον ταῦτα ποιεῦντα, ἵνα μὴ οἰκηίῳ πολέμῳ συνέχῃ· τρόπῳ δὲ ἠπίῳ μεταπεμψάμενος παῦσον· ἐπεὰν δὲ αὐτὸν περιλάβῃς, ποίειν ὅκως μηκέτι κεῖνος ἐς Ἕλληνας ἀπίξεται." (**24**) ταῦτα λέγων ὁ Μεγάβαζος εὐπετέως ἔπειθε Δαρεῖον ὡς εὖ προορῶν τὸ μέλλον γίνεσθαι. μετὰ δὲ πέμψας ἄγγελον ἐς τὴν Μύρκινον ὁ Δαρεῖος ἔλεγε τάδε· "Ἱστιαῖε, βασιλεὺς Δαρεῖος τάδε λέγει· ἐγὼ φροντίζων εὑρίσκω ἐμοί τε καὶ τοῖσι ἐμοῖσι πρήγμασι εἶναι οὐδένα σεῦ ἄνδρα εὐνοέστερον, τοῦτο δὲ οὐ λόγοισι ἀλλ' ἔργοισι οἶδα μαθών. (*2*) νῦν ὦν, ἐπινοέω γὰρ πρήγματα μεγάλα κατεργάσασθαι, ἀπίκεό μοι πάντως, ἵνα τοι αὐτὰ ὑπερθέωμαι." τούτοισι τοῖσι ἔπεσι πιστεύσας ὁ Ἱστιαῖος, καὶ ἅμα μέγα ποιεύμενος βασιλέος σύμβουλος γενέσθαι, ἀπίκετο ἐς τὰς Σάρδις. (*3*) ἀπικομένῳ δέ οἱ ἔλεγε Δαρεῖος τάδε· "Ἱστιαῖε, ἐγώ σε μετεπεμψάμην τῶνδε εἵνεκεν. ἐπείτε τάχιστα ἐνόστησα ἀπὸ Σκυθέων καὶ σύ μοι ἐγένεο ἐξ ὀφθαλμῶν, οὐδέν κω ἄλλο χρῆμα οὕτω ἐν βραχέϊ ἐπεζήτησα ὡς σὲ ἰδεῖν τε καὶ ἐς λόγους μοι ἀπικέσθαι, ἐγνωκὼς ὅτι κτημάτων πάντων ἐστὶ τιμιώτατον ἀνὴρ

---

23. 1.   Μύρκινον inserted after Μιλησίου Steger.
   μισθὸν δωρεὴν MSS: μισθὸν deleted Schaefer, δωρεὴν deleted Dobree, δωρεὴν μισθὸν Abicht, δωρεὴν <ἅτε> μισθὸν Wilson.
   τῷ οὔνομα ἐστὶ Μύρκινος deleted Powell.
24. 3.   ἐν βραχέϊ obelised Maas, deleted Powell, perhaps to be placed after σύ μοι or before ἀπίκεσθαι Wilson.

(**23**) Megabazus took the Paeonians and reached the Hellespont, and then he crossed over and reached Sardis. Histiaeus the Milesian was now fortifying the gift which he had asked and received from Darius as payment for guarding the bridge, the place being by the River Strymon and named Myrcinus. Megabazus learned what was being done by Histiaeus, and as soon as he had gone to Sardis taking the Paeonians he said this to Darius: (*2*) 'O King, what a thing you have done in granting to a dangerous and clever Greek man to found a city in Thrace, where there are abundant shipbuilding timber, many oars and silver mines, and there lives around it a great crowd both of Greeks and of barbarians, who will take him as their leader and both by day and by night do what he expounds! (*3*) You must stop this man from doing these things, if you are not to be caught up in a domestic war. Stop him by sending for him in a kindly way; and when you have him in your hands see that he no longer travels to the Greeks.' (**24**) By saying this Megabazus easily persuaded Darius that he could well foresee what was likely to happen. Then Darius sent a messenger to Myrcinus saying this: 'Histiaeus, King Darius says this: On considering the matter I find that no man is better disposed to me and my affairs than you, and I have come to the knowledge of this not from words but from deeds. (*2*) Now therefore, since I am planning to accomplish great deeds, come to me unhesitatingly, so that I can impart them to you.' Histiaeus trusted in these words and thought it a great matter to be an adviser of the King, and he came to Sardis. (*3*) When he had come, Darius said this to him: 'Histiaeus, I have sent for you for this reason: as soon as I had returned from the Scythians and you had departed from my presence, I have desired no other thing (in short) than to see you and have you come and converse with me, knowing that the most valuable of all possessions is a friend who is

φίλος συνετός τε καὶ εὔνοος, τά τοι ἐγὼ καὶ ἀμφότερα συνειδὼς ἔχω μαρτυρέειν ἐς πρήγματα τὰ ἐμά. (*4*) νῦν ὦν, εὖ γὰρ ἐποίησας ἀπικόμενος, τάδε τοι ἐγὼ προτείνομαι· Μίλητον μὲν ἔα καὶ τὴν νεόκτιστον ἐν Θρηίκῃ πόλιν, σὺ δέ μοι ἑπόμενος ἐς Σοῦσα ἔχε τά περ ἂν ἐγὼ ἔχω, ἐμός τε σύσσιτος ἐὼν καὶ σύμβουλος."

(**25**) ταῦτα Δαρεῖος εἴπας, καὶ καταστήσας Ἀρταφρένεα ἀδελφεὸν ἑωυτοῦ ὁμοπάτριον ὕπαρχον εἶναι Σαρδίων, ἀπήλαυνε ἐς Σοῦσα ἅμα ἀγόμενος Ἱστιαῖον, Ὀτάνεα δὲ ἀποδέξας στρατηγὸν εἶναι τῶν παραθαλασσίων ἀνδρῶν, τοῦ τὸν πατέρα Σισάμνην βασιλεὺς Καμβύσης γενόμενον τῶν βασιληίων δικαστέων, ὅτι ἐπὶ χρήμασι δίκην ἄδικον ἐδίκασε, σφάξας ἀπέδειρε πᾶσαν τὴν ἀνθρωπέην, σπαδίξας δὲ αὐτοῦ τὸ δέρμα ἱμάντας ἐξ αὐτοῦ ἔταμε καὶ ἐνέτεινε τὸν θρόνον ἐς τὸν ἵζων ἐδίκαζε. (*2*) ἐντανύσας δὲ ὁ Καμβύσης ἀπέδεξε δικαστὴν εἶναι ἀντὶ τοῦ Σισάμνεω, τὸν ἀποκτείνας ἀπέδειρε, τὸν παῖδα τοῦ Σισάμνεω, ἐντειλάμενός οἱ μεμνῆσθαι ἐν τῷ κατίζων θρόνῳ δικάζει.

(**26**) οὗτος ὦν ὁ Ὀτάνης ὁ ἐγκατιζόμενος ἐς τοῦτον τὸν θρόνον, τότε διάδοχος γενόμενος Μεγαβάζῳ τῆς στρατηγίης Βυζαντίους τε εἷλε καὶ Καλχηδονίους, εἷλε δὲ Ἄντανδρον τὴν ἐν τῇ Τρῳάδι γῇ, εἷλε δὲ Λαμπώνιον, λαβὼν δὲ παρὰ Λεσβίων νέας εἷλε Λῆμνόν τε καὶ Ἴμβρον, ἀμφοτέρας ἔτι τότε ὑπὸ Πελασγῶν οἰκεομένας. (**27**) οἱ μὲν δὴ Λήμνιοι καὶ ἐμαχέσαντο εὖ καὶ ἀμυνόμενοι ἀνὰ χρόνον ἐκακώθησαν, τοῖσι δὲ περιεοῦσι αὐτῶν οἱ Πέρσαι ὕπαρχον ἐπιστᾶσι Λυκάρητον τὸν Μαιανδρίου τοῦ βασιλεύσαντος Σάμου ἀδελφεόν. (*2*) οὗτος ὁ Λυκάρητος ἄρχων ἐν Λήμνῳ τελευτᾷ. – – – αἰτίη δὲ τούτου ἥδε· πάντας ἠνδραποδίζετο καὶ κατεστρέφετο, τοὺς μὲν λιποστρατίης ἐπὶ Σκύθας αἰτιώμενος, τοὺς δὲ σίνασθαι τὸν Δαρείου στρατὸν ἀπὸ Σκυθέων ὀπίσω ἀποκομιζόμενον.

(**28**) οὗτος μέν νυν τοσαῦτα ἐξεργάσατο στρατηγήσας. μετὰ δὲ οὐ πολλὸν χρόνον ἀνανέωσις κακῶν ἦν, καὶ ἤρχετο τὸ δεύτερον ἐκ

25. 5. ἀντὶ τοῦ Σισάμνεω, τὸν ἀποκτείνας ἀπέδειρε deleted Powell.
27. 1. Λήμνιοι καὶ <Ἴμβριοι> ἐμαχέσαντο εὖ [καὶ] ἀμυνομένοι <δ᾽> Powell.
27. 2 τελευτᾷ – – – αἰτίη: lacuna Valckenaer.
28. ἀνανέωσις Gebhardt: ἄνεος or ἄνεως MSS, ἄνεσις Scaliger, νέα Ἴωσι κακὰ ἦν Griffiths *ap.* Hornblower, perhaps ἀνὰ τὰς νήσους κακὰ ἦν Hornblower (commentary).

intelligent and well disposed, and I can testify that you have both of these qualities with regard to my affairs. (*4*) Now therefore, since you have done well in coming to me, I put this before you: let go Miletus and the newly-founded city in Thrace, come to Susa with me and have what I have, being my eating-companion and adviser.'

(**25**) After saying that, Darius installed Artaphernes, his brother by the same father, as governor of Sardis. He drove away to Susa, taking Histiaeus with him, and he appointed Otanes as general of the men by the sea. Otanes' father Sisamnes, who was one of the royal judges, King Cambyses had had killed and all his skin flayed, for taking a bribe to give an unjust judgment: he had his skin tanned and strips cut from it, and he stretched these across the throne on which Sisamnes used to sit to give judgment. (*2*) After stringing the throne, Cambyses appointed as judge in place of Sisamnes, whom he had killed and flayed, Sisamnes' son, and instructed him to remember what the throne was on which he sat to give judgment.

(**26**) This Otanes, who had sat on that throne, then became successor to Megabazus in his command. He captured Byzantium and Calchedon, he captured Antandrus in the land of the Troad, and he captured Lamponium. Taking ships from the Lesbians, he captured Lemnos and Imbros, both at that time occupied by Pelasgians. (**27**) The Lemnians fought well but after resisting for a time were worsted, and on those who survived the Persians imposed as governor Lycaretus, the brother of Maeandrius who had been king over Samos. (*2*) This Lycaretus after ruling in Lesbos died – – – The reason is this: he enslaved and reduced them all, accusing some of deserting the campaign against the Scythians and others of harassing Darius' force when it was making its way back from the Scythians.

(**28**) That is what Otanes did as general. After no long time there was a renewal of evil, and evil began to come to the Ionians for a

Νάξου τε καὶ Μιλήτου Ἴωσι γίνεσθαι κακά. τοῦτο μὲν γὰρ ἡ Νάξος
εὐδαιμονίη τῶν νήσων προέφερε, τοῦτο δὲ κατὰ τὸν αὐτὸν χρόνον ἡ
Μίλητος αὐτή τε ἑωυτῆς μάλιστα δὴ τότε ἀκμάσασα καὶ δὴ καὶ τῆς
Ἰωνίης ἦν πρόσχημα, κατύπερθε δὲ τούτων ἐπὶ δύο γενεὰς ἀνδρῶν
νοσήσασα ἐς τὰ μάλιστα στάσι, μέχρι οὗ μιν Πάριοι κατήρτισαν·
τούτους γὰρ καταρτιστῆρας ἐκ πάντων Ἑλλήνων εἵλοντο οἱ Μιλήσιοι.
(**29**) κατήλλαξαν δὲ σφέας ὧδε Πάριοι. ὡς ἀπίκοντο αὐτῶν ἄνδρες οἱ
ἄριστοι ἐς τὴν Μίλητον, ὥρων γὰρ δή σφεας δεινῶς οἰκοφθορημένους,
ἔφασαν αὐτῶν βούλεσθαι διεξελθεῖν τὴν χώρην. ποιεῦντες δὲ
ταῦτα καὶ διεξιόντες πᾶσαν τὴν Μιλησίην, ὅκως τινὰ ἴδοιεν <ἐν>
ἀνεστηκυίη τῇ χώρῃ ἀγρὸν εὖ ἐξεργασμένον, ἀπεγράφοντο τὸ οὔνομα
τοῦ δεσπότεω τοῦ ἀγροῦ. (*2*) διεξελάσαντες δὲ πᾶσαν τὴν χώρην καὶ
σπανίους εὑρόντες τούτους, ὡς τάχιστα κατέβησαν ἐς τὸ ἄστυ, ἁλίην
ποιησάμενοι ἀπέδεξαν τούτους μὲν πόλιν νέμειν τῶν εὗρον τοὺς
ἀγροὺς εὖ ἐξεργασμένους· δοκέειν γὰρ ἔφασαν καὶ τῶν δημοσίων
οὕτω δή σφεας ἐπιμελήσεσθαι ὥσπερ τῶν σφετέρων· τοὺς δὲ ἄλλους
Μιλησίους τοὺς πρὶν στασιάζοντας τούτων ἔταξαν πείθεσθαι.

(**30**) Πάριοι μέν νυν Μιλησίους οὕτω κατήρτισαν. τότε δὲ
ἐκ τουτέων τῶν πολίων ὧδε ἤρχετο κακὰ γίνεσθαι τῇ Ἰωνίῃ. ἐκ
Νάξου ἔφυγον ἄνδρες τῶν παχέων ὑπὸ τοῦ δήμου, φυγόντες δὲ
ἀπίκοντο ἐς Μίλητον. (*2*) τῆς δὲ Μιλήτου ἐτύγχανε ἐπίτροπος ἐὼν
Ἀρισταγόρης ὁ Μολπαγόρεω, γαμβρός τε ἐὼν καὶ ἀνεψιὸς Ἱστιαίου
τοῦ Λυσαγόρεω, τὸν ὁ Δαρεῖος ἐν Σούσοισι κατεῖχε· ὁ γὰρ Ἱστιαῖος
τύραννος ἦν Μιλήτου καὶ ἐτύγχανε τοῦτον τὸν χρόνον ἐὼν ἐν
Σούσοισι, ὅτε οἱ Νάξιοι ἦλθον, ξεῖνοι πρὶν ἐόντες τῷ Ἱστιαίῳ. (*3*)
ἀπικόμενοι δὲ οἱ Νάξιοι ἐς τὴν Μίλητον ἐδέοντο τοῦ Ἀρισταγόρεω
εἴ κως αὐτοῖσι παράσχοι δύναμίν τινα καὶ κατέλθοιεν ἐς τὴν ἑωυτῶν.
ὁ δὲ ἐπιλεξάμενος ὡς ἢν δι' αὐτοῦ κατέλθωσι ἐς τὴν πόλιν, ἄρξει
τῆς Νάξου, σκῆψιν δὲ ποιεύμενος τὴν ξεινίην τὴν Ἱστιαίου, τόνδε
σφι λόγον προσέφερε· (*4*) "αὐτὸς μὲν ὑμῖν οὐ φερέγγυός εἰμι δύναμιν
παρασχεῖν τοσαύτην ὥστε κατάγειν ἀεκόντων τῶν τὴν πόλιν ἐχόντων
Ναξίων· πυνθάνομαι γὰρ ὀκτακισχιλίην ἀσπίδα Ναξίοισι εἶναι καὶ

---

29. 1.   ἐν inserted Reiske.

second time, from Naxos and Miletus. Naxos, on one side, ranked first among the islands in prosperity; and at the same time Miletus, on the other hand, had itself reached its greatest height and moreover was the glory of Ionia. Before this for two generations of men it had ailed particularly from internal dissension, until the Parians rectified it: for the Milesians chose these out of all the Greeks to be rectifiers. (**29**) When their best men came to Miletus, they saw that they were in a dreadful state of domestic ruin, and they said that they would like to make a tour through their land. When they did this and made a tour through all Miletus' territory, whenever they saw a plot well worked in the devastated land, they recorded the name of the master of the plot. (*2*) Exploring all the land, and finding few of these, as soon as they went down to the city they held an assembly and declared that those men whose plots they found well worked should administer the city: for they said they thought these men would take care of public property as they did of their own. They instructed the other Milesians, who previously had been in dissension, to obey them.

(**30**) That is how the Parians rectified the Milesians. But now it was from those cities, Naxos and Miletus, that evil began to occur for Ionia, as follows. Men of the bloated class from Naxos were exiled by the people, and having been exiled they came to Miletus. (*2*) It happened that Aristagoras son of Molpagoras was deputy in Miletus, being both son-in-law and cousin of Histiaeus son of Lysagoras, whom Darius was detaining in Susa when the Naxians arrived. They had previously been guest-friends of Histiaeus. (*3*) On coming to Miletus the Naxians asked Aristagoras if he could somehow provide them with a force and they could be restored to their own territory. He reckoned that if it was through him that they were restored to their city he would be able to rule Naxos; and, using Histiaeus' guest-friendship with Naxos as a pretext, he put this proposal to them: (*4*) 'I cannot myself undertake to provide a sufficient force to reinstate you against the will of the Naxians in possession of the city, for I am aware that the Naxians have

πλοῖα μακρὰ πολλά. μηχανήσομαι δὲ πᾶσαν σπουδὴν ποιεύμενος. (5) ἐπινοέω δὲ τῇδε. Ἀρταφρένης μοι τυγχάνει ἐὼν φίλος· ὁ δὲ Ἀρταφρένης ὑμῖν Ὑστάσπεος μέν ἐστι παῖς, Δαρείου δὲ τοῦ βασιλέος ἀδελφεός, τῶν δ᾽ ἐπιθαλασσίων τῶν ἐν τῇ Ἀσίῃ ἄρχει πάντων, ἔχων στρατιήν τε πολλὴν καὶ πολλὰς νέας. τοῦτον ὦν δοκέω τὸν ἄνδρα ποιήσειν τῶν ἂν χρηίζωμεν.” (6) ταῦτα ἀκούσαντες οἱ Νάξιοι προσέθεσαν τῷ Ἀρισταγόρῃ πρήσσειν τῇ δύναιτο ἄριστα, καὶ ὑπίσχεσθαι δῶρα ἐκέλευον καὶ δαπάνην τῇ στρατιῇ ὡς αὐτοὶ διαλύσοντες, ἐλπίδας πολλὰς ἔχοντες, ὅταν ἐπιφανέωσι ἐς τὴν Νάξον, πάντα ποιήσειν τοὺς Ναξίους τὰ ἂν αὐτοὶ κελεύωσι, ὣς δὲ καὶ τοὺς ἄλλους νησιώτας. τῶν γὰρ νήσων τουτέων [τῶν Κυκλάδων] οὐδεμία κω ἦν ὑπὸ Δαρείῳ.

(31) ἀπικόμενος δὲ ὁ Ἀρισταγόρης ἐς τὰς Σάρδις λέγει πρὸς τὸν Ἀρταφρένεα ὡς Νάξος εἴη νῆσος μεγάθεϊ μὲν οὐ μεγάλη, ἄλλως δὲ καλή τε καὶ ἀγαθὴ καὶ ἀγχοῦ Ἰωνίης, χρήματα δὲ ἔνι πολλὰ καὶ ἀνδράποδα. “σὺ ὦν ἐπὶ ταύτην τὴν χώρην στρατηλάτεε, κατάγων ἐς αὐτὴν τοὺς φυγάδας ἐξ αὐτῆς. (2) καί τοι ταῦτα ποιήσαντι τοῦτο μὲν ἐστὶ ἕτοιμα παρ᾽ ἐμοὶ χρήματα μεγάλα πάρεξ τῶν ἀναισιμωμάτων τῇ στρατιῇ (ταῦτα μὲν γὰρ δίκαιον ἡμέας τοὺς ἄγοντας παρέχειν ἐστί), τοῦτο δὲ νήσους βασιλέϊ προσκτήσεαι αὐτήν τε Νάξον καὶ τὰς ἐκ ταύτης ἠρτημένας, Πάρον καὶ Ἄνδρον καὶ ἄλλας τὰς Κυκλάδας καλευμένας. (3) ἐνθεῦτεν δὲ ὁρμώμενος εὐπετέως ἐπιθήσεαι Εὐβοίῃ, νήσῳ μεγάλῃ τε καὶ εὐδαίμονι, οὐκ ἐλάσσονι Κύπρου καὶ κάρτα εὐπετέϊ αἱρεθῆναι. ἀποχρῶσι δὲ ἑκατὸν νέες ταύτας πάσας χειρώσασθαι.” ὁ δὲ ἀμείβετο αὐτὸν τοῖσιδε· (4) “σὺ ἐς οἶκον τὸν βασιλέος ἐξηγητὴς γίνεαι πρηγμάτων ἀγαθῶν, καὶ ταῦτα εὖ παραινέεις πάντα, πλὴν τῶν νεῶν τοῦ ἀριθμοῦ· ἀντὶ δὲ ἑκατὸν νεῶν διηκόσιαί τοι ἕτοιμοι ἔσονται ἅμα τῷ ἔαρι. δεῖ δὲ τούτοισι καὶ αὐτὸν βασιλέα συνέπαινον γίνεσθαι.”

(32) ὁ μὲν δὴ Ἀρισταγόρης, ὡς ταῦτα ἤκουσε, περιχαρὴς ἐὼν ἀπήιε ἐς Μίλητον. ὁ δὲ Ἀρταφρένης, ὥς οἱ πέμψαντι ἐς Σοῦσα καὶ ὑπερθέντι τὰ ἐκ τοῦ Ἀρισταγόρεω λεγόμενα συνέπαινος καὶ αὐτὸς Δαρεῖος ἐγένετο, παρεσκευάσατο μὲν διηκοσίας τριήρεας, πολλὸν δὲ κάρτα ὅμιλον Περσέων τε καὶ τῶν ἄλλων συμμάχων, στρατηγὸν δὲ τούτων ἀπέδεξε Μεγαβάτην ἄνδρα Πέρσην τῶν Ἀχαιμενιδέων,

30. 6.   τῶν Κυκλάδων deleted Hude.

eight thousand shields and many long ships. But I shall contrive with all the urgency I can. (*5*) What I plan is this. Artaphernes happens to be a friend of mine; and Artaphernes (I tell you) is a son of Hystaspes, and a brother of King Darius, and he rules over all the coastal people in Asia, and has a large army and many ships. This man, I think, will do what we want.' (*6*) On hearing this the Naxians told Aristagoras to do the best he could, and they instructed him to promise gifts and expenses for the force, which they themselves would pay; since they had great hopes that when they appeared at Naxos the Naxians would do everything which they instructed – and so too the other islanders, for none of these islands was yet under Darius.

(**31**) When Aristagoras went to Sardis he said to Artaphernes that Naxos was an island not of a great size, and in general that it was fine and good and near to Ionia, and had plentiful money and slaves. 'So you must campaign against this land, and reinstate in it the men exiled from it. (*2*) If you do this, on the one hand there is available from me a great sum of money, apart from the costs of the campaign (for it is right that we who are taking you there should provide them), and on the other hand you will gain for the King the islands, Naxos itself and those dependent on it, Paros, Andros and the rest of what are called the Cyclades. (*3*) If you set out from there, you will easily attack Euboea, which is a large and prosperous island, no smaller than Cyprus and very easy to capture. A hundred ships will be enough to subdue all of these.' Artaphernes responded to him as follows: (*4*) 'You are proposing good things for the King's house, and all of this that you recommend is good, except for the number of the ships. Instead of one hundred ships two hundred will be ready at the beginning of spring. But the King too needs to join in approving this.'

(**32**) When Aristagoras heard this, he was delighted and went back to Miletus. When Artaphernes sent to Susa and communicated what was said by Aristagoras, and Darius himself did join in approval, he prepared two hundred triremes and a great crowd of Persians and the other allies. He appointed as general of these Megabates, a Persian man of the Achaemenids, a cousin of himself and Darius, whose daughter was taken in marriage by Pausanias son of Cleombrotus the

ἑωυτοῦ τε καὶ Δαρείου ἀνεψιόν, τοῦ Παυσανίης ὁ Κλεομβρότου Λακεδαιμόνιος, εἰ δὴ ἀληθής γε ἐστὶ ὁ λόγος, ὑστέρῳ χρόνῳ τούτων ἡρμόσατο θυγατέρα, ἔρωτα σχὼν τῆς Ἑλλάδος τύραννος γενέσθαι. ἀποδέξας δὲ Μεγαβάτην στρατηγὸν Ἀρταφρένης ἀπέστειλε τὸν στρατὸν παρὰ τὸν Ἀρισταγόρεα.

(**33**) παραλαβὼν δὲ ὁ Μεγαβάτης ἐκ τῆς Μιλήτου τόν τε Ἀρισταγόρεα καὶ τὴν Ἰάδα στρατιὴν καὶ τοὺς Ναξίους, ἔπλεε πρόφασιν ἐπ᾽ Ἑλλησπόντου, ἐπείτε δὲ ἐγένετο ἐν Χίῳ, ἔσχε τὰς νέας ἐς Καύκασα, ὡς ἐνθεῦτεν βορέῃ ἀνέμῳ ἐς τὴν Νάξον διαβάλοι. (*2*) καὶ οὐ γὰρ ἔδεε τούτῳ τῷ στόλῳ Ναξίους ἀπολέσθαι, πρῆγμα τοιόνδε συνηνείχθη γενέσθαι. περιιόντος Μεγαβάτεω τὰς ἐπὶ τῶν νεῶν φυλακάς, ἐπὶ νεὸς Μυνδίης ἔτυχε οὐδεὶς φυλάσσων· ὁ δὲ δεινόν τι ποιησάμενος ἐκέλευσε τοὺς δορυφόρους ἐξευρόντας τὸν ἄρχοντα ταύτης τῆς νεός, τῷ οὔνομα ἦν Σκύλαξ, τοῦτον δῆσαι διὰ θαλαμίης διελόντας τῆς νεὸς κατὰ τοῦτο, ἔξω μὲν <τὴν> κεφαλὴν ποιεῦντας ἔσω δὲ τὸ σῶμα. (*3*) δεθέντος δὲ τοῦ Σκύλακος, ἐξαγγέλλει τις τῷ Ἀρισταγόρῃ ὅτι τὸν ξεῖνόν οἱ τὸν Μύνδιον Μεγαβάτης δήσας λυμαίνοιτο. ὁ δ᾽ ἐλθὼν παραιτέετο τὸν Πέρσην, τυγχάνων δὲ οὐδενὸς τῶν ἐδέετο αὐτὸς ἐλθὼν ἔλυσε. πυθόμενος δὲ κάρτα δεινὸν ἐποιήσατο ὁ Μεγαβάτης καὶ ἐσπέρχετο τῷ Ἀρισταγόρῃ, (*4*) ὁ δὲ εἶπε· "σοὶ δὲ καὶ τούτοισι τοῖσι πρήγμασι τί ἐστι; οὐ σὲ ἀπέστειλε Ἀρταφρένης ἐμέο πείθεσθαι καὶ πλέειν τῇ ἂν ἐγὼ κελεύω; τί πολλὰ πρήσσεις;" ταῦτα εἶπε ὁ Ἀρισταγόρης.

ὁ δὲ θυμωθεὶς τούτοισι, ὡς νὺξ ἐγένετο, ἔπεμπε ἐς Νάξον πλοίῳ ἄνδρας φράσοντας τοῖσι Ναξίοισι πάντα τὰ παρεόντα σφι πρήγματα. (**34**) οἱ γὰρ ὦν Νάξιοι οὐδὲν πάντως προσεδέκοντο ἐπὶ σφέας τὸν στόλον τοῦτον ὁρμήσεσθαι. ἐπεὶ μέντοι ἐπύθοντο, αὐτίκα μὲν ἐσηνείκαντο τὰ ἐκ τῶν ἀγρῶν ἐς τὸ τεῖχος, παρεσκευάσαντο δὲ ὡς πολιορκησόμενοι καὶ σῖτα καὶ ποτά, καὶ τὸ τεῖχος ἐσάξαντο. (*2*) καὶ

---

33. 1. ἐκ τῆς Μιλήτου τόν τε Ἀρισταγόρεα: τόν τε Ἀρισταγόρεα ἐκ Μιλήτου A.
33. 2. διελόντας MSS: διέλκοντας Stein, διέχοντας Powell.
   <τὴν> Hude *apparatus*.
33. 4. ἀπέστειλε: perhaps ἐπέστειλε Wilson *apparatus*.
34. 1. τι inserted after οὐδέν Krüger (cf. 65. 1, VI. 3).

Spartan (if the story is true) at a time later than this, when he had a passion to become tyrant of Greece. After appointing Megabates as general, Artaphernes sent the force to Aristagoras.

(**33**) Megabates took over from Miletus Aristagoras, and the Ionian force and the Naxians, and he set sail ostensibly for the Hellespont, but when he was at Chios he kept his ships at Caucasa, so that with a north wind he could cross from there to Naxos. (*2*) For the Naxians were not bound to be brought to ruin by this expedition, but the following kind of thing came about. When Megabates went around the guards on the ships, he found nobody guarding a Myndian ship; taking that hard, he ordered the spear-bearers to find the commander of the ship, whose name was Scylax, and to bind him, partitioning him through a lower oar-port of the ship in such a way that they put his head outside and his body inside. (*3*) When Scylax had been bound, somebody reported to Anaxagoras that Megabates had bound and was maltreating his Myndian guest-friend. He went and tried to dissuade the Persian, but obtained nothing that he asked for, and so himself went and freed him. When Megabates learned of that he took it very hard, and was angry with Aristagoras. (*4*) Aristagoras said, 'What are these matters to do with you? Didn't Artaphernes send you to obey me and sail wherever I order? Why are you causing trouble?' That is what Aristagoras said.

Megabates, incensed by that, when night fell sent men in a boat to Naxos to tell the Naxians all that was going on with regard to them. (**34**) For the Naxians had no expectation at all that this mission was aimed at them. But, when they learned it, they immediately brought their things from the fields inside the wall, prepared food and drink to withstand a siege and strengthened their wall. (*2*) So they prepared for war to come upon them, and when the attackers had taken their

οὗτοι μὲν παρεσκευάζοντο ὡς παρεσομένου σφι πολέμου· οἱ δ' ἐπείτε διέβαλον ἐκ τῆς Χίου τὰς νέας ἐς τὴν Νάξον, πρὸς πεφραγμένους προσεφέροντο καὶ ἐπολιόρκεον μῆνας τέσσερα. (3) ὡς δὲ τά τε ἔχοντες ἦλθον χρήματα οἱ Πέρσαι, ταῦτα κατεδεδαπάνητό σφι, καὶ αὐτῷ τῷ Ἀρισταγόρῃ προσαναισίμωτο πολλά, τοῦ πλεῦνός τε ἐδέετο ἡ πολιορκίη, ἐνθαῦτα τείχεα τοῖσι φυγάσι τῶν Ναξίων οἰκοδομήσαντες ἀπαλλάσσοντο ἐς τὴν ἤπειρον κακῶς πρήσσοντες.

(35) Ἀρισταγόρης δὲ οὐκ εἶχε τὴν ὑπόσχεσιν τῷ Ἀρταφρένεϊ ἐκτελέσαι· ἅμα δὲ ἐπίεζέ μιν ἡ δαπάνη τῆς στρατιῆς ἀπαιτεομένη, ἀρρώδεέ τε τοῦ στρατοῦ πρήξαντος κακῶς καὶ Μεγαβάτῃ διαβεβλημένος, ἐδόκεέ τε τὴν βασιληίην τῆς Μιλήτου ἀπαιρεθήσεσθαι. (2) ἀρρωδέων δὲ τούτων ἕκαστα ἐβουλεύετο ἀπόστασιν· συνέπιπτε γὰρ καὶ τὸν ἐστιγμένον τὴν κεφαλὴν ἀπῖχθαι ἐκ Σούσων παρὰ Ἱστιαίου, σημαίνοντα ἀπίστασθαι Ἀρισταγόρην ἀπὸ βασιλέος. (3) ὁ γὰρ Ἱστιαῖος βουλόμενος τῷ Ἀρισταγόρῃ σημῆναι ἀποστῆναι ἄλλως μὲν οὐδαμῶς εἶχε ἀσφαλέως σημῆναι ὥστε φυλασσομενέων τῶν ὁδῶν, ὁ δὲ τῶν δούλων τὸν πιστότατον ἀποξυρήσας τὴν κεφαλὴν ἔστιξε καὶ ἀνέμεινε ἀναφῦναι τὰς τρίχας, ὡς δὲ ἀνέφυσαν τάχιστα, ἀπέπεμπε ἐς Μίλητον ἐντειλάμενος αὐτῷ ἄλλο μὲν οὐδέν, ἐπεὰν δὲ ἀπίκηται ἐς Μίλητον, κελεύειν Ἀρισταγόρην ξυρήσαντά μιν τὰς τρίχας κατιδέσθαι ἐς τὴν κεφαλήν. τὰ δὲ στίγματα ἐσήμαινε, ὡς καὶ πρότερόν μοι εἴρηται, ἀπόστασιν. (4) ταῦτα δὲ ὁ Ἱστιαῖος ἐποίεε συμφορὴν ποιεύμενος μεγάλην τὴν ἑωυτοῦ κατοχὴν τὴν ἐν Σούσοισι· ἀποστάσιος ὦν γινομένης πολλὰς εἶχε ἐλπίδας μετήσεσθαι ἐπὶ θάλασσαν, μὴ δὲ νεώτερόν τι ποιεύσης τῆς Μιλήτου οὐδαμὰ ἐς αὐτὴν ἥξειν ἔτι ἐλογίζετο.

(36) Ἱστιαῖος μέν νυν ταῦτα διανοεύμενος ἀπέπεμπε τὸν ἄγγελον, Ἀρισταγόρῃ δὲ συνέπιπτε τοῦ αὐτοῦ χρόνου πάντα ταῦτα συνελθόντα. ἐβουλεύετο ὦν μετὰ τῶν στασιωτέων, ἐκφήνας τήν τε ἑωυτοῦ γνώμην καὶ τὰ παρὰ τοῦ Ἱστιαίου ἀπιγμένα. (2) οἱ μὲν δὴ ἄλλοι πάντες γνώμην κατὰ τώυτὸ ἐξεφέροντο, κελεύοντες ἀπίστασθαι· Ἑκαταῖος δ' ὁ λογοποιὸς πρῶτα μὲν οὐκ ἔα πόλεμον βασιλέϊ τῶν Περσέων ἀναιρέεσθαι, καταλέγων τά τε ἔθνεα πάντα τῶν ἦρχε Δαρεῖος καὶ τὴν δύναμιν αὐτοῦ. ἐπείτε δὲ οὐκ ἔπειθε, δεύτερα συνεβούλευε ποιέειν ὅκως ναυκρατέες τῆς θαλάσσης ἔσονται. (3) ἄλλως μέν νυν οὐδαμῶς

ships across from Chios to Naxos they assailed a defended enemy, and they carried on the siege for four months. (*3*) When the money which the Persians had brought with them had all been spent, much had been used up by Aristagoras in addition, and the siege needed more, then the attackers built forts for the Naxian exiles and departed for the mainland, having done badly.

(**35**) Aristagoras was unable to keep his promise to Artaphernes. At the same time he was under pressure from the request for the expenses of the campaign, and was worried since the force had done badly and he had quarrelled with Megabates, and thought he might be deprived of his kingship of Miletus. (*2*) Since he was worried on each of these counts, he chose to revolt. For it happened that the man with a tattooed head had arrived from Histiaeus in Susa, indicating that Aristagoras should revolt from the King. (*3*) For Histiaeus wanted to indicate to Aristagoras that he should revolt, but had no other way to indicate safely since the roads were guarded. He shaved bare the head of the most trustworthy of his slaves, tattooed it and waited for the hair to grow; and as soon as it had grown he sent the slave to Miletus, giving him no other instruction than that, when he reached Miletus, he was to tell Anaxagoras to shave his hair and examine his head. The tattoo, as I have said before, indicated revolt. (*4*) Histiaeus did this because he considered his detention in Susa a great disaster: he had great hope that when the revolt broke out he would be released to go to the sea, whereas if Miletus took no drastic action he reckoned that he would never return there.

(**36**) Histiaeus had that intention in sending his messenger, and for Aristagoras all these things happened to come together at the same time. So he began to deliberate with the dissidents, declaring his own opinion and what had arrived from Histiaeus. (*2*) All the others put forward the same opinion, saying that they should revolt. But Hecataeus the prose-writer first did not approve of undertaking a war against the King of the Persians, reviewing all the peoples whom Darius ruled and his power. When he failed to persuade them, his alternative advice was to see that they became masters of the sea. (*3*) He said that he could see no other way in which this could come about

ἔφη λέγων ἐνορᾶν ἐσόμενον τοῦτο (ἐπίστασθαι γὰρ τὴν δύναμιν τῶν Μιλησίων ἐοῦσαν ἀσθενέα) εἰ δὲ τὰ χρήματα καταιρεθείη τὰ ἐκ τοῦ ἱροῦ τοῦ ἐν Βραγχίδῃσι, τὰ Κροῖσος ὁ Λυδὸς ἀνέθηκε, πολλὰς εἶχε ἐλπίδας ἐπικρατήσειν τῆς θαλάσσης, καὶ οὕτω αὐτούς τε ἕξειν <τοῖσι> χρήμασι χρᾶσθαι καὶ τοὺς πολεμίους οὐ συλήσειν αὐτά. (*4*) τὰ δὲ χρήματα ἦν ταῦτα μεγάλα, ὡς δεδήλωταί μοι ἐν τῷ πρώτῳ τῶν λόγων. αὕτη μὲν δὴ οὐκ ἐνίκα ἡ γνώμη, ἐδόκεε δὲ ὅμως ἀπίστασθαι, ἕνα τε αὐτῶν πλώσαντα ἐς Μυοῦντα ἐς τὸ στρατόπεδον τὸ ἀπὸ τῆς Νάξου ἀπελθόν, ἐὸν ἐνθαῦτα, συλλαμβάνειν πειρᾶσθαι τοὺς ἐπὶ τῶν νεῶν ἐπιπλέοντας στρατηγούς.

(**37**) ἀποπεμφθέντος δὲ Ἰητραγόρεω κατ' αὐτὸ τοῦτο καὶ συλλαβόντος δόλῳ Ὀλίατον Ἰβανώλλιος Μυλασσέα καὶ Ἰστιαῖον Τύμνεω Τερμερέα καὶ Κώην Ἐρξάνδρου, τῷ Δαρεῖος Μυτιλήνην ἐδωρήσατο, καὶ Ἀρισταγόρην Ἡρακλείδεω Κυμαῖον καὶ ἄλλους συχνούς, οὕτω δὴ ἐκ τοῦ ἐμφανέος ὁ Ἀρισταγόρης ἀπεστήκεε, πᾶν ἐπὶ Δαρείῳ μηχανώμενος. (*2*) καὶ πρῶτα μὲν λόγῳ μετεὶς τὴν τυραννίδα ἰσονομίην ἐποίεε τῇ Μιλήτῳ, ὡς ἂν ἑκόντες αὐτῷ οἱ Μιλήσιοι συναπισταίατο, μετὰ δὲ καὶ ἐν τῇ ἄλλῃ Ἰωνίῃ τὠυτὸ τοῦτο ἐποίεε, τοὺς μὲν ἐξελαύνων τῶν τυράννων, τοὺς δ' ἔλαβε τυράννους ἀπὸ τῶν νεῶν τῶν συμπλευσασέων ἐπὶ Νάξον, τούτους δὲ φίλα βουλόμενος ποιέεσθαι τῇσι πόλισι ἐξεδίδου, ἄλλον ἐς ἄλλην πόλιν παραδιδούς, ὅθεν εἴη ἕκαστος. (**38**) Κώην μέν νυν Μυτιληναῖοι ἐπείτε τάχιστα παρέλαβον, ἐξαγαγόντες κατέλευσαν, Κυμαῖοι δὲ τὸν σφέτερον αὐτῶν ἀπῆκαν· ὣς δὲ καὶ ἄλλοι οἱ πλεῦνες ἀπίεσαν. (*2*) τυράννων μέν νυν κατάπαυσις ἐγίνετο ἀνὰ τὰς πόλιας· Ἀρισταγόρης δὲ ὁ Μιλήσιος ὡς τοὺς τυράννους κατέπαυσε, στρατηγοὺς ἐν ἑκάστῃ τῶν πολίων κελεύσας ἑκάστους καταστῆσαι, δεύτερα αὐτὸς ἐς Λακεδαίμονα τριήρεϊ ἀπόστολος ἐγίνετο· ἔδεε γὰρ δὴ συμμαχίης τινός οἱ μεγάλης ἐξευρεθῆναι.

(**39**) τῆς δὲ Σπάρτης Ἀναξανδρίδης μὲν ὁ Λέοντος οὐκέτι περιεὼν ἐβασίλευε ἀλλὰ ἐτετελευτήκεε, Κλεομένης δὲ ὁ Ἀναξανδρίδεω εἶχε τὴν βασιληίην, οὐ κατ' ἀνδραγαθίην σχὼν ἀλλὰ κατὰ γένος. Ἀναξανδρίδῃ

---

36. 3.   τοῖσι inserted Stein.
37. 2.   λόγῳ MSS: <τῷ> λεῷ Griffiths *ap.* Hornblower, <ἐν συλ>λόγῳ Wilson.

(for he knew that the condition of Miletus was weak); but if they were to take from the temple at Branchidae the funds which Croesus the Lydian had dedicated, then he had great hope that they would get mastery of the sea, and in that case they would be able to make use of the funds and the enemy would not be able to pillage them. (*4*) These funds were substantial, as I have indicated in the first of my accounts. That opinion did not prevail, but nevertheless they decided to revolt; and one of them was to sail to Myus to the force which had returned from Naxos, and when there should try to persuade the men sailing on the ships to arrest the generals.

(**37**) Iatragoras was sent for this very purpose. By trickery he captured Olliatus son of Ibanollis of Mylasa, Histiaeus son of Tymnes of Termera, Coes son of Erxandrus (to whom Darius had presented Mytilene), Aristagoras son of Heraclides of Cyme and many others. Then Aristagoras revolted openly, contriving all that he could against Darius. (*2*) First he in theory laid aside his tyranny, creating legal equality for Miletus so that the Milesians should willingly join him in revolt; and afterwards he did the same for the rest of Ionia, driving out some of the tyrants, whereas the tyrants whom he took from the ships which had joined in sailing aganst Naxos he gave up to their cities, wanting to make friends of them: he handed over the different men to the different cities from which each had come. (**38**) Coes, as soon as the Mytilenaeans had taken him over, they took outside and stoned him to death; but the Cymaeans set theirs free, and similarly most of the others set theirs free. (*2*) So the ending of tyrants occurred among the cities; and Aristagoras of Miletus, when he had ended the tyrants, told them each to appoint generals in each of the cities, and secondly he went as an emissary in a trireme to Sparta: for he needed to find some great alliance.

(**39**) In Sparta Anaxandridas the son of Leon was no longer surviving as king but had died, and Cleomenes the son of Anaxandridas held the kingship, in accordance not with personal merit but with descent. For Anaxandridas had as wife the daughter of his own sister, and although

γὰρ ἔχοντι γυναῖκα ἀδελφεῆς ἑωυτοῦ θυγατέρα, καὶ ἐούσης ταύτης οἱ καταθυμίης, παῖδες οὐκ ἐγίνοντο. (*2*) τούτου δὲ τοιούτου ἐόντος, οἱ ἔφοροι εἶπαν ἐπικαλεσάμενοι αὐτόν· "εἴ τοι σὺ σεωυτοῦ μὴ προορᾶς, ἀλλ᾽ ἡμῖν τοῦτό ἐστι οὐ περιοπτέον, γένος τὸ Εὐρυσθένεος γενέσθαι ἐξίτηλον. σὺ νυν τὴν μὲν ἔχεις γυναῖκα, ἐπείτε τοι οὐ τίκτει, ἔξεο, ἄλλην δὲ γῆμον· καὶ ποιέων ταῦτα Σπαρτιήτῃσι ἁδήσεις." ὁ δ᾽ ἀμείβετο φὰς τούτων οὐδέτερα ποιήσειν, ἐκείνους τε οὐ καλῶς συμβουλεύειν παραινέοντας, τὴν ἔχει γυναῖκα, ἐοῦσαν ἀναμάρτητον ἑωυτῷ, ταύτην ἀπέντα ἄλλην ἐσαγαγέσθαι· οὐδέ σφι πείσεσθαι. (**40**) πρὸς ταῦτα οἱ ἔφοροι καὶ οἱ γέροντες βουλευσάμενοι προσέφερον Ἀναξανδρίδῃ τάδε· "ἐπεὶ τοίνυν [τοι] περιεχόμενόν σε ὁρῶμεν τῆς ἔχεις γυναικός, σὺ δὲ ταῦτα ποίεε, καὶ μὴ ἀντίβαινε τούτοισι, ἵνα μή τι ἀλλοῖον περὶ σεῦ Σπαρτιῆται βουλεύσωνται. (*2*) γυναικὸς μὲν τῆς ἔχεις οὐ προσδεόμεθά σευ τῆς ἐξέσιος, σὺ δὲ ταύτῃ τε πάντα ὅσα νῦν παρέχεις πάρεχε καὶ ἄλλην πρὸς ταύτῃ ἐσάγαγε γυναῖκα τεκνοποιόν." ταῦτά κῃ λεγόντων συνεχώρησε ὁ Ἀναξανδρίδης, μετὰ δὲ γυναῖκας ἔχων δύο διξὰς ἱστίας οἴκεε, ποιέων οὐδαμῶς Σπαρτιητικά.

(**41**) χρόνου δὲ οὐ πολλοῦ διελθόντος ἡ ἐσύστερον ἐπελθοῦσα γυνὴ τίκτει τὸν δὴ Κλεομένεα τοῦτον. καὶ αὕτη τε ἔφεδρον βασιλέα Σπαρτιήτῃσι ἀπέφαινε, καὶ ἡ προτέρη γυνὴ τὸν πρότερον χρόνον ἄτοκος ἐοῦσα τότε κως ἐκύησε, συντυχίῃ ταύτῃ χρησαμένη. (*2*) ἔχουσαν δὲ αὐτὴν ἀληθέϊ λόγῳ οἱ τῆς ἐπελθούσης γυναικὸς οἰκήιοι πυθόμενοι ὤχλεον, φάμενοι αὐτὴν κομπέειν ἄλλως βουλομένην ὑποβαλέσθαι. δεινὰ δὲ ποιεύντων αὐτῶν, τοῦ χρόνου συντάμνοντος, ὑπ᾽ ἀπιστίης οἱ ἔφοροι τίκτουσαν τὴν γυναῖκα περιιζόμενοι ἐφύλαξαν. (*3*) ἡ δὲ ὡς ἔτεκε Δωριέα ἰθέως ἴσχει Λεωνίδην, καὶ μετὰ τοῦτον ἰθέως ἴσχει Κλεόμβροτον· οἱ δὲ καὶ διδύμους λέγουσι Κλεόμβροτον

40. 1.   τοι omitted S.
41. 1.   συντυχίῃ ταύτῃ MSS: συντυχίῃ θείῃ Powell.
41. 2.   ἐν γαστρὶ inserted after ἔχουσαν δὲ αὐτὴν, and perhaps κυοῦσαν for ἔχουσαν, van Herwerden.
41. 3.   καὶ τὸ δευτέρον ἐπελθοῦσα γυνή, ἐοῦσα θυγάτηρ Πρινητάδεω τοῦ Δημαρμένου: τὸ deleted Stein, whole passage deleted here and ἐοῦσα θυγάτηρ Πρινητάδεω τοῦ Δημαρμένου inserted in 41. 1 after ἐπελθοῦσα γυνή Maas.

she was dear to him they had no sons. (*2*) This being the case, the ephors summoned him and said, 'Even if you do not look to your interest, this is something which we cannot overlook, that the line of Eurysthenes should be obliterated. The wife whom you have, since she has not given birth, divorce, and marry another: if you do this you will gratify the Spartiates.' He replied that he would do neither of those things, and that they were not giving good advice in urging him to dismiss the wife he had, who had done him no wrong, and bring in another: he would not agree to that. (**40**) In response to that the ephors and the elders debated and put this proposal to Anaxandridas: 'Since we see that you are attached to the wife whom you have, do this and do not oppose it, unless the Spartiates are to take another kind of decision about you. (*2*) We do not insist on your divorcing the wife whom you have, but while continuing to grant her all that you do grant her now you must bring in another wife in addition to her, to bear a son.' When they said that Anaxandridas agreed, and afterwards he had two wives and maintained two households, a totally un-Spartiate practice.

(**41**) After no long time the wife who came in more recently bore this son Cleomenes. She revealed him to the Spartiates as king in waiting; and the previous wife, who in the previous time had been childless, did then become pregnant, as a matter of coincidence. (*2*) Although in very truth she was pregnant, when the relatives of the additional wife learned of it they began to cause trouble, saying that she was making an empty boast and intended to substitute a child. Since they made a dreadful thing of this, when her time was short the ephors in distrust sat around the woman and watched her giving birth. (*3*) When she had borne Dorieus, she soon conceived Leonidas, and after him she soon conceived Cleombrotus; some say that Cleombrotus and Leonidas were actually twins. The wife who had borne Cleomenes,

καὶ Λεωνίδην γενέσθαι. ἡ δὲ Κλεομένεα τεκοῦσα καὶ τὸ δεύτερον ἐπελθοῦσα γυνή, ἐοῦσα θυγάτηρ Πρινητάδεω τοῦ Δημαρμένου, οὐκέτι ἔτικτε τὸ δεύτερον.

(42) ὁ μὲν δὴ Κλεομένης, ὡς λέγεται, ἦν τε οὐ φρενήρης ἀκρομανής τε· ὁ δὲ Δωριεὺς ἦν τῶν ἡλίκων πάντων πρῶτος, εὖ τε ἐπίστατο κατ᾽ ἀνδραγαθίην αὐτὸς σχήσων τὴν βασιληίην. (2) ὥστε ὦν οὕτω φρονέων, ἐπειδὴ ὅ τε Ἀναξανδρίδης ἀπέθανε καὶ οἱ Λακεδαιμόνιοι χρεώμενοι τῷ νόμῳ ἐστήσαντο βασιλέα τὸν πρεσβύτατον Κλεομένεα, ὁ Δωριεύς, δεινόν τε ποιεύμενος καὶ οὐκ ἀξιῶν ὑπὸ Κλεομένεος βασιλεύεσθαι, αἰτήσας λεὼν Σπαρτιήτας ἦγε ἐς ἀποικίην, οὔτε τῷ ἐν Δελφοῖσι χρηστηρίῳ χρησάμενος ἐς ἥντινα γῆν κτίσων ἴῃ, οὔτε ποιήσας οὐδὲν τῶν νομιζομένων. οἷα δὲ βαρέως φέρων, ἀπίει ἐς τὴν Λιβύην τὰ πλοῖα· κατηγέοντο δέ οἱ ἄνδρες Θηραῖοι. (3) ἀπικόμενος δὲ ἐς Λιβύην οἴκισε χῶρον κάλλιστον τῶν Λιβύων παρὰ Κίνυπα ποταμόν. ἐξελαθεὶς δὲ ἐνθεῦτεν τρίτῳ ἔτεϊ ὑπὸ Μακέων τε [καὶ] Λιβύων καὶ Καρχηδονίων ἀπίκετο ἐς Πελοπόννησον.

(43) ἐνθαῦτα δέ οἱ Ἀντιχάρης ἀνὴρ Ἐλεώνιος συνεβούλευσε ἐκ τῶν Λαΐου χρησμῶν Ἡρακλείην τὴν ἐν Σικελίῃ κτίζειν, φὰς τὴν Ἔρυκος χώρην πᾶσαν εἶναι Ἡρακλειδέων αὐτοῦ Ἡρακλέος κτησαμένου. ὁ δὲ ἀκούσας ταῦτα ἐς Δελφοὺς οἴχετο χρησόμενος τῷ χρηστηρίῳ, εἰ αἱρέει ἐπ᾽ ἣν στέλλεται χώρην· ἡ δὲ Πυθίη οἱ χρᾷ αἱρήσειν. παραλαβὼν δὲ Δωριεὺς τὸν στόλον τὸν καὶ ἐς Λιβύην ἦγε, ἐκομίζετο παρὰ τὴν Ἰταλίην. (44) τὸν χρόνον δὲ τοῦτον, ὡς λέγουσι Συβαρῖται, σφέας τε αὐτοὺς καὶ Τῆλυν τὸν ἑωυτῶν βασιλέα ἐπὶ Κρότωνα μέλλειν στρατεύεσθαι, τοὺς δὲ Κροτωνιήτας περιδεέας γενομένους δεηθῆναι Δωριέος σφίσι τιμωρῆσαι καὶ τυχεῖν δεηθέντας· συστρατεύεσθαί τε δὴ ἐπὶ Σύβαριν Δωριέα καὶ συνελεῖν τὴν Σύβαριν. (2) ταῦτα μέν νυν Συβαρῖται λέγουσι ποιῆσαι Δωριέα τε καὶ τοὺς μετ᾽

---

42. 2.   οἷα δὲ S: δὲ omitted other MSS.
42. 3.   ἐς Λιβύην ... παρὰ Κίνυπα ποταμόν Stein: ἐς Κίνυπα ... παρὰ
         ποταμόν MSS.
         ἐξελαθεὶς A: ἐξελασθεὶς other MSS.
         καὶ deleted Niebuhr.
43.   Λαΐου MSS: Λάσου Schneidewin, Ἰάμου Valckenaer.
         γῆν inserted after Ἡρακλείην Stein.

who had come in second, being the daughter of Prinetadas son of Demarmenus, did not give birth a second time.

(**42**) Now Cleomenes, as it is said, was not of sound mind but was slightly mad. But Dorieus was first among all his contemporaries, and was confident that in accordance with personal merit he would have the kingship. (*2*) So, that being his view, when Anaxandridas died, and the Spartans followed their custom and installed the eldest son Cleomenes as king, Dorieus made a dreadful thing of this. Not thinking it right that he should be subject to Cleomenes as king, he asked the Spartiates for a body of men and took them to found a colony, though he did not ask the oracle at Delphi which territory he should go to for his foundation, or do any of the customary things. Taking it hard, he sent his boats to Libya; they were guided by men of Thera. (*3*) On arrival in Libya he settled the finest site of the Libyans by the River Cinyps. But he was driven out from there in the third year by the Macian Libyans and the Carthaginians, and went to the Peloponnese.

(**43**) Then Antichares, a man of Eleon, advised him from the oracles of Laïus to found Heraclea in Sicily, saying that all the land of Eryx belonged to the Heraclidae because Heracles himself had gained it. On hearing this he went to Delphi to ask the oracle whether he would take the land for which he was setting out; and the Pythia answered that he would take it. Dorieus took up the force which he had taken to Libya also, and made his way past Italy. (**44**) At this time, as the Sybarites say, they and their king Telys were about to campaign against Croton. In great fear the Crotoniates begged Dorieus to succour them, and they obtained what they begged for. Dorieus joined them in campaigning against Sybaris and in taking Sybaris. (*2*) The Sybarites say that that is what was done by Dorieus and those with him; but the Crotoniates

αὐτοῦ, Κροτωνιῆται δὲ οὐδένα σφίσι φασὶ ξεῖνον προσεπιλαβέσθαι τοῦ πρὸς Συβαρίτας πολέμου εἰ μὴ Καλλίην τῶν Ἰαμιδέων μάντιν Ἠλεῖον μοῦνον, καὶ τοῦτον τρόπῳ τοιῷδε· παρὰ Τήλυος τοῦ Συβαριτέων τυράννου ἀποδράντα ἀπικέσθαι παρὰ σφέας, ἐπείτε οἱ τὰ ἱρὰ οὐ προεχώρεε χρηστὰ θυομένῳ ἐπὶ Κρότωνα. (45) ταῦτα δὲ οὗτοι λέγουσι. μαρτύρια δὲ τούτων ἑκάτεροι ἀποδεικνύουσι τάδε. Συβαρῖται μὲν τέμενός τε καὶ νηὸν ἐόντα παρὰ τὸν ξηρὸν Κρᾶθιν, τὸν ἱδρύσασθαι συνελόντα τὴν πόλιν Δωριέα λέγουσι Ἀθηναίῃ ἐπωνύμῳ Κραθίῃ· τοῦτο δὲ αὐτοῦ Δωριέος τὸν θάνατον μαρτύριον μέγιστον ποιεῦνται, ὅτι παρὰ τὰ μεμαντευμένα ποιέων διεφθάρη· εἰ γὰρ δὴ μὴ παρέπρηξε μηδέν, ἐπ' ὃ δὲ ἐστάλη ἐποίεε, εἷλε ἂν τὴν Ἐρυκίνην χώρην καὶ ἑλὼν κατέσχε, οὐδ' ἂν αὐτός τε καὶ ἡ στρατιὴ διεφθάρη. (2) οἱ δ' αὖ Κροτωνιῆται ἀποδεικνῦσι Καλλίῃ μὲν τῷ Ἠλείῳ ἐξαίρετα ἐν γῇ τῇ Κροτωνιήτιδι πολλὰ δοθέντα, τὰ καὶ ἐς ἐμὲ ἔτι ἐνέμοντο οἱ Καλλίεω ἀπόγονοι, Δωριέϊ δὲ καὶ τοῖσι Δωριέος ἀπογόνοισι οὐδέν· καίτοι εἰ συνεπελάβετό γε τοῦ Συβαριτικοῦ πολέμου Δωριεύς, δοθῆναι ἄν οἱ πολλαπλήσια ἢ Καλλίῃ. ταῦτα μέν νυν ἑκάτεροι αὐτῶν μαρτύρια ἀποφαίνονται, καὶ πάρεστι, ὁκοτέροισί τις πείθεται αὐτῶν, τούτοισι προσχωρέειν.

(46) συνέπλεον δὲ Δωριέϊ καὶ ἄλλοι συγκτίσται Σπαρτιητέων, Θεσσαλὸς καὶ Παραιβάτης καὶ Κελέης καὶ Εὐρυλέων, οἳ ἐπείτε ἀπίκοντο παντὶ στόλῳ ἐς τὴν Σικελίην ἀπέθανον μάχῃ ἑσσωθέντες ὑπό τε Φοινίκων καὶ Ἐγεσταίων· μοῦνος δὲ Εὐρυλέων τῶν συγκτιστέων περιεγένετο τούτου τοῦ πάθεος. (2) συλλαβὼν δὲ οὗτος τῆς στρατιῆς τοὺς περιγενομένους ἔσχε Μινώην τὴν Σελινουσίων ἀποικίην, καὶ συνελευθέρου Σελινουσίους τοῦ μουνάρχου Πειθαγόρεω. μετὰ δὲ ὡς τοῦτον κατεῖλε, αὐτὸς τυραννίδι ἐπεχείρησε Σελινοῦντος καὶ ἐμουνάρχησε χρόνον ἐπ' ὀλίγον· οἱ γάρ μιν Σελινούσιοι ἐπαναστάντες ἀπέκτειναν καταφυγόντα ἐπὶ Διὸς ἀγοραίου βωμόν. (47) συνέσπετο δὲ Δωριέϊ καὶ συναπέθανε Φίλιππος ὁ Βουτακίδεω Κροτωνιήτης ἀνήρ, ὃς ἁρμοσάμενος Τήλυος τοῦ Συβαρίτεω θυγατέρα ἔφυγε ἐκ Κρότωνος, ψευσθεὶς δὲ τοῦ γάμου οἴχετο πλέων ἐς Κυρήνην, ἐκ

45. 1. ὧν de la Barre, Wilson: οὐχ or οὐκ MSS, αὖ Bekker, δὴ Legrand.
47. 1. δυνάμι Powell: δαπάνῃ MSS.

say that no foreigner took a share with them in the war against the Sybarites, save only Callias of the Iamidae, a seer from Elis, and he did so in this kind of way. He ran away from Telys the tyrant of the Sybarites and came to them, because when he sacrificed for the campaign against Croton the auspices were not good. (**45**) That, then, is what they say. Each cite evidence of this, as follows. The Sybarites say there is a precinct and temple by the dried-up Crathis, which after he joined in taking the city Dorieus founded for Athena with the cult name Crathias; and they consider as the greatest evidence the death of Dorieus himself, that he was destroyed through acting contrary to the oracle: for if he had not done anything on the side, but had done what he was sent to do, he would have taken the land of Eryx and having taken it would have been able to hold it, and he and his force would not have been destroyed. (*2*) The Crotoniates for their part cite great quantities of land set aside and given to Callias the Elean in Crotoniate territory, which the descendants of Callias were continuing to cultivate to my time, but none given to Dorieus and the descendants of Dorieus. Yet, if Dorieus had taken a share in the Sybarite war, much the same would have been given to him as to Callias. That is the evidence cited by each of them, and it is possible to go along with whichever one finds persuasive.

(**46**) There sailed with Dorieus other joint founders from the Spartiates, Thessalus, Paraebatas, Celeas and Euryleon. When they had reached Sicily with their whole expedition they died, defeated in battle by the Phoenicians and Egestaeans: of the joint founders only Euryleon survived this disaster. (*2*) He took over the survivors of the force, captured Minoa the colony of Selinus, and joined in freeing the Selinuntines from their ruler Peithagoras. Afterwards, when he had overthrown him, he himself made a bid for tyranny over Selinus, and ruled only for a short time; for the Selinuntines rose up and killed him, though he took refuge at the altar of Zeus Agoraios. (**47**) There joined Dorieus and died with him Philippus son of Butacides, a man of Croton, who was betrothed to the daughter of Telys the Sybarite but was exiled from Croton. Deprived of his marriage he went and sailed to Cyrene; setting out from there, he joined Dorieus with his

ταύτης δὲ ὁρμώμενος συνέσπετο οἰκηίῃ τε τριήρεϊ καὶ οἰκηίῃ ἀνδρῶν δυνάμι, ἐών τε Ὀλυμπιονίκης καὶ κάλλιστος Ἑλλήνων τῶν κατ' ἑωυτόν. (*2*) διὰ δὲ τὸ ἑωυτοῦ κάλλος ἠνείκατο παρὰ Ἐγεσταίων τὰ οὐδεὶς ἄλλος· ἐπὶ γὰρ τοῦ τάφου αὐτοῦ ἡρώιον ἱδρυσάμενοι θυσίῃσι αὐτὸν ἱλάσκονται.

(**48**) Δωριεὺς μέν νυν τρόπῳ τοιούτῳ ἐτελεύτησε· εἰ δὲ ἠνέσχετο βασιλευόμενος ὑπὸ Κλεομένεος καὶ κατέμενε ἐν Σπάρτῃ, ἐβασίλευσε ἂν Λακεδαίμονος· οὐ γάρ τινα πολλὸν χρόνον ἦρξε ὁ Κλεομένης, ἀλλ' ἀπέθανε ἄπαις, θυγατέρα μούνην λιπών, τῇ οὔνομα ἦν Γοργώ.

(**49**) ἀπικνέεται δὲ ὦν ὁ Ἀρισταγόρης ὁ Μιλήτου τύραννος ἐς τὴν Σπάρτην Κλεομένεος ἔχοντος τὴν ἀρχήν· τῷ δὴ ἐς λόγους ἤιε, ὡς Λακεδαιμόνιοι λέγουσι, ἔχων χάλκεον πίνακα ἐν τῷ γῆς ἁπάσης περίοδος ἐνετέτμητο καὶ θάλασσά τε πᾶσα καὶ ποταμοὶ πάντες. (*2*) ἀπικνεόμενος δὲ ἐς λόγους ὁ Ἀρισταγόρης ἔλεγε πρὸς αὐτὸν τάδε· "Κλεόμενες, σπουδὴν μὲν τὴν ἐμὴν μὴ θωμάσῃς τῆς ἐνθαῦτα ἀπίξιος. τὰ γὰρ κατήκοντα ἐστὶ τοιαῦτα· Ἰώνων παῖδας δούλους εἶναι ἀντ' ἐλευθέρων ὄνειδος καὶ ἄλγος μέγιστον μὲν αὐτοῖσι ἡμῖν, ἔτι δὲ τῶν λοιπῶν ὑμῖν, ὅσῳ προέστατε τῆς Ἑλλάδος. (*3*) νῦν ὦν πρὸς θεῶν τῶν Ἑλληνίων ῥύσασθε Ἴωνας ἐκ δουλοσύνης, ἄνδρας ὁμαίμονας. εὐπετέως δὲ ὑμῖν ταῦτα οἷά τε χωρέειν ἐστί· οὔτε γὰρ οἱ βάρβαροι ἄλκιμοι εἰσί, ὑμεῖς τε τὰ ἐς τὸν πόλεμον ἐς τὰ μέγιστα ἀνήκετε ἀρετῆς πέρι. ἥ τε μάχη αὐτῶν ἐστὶ τοιήδε, τόξα καὶ αἰχμὴ βραχέα· ἀναξυρίδας δὲ ἔχοντες ἔρχονται ἐς τὰς μάχας καὶ κυρβασίας ἐπὶ τῇσι κεφαλῇσι. (*4*) οὕτω εὐπετέες χειρωθῆναι εἰσί. ἔστι δὲ καὶ ἀγαθὰ τοῖσι τὴν ἤπειρον ἐκείνην νεμομένοισι ὅσα οὐδὲ τοῖσι συνάπασι ἄλλοισι, ἀπὸ χρυσοῦ ἀρξαμένοισι, ἄργυρος καὶ χαλκὸς καὶ ἐσθὴς ποικίλη καὶ ὑποζύγιά τε καὶ ἀνδράποδα· τὰ θυμῷ βουλόμενοι αὐτοὶ ἂν ἔχοιτε. (*5*) κατοίκηνται δὲ ἀλλήλων ἐχόμενοι ὡς ἐγὼ φράσω. Ἰώνων μὲν τῶνδε οἵδε Λυδοί, οἰκέοντές τε χώρην ἀγαθὴν καὶ πολυαργυρώτατοι ἐόντες." δεικνὺς δὲ ἔλεγε ταῦτα ἐς τῆς γῆς τὴν περίοδον, τὴν ἐφέρετο ἐν τῷ πίνακι ἐντετμημένην. "Λυδῶν δέ", ἔφη λέγων ὁ Ἀρισταγόρης, "οἵδε ἔχονται

---

48.   οὐ γάρ τινα πολλὸν MSS: εἰ γάρ Griffiths *ap.* Hornblower, οὐ γὰρ ἔτι πολλὸν Wilson.

49. 5.   Φρύγες οἱ: οἱ deleted Powell.

own trireme and his own force of men. He was an Olympic victor and the most handsome of the men of his time. (*2*) Because of his handsomeness he won from the Egestaeans what nobody else won: for at his tomb they founded a hero's shrine, and they sacrifice to propitiate him.

(**48**) Dorieus died in that kind of way. But if he had put up with being under the kingship of Cleomenes and had remained in Sparta he would have become king of Sparta; for Cleomenes did not rule for a long time, but he died without a son, leaving a sole daughter, whose name was Gorgo.

(**49**) So Aristagoras the tyrant of Miletus came to Sparta when Cleomenes was ruling. He went to speak to him, as the Spartans say, taking a bronze tablet on which the circuit of the whole earth was engraved, with all the sea and all the rivers. (*2*) When they came to speak to each other Aristagoras said this to him: 'Cleomenes, do not be surprised at my urgency in coming here; for the situation is like this. That the sons of the Ionians are slaves instead of free is the greatest disgrace and grief both to us and to you among the others, in so far as you are the leaders of Greece. (*3*) So now, by the gods of the Greeks, rescue from slavery the Ionians, who are men of the same blood as you. It will be easy for you to succeed in this: for the barbarians are not valiant, while you with regard to warfare have reached the greatest height in respect of excellence. Their mode of battle is like this: the bow and short sword; and they go into battle wearing trousers, and peaked caps on their heads. (*4*) So they are easy to subdue. And in addition those who occupy that continent have more good things than everybody else together: starting with gold, they have silver and bronze and embroidered clothing and beasts of burden and slaves. If in your hearts you want it you could have this. (*5*) They live one in succession to another as I shall indicate. Next to these Ionians here are the Lydians, living in a good land and rich in money.' He said this pointing to the circuit of the earth which he had brought, engraved on the tablet. 'Adjoining the Lydians', said Aristagoras, 'here are the Phrygians to the east, the richest in flocks of all whom I know, and

Φρύγες οἱ πρὸς τὴν ἠῶ, πολυπροβατώτατοί τε ἐόντες πάντων τῶν ἐγὼ οἶδα καὶ πολυκαρπότατοι. (6) Φρυγῶν δὲ ἔχονται Καππαδόκαι, τοὺς ἡμεῖς Συρίους καλέομεν. τούτοισι δὲ πρόσουροι Κίλικες, κατήκοντες ἐπὶ θάλασσαν τήνδε, ἐν τῇ ἥδε Κύπρος νῆσος κέεται· οἳ πεντακόσια τάλαντα βασιλέϊ τὸν ἐπέτειον φόρον ἐπιτελεῦσι. Κιλίκων δὲ τῶνδε ἔχονται Ἀρμένιοι οἵδε, καὶ οὗτοι ἐόντες πολυπρόβατοι, Ἀρμενίων δὲ Ματιηνοὶ χώρην τήνδε ἔχοντες. (7) ἔχεται δὲ τούτων γῆ ἥδε Κισσίη, ἐν τῇ δὴ παρὰ ποταμὸν τόνδε Χοάσπην κείμενα ἐστὶ τὰ Σοῦσα ταῦτα, ἔνθα βασιλεύς τε μέγας δίαιταν ποιέεται, καὶ τῶν χρημάτων οἱ θησαυροὶ ἐνθαῦτά εἰσι· ἑλόντες δὲ ταύτην τὴν πόλιν θαρσέοντες ἤδη τῷ Διὶ πλούτου πέρι ἐρίζετε. (8) ἀλλὰ περὶ μὲν χώρης ἄρα οὐ πολλῆς οὐδὲ οὕτω χρηστῆς καὶ οὔρων σμικρῶν χρεόν ἐστι ὑμέας μάχας ἀναβάλλεσθαι πρός τε Μεσσηνίους ἐόντας ἰσοπαλέας καὶ Ἀρκάδας τε καὶ Ἀργείους, τοῖσι οὔτε χρυσοῦ ἐχόμενόν ἐστι οὐδὲν οὔτε ἀργύρου, τῶν πέρι καί τινα ἐνάγει προθυμίη μαχόμενον ἀποθνήσκειν. παρέχον δὲ τῆς Ἀσίης πάσης ἄρχειν εὐπετέως, ἄλλο τι αἱρήσεσθε;"

(9) Ἀρισταγόρης μὲν ταῦτα ἔλεξε, Κλεομένης δὲ ἀμείβετο τοῖσιδε· "ὦ ξεῖνε Μιλήσιε, ἀναβάλλομαί τοι ἐς τρίτην ἡμέρην ὑποκρινέεσθαι." (50) τότε μὲν ἐς τοσοῦτον ἤλασαν· ἐπείτε δὲ ἡ κυρίη ἡμέρη ἐγένετο τῆς ὑποκρίσιος καὶ ἦλθον ἐς τὸ συγκείμενον, εἴρετο ὁ Κλεομένης τὸν Ἀρισταγόρην ὁκοσέων ἡμερέων ἀπὸ θαλάσσης τῆς Ἰώνων ὁδὸς εἴη παρὰ βασιλέα. (2) ὁ δὲ Ἀρισταγόρης τἆλλα ἐὼν σοφὸς καὶ διαβάλλων ἐκεῖνον εὖ ἐν τούτῳ ἐσφάλη· χρεὸν γάρ μιν μὴ λέγειν τὸ ἐόν, βουλόμενόν γε Σπαρτιήτας ἐξαγαγεῖν ἐς τὴν Ἀσίην, λέγει δ' ὦν τριῶν μηνῶν φὰς εἶναι τὴν ἄνοδον. (3) ὁ δὲ ὑπαρπάσας τὸν ἐπίλοιπον λόγον τὸν ὁ Ἀρισταγόρης ὥρμητο λέγειν περὶ τῆς ὁδοῦ, εἶπε· "ὦ ξεῖνε Μιλήσιε, ἀπαλλάσσεο ἐκ Σπάρτης πρὸ δύντος ἡλίου· οὐδένα γὰρ λόγον εὐεπέα λέγεις Λακεδαιμονίοισι, ἐθέλων σφέας ἀπὸ θαλάσσης τριῶν μηνῶν ὁδὸν ἀγαγεῖν."

(51) ὁ μὲν Κλεομένης ταῦτα εἴπας ἤιε ἐς τὰ οἰκία, ὁ δὲ Ἀρισταγόρης λαβὼν ἱκετηρίην ἤιε ἐς τοῦ Κλεομένεος, ἐσελθὼν δὲ ἔσω ἅτε ἱκετεύων ἐπακοῦσαι ἐκέλευε τὸν Κλεομένεα ἀποπέμψαντα τὸ παιδίον· προσεστήκεε γὰρ δὴ τῷ Κλεομένεϊ ἡ θυγάτηρ, τῇ οὔνομα

50. 3. εὐεπέα: εὐπρεπέα Richards.

in crops. (*6*) Adjoining the Phrygians are the Cappadocians, whom we call Syrians. Bordering on these are the Cilicians, reaching to this sea in which the island of Cyprus lies: they pay fifty talents to the King in annual tribute. Here next to these Cilicians are the Armenians, and they too are rich in flocks. This land next to the Armenians the Matienians occupy. (*7*) This territory next to them is Cissia, in which by this River Choaspes here is Susa, where the great King leads his life, and where the treasuries with his money are. If you took this city you could have the confidence to rival even Zeus for wealth. (*8*) You can set aside your battles for land which is not large or particularly good, with short borders, against the Messenians, who are on a level with you, and the Arcadians and Argives, who have nothing in the way of gold or silver for which a desire might come upon men to fight and die. When it is possible for you easily to gain rule over all Asia, what else would you choose?'

(*9*) That is what Aristagoras said; and Cleomenes gave this reply: 'Foreigner from Miletus, I shall delay my reply until the third day from now.' (**50**) That is as far as they went then. When the day fixed for the reply came, and they went to the agreed place, Cleomenes asked Aristagoras how many days from the Ionians' sea the journey was to the King. (*2*) Aristagoras had in other respects been clever and had misled him well, but in this respect he slipped: for he ought not to have told the truth, if he wanted to lead the Spartiates to Asia, but he said that the journey inland was of three months. (*3*) Cleomenes cut off the rest of the account which Aristagoras had started to tell him about the journey, and said, 'Foreigner from Miletus, be gone from Sparta before sunset; for you are not at all putting an acceptable account to the Spartans, when you want to lead us on a journey of three months from the sea'.

(**51**) Cleomenes said that and went to his house. Aristagoras took a suppliant's branch and went to Cleomenes' house. When he went in, he told Cleomenes to listen to him as a suppliant, and to send the child away. For Cleomenes' daughter, whose name was Gorgo, was standing beside him: she was his only child, and was eight or

ἦν Γοργώ· τοῦτο δέ οἱ καὶ μοῦνον τέκνον ἐτύγχανε ἐὸν ἐτέων ὀκτὼ ἢ ἐννέα ἡλικίην. Κλεομένης δὲ λέγειν μιν ἐκέλευε τὰ βούλεται μηδὲ ἐπισχεῖν τοῦ παιδίου εἵνεκα. (2) ἐνθαῦτα δὴ ὁ Ἀρισταγόρης ἄρχετο ἐκ δέκα ταλάντων ὑπισχνεόμενος, ἤν οἱ ἐπιτελέσῃ τῶν ἐδέετο. ἀνανεύοντος δὲ τοῦ Κλεομένεος προέβαινε τοῖσι χρήμασι ὑπερβάλλων ὁ Ἀρισταγόρης, ἐς οὗ πεντήκοντά τε τάλαντα ὑπεδέδεκτο καὶ τὸ παιδίον ηὐδάξατο· "πάτερ, διαφθερέει σε ὁ ξεῖνος, ἢν μὴ ἀποστὰς ἴῃς." (3) ὅ τε δὴ Κλεομένης ἠσθεὶς τοῦ παιδίου τῇ παραινέσι ἤιε ἐς ἕτερον οἴκημα, καὶ ὁ Ἀρισταγόρης ἀπαλλάσσετο τὸ παράπαν ἐκ τῆς Σπάρτης, οὐδέ οἱ ἐξεγένετο ἐπὶ πλέον ἔτι σημῆναι περὶ τῆς ἀνόδου τῆς παρὰ βασιλέα.

(52) ἔχει γὰρ ἀμφὶ τῇ ὁδῷ ταύτῃ ὧδε. σταθμοί τε πανταχῇ εἰσι βασιλήιοι καὶ καταλύσιες κάλλισται, διὰ οἰκεομένης τε ἡ ὁδὸς ἅπασα καὶ ἀσφαλέος. διὰ μέν γε Λυδίης καὶ Φρυγίης σταθμοὶ τείνοντες εἴκοσι εἰσί, παρασάγγαι δὲ τέσσερες καὶ ἐνενήκοντα καὶ ἥμισυ. (2) ἐκδέκεται δὲ ἐκ τῆς Φρυγίης ὁ Ἅλυς ποταμός, ἐπ᾽ ᾧ πύλαι τε ἔπεισι, τὰς διεξελάσαι πᾶσα ἀνάγκη καὶ οὕτω διεκπερᾶν τὸν ποταμόν, καὶ φυλακτήριον μέγα ἐπ᾽ αὐτῷ. διαβάντι δὲ ἐς τὴν Καππαδοκίην καὶ ταύτῃ πορευομένῳ μέχρι οὔρων τῶν Κιλικίων σταθμοὶ δυῶν δέοντες εἰσὶ τριήκοντα, παρασάγγαι δὲ τέσσερες καὶ ἑκατόν. ἐπὶ δὲ τοῖσι τούτων οὔροισι διξάς τε πύλας διεξελᾷς καὶ διξὰ φυλακτήρια παραμείψεαι. (3) ταῦτα δὲ διεξελάσαντι καὶ διὰ τῆς Κιλικίης ὁδὸν ποιευμένῳ τρεῖς εἰσι σταθμοί, παρασάγγαι δὲ πεντεκαίδεκα καὶ ἥμισυ. οὖρος δὲ Κιλικίης καὶ τῆς Ἀρμενίης ἐστὶ ποταμὸς νηυσιπέρητος, τῷ οὔνομα Εὐφρήτης. ἐν δὲ τῇ Ἀρμενίῃ σταθμοὶ μὲν εἰσὶ [καταγωγέων] πεντεκαίδεκα, παρασάγγαι δὲ ἒξ καὶ πεντήκοντα καὶ ἥμισυ, καὶ φυλακτήριον ἐν αὐτοῖσι. (4) ποταμοὶ δὲ νηυσιπέρητοι τέσσερες διὰ ταύτης ῥέουσι, τοὺς πᾶσα ἀνάγκη διαπορθμεῦσαί ἐστι, πρῶτος μὲν Τίγρης, μετὰ δὲ δεύτερός τε καὶ τρίτος Ζάβατος ὀνομαζόμενος, οὐκ

52. 1. τείνοντες obelised Wilson: <ἰόντι> σταθμοὶ [τείνοντες] Powell.
52. 3. καταγωγέων deleted Powell, Maas.
καὶ φυλακτήριον ἐν αὐτοῖσι: Powell placed after διαπορθμεῦσαί ἐστι in §4 and emended to καὶ φυλακτήρια τέσσερα ἐπ᾽ αὐτοῖσι.
52. 4. Ζάβατος Weissenborn: ὠυτὸς MSS.

nine years old. Cleomenes told him to say what he wanted and not to hold back on account of the child. (*2*) Then Aristagoras began with a promise of ten talents, if Cleomenes would accomplish what he begged for. When Cleomenes nodded his disagreement, Aristagoras proceeded to increase the money, until he had promised fifty talents. Then the child broke silence: 'Father, the foreigner will corrupt you, if you don't go and leave him'. (*3*) Cleomenes was pleased at the child's advice and went to another room; and Aristagoras left Sparta altogether, and did not have the opportunity to reveal any more about the road into the interior to the King.

(**52**) The situation with regard to this road is as follows. Everywhere there are royal staging-posts and highest-quality inns, and the whole road runs through inhabited and safe territory. Stretching through Lydia and Phrygia there are twenty staging-posts, amounting to 94½ parasangs. (*2*) Following on Phrygia is the River Halys, on which there are gates, through which it is absolutely necessary to pass and so to cross the river, and there is a great guard-post on it. When one crosses into Cappadocia and journeys through that to the borders of Cilicia there are twenty-eight staging-posts, 104 parasangs: at these borders you drive through double gates and pass double guard-posts. (*3*) When you have driven through that and take the road through Cilicia there are three staging-posts, 15½ parasangs. The border of Cilicia and Armenia is a navigable river, whose name is Euphrates. In Armenia there are fifteen staging-posts, 56½ parasangs, and a guard-post there. (*4*) Four navigable rivers flow through that, and it is absolutely necessary to make the crossing of these: first the Tigris; then the second and third named Zabatus (but not the same river or flowing from the same source: for the first one mentioned flows

ὡυτὸς ἐὼν ποταμὸς οὐδὲ ἐκ τοῦ αὐτοῦ ῥέων· ὁ μὲν γὰρ πρότερον αὐτῶν καταλεχθεὶς ἐξ Ἀρμενίων ῥέει, ὁ δ᾽ ὕστερον ἐκ Ματιηνῶν. (5) ὁ δὲ τέταρτος τῶν ποταμῶν οὔνομα ἔχει Γύνδης, τὸν Κῦρος διέλαβέ κοτε ἐς διώρυχας ἑξήκοντα καὶ τριηκοσίας. ἐκ δὲ ταύτης τῆς Ἀρμενίης ἐς βάλλοντι ἐς τὴν Ματιηνὴν γῆν σταθμοί εἰσι τέσσερες <καὶ τριήκοντα, παρασάγγαι δὲ ἑπτὰ καὶ τριήκοντα καὶ ἑκατόν>. (6) ἐκ δὲ ταύτης ἐς τὴν Κισσίην χώρην μεταβαίνοντι ἕνδεκα σταθμοί, παρασάγγαι δὲ δύο καὶ τεσσεράκοντα καὶ ἥμισυ ἔστι ἐπὶ ποταμὸν Χοάσπην, ἐόντα καὶ τοῦτον νηυσιπέρητον, ἐπ᾽ ᾧ Σοῦσα πόλις πεπόλισται. οὗτοι οἱ πάντες σταθμοί εἰσι ἕνδεκα καὶ ἑκατόν. καταγωγαὶ μέν νυν σταθμῶν τοσαῦται εἰσὶ ἐκ Σαρδίων ἐς Σοῦσα ἀναβαίνοντι.

(53) εἰ δὲ ὀρθῶς μεμέτρηται ἡ ὁδὸς ἡ βασιληίη τοῖσι παρασάγγῃσι καὶ ὁ παρασάγγης δύναται τριήκοντα στάδια, ὥσπερ οὗτός γε δύναται ταῦτα, ἐκ Σαρδίων στάδιά ἐστι ἐς τὰ βασιλήια τὰ Μεμνόνεια καλεόμενα πεντακόσια καὶ τρισχίλια καὶ μύρια, παρασαγγέων ἐόντων πεντήκοντα καὶ τετρακοσίων. πεντήκοντα δὲ καὶ ἑκατὸν στάδια ἐπ᾽ ἡμέρῃ ἑκάστῃ διεξιοῦσι ἀναισιμοῦνται ἡμέραι ἀπαρτὶ ἐνενήκοντα. (54) οὕτω τῷ Μιλησίῳ Ἀρισταγόρῃ εἴπαντι πρὸς Κλεομένεα τὸν Λακεδαιμόνιον εἶναι τριῶν μηνῶν τὴν ἄνοδον τὴν παρὰ βασιλέα ὀρθῶς εἴρητο. εἰ δέ τις τὸ ἀτρεκέστερον τούτων ἔτι δίζηται, ἐγὼ καὶ τοῦτο σημανέω· τὴν γὰρ ἐξ Ἐφέσου ἐς Σάρδις ὁδὸν δεῖ προσλογίσασθαι ταύτῃ. (2) καὶ δὴ λέγω σταδίους εἶναι τοὺς πάντας ἀπὸ θαλάσσης τῆς Ἑλληνικῆς μέχρι Σούσων (τοῦτο γὰρ Μεμνόνειον ἄστυ καλέεται), τεσσεράκοντα καὶ τετρακισχιλίους καὶ μυρίους· οἱ γὰρ ἐξ Ἐφέσου ἐς Σάρδις εἰσὶ τεσσεράκοντα καὶ πεντακόσιοι στάδιοι, καὶ οὕτω τρισὶ ἡμέρῃσι μηκύνεται ἡ τρίμηνος ὁδός.

(55) ἀπελαυνόμενος δὲ ὁ Ἀρισταγόρης ἐκ τῆς Σπάρτης ἤιε ἐς τὰς Ἀθήνας, γενομένας τυράννων ὧδε ἐλευθέρας. ἐπεὶ Ἵππαρχον τὸν Πεισιστράτου, Ἱππίεω δὲ τοῦ τυράννου ἀδελφεόν, ἰδόντα ὄψιν ἐνυπνίου τῷ ἑωυτοῦ πάθεϊ ἐμφερεστάτην κτείνουσι Ἀριστογείτων

---

52. 5 <καὶ τριήκοντα, παρασάγγαι δὲ ἑπτὰ καὶ τριήκοντα καὶ ἑκατόν> de la Barre: ἐκ δὲ ταύτης [τῆς Ἀρμενίης] ἐσβάλλοντι ... καὶ ἑκατόν> transposed to end of §3 after φυλακτήριον ἐν αὐτοῖσι Stein.

55. ἐμφερεστάτην Wyttenbach: ἐναργεστάτην MSS.

from Armenia and the other from Matiene); (*5*) and the fourth of the rivers has the name Gyndes, the river which Cyrus once divided into three hundred and sixty channels. When from this place Armenia you advance into the Matienian territory there are thirty-four staging-posts, and 137 parasangs. (*6*) When you move from there into the land of Cissia there are eleven staging-posts, 42½ parasangs, to the River Choaspes, which also is navigable, on which the city of Susa has been built. The total number of staging-posts is a hundred and eleven. That is the number of staging-posts to pause at if you go inland from Sardis to Susa.

(**53**) If the Royal Road has been correctly measured in parasangs, and if a parasang is equivalent to 30 stades (and that is indeed the equivalence), then from Sardis to what is called Memnon's Palace is 13,500 stades (450 parasangs). If you complete 150 stades each day, you take exactly ninety days. (**54**) So, when Aristagoras the Milesian said to Cleomenes the Spartan that the journey inland to the King was of three months, he spoke correctly. If one wants something more precise than that, I can add this. One needs to add to the reckoning the road from Epehsus to Sardis; (*2*) and I can state that the total number of stades from the Greek sea to Susa is 14,040; for from Ephesus to Sardis there are 540 stades, and so the three-month journey is lengthened by three days.

(**55**) Aristagoras left Sparta and went to Athens. It had become free from tyrants in this way. Hipparchus son of Pisistratus, brother of Hippias the tyrant, though he had seen in his sleep a vision very similar to his disaster, was killed by Harmodius and Aristogeiton, whose family was descended from the Gephyraei; but after that the

καὶ Ἁρμόδιος, γένος ἐόντες τὰ ἀνέκαθεν Γεφυραῖοι, μετὰ ταῦτα ἐτυραννεύοντο Ἀθηναῖοι ἐπ' ἔτεα τέσσερα οὐδὲν ἧσσον ἀλλὰ καὶ μᾶλλον ἢ πρὸ τοῦ. (56) ἡ μέν νυν ὄψις τοῦ Ἱππάρχου ἐνυπνίου ἦν ἥδε. ἐν τῇ προτέρῃ νυκτὶ τῶν Παναθηναίων ἐδόκεε ὁ Ἵππαρχος ἄνδρα οἱ ἐπιστάντα μέγαν καὶ εὐειδέα αἰνίσσεσθαι τάδε τὰ ἔπεα·

> τλῆθι λέων ἄτλητα παθὼν τετληότι θυμῷ·
> οὐδεὶς ἀνθρώπων ἀδικῶν τίσιν οὐκ ἀποτίσει.

(2) ταῦτα δέ, ὡς ἡμέρη ἐγένετο τάχιστα, φανερὸς ἦν ὑπερτιθέμενος ὀνειροπόλοισι· μετὰ δὲ ἀπειπάμενος τὴν ὄψιν ἔπεμπε τὴν πομπήν, ἐν τῇ δὴ τελευτᾷ.

(57) οἱ δὲ Γεφυραῖοι, τῶν ἦσαν οἱ φονέες οἱ Ἱππάρχου, ὡς μὲν αὐτοὶ λέγουσι, ἐγεγόνεσαν ἐξ Ἐρετρίης τὴν ἀρχήν, ὡς δὲ ἐγὼ ἀναπυνθανόμενος εὑρίσκω, ἦσαν Φοίνικες τῶν σὺν Κάδμῳ ἀπικομένων Φοινίκων ἐς γῆν τὴν νῦν Βοιωτίην καλεομένην, οἴκεον δὲ τῆς χώρης ταύτης ἀπολαχόντες τὴν Ταναγρικὴν μοῖραν. (2) ἐνθεῦτεν δὲ Καδμείων πρότερον ἐξαναστάντων ὑπ' Ἀργείων, οἱ Γεφυραῖοι οὗτοι δεύτερα ὑπὸ Βοιωτῶν ἐξαναστάντες ἐτράποντο ἐπ' Ἀθηνέων. Ἀθηναῖοι δὲ σφέας ἐπὶ ῥητοῖσι ἐδέξαντο σφέων αὐτῶν εἶναι πολιήτας, ὀλίγων τεῶν καὶ οὐκ ἀξιαπηγήτων ἐπιτάξαντες ἔργεσθαι.

(58) οἱ δὲ Φοίνικες οὗτοι οἱ σὺν Κάδμῳ ἀπικόμενοι, τῶν ἦσαν οἱ Γεφυραῖοι, ἄλλα τε πολλὰ οἰκήσαντες ταύτην τὴν χώρην ἐσήγαγον διδασκάλια ἐς τοὺς Ἕλληνας καὶ δὴ καὶ γράμματα, οὐκ ἐόντα πρὶν Ἕλλησι ὡς ἐμοὶ δοκέειν, πρῶτα μὲν τοῖσι καὶ ἅπαντες χρέωνται Φοίνικες· μετὰ δὲ χρόνου προβαίνοντος ἅμα τῇ φωνῇ μετέβαλλον καὶ τὸν ῥυθμὸν τῶν γραμμάτων. (2) περιοίκεον δὲ σφέας τὰ πολλὰ τῶν χώρων τοῦτον τὸν χρόνον Ἑλλήνων Ἴωνες· οἳ παραλαβόντες διδαχῇ παρὰ τῶν Φοινίκων τὰ γράμματα, μεταρρυθμίσαντες σφέων ὀλίγα ἐχρέωντο, χρεώμενοι δὲ ἐφάτισαν, ὥσπερ καὶ τὸ δίκαιον ἔφερε, ἐσαγαγόντων Φοινίκων ἐς τὴν Ἑλλάδα, Φοινικήια κεκλῆσθαι. (3) καὶ τὰς βύβλους διφθέρας καλέουσι ἀπὸ τοῦ παλαιοῦ οἱ Ἴωνες, ὅτι κοτὲ ἐν σπάνι βύβλων ἐχρέωντο διφθέρῃσι αἰγέῃσί τε καὶ οἰέῃσι· ἔτι δὲ καὶ

---

57. 2.   ὀλίγων Scheibe: πολλῶν MSS, <οὐ> πολλῶν Madvig.
58. 1.   οἰκήσαντες: οἰκίσαντες van Herwerden.

Athenians were for four years subject to tyranny, no less than before but indeed more. (**56**) Hipparchus' vision in his sleep was this. In the night before the Panathenaea he seemed to see a large and handsome man standing over him and speaking these riddling words:

> Endure, lion, you who have suffered the unendurable with an enduring heart:
> No man who does wrong will avoid paying the penalty.

(*2*) As soon as day broke, he could be seen communicating this to the expounders of dreams; but afterwards he rejected the dream, and dispatched the procession, in the course of which he died.

(**57**) The Gephyraei, to whom the killers of Hipparchus belonged, were according to what they themselves say originally from Eretria, but as I have discovered in my investigation they were Phoenicians, of those Phoenicians who came with Cadmus to the land now called Boeotia, and they were allotted Tanagra as their portion of land and lived there. (*2*) Then, after the Cadmeans had previously been expelled by the Argives, secondly these Gephyraei were expelled by the Boeotians and turned to Athens. The Athenians accepted them to be citizens of their own on stated terms, prescribing that they were to be excluded from a few matters not worthy of mention.

(**58**) These Phoenicians who came with Cadmus, to whom the Gephyraei belonged, among many other things, when they occupied this land, brought to the Greeks accomplishments and indeed writing, which did not previously exist among the Greeks, as far as I can judge. At first they used the same characters as all the Phoenicians, but afterwards in the passage of time along with their speech they changed also the form of their letters. (*2*) It was the Ionians who at that time lived around them in most of the localities. They took over these letters by learning them from the Phoenicians, and used them while making slight changes in the letters; and in using them they named them, as was right since the Phoenicians had brought them to Greece, calling them *phoinikeia*. (*3*) Since long ago the Ionians have called scrolls skins, because once when there was a shortage of papyrus they used goat and sheep skins; and still in my time many of the barbarians write on skins of that kind.

τὸ κατ’ ἐμὲ πολλοὶ τῶν βαρβάρων ἐς τοιαύτας διφθέρας γράφουσι.

(59) εἶδον δὲ καὶ αὐτὸς Καδμήια γράμματα ἐν τῷ ἱρῷ τοῦ Ἀπόλλωνος τοῦ Ἰσμηνίου ἐν Θήβῃσι τῇσι Βοιωτῶν, ἐπὶ τρίποσί τισι ἐγκεκολαμμένα, τὰ πολλὰ ὅμοια ἐόντα τοῖσι Ἰωνικοῖσι. ὁ μὲν δὴ εἷς τῶν τριπόδων ἐπίγραμμα ἔχει·

> Ἀμφιτρύων μ’ ἀνέθηκεν †ἐὼν† ἀπὸ Τηλεβοάων.

ταῦτα ἡλικίην εἴη ἂν κατὰ Λάιον τὸν Λαβδάκου τοῦ Πολυδώρου τοῦ Κάδμου. (60) ἕτερος δὲ τρίπους ἐν ἑξαμέτρῳ τόνῳ λέγει·

> Σκαῖος πυγμαχέων με ἐκηβόλῳ Ἀπόλλωνι
> νικήσας ἀνέθηκε τεῒν περικαλλὲς ἄγαλμα.

Σκαῖος δ’ ἂν εἴη ὁ Ἱπποκόωντος, εἰ δὴ οὗτός γε ἐστὶ ὁ ἀναθεὶς καὶ μὴ ἄλλος τὠυτὸ οὔνομα ἔχων τῷ Ἱπποκόωντος, ἡλικίην κατὰ Οἰδίπουν τὸν Λαΐου. (61) τρίτος δὲ τρίπους λέγει καὶ οὗτος ἐν ἑξαμέτρῳ·

> Λαοδάμας τρίποδ’ †αὐτὸν† εὐσκόπῳ Ἀπόλλωνι
> μουναρχέων ἀνέθηκε τεῒν περικαλλὲς ἄγαλμα.

(2) ἐπὶ τούτου δὴ τοῦ Λαοδάμαντος τοῦ Ἐτεοκλέος μουναρχέοντος ἐξανιστέαται Καδμεῖοι ὑπ’ Ἀργείων καὶ τρέπονται ἐς τοὺς Ἐγχελέας. οἱ δὲ Γεφυραῖοι ὑπολειφθέντες ὕστερον ὑπὸ Βοιωτῶν ἀναχωρέουσι ἐς Ἀθήνας· καί σφι ἱρὰ ἔστι ἐν Ἀθήνῃσι ἱδρυμένα, τῶν οὐδὲν μέτα τοῖσι λοιποῖσι Ἀθηναίοισι, ἄλλα τε κεχωρισμένα τῶν ἄλλων ἱρῶν καὶ δὴ καὶ Ἀχαιίης Δήμητρος ἱρόν τε καὶ ὄργια.

(62) ἡ μὲν δὴ ὄψις τοῦ Ἱππάρχου ἐνυπνίου καὶ οἱ Γεφυραῖοι ὅθεν ἐγεγόνεσαν, τῶν ἦσαν οἱ Ἱππάρχου φονέες, ἀπήγηταί μοι· δεῖ δὲ πρὸς τούτοισι ἔτι ἀναλαβεῖν τὸν κατ’ ἀρχὰς ἦια λέξων λόγον, ὡς τυράννων ἐλευθερώθησαν Ἀθηναῖοι. (2) Ἱππίεω τυραννεύοντος καὶ ἐμπικραινομένου Ἀθηναίοισι διὰ τὸν Ἱππάρχου θάνατον, Ἀλκμεωνίδαι, γένος ἐόντες Ἀθηναῖοι καὶ φεύγοντες Πεισιστρατίδας, ἐπείτε σφι ἅμα τοῖσι ἄλλοισι Ἀθηναίων φυγάσι πειρωμένοισι κατὰ

---

59. ἐὼν obelised Wilson: ἰὼν Bergler, ἐόντ’ Valckenaer, ἐλὼν Meineke, θεῷ Stein, νέων Bentley, perhaps νεῶν Wilson.

61. 1. αὐτὸν obelised Powell, Wilson: αὐτὸς Schweighäuser, ὄντα μ’ Blaydes, ἆθλον Stein.

(**59**) I myself actually saw Cadmean letters in the sanctuary of Apollo Ismenias at Thebes in Boeotia, which in general are like those of the Ionians, carved on three tripods. One of the tripods has this inscription:

> Amphitryon dedicated me, †being† from the Teleboeans.

This would be from the time of Laïus son of Labdacus son of Polydorus son of Cadmus. (**60**) A second tripod says in hexameter rhythm:

> Scaeus the boxer to you, far-shooting Apollo,
> Having won a victory dedicated me, this very fine treasure.

Scaeus would be the son of Hippocoön, if this is the dedicator and not another man with the same name as Hippocoön's son, from the time of Oedipus son of Laïus. (**61**) The third tripod, this also in hexameters, says:

> Leodamas as monarch dedicated to you, well-aiming Apollo,
> This tripod, a very fine treasure.

(*2*) It was in the monarchy of this Laodamas son of Eteocles that the Cadmeans were expelled and turned to the Encheleis; and the Gephyraei were left behind but later were forced by the Boeotians to move to Athens. They have sanctuaries founded in Athens, which have nothing to do with the rest of the Athenians: others which are set apart from the other sanctuaries, and in particular a sanctuary and secret rites of Demeter Achaea.

(**62**) Hipparchus' vision in his sleep, and the origin of the Gephyraei, to whom the killers of Hipparchus belonged, I have set out. In addition to this I still need to take up the account on which I embarked at the beginning, of how the Athenians were freed from tyrants. (*2*) When Hippias was tyrant, he was becoming embittered against the Athenians because of the death of Hipparchus. The Alcmaeonids, an Athenian family who were exiled by the Pisistratids, tried together with the other Athenian exiles, as far as their strength allowed, but

τὸ ἰσχυρὸν οὐ προεχώρεε <ἡ> κάτοδος, ἀλλὰ προσέπταιον μεγάλως πειρώμενοι κατιέναι τε καὶ ἐλευθεροῦν τὰς Ἀθήνας, Λειψύδριον τὸ ὑπὲρ Παιονίης τειχίσαντες, ἐνθαῦτα οἱ Ἀλκμεωνίδαι πᾶν ἐπὶ τοῖσι Πεισιστρατίδῃσι μηχανώμενοι παρ' Ἀμφικτυόνων τὸν νηὸν μισθοῦνται τὸν ἐν Δελφοῖσι, τὸν νῦν <μὲν> ἐόντα τότε δὲ οὔκω, τοῦτον ἐξοικοδομῆσαι. (*3*) οἷα δὲ χρημάτων εὖ ἥκοντες καὶ ἐόντες ἄνδρες δόκιμοι ἀνέκαθεν ἔτι τε τὸν νηὸν ἐξεργάσαντο τοῦ παραδείγματος κάλλιον τά τε ἄλλα καὶ συγκειμένου σφι πωρίνου λίθου ποιέειν τὸν νηόν, Παρίου τὰ ἔμπροσθε αὐτοῦ ἐξεποίησαν.

(**63**) ὡς ὦν δὴ οἱ Λακεδαιμόνιοι λέγουσι, οὗτοι οἱ ἄνδρες ἐν Δελφοῖσι κατήμενοι ἀνέπειθον τὴν Πυθίην χρήμασι, ὅκως ἔλθοιεν Σπαρτιητέων ἄνδρες εἴτε ἰδίῳ στόλῳ εἴτε δημοσίῳ χρησόμενοι, προφέρειν σφι τὰς Ἀθήνας ἐλευθεροῦν. (*2*) Λακεδαιμόνιοι δέ, ὥς σφι αἰεὶ τὠυτὸ πρόφαντον ἐγίνετο, πέμπουσι Ἀγχίμολον τὸν Ἀστέρος, ἐόντα τῶν ἀστῶν ἄνδρα δόκιμον, σὺν στρατῷ ἐξελῶντα Πεισιστρατίδας ἐξ Ἀθηνέων ὅμως καὶ ξεινίους σφι ἐόντας τὰ μάλιστα· τὰ γὰρ τοῦ θεοῦ πρεσβύτερα ἐποιεῦντο ἢ τὰ τῶν ἀνδρῶν. (*3*) πέμπουσι δὲ τούτους κατὰ θάλασσαν πλοίοισι. ὁ μὲν δὴ προσσχὼν ἐς Φάληρον τὴν στρατιὴν ἀπέβησε, οἱ δὲ Πεισιστρατίδαι προπυνθανόμενοι ταῦτα ἐπεκαλέοντο ἐκ Θεσσαλίης ἐπικουρίην· ἐπεποίητο γάρ σφι συμμαχίη πρὸς αὐτούς. Θεσσαλοὶ δέ σφι δεομένοισι ἀπέπεμψαν κοινῇ γνώμῃ χρεώμενοι χιλίην τε ἵππον καὶ τὸν βασιλέα τὸν σφέτερον Κινέην ἄνδρα Κονδαῖον· τοὺς ἐπείτε ἔσχον συμμάχους οἱ Πεισιστρατίδαι, ἐμηχανῶντο τοιάδε. (*4*) κείραντες τῶν Φαληρέων τὸ πεδίον καὶ ἱππάσιμον ποιήσαντες τοῦτον τὸν χῶρον ἐπῆκαν τῷ στρατοπέδῳ τὴν ἵππον· ἐμπεσοῦσα δὲ διέφθειρε

---

62. 2   ἡ inserted Schaefer: κάτοδος deleted Krüger.
  μὲν inserted van Herwerden.
  Παιονίης: Παιονιδέων Holford-Strevens (cf. Wilson, *Herodotea*, 101–2).
62. 3.   οἷα δὲ: οἷά τε Powell.
  ἔτι τε τὸν Maas (cf. 90. 2): ἔτι τόν τε MSS, τε deleted Krüger.
63. 1.   Λακεδαιμόνιοι Schwieghäuser: Ἀθηναῖοι MSS.
63. 2.   Ἀγχίμολον Wilson (cf. *Ath. Pol.* 19. 5): Ἀγχιμόλιον MSS.
63. 3.   Κονδαῖον Kip: Κονιαῖον MSS, Γόνναιον Wachsmuth.
63. 4.   Ἀγχίμολον, Ἀγχιμόλου Wilson (cf. *Ath. Pol.* 19.5): Ἀγχιμόλιον, Ἀγχιμολίου MSS.

their return did not progress; and they failed greatly in their attempt to return and free Athens when they fortified Leipsydrium above Paeonia. Then, contriving all against the Pisistratids, they took the contract from the Amphictyons to build the temple at Delphi (the one which is standing now but was not standing then). (*3*) Since they were well furnished with money, and were distinguished men by descent, they completed the work on the temple even more finely than the schedule: in particular, when it had been agreed that they were to make the temple of limestone, they finished its façade with Parian marble.

(**63**) As the Spartans say, these men sat at Delphi and by payment induced the Pythia, whenever men of the Spartiates came either on a private or on a public mission to consult the oracle, to put it to them that they should liberate Athens. (*2*) The Spartans, since the same prophecy was always given to them, sent Anchimolus the son of Aster, a distinguished man among their citizens, with a force to drive the Pisistratids out of Athens, even though they were particular guest-friends of the Spartans; for they considered the obligations of the gods greater than those of men. (*3*) They sent these by sea in boats. He put in to Phalerum and disembarked his force, but the Pisistratids learned of this in advance and invited support from Thessaly: for they had made an alliance with the Thessalians. In response to their request the Thessalians took a common decision and sent them a thousand cavalry and their king Cineas, a man of Condaea. When they had these present as allies the Pisistratids contrived this kind of thing: (*4*) they cleared the plain of Phalerum and made it usable for horses, and then launched the cavalry against the enemy army. Falling on them, they

ἄλλους τε πολλοὺς τῶν Λακεδαιμονίων καὶ δὴ καὶ τὸν Ἀγχίμολον· τοὺς δὲ περιγενομένους αὐτῶν ἐς τὰς νέας κατεῖρξαν. ὁ μὲν δὴ πρῶτος στόλος ἐκ Λακεδαίμονος οὕτω ἀπήλλαξε, καὶ Ἀγχιμόλου εἰσὶ ταφαὶ τῆς Ἀττικῆς Ἀλωπεκῆσι, ἀγχοῦ τοῦ Ἡρακλείου τοῦ ἐν Κυνοσάργεϊ. (64) μετὰ δὲ Λακεδαιμόνιοι μέζω στόλον στείλαντες ἀπέπεμψαν ἐπὶ τὰς Ἀθήνας, στρατηγὸν τῆς στρατιῆς ἀποδέξαντες βασιλέα Κλεομένεα τὸν Ἀναξανδρίδεω, οὐκέτι κατὰ θάλασσαν στείλαντες ἀλλὰ κατ' ἤπειρον. (2) τοῖσι ἐσβαλοῦσι ἐς τὴν Ἀττικὴν χώρην ἡ τῶν Θεσσαλῶν ἵππος πρώτη προσέμειξε καὶ οὐ μετὰ πολλὸν ἐτράπετο, καὶ σφεων ἔπεσον ὑπὲρ τεσσεράκοντα ἄνδρας· οἱ δὲ περιγενόμενοι ἀπαλλάσσοντο ὡς εἶχον εὐθὺς ἐπὶ Θεσσαλίης. Κλεομένης δὲ ἀπικόμενος ἐς τὸ ἄστυ ἅμα Ἀθηναίων τοῖσι βουλομένοισι εἶναι ἐλευθέροισι ἐπολιόρκεε τοὺς τυράννους ἀπεργμένους ἐν τῷ Πελαργικῷ τείχεϊ. (65) καὶ οὐδέν τι πάντως ἂν ἐξεῖλον Πεισιστρατίδας οἱ Λακεδαιμόνιοι (οὔτε γὰρ ἐπέδρην ἐπενόεον ποιήσασθαι, οἵ τε Πεισιστρατίδαι σίτοισι καὶ ποτοῖσι εὖ παρεσκευάδατο), πολιορκήσαντές τε ἂν ἡμέρας ὀλίγας ἀπαλλάσσοντο ἐς τὴν Σπάρτην. νῦν δὲ συντυχίη τοῖσι μὲν κακὴ ἐπεγένετο, τοῖσι δὲ ἡ αὐτὴ αὕτη σύμμαχος· ὑπεκτιθέμενοι γὰρ ἔξω τῆς χώρης οἱ παῖδες τῶν Πεισιστρατιδέων ἥλωσαν. (2) τοῦτο δὲ ὡς ἐγένετο, πάντα αὐτῶν τὰ πρήγματα συνετετάρακτο, παρέστησαν δὲ ἐπὶ μισθῷ τοῖσι τέκνοισι, ἐπ' οἷσι ἐβούλοντο οἱ Ἀθηναῖοι, ὥστε ἐν πέντε ἡμέρῃσι ἐκχωρῆσαι ἐκ τῆς Ἀττικῆς. (3) μετὰ δὲ ἐξεχώρησαν ἐς Σίγειον τὸ ἐπὶ τῷ Σκαμάνδρῳ, ἄρξαντες μὲν Ἀθηναίων ἐπ' ἔτεα ἕξ τε καὶ τριήκοντα, ἐόντες δὲ καὶ οὗτοι ἀνέκαθεν Πύλιοί τε καὶ Νηλεῖδαι, ἐκ τῶν αὐτῶν γεγονότες καὶ οἱ ἀμφὶ Κόδρον τε καὶ Μέλανθον, οἳ πρότερον ἐπήλυδες ἐόντες ἐγένοντο Ἀθηναίων βασιλέες. (4) ἐπὶ τούτου δὲ καὶ τὠυτὸ οὔνομα ἀπεμνημόνευσε Ἱπποκράτης τῷ παιδὶ θέσθαι τὸν Πεισίστρατον, ἐπὶ τοῦ Νέστορος Πεισιστράτου ποιεύμενος τὴν ἐπωνυμίην. (5) οὕτω μὲν Ἀθηναῖοι τυράννων ἀπαλλάχθησαν·

---

64. 2.   Πελαργικῷ V (cf. *Ath. Pol.* 19. 5): Πελασιγκῷ other MSS.
65. 4.   ἀπεμνημόνευσε obelised Powell: perhaps ἀπεμνημονεύ<ων ἠθέλη>σε Wilson.
          τὸν Πεισίστρατον deleted van Herwerden.

destroyed many others of the Spartans and in particular Anchimolus, and they confined the survivors in the ships. The first mission from Sparta ended like that, and Anchimolus' tomb is in Attica at Alopece, near the Heracleum in Cynosarges.

(**64**) Afterwards the Spartans dispatched a larger mission and sent it against Athens, appointing as general of the force the king Cleomenes son of Anaxandridas, and they no longer dispatched it by sea but by land. (*2*) When they invaded the land of Attica the Thessalian cavalry first engaged with them but after no long time was defeated; and there fell of them more than forty men. The survivors departed for Thessaly as soon as they could. When Cleomenes reached the city, together with those of the Athenians who wanted to be free he blockaded the tyrants, confining them in the Pelargic Wall. (**65**) But the Spartans would not at all have been able to capture the Pisistratids (for they had not planned to mount a siege, and the Pisistratids were well provided with food and drink), but after blockading them for a few days would have departed for Sparta. Now, however, there occurred a chance incident, which was bad for the Pisistratids, while this same thing became a support for their attackers: for the children of the Pisistratids, who were being smuggled outside the land, were captured. (*2*) When that happened, all the Pisistratids' plans were thrown into confusion; and they accepted as the price of their children the terms which the Athenians wanted, that they should leave Attica in five days. (*3*) Afterwards they left for Sigeum on the Scamander. They had ruled over the Athenians for thirty-six years, and were themselves by descent Pylians and Neleïds, born from the same stock as that of Codrus and Melanthus, who had originally been immigrants but became kings of the Athenians. (*4*) Hippocrates was acting in memory of this when he gave the same name Pisistratus to his son, taking the name from Pisistratus son of Nestor. (*5*) In this way the Athenians were rid of tyrants. What they did or had done to them

ὅσα δὲ ἐλευθερωθέντες ἔρξαν ἢ ἔπαθον ἀξιόχρεα ἀπηγήσιος, πρὶν ἢ Ἰωνίην τε ἀποστῆναι ἀπὸ Δαρείου καὶ Ἀρισταγόρεα τὸν Μιλήσιον ἀπικόμενον ἐς Ἀθήνας χρηίσαι σφέων βοηθέειν, ταῦτα πρῶτα φράσω. (66) Ἀθῆναι, ἐοῦσαι καὶ πρὶν μεγάλαι, τότε ἀπαλλαχθεῖσαι τυράννων ἐγίνοντο μέζονες. ἐν δὲ αὐτῇσι δύο ἄνδρες ἐδυνάστευον, Κλεισθένης τε ἀνὴρ Ἀλκμεωνίδης, ὅς περ δὴ λόγον ἔχει τὴν Πυθίην ἀναπεῖσαι, καὶ Ἰσαγόρης Τισάνδρου οἰκίης μὲν ἐὼν δοκίμου, ἀτὰρ τὰ ἀνέκαθεν οὐκ ἔχω φράσαι· θύουσι δὲ οἱ συγγενέες αὐτοῦ Διὶ Ἰκαρίῳ. (2) οὗτοι οἱ ἄνδρες ἐστασίασαν περὶ δυνάμιος, ἐσσούμενος δὲ ὁ Κλεισθένης τὸν δῆμον προσεταιρίζεται. μετὰ δὲ τετραφύλους ἐόντας Ἀθηναίους δεκαφύλους ἐποίησε, τῶν Ἴωνος παίδων Γελέοντος καὶ Αἰγικόρεος καὶ Ἀργάδεω καὶ Ὅπλητος ἀπαλλάξας τὰς ἐπωνυμίας, ἐξευρὼν δὲ ἑτέρων ἡρώων ἐπωνυμίας ἐπιχωρίων, πάρεξ Αἴαντος· τοῦτον δέ, ἅτε ἀστυγείτονα καὶ σύμμαχον, ξεῖνον ἐόντα προσέθετο. (67) ταῦτα δέ, δοκέειν ἐμοί, ἐμιμέετο ὁ Κλεισθένης οὗτος τὸν ἑωυτοῦ μητροπάτορα Κλεισθένεα τὸν Σικυῶνος τύραννον. Κλεισθένης γὰρ Ἀργείοισι πολεμήσας τοῦτο μὲν ῥαψῳδοὺς ἔπαυσε ἐν Σικυῶνι ἀγωνίζεσθαι τῶν Ὁμηρείων ἐπέων εἵνεκα, ὅτι Ἀργεῖοί τε καὶ Ἄργος τὰ πολλὰ πάντα ὑμνέαται· τοῦτο δέ, ἡρώιον γὰρ ἦν καὶ ἔστι ἐν αὐτῇ τῇ ἀγορῇ τῶν Σικυωνίων Ἀδρήστου τοῦ Ταλαοῦ, τοῦτον ἐπεθύμησε ὁ Κλεισθένης ἐόντα Ἀργεῖον ἐκβαλεῖν ἐκ τῆς χώρης. (2) ἐλθὼν δὲ ἐς Δελφοὺς ἐχρηστηριάζετο εἰ ἐκβάλοι τὸν Ἄδρηστον· ἡ δὲ Πυθίη οἱ χρᾷ φᾶσα Ἄδρηστον μὲν εἶναι Σικυωνίων βασιλέα, κεῖνον δὲ λευστῆρα. ἐπεὶ δὲ ὁ θεὸς τοῦτό γε οὐ παρεδίδου, ἀπελθὼν ὀπίσω ἐφρόντιζε μηχανὴν τῇ αὐτὸς ὁ Ἄδρηστος ἀπαλλάξεται. ὡς δέ οἱ ἐξευρῆσθαι ἐδόκεε, πέμψας ἐς Θήβας τὰς Βοιωτίας ἔφη θέλειν ἐπαγαγέσθαι Μελάνιππον τὸν Ἀστακοῦ· οἱ δὲ Θηβαῖοι ἔδοσαν. (3) ἐπαγαγόμενος δὲ ὁ Κλεισθένης τὸν Μελάνιππον τέμενός οἱ ἀπέδεξε ἐν αὐτῷ τῷ πρυτανηίῳ καί μιν ἵδρυσε ἐνθαῦτα ἐν τῷ ἰσχυροτάτῳ. ἐπηγάγετο δὲ τὸν Μελάνιππον ὁ Κλεισθένης (καὶ γὰρ τοῦτο δεῖ ἀπηγήσασθαι) ὡς ἔχθιστον ἐόντα Ἀδρήστῳ, ὅς τόν τε ἀδελφεόν οἱ Μηκιστέα ἀπεκτόνεε καὶ τὸν γαμβρὸν Τυδέα. (4) ἐπείτε δέ οἱ τὸ

---

66. 1.   ὅς περ δὴ λόγον: ὅν περ δὴ λόγος Blaydes.
   Διὶ Ἰκαρίῳ Rhodes: Διὶ Καρίῳ MSS.

that is worthy of being set out, after they had been freed, before Ionia revolted against Darius and Aristagoras of Miletus went to Athens to ask them to give support, that I shall expound first.

(**66**) Athens had been great even before, but then, when it was rid of tyrants, it became greater. In it two men held preponderant positions: Cleisthenes, an Alcmaeonid man, who is reputed to have persuaded the Pythia, and Isagoras son of Teisandrus, who was of a distinguished family but I am not able to report his descent; but his kin sacrifice to Zeus Ikarios. (*2*) These men were striving against each other for power; and Cleisthenes, getting the worse of it, added the people to his following. Afterwards he made the Athenians a people of ten tribes when they had been of four, and he got rid of the tribes named after Ion's sons, Geleon, Aegicores, Argades and Hoples, and he devised names from other heroes, local apart from Ajax, whom he added because, though a foreigner, he had been a neighbour and ally.

(**67**) In this matter, I think, this Cleisthenes was imitating his maternal grandfather Cleisthenes the tyrant of Sicyon. For when Cleisthenes had fought a war against the Argives, first, he stopped the reciters at Sicyon competing over the Homeric poems, because for the most part Argives and Argos are sung of everywhere; and also, since right in the agora of Sicyon there was and indeed is a hero's shrine of Adrastus son of Talaus, Cleisthenes conceived a desire to expel him from the land becauase he was an Argive. (*2*) He went to Delphi and asked the oracle if he should expel Adrastus; and the Pythia responded to him saying that Adrastus was a king of Sicyon but Cleisthenes was a stone-thrower. Since the God would not grant him this, he went back and thought of a contrivance by which Adrastus would be gone of his own accord. When he thought he had found one, he sent to Thebes in Boeotia saying that he wanted to bring in Melanippus son of Astacus; and the Thebans granted that. (*3*) When Cleisthenes brought in Melanippus he designated a precinct for him right in the *prytaneion*, and established it there in the strongest place. Cleisthenes brought in Melanippus (for I must expound this too) as being the greatest enemy of Adrastus, who had killed both his brother Mecisteus and his son-in-law Tydeus. (*4*) When he had designated the precinct for

τέμενος ἀπέδεξε, θυσίας τε καὶ ὁρτὰς Ἀδρήστου ἀπελόμενος ἔδωκε τῷ Μελανίππῳ. οἱ δὲ Σικυώνιοι ἐώθεσαν μεγαλωστὶ κάρτα τιμᾶν τὸν Ἄδρηστον· ἡ γὰρ χώρη ἦν αὕτη Πολύβου, ὁ δὲ Ἄδρηστος ἦν Πολύβου θυγατριδέος, ἄπαις δὲ Πόλυβος τελευτῶν διδοῖ Ἀδρήστῳ τὴν ἀρχήν. (5) τά τε δὴ ἄλλα οἱ Σικυώνιοι ἐτίμων τὸν Ἄδρηστον καὶ δὴ πρὸς τὰ πάθεα αὐτοῦ τραγικοῖσι χοροῖσι ἐγέραιρον, τὸν μὲν Διόνυσον οὐ τιμῶντες, τὸν δὲ Ἄδρηστον. Κλεισθένης δὲ χοροὺς μὲν τῷ Διονύσῳ ἀπέδωκε, τὴν δὲ ἄλλην θυσίην Μελανίππῳ.

(68) ταῦτα μὲν ἐς Ἄδρηστόν οἱ ἐπεποίητο, φυλὰς δὲ τὰς Δωριέων, ἵνα δὴ μὴ αἱ αὐταὶ ἔωσι τοῖσι Σικυωνίοισι καὶ τοῖσι Ἀργείοισι, μετέβαλε ἐς ἄλλα οὐνόματα. ἔνθα καὶ πλεῖστον κατεγέλασε τῶν Σικυωνίων· ἐπὶ γὰρ ὑός τε καὶ ὄνου <καὶ χοίρου> τὰς ἐπωνυμίας μετατιθεὶς αὐτὰ τὰ τελευταῖα ἐπέθηκε, πλὴν τῆς ἑωυτοῦ φυλῆς· ταύτῃ δὲ τὸ οὔνομα ἀπὸ τῆς ἑωυτοῦ ἀρχῆς ἔθετο. οὗτοι μὲν δὴ Ἀρχέλαοι ἐκαλέοντο, ἕτεροι δὲ Ὑᾶται, ἄλλοι δὲ Ὀνεᾶται, ἕτεροι δὲ Χοιρεᾶται. (2) τούτοισι τοῖσι οὐνόμασι τῶν φυλέων ἐχρέωντο οἱ Σικυώνιοι καὶ ἐπὶ Κλεισθένεος ἄρχοντος καὶ ἐκείνου τεθνεῶτος ἔτι ἐπ' ἔτεα ἑξήκοντα· μετέπειτα μέντοι λόγον σφίσι δόντες μετέβαλον ἐς τοὺς Ὑλλέας καὶ Παμφύλους καὶ Δυμανάτας, τετάρτους δὲ αὐτοῖσι προσέθεντο ἐπὶ τοῦ Ἀδρήστου παιδὸς Αἰγιαλέος τὴν ἐπωνυμίην ποιεύμενοι κεκλῆσθαι Αἰγιαλέας.

(69) ταῦτα μέν νυν ὁ Σικυώνιος Κλεισθένης ἐπεποιήκεε· ὁ δὲ δὴ Ἀθηναῖος Κλεισθένης, ἐὼν τοῦ Σικυωνίου τούτου θυγατριδέος καὶ τὸ οὔνομα ἐπὶ τούτου ἔχων, δοκέειν ἐμοὶ καὶ οὗτος ὑπεριδὼν Ἴωνας, ἵνα μὴ σφίσι αἱ αὐταὶ ἔωσι φυλαὶ καὶ Ἴωσι, τὸν ὁμώνυμον Κλεισθένεα ἐμιμήσατο. (2) ὡς γὰρ δὴ τὸν Ἀθηναίων δῆμον πρότερον ἀπωσμένον τότε πάντως πρὸς τὴν ἑωυτοῦ μοῖραν προσεθήκατο, τὰς φυλὰς μετωνόμασε καὶ ἐποίησε πλεῦνας ἐξ ἐλασσόνων· δέκα τε δὴ φυλάρχους ἀντὶ τεσσέρων ἐποίησε, δέκαχα δὲ καὶ τοὺς δήμους κατένειμε ἐς τὰς φυλάς. ἦν τε τὸν δῆμον προσθέμενος πολλῷ κατύπερθε τῶν ἀντιστασιωτέων.

68. 1.   καὶ χοίρου inserted Sauppe: ἕτεροι δὲ Χοιρεᾶται deleted Bicknell. See Wilson, *Herodotea*, 103.
69. 2.   τότε πάντως Bekker: τότε πάντων MSS, τότε <μεταδιδοὺς τῶν> πάντων Stein.
     δέκαχα Lolling: δέκα MSS, δέκα τε δὴ ... ἐς τὰς φυλάς deleted Powell.

him, he took away the sacrifices and festivals of Adrastus and gave them to Melanippus. The Sicyonians had been accustomed to honour Adrastus very greatly: for the land had belonged to Polybus, Adrastus was maternal grandson of Polybus, and Polybus when he died without a son had granted the rule to Adrastus. (*5*) The Sicyonians used to honour Adrastus in other respects, and in particular they showed respect to his sufferings with tragic choruses, honouring not Dionysus but Adrastus. But Cleisthenes gave over the choruses to Dionysus, and the rest of the sacrificial programme to Melanippus.

(**68**) That is what he did towards Adrastus. The tribes of the Dorians, so that they should not be the same for the Sicyonians as they were for the Argives, he changed to other names. In that he made the greatest laughing-stock of the Sicyonians. For he gave the tribes names derived from pig, ass and swine, changing just the endings, apart from his own tribe: to that he gave a name derived from his own rule. So they were called Archelaoi [ruling people], while others were called respectively Hyatai [pigites], Orneatai [assites] and Choireatai [swinites]. (*2*) The Sicyonians both used these names for the tribes under the rule of Cleisthenes and still continued to use them after his death for sixty years. After that they discussed it among themselves and changed to Hylleis, Pamphyloi and Dymanatai, and to the fourth they attached a name from Adrastus' son Aegialeos, and made them to be called Aegialeis.

(**69**) That is what Cleisthenes of Sicyon had done. The Athenian Cleisthenes, being a maternal grandson of that Sicyonian and having his name from him, I think in his case looked down on the Ionians, so that the tribes should not be the same for the Athenians as for the Ionians, and so imitated the other man named Cleisthenes. (*2*) While previously he had spurned the Athenian people but now he attached it entirely to his own side, he renamed the tribes and made them more instead of fewer: for he created ten phylarchs instead of four, and distributed the demes on a basis of ten among the tribes. Having attached the people, he was far superior to those opposed to him.

(70) ἐν τῷ μέρεϊ δὲ ἑσσούμενος ὁ Ἰσαγόρης ἀντιτεχνᾶται τάδε· ἐπικαλέεται Κλεομένεα τὸν Λακεδαιμόνιον, γενόμενον ἑωυτῷ ξεῖνον ἀπὸ τῆς Πεισιστρατιδέων πολιορκίης. τὸν δὲ Κλεομένεα εἶχε αἰτίη φοιτᾶν παρὰ τοῦ Ἰσαγόρεω τὴν γυναῖκα. (2) τὰ μὲν δὴ πρῶτα πέμπων ὁ Κλεομένης ἐς τὰς Ἀθήνας κήρυκα ἐξέβαλλε Κλεισθένεα καὶ μετ' αὐτοῦ ἄλλους πολλοὺς Ἀθηναίων, τοὺς ἐναγέας ἐπιλέγων. ταῦτα δὲ πέμπων ἔλεγε ἐκ διδαχῆς τοῦ Ἰσαγόρεω. οἱ μὲν γὰρ Ἀλκμεωνίδαι καὶ οἱ συστασιῶται αὐτῶν εἶχον αἰτίην τοῦ φόνου τούτου, αὐτὸς δὲ οὐ μετεῖχε οὐδ' οἱ φίλοι αὐτοῦ. (71) οἱ δ' ἐναγέες Ἀθηναίων ὧδε ὠνομάσθησαν. ἦν Κύλων τῶν Ἀθηναίων ἀνὴρ Ὀλυμπιονίκης· οὗτος ἐπὶ τυραννίδι ἐκόμησε, προσποιησάμενος δὲ ἑταιρηίην τῶν ἡλικιωτέων καταλαβεῖν τὴν ἀκρόπολιν ἐπειρήθη, οὐ δυνάμενος δὲ ἐπικρατῆσαι ἱκέτης ἵζετο πρὸς τὸ ἄγαλμα. (2) τούτους ἀνιστᾶσι μὲν οἱ πρυτάνιες τῶν ναυκράρων, οἵπερ ἔνεμον τότε τὰς Ἀθήνας, ὑπεγγύους πλὴν θανάτου· φονεῦσαι δὲ αὐτοὺς αἰτίη ἔχει Ἀλκμεωνίδας. ταῦτα πρὸ τῆς Πεισιστράτου ἡλικίης ἐγένετο.

(72) Κλεομένης δὲ ὡς πέμπων ἐξέβαλλε Κλεισθένεα καὶ τοὺς ἐναγέας, Κλεισθένης μὲν αὐτὸς ὑπεξέσχε, μετὰ δὲ οὐδὲν ἧσσον παρῆν ἐς τὰς Ἀθήνας ὁ Κλεομένης οὐ σὺν μεγάλῃ χειρί, ἀπικόμενος δὲ ἀγηλατέει ἑπτακόσια ἐπίστια Ἀθηναίων, τά οἱ ὑπέθετο ὁ Ἰσαγόρης. ταῦτα δὲ ποιήσας δεύτερα τὴν βουλὴν καταλύειν ἐπειρᾶτο, τριηκοσίοισι δὲ τοῖσι Ἰσαγόρεω στασιώτῃσι τὰς ἀρχὰς ἐνεχείριζε. (2) ἀντισταθείσης δὲ τῆς βουλῆς καὶ οὐ βουλομένης πείθεσθαι, ὅ τε Κλεομένης καὶ ὁ Ἰσαγόρης καὶ οἱ στασιῶται αὐτοῦ καταλαμβάνουσι τὴν ἀκρόπολιν. Ἀθηναίων δὲ οἱ λοιποὶ τὰ αὐτὰ φρονήσαντες ἐπολιόρκεον αὐτοὺς ἡμέρας δύο· τῇ δὲ τρίτῃ ὑπόσπονδοι ἐξέρχονται ἐκ τῆς χώρης ὅσοι ἦσαν αὐτῶν Λακεδαιμόνιοι (3). ἐπετελέετο δὲ τῷ Κλεομένεϊ ἡ φήμη· ὡς γὰρ ἀνέβη ἐς τὴν ἀκρόπολιν μέλλων δὴ αὐτὴν κατασχήσειν, ἤιε ἐς τὸ ἄδυτον τῆς θεοῦ ὡς προσερέων· ἡ δὲ ἱερείη, ἐξαναστᾶσα ἐκ τοῦ θρόνου πρὶν ἢ τὰς θύρας αὐτὸν ἀμεῖψαι, εἶπε· "ὦ ξεῖνε Λακεδαιμόνιε, πάλιν χώρεε μηδὲ ἔσιθι ἐς τὸ ἱρόν· οὐ γὰρ θεμιτὸν Δωριεῦσι παριέναι ἐνθαῦτα." ὁ δὲ εἶπε· "ὦ γύναι, ἀλλ' οὐ

---

70. 2.   οἱ μὲν γὰρ ... οἱ φίλοι αὐτοῦ deleted Powell.

(**70**) Isagoras, getting the worse of it in turn, contrived this in response: he invited Cleomenes the Spartan, who had become a guest-friend of his from the blockade of the Pisistratids (and it was charged against Cleomenes that he had intercourse with Isagoras' wife). (*2*) First Cleomenes sent a herald to Athens, ordering the expulsion of Cleisthenes and many others of the Athenians with him, calling them the accursed. In sending that message he was following the instruction of Isagoras: for the Alcmaeonids and their partisans were charged with this killing, but Isagoras and his friends were not involved. (**71**) This is how the accursed among the Athenians acquired that appellation. There was an Athenian man called Cylon, an Olympic victor, who preened himself for tyranny. He attached to himself a following of his contemporaries and tried to seize the acropolis; and when he was not able to get control of that he sat as a suppliant at the image. (*2*) These men were removed by the *prytaneis* of the *naukraroi*, who at that time administered Athens, making them liable to anything except death; and it is charged that the Alcmaeonids slaughtered them. This happened before the time of Pisistratus.

(**72**) Cleomenes sent instructions to expel Cleisthenes and the accursed, and Cleisthenes himself withdrew. Afterwards none the less Cleomenes arrived at Athens, without a large force, and when he had come he drove out as accursed seven hundred Athenian households which Isagoras suggested to him. After doing that he next tried to dissolve the council, and entrusted the offices to the three hundred striving on Isagoras' side. (*2*) When the council resisted and was not willing to obey, Cleomenes, Isagoras and those striving on his side seized the acropolis. The rest of the Athenians agreed among themselves and blockaded them for two days; on the third day those of them who were Spartans departed from the land under a truce. (*3*) The saying for Cleomenes was fulfilled: for, when he went up to the acropolis intending to take control of it, he went into the shrine of the Goddess to address her, and the priestess rose up from her throne before he had passed through the doors, and said, 'Spartan foreigner, go back and do not enter the temple, for it is not rightful for a Dorian to come here'. He said, 'Woman, I am not a Dorian but an Achaean'.

Δωριεύς εἰμι ἀλλ᾽ Ἀχαιός." (*4*) ὁ μὲν δὴ τῇ κληηδόνι οὐδὲν χρεώμενος ἐπεχείρησέ τε καὶ τότε πάλιν ἐξέπιπτε μετὰ τῶν Λακεδαιμονίων· τοὺς δὲ ἄλλους Ἀθηναῖοι κατέδησαν τὴν ἐπὶ θανάτῳ, ἐν δὲ αὐτοῖσι καὶ Τιμησίθεον τὸν Δελφόν, τοῦ ἔργα χειρῶν τε καὶ λήματος ἔχοιμ᾽ ἂν μέγιστα καταλέξαι.

(**73**) οὗτοι μέν νυν δεδεμένοι ἐτελεύτησαν. Ἀθηναῖοι δὲ μετὰ ταῦτα Κλεισθένεα καὶ τὰ ἑπτακόσια ἐπίστια τὰ διωχθέντα ὑπὸ Κλεομένεος μεταπεμψάμενοι πέμπουσι ἀγγέλους ἐς Σάρδις, συμμαχίην βουλόμενοι ποιήσασθαι πρὸς Πέρσας· ἠπιστέατο γὰρ σφίσι [πρὸς] Λακεδαιμονίους τε καὶ Κλεομένεα ἐκπεπολεμῶσθαι. (*2*) ἀπικομένων δὲ τῶν ἀγγέλων ἐς τὰς Σάρδις καὶ λεγόντων τὰ ἐντεταλμένα, Ἀρταφρένης ὁ Ὑστάσπεος Σαρδίων ὕπαρχος ἐπειρώτα τίνες ἐόντες ἄνθρωποι καὶ κοῦ γῆς οἰκημένοι δεοίατο Περσέων σύμμαχοι γενέσθαι, πυθόμενος δὲ πρὸς τῶν ἀγγέλων ἀπεκορύφου σφι τάδε· εἰ μὲν διδοῦσι βασιλέι Δαρείῳ Ἀθηναῖοι γῆν τε καὶ ὕδωρ, ὁ δὲ συμμαχίην σφι συνετίθετο, εἰ δὲ μὴ διδοῦσι, ἀπαλλάσσεσθαι αὐτοὺς ἐκέλευε. (*3*) οἱ δὲ ἄγγελοι ἐπὶ σφέων αὐτῶν βαλόμενοι διδόναι ἔφασαν, βουλόμενοι τὴν συμμαχίην ποιήσασθαι. οὗτοι μὲν δὴ ἀπελθόντες ἐς τὴν ἑωυτῶν αἰτίας μεγάλας εἶχον.

(**74**) Κλεομένης δὲ ἐπιστάμενος περιυβρίσθαι ἔπεσι καὶ ἔργοισι ὑπ᾽ Ἀθηναίων συνέλεγε ἐκ πάσης Πελοποννήσου στρατόν, οὐ φράζων ἐς τὸ συλλέγει, τίσασθαί τε ἐθέλων τὸν δῆμον τὸν Ἀθηναίων καὶ Ἰσαγόρην βουλόμενος τύραννον καταστῆσαι· συνεξῆλθε γάρ οἱ οὗτος ἐκ τῆς ἀκροπόλιος. (*2*) Κλεομένης τε δὴ στόλῳ μεγάλῳ ἐσέβαλε ἐς Ἐλευσῖνα, καὶ οἱ Βοιωτοὶ ἀπὸ συνθήματος Οἰνόην αἱρέουσι καὶ Ὑσιὰς, δήμους τοὺς ἐσχάτους τῆς Ἀττικῆς, Χαλκιδέες τε ἐπὶ τὰ ἕτερα ἐσίνοντο ἐπιόντες χώρους τῆς Ἀττικῆς. Ἀθηναῖοι δέ, καίπερ ἀμφιβολίῃ ἐχόμενοι, Βοιωτῶν μὲν καὶ Χαλκιδέων ἐς ὕστερον ἔμελλον μνήμην ποιήσεσθαι, Πελοποννησίοισι δὲ ἐοῦσι ἐν Ἐλευσῖνι ἀντία ἔθεντο τὰ ὅπλα. (**75**) μελλόντων δὲ συνάψειν τὰ στρατόπεδα ἐς μάχην, Κορίνθιοι μὲν πρῶτοι σφίσι αὐτοῖσι δόντες λόγον ὡς οὐ ποιέοιεν δίκαια μετεβάλλοντό τε καὶ ἀπαλλάσσοντο, μετὰ δὲ Δημάρητος ὁ Ἀρίστωνος, ἐὼν καὶ οὗτος βασιλεὺς Σπαρτιητέων καὶ συνεξαγαγών τε

---

72. 4. Δελφόν Palmerius: ἀδελφεόν MSS.
73. 1. πρὸς deleted Schweighäuser.

(4) He took no notice of the omen, but made his attempt and then was driven out with the Spartans. The others the Athenians imprisoned to put them to death, among them Timesitheus the Delphian (and about his deeds of strength and courage I could say very much).

(**73**) They, then, were imprisoned and perished. The Athenians after this sent to recall Cleisthenes and the seven hundred households banished by Cleomenes; and they sent to Sardis, wanting to make an alliance with the Persians; for they understood that they were in a state of war with the Spartans and Cleomenes. (*2*) When the messengers reached Sardis and said what they had been instructed to say, Artaphernes son of Hystaspes, the governor of Sardis, asked who were these people and where on the earth they lived, who asked to become allies of the Persians. When he found out from the messengers, he gave them this summary answer: 'If the Athenians will give King Darius earth and water he will make an alliance with them; but if they will not give these he bids them be gone'. (*3*) The messengers on their own initiative said they would give them, since they wanted to make the alliance. But when they returned to their own land they incurred great blame.

(**74**) Cleomenes understood that he had been greatly insulted in word and deed by the Athenians; and he collected an army from the whole Peloponnese, not stating the purpose for which he was collecting it, but wishing to take revenge on the Athenian people and wanting to install Isagoras as tyrant: for Isagoras had withdrawn from the acropolis with him. (*2*) So Cleomenes with a large force invaded Eleusis, and the Boeotians by agreement captured Oenoë and Hysiae, the remotest demes of Attica, and the Chalcidians attacked on the other side and ravaged sites in Attica. The Athenians, though caught in a dilemma, planned to take account of the Boeotians and Chalcidians later, and they took up arms against the Peloponnesians who were at Eleusis. (**75**) But, when the two forces were about to join battle, first the Corinthians discussed among themselves that they would not be acting rightly, and changed their minds and were gone; and so afterwards did Demaratus son of Ariston, who was himself king of the Spartiates, had joined in leading the force out from Sparta and had

τὴν στρατιὴν ἐκ Λακεδαίμονος, καὶ οὐκ ἐὼν διάφορος ἐν τῷ πρόσθε χρόνῳ Κλεομένεϊ. (*2*) ἀπὸ δὲ ταύτης τῆς διχοστασίης ἐτέθη νόμος ἐν Σπάρτῃ μὴ ἐξεῖναι ἕπεσθαι ἀμφοτέρους τοὺς βασιλέας ἐξιούσης στρατιῆς· τέως γὰρ ἀμφότεροι εἵποντο. παραλυομένου δὲ τούτων τοῦ ἑτέρου καταλείπεσθαι καὶ τῶν Τυνδαριδέων τὸν ἕτερον· πρὸ τοῦ γὰρ δὴ καὶ οὗτοι ἀμφότεροι ἐπίκλητοί σφι ἐόντες εἵποντο. (*3*) τότε δή, ἐν τῇ Ἐλευσῖνι ὁρῶντες οἱ λοιποὶ τῶν συμμάχων τούς τε βασιλέας τῶν Λακεδαιμονίων οὐκ ὁμολογέοντας καὶ Κορινθίους ἐκλιπόντας τὴν τάξιν, οἴχοντο καὶ αὐτοὶ ἀπαλλασσόμενοι,

(**76**) τέταρτον δὴ τοῦτο ἐπὶ τὴν Ἀττικὴν ἀπικόμενοι Δωριέες, δίς τε ἐπὶ πολέμῳ ἐσβαλόντες καὶ δὶς ἐπ᾽ ἀγαθῷ τοῦ πλήθεος τοῦ Ἀθηναίων, πρῶτον μὲν ὅτε καὶ Μέγαρα κατοίκισαν (οὗτος ὁ στόλος ἐπὶ Κόδρου βασιλεύοντος Ἀθηναίων ὀρθῶς ἂν <πολέμιος> καλέοιτο), δεύτερον δὲ καὶ τρίτον ὅτε ἐπὶ Πεισιστρατιδέων ἐξέλασιν ὁρμηθέντες ἐκ Σπάρτης ἀπίκοντο, τέταρτον δὲ τότε ὅτε ἐς Ἐλευσῖνα Κλεομένης ἄγων Πελοποννησίους ἐσέβαλε. οὕτω τέταρτον τότε Δωριέες ἐσέβαλον ἐς Ἀθήνας.

(**77**) διαλυθέντος ὦν τοῦ στόλου τούτου ἀκλεῶς, ἐνθαῦτα Ἀθηναῖοι τίνυσθαι βουλόμενοι πρῶτα στρατηίην ποιεῦνται ἐπὶ Χαλκιδέας. Βοιωτοὶ δὲ τοῖσι Χαλκιδεῦσι βοηθέουσι ἐπὶ τὸν Εὔριπον. Ἀθηναίοισι δὲ ἰδοῦσι τοὺς βοηθοὺς ἔδοξε πρότερον τοῖσι Βοιωτοῖσι ἢ τοῖσι Χαλκιδεῦσι ἐπιχειρέειν. (*2*) συμβάλλουσί τε δὴ τοῖσι Βοιωτοῖσι οἱ Ἀθηναῖοι καὶ πολλῷ ἐκράτησαν, κάρτα δὲ πολλοὺς φονεύσαντες ἑπτακοσίους αὐτῶν ἐζώγρησαν. τῆς δὲ αὐτῆς ταύτης ἡμέρης οἱ Ἀθηναῖοι διαβάντες ἐς τὴν Εὔβοιαν συμβάλλουσι καὶ τοῖσι Χαλκιδεῦσι, νικήσαντες δὲ καὶ τούτους τετρακισχιλίους κληρούχους ἐπὶ τῶν ἱπποβοτέων τῇ χώρῃ λείπουσι· οἱ δὲ ἱπποβόται ἐκαλέοντο οἱ παχέες τῶν Χαλκιδέων. (*3*) ὅσους δὲ καὶ τούτων ἐζώγρησαν, ἅμα τοῖσι Βοιωτῶν ἐζωγρημένοισι εἶχον ἐν φυλακῇ ἐς πέδας δήσαντες·

---

76. τοῦτο: τότε Powell.
   πολέμιος inserted Richards: πρῶτος inserted Naber, οὗτος ... καλέοιτο deleted
   Powell, perhaps οὗτος <γὰρ> Wilson.
77. 1. βοηθοὺς DSV: Βοιωτοὺς other MSS.

not previously been at odds with Cleomenes. (*2*) As a result of this difference a law was enacted at Sparta that it should not be permitted to both kings to accompany an army when it set out. Until then both had accompanied the army; and when one of these was relieved of the duty one also of the Tyndarids was left behind; for before this both of these had accompanied the army as invited supporters. (*3*) On this occasion at Eleusis the rest of the allies saw that the Spartans' kings were not in agreement and that the Corinthians had left the ranks, and so they themselves went and were gone.

(**76**) This was the fourth time the Dorians had gone to Attica: twice they had invaded for war and twice they had gone for the good of the mass of the Athenians. The first time was when they had founded Megara (this mission when Codrus was king of Athens would rightly be called warlike); the second and third were when they set out from Sparta and went to drive out the Pisistratids; and the fourth was on this occasion when Cleomenes invaded Eleusis taking the Peloponnesians: so this was the fourth Dorian invasion of Athens.

(**77**) When this mission had broken up ingloriously, the Athenians wanted to take revenge, and first made an expedition against the Chalcidians. The Boeotians went to the Euripus in support of the Chalcidians. When the Athenians saw the supporting force, they decided to make an attempt against the Boeotians before the Chalcidians. (*2*) The Athenians attacked the Boeotians and were by far the masters, and they killed very many of them and took seven hundred prisoners. That very same day the Athenians crossed to Euboea and attacked the Chalcidians too; and they defeated them too, and left four thousand cleruchs on the land of the horse-rearers (horse-rearers is what the bloated class of the Chalcidians are called). (*3*) Those of the Chalcidians who were taken prisoner, together with those of the Boeotians who had been taken, they kept under guard,

χρόνῳ δὲ ἔλυσαν σφέας δίμνεως ἀποτιμησάμενοι. τὰς δὲ πέδας αὐτῶν, ἐν τῇσι ἐδεδέατο, ἀνεκρέμασαν ἐς τὴν ἀκρόπολιν· αἵ περ ἔτι καὶ ἐς ἐμὲ ἦσαν περιεοῦσαι, κρεμάμεναι ἐκ τειχέων περιπεφλευσμένων πυρὶ ὑπὸ τοῦ Μήδου, ἀντίον δὲ τοῦ μεγάρου τοῦ πρὸς ἑσπέρην τετραμμένου. (4) καὶ τῶν λύτρων τὴν δεκάτην ἀνέθηκαν ποιησάμενοι τέθριππον χάλκεον· τὸ δὲ ἀριστερῆς χειρὸς ἕστηκε πρῶτον ἐσιόντι ἐς τὰ προπύλαια τὰ ἐν τῇ ἀκροπόλι· ἐπιγέγραπται δέ οἱ τάδε·

ἔθνεα Βοιωτῶν καὶ Χαλκιδέων δαμάσαντες
παῖδες Ἀθηναίων ἔργμασιν ἐν πολέμου,
δεσμῷ ἐν ἀχλυόεντι σιδηρέῳ ἔσβεσαν ὕβριν·
τῶν ἵππους δεκάτην Παλλάδι τάσδ' ἔθεσαν.

(78) Ἀθηναῖοι μέν νυν ηὔξηντο. δηλοῖ δὲ οὐ κατ' ἓν μοῦνον ἀλλὰ πανταχῇ ἡ ἰσηγορίη ὡς ἔστι χρῆμα σπουδαῖον, εἰ καὶ Ἀθηναῖοι τυραννευόμενοι μὲν οὐδαμῶν τῶν σφέας περιοικεόντων ἦσαν τὰ πολέμια ἀμείνους, ἀπαλλαχθέντες δὲ τυράννων μακρῷ πρῶτοι ἐγένοντο. δηλοῖ ὦν ταῦτα ὅτι κατεχόμενοι μὲν ἐθελοκάκεον ὡς δεσπότῃ ἐργαζόμενοι, ἐλευθερωθέντων δὲ αὐτὸς ἕκαστος ἑωυτῷ προεθυμέετο κατεργάζεσθαι.

(79) οὗτοι μέν νυν ταῦτα ἔπρησσον. Θηβαῖοι δὲ μετὰ ταῦτα ἐς θεὸν ἔπεμπον, βουλόμενοι τείσασθαι Ἀθηναίους. ἡ δὲ Πυθίη ἀπὸ σφέων μὲν αὐτῶν οὐκ ἔφη αὐτοῖσι εἶναι τίσιν, ἐς πολύφημον δὲ ἐξενείκαντας ἐκέλευε τῶν ἄγχιστα δέεσθαι. (2) ἀπελθόντων ὦν τῶν θεοπρόπων, ἐξέφερον τὸ χρηστήριον ἁλίην ποιησάμενοι· ὡς ἐπυνθάνοντο δὲ λεγόντων αὐτῶν τῶν ἄγχιστα δέεσθαι, εἶπαν οἱ Θηβαῖοι ἀκούσαντες τούτων· "οὐκ ὦν ἄγχιστα ἡμέων οἰκέουσι Ταναγραῖοί τε καὶ Κορωναῖοι καὶ Θεσπιέες; καὶ οὗτοί γε ἅμα ἡμῖν

77. 4.   ἐς τὰ προπύλαια τὰ deleted Powell, τὰ ἐν τῇ ἀκροπόλει better deletion
Wilson *apparatus*.
ἀχνυόεντι Hecker: ἀχνυνθέντι AB (and *Anth. Pal.* VI. 343), ἀχνυθέντι
C, ἀχλυόεντι other MSS (and Diod. Sic. X. 24. 3). There is room on the
inscription for only eight letters, so none of these readings can be correct unless
τι was inscribed in a single space.
78.   τι inserted before κατεργάζεσθαι Powell.
79. 1.   ἀγορὴν inserted before πολύφημον Wilson.

binding them in fetters; and in time they released them after setting a price of 2 minas. The fetters in which they had been bound they hung up on the acropolis, and they still survived to my time, hanging from the walls which had been scorched by fire by the Medes, opposite the building which faces west. (*4*) From the ransom they dedicated a tithe, making a bronze four-horse chariot: that stands on the left as soon as you enter the propylaea on the acropolis. Inscribed on it is this:

> Subduing the peoples of the Boeotians and Chalcidians,
>
> The sons of the Athenians in deeds of war
>
> Quenched their arrogance in painful bonds of iron,
>
> From which they dedicated these mares to Pallas as a tithe.

(**78**) The Athenians had increased, then. It can be demonstrated not just in one respect but altogether that freedom of speech is a valuable thing, if the Athenians when they were under tyrants were not superior in warfare to any of those living around them, but when rid of tyrants became by far the first. This shows that when they were under constraint they were weak-spirited because they were labouring for a master, but when they were freed every one of them was eager to achieve something for himself.

(**79**) So that is what they did. The Thebans after that sent to the God, wanting to take revenge on the Athenians. The Pythia said that revenge would not come to them from themselves, but ordered them to bring the matter forward to the many-voiced, and to ask those nearest. (*2*) When the consultants went back, the Thebans held an assembly and brought forward the oracle. On hearing this the Thebans said, 'Are not those who live nearest to us the people of Tanagra, Coronea and Thespiae? But they have always fought enthusiastically

αἰεὶ μαχόμενοι προθύμως συνδιαφέρουσι τὸν πόλεμον. τί δεῖ τούτων γε δέεσθαι; ἀλλὰ μᾶλλον μὴ οὐ τοῦτο ᾖ τὸ χρηστήριον." (**80**) τοιαῦτα ἐπιλεγομένων εἶπε δή κοτε μαθών τις· "ἐγώ μοι δοκέω συνιέναι τὸ θέλει λέγειν ἡμῖν τὸ μαντήιον. Ἀσωποῦ λέγονται γενέσθαι θυγατέρες Θήβη τε καὶ Αἴγινα· τουτέων ἀδελφεῶν ἐουσέων, δοκέω ἡμῖν Αἰγινητέων δέεσθαι τὸν θεὸν χρῆσαι τιμωρητήρων γενέσθαι." (*2*) καὶ οὐ γάρ τις ταύτης ἀμείνων γνώμη ἐδόκεε φαίνεσθαι, αὐτίκα πέμψαντες ἐδέοντο Αἰγινητέων ἐπικαλεόμενοι κατὰ τὸ χρηστήριόν σφι βοηθέειν, ὡς ἐόντων ἀγχίστων· οἱ δέ σφι αἰτέουσι ἐπικουρίην τοὺς Αἰακίδας συμπέμπειν ἔφασαν. (**81**) πειρησαμένων δὲ τῶν Θηβαίων κατὰ τὴν συμμαχίην τῶν Αἰακιδέων καὶ τρηχέως περιεφθέντων ὑπὸ τῶν Ἀθηναίων, αὖτις οἱ Θηβαῖοι πέμψαντες τοὺς μὲν Αἰακίδας σφι ἀπεδίδοσαν, τῶν δὲ ἀνδρῶν ἐδέοντο. (*2*) Αἰγινῆται δέ, εὐδαιμονίη τε μεγάλῃ ἐπαρθέντες καὶ ἔχθρης παλαιῆς ἀναμνησθέντες ἐχούσης ἐς Ἀθηναίους, τότε Θηβαίων δεηθέντων πόλεμον ἀκήρυκτον Ἀθηναίοισι ἐπέφερον. (*3*) ἐπικειμένων γὰρ αὐτῶν Βοιωτοῖσι, ἐπιπλώσαντες μακρῇσι νηυσὶ ἐς τὴν Ἀττικὴν κατὰ μὲν ἔσυραν Φάληρον κατὰ δὲ τῆς ἄλλης παραλίης πολλοὺς δήμους, ποιεῦντες δὲ ταῦτα μεγάλως Ἀθηναίους ἐσινέοντο.

(**82**) ἡ δὲ ἔχθρη ἡ προοφειλομένη ἐς Ἀθηναίους ἐκ τῶν Αἰγινητέων ἐγένετο ἐξ ἀρχῆς τοιῆσδε. Ἐπιδαυρίοισι ἡ γῆ καρπὸν οὐδένα ἀνεδίδου. περὶ ταύτης ὦν τῆς συμφορῆς οἱ Ἐπιδαύριοι ἐχρέωντο ἐν Δελφοῖσι· ἡ δὲ Πυθίη σφέας ἐκέλευε Δαμίης τε καὶ Αὐξησίης ἀγάλματα ἱδρύσασθαι καί σφι ἱδρυσαμένοισι ἄμεινον συνοίσεσθαι. (*2*) ἐπειρώτεον ὦν οἱ Ἐπιδαύριοι κότερα χαλκοῦ ποιέωνται τὰ ἀγάλματα ἢ λίθου· ἡ δὲ Πυθίη οὐδέτερα τούτων ἔα, ἀλλὰ ξύλου ἡμέρης ἐλαίης. ἐδέοντο ὦν οἱ Ἐπιδαύριοι Ἀθηναίων ἐλαίας σφι δοῦναι ταμέσθαι, ἱρωτάτας δὴ κείνας νομίζοντες εἶναι· λέγεται δὲ καὶ ὡς ἐλαῖαι ἦσαν ἄλλοθι γῆς

---

80. 2.   συν<πεισθέντας> πέμπειν Wilson *apparatus*: συμπέμπειν other MSS, συμπείθειν ABC.
82. 2.   ἡμέρης: ἱρῆς Griffiths *ap.* Hornblower.
        ἐλαίας Powell: ἐλαίην MSS.

on our side and helped us in waging war. Why do we need to ask these? But perhaps that is not what the oracle means.' (**80**) As they were considering such matters, one of them eventually realised, and said, 'I think I understand what the prophecy means to say to us. It is said that the daughters of Asopus were Thebe and Aegina: since they were sisters, I think the God's response was was that we should ask the Aeginetans to be our avengers.' (*2*) No other opinion was thought to seem better than this, so immediately they sent and asked the Aeginetans, inviting them to give them support in accordance with the oracle, since they were their nearest; and they were persuaded and said in answer to their request that they would send them the sons of Aeacus. (**81**) The Thebans made their attempt with the sons of Aeacus as allies, but were harshly treated by the Athenians, They then sent again, returning the sons of Aeacus to them and asking for men. (*2*) The Aeginetans were buoyed up by great prosperity, and, mindful of their ancient enmity towards the Athenians, then as the Thebans asked they began to wage a war without heralds against the Athenians. (*3*) While the Athenians were attacking the Boeotians, they sailed against Attica in long ships, and devastated both Phalerum and many other demes along the rest of the coast, and by doing that they did great harm to the Athenians.

(**82**) The enmity which the Athenians had already incurred from the Aeginetans had an origin of this kind. The territory of the Epidaurians was bearing them no crops. The Epidaurians consulted at Delphi about this disaster, and the Pythia ordered them to set up images of Damia and Auxesia, and things would turn out better when they had set these up. (*2*) So the Epidaurians asked whether they should make the images of bronze or of stone, and the Pythia would not allow either of those, but cultivated olive wood. So the Epidaurians asked the Athenians to let them cut some olive wood, thinking that theirs were the most sacred olives (and it is said that at that time there were

οὐδαμοῦ κατὰ χρόνον κεῖνον ἢ ἐν Ἀθήνησι. (*3*) οἱ δὲ ἐπὶ τοῖσιδε δώσειν ἔφασαν ἐπ' ᾧ ἀπάξουσι ἔτεος ἑκάστου τῇ τε Ἀθηναίῃ τῇ Πολιάδι ἱρὰ καὶ τῷ Ἐρεχθέϊ. καταινέσαντες δὲ ἐπὶ τούτοισι οἱ Ἐπιδαύριοι τῶν τε ἐδέοντο ἔτυχον καὶ ἀγάλματα ἐκ τῶν ἐλαιέων τουτέων ποιησάμενοι ἱδρύσαντο· καὶ ἥ τε γῆ σφι ἔφερε καρπὸν καὶ Ἀθηναίοισι ἐπετέλεον τὰ συνέθεντο.

(**83**) τοῦτον δ' ἔτι τὸν χρόνον καὶ πρὸ τοῦ Αἰγινῆται Ἐπιδαυρίων ἤκουον τά τε ἄλλα καὶ δίκας διαβαίνοντες ἐς Ἐπίδαυρον ἐδίδοσάν τε καὶ ἐλάμβανον παρ' ἀλλήλων [οἱ Αἰγινῆται]. τὸ δὲ ἀπὸ τοῦδε νέας τε πηξάμενοι καὶ ἀγνωμοσύνῃ χρησάμενοι ἀπέστησαν ἀπὸ τῶν Ἐπιδαυρίων. (*2*) ἅτε δὲ ἐόντες διάφοροι ἐδηλέοντο αὐτούς, ὥστε θαλασσοκράτορες ἐόντες, καὶ δὴ καὶ τὰ ἀγάλματα ταῦτα τῆς τε Δαμίης καὶ τῆς Αὐξησίης ὑπαιρέονται αὐτῶν, καί σφεα ἐκόμισάν τε καὶ ἱδρύσαντο τῆς σφετέρης χώρης ἐς τὴν μεσόγαιαν, τῇ Οἴῃ μὲν ἐστὶ οὔνομα, στάδια δὲ μάλιστά κῃ ἀπὸ τῆς πόλιος ὡς εἴκοσι ἀπέχει. (*3*) ἱδρυσάμενοι δὲ ἐν τούτῳ τῷ χώρῳ θυσίῃσί τε σφέα καὶ χοροῖσι γυναικηίοισι κερτομίοισι ἱλάσκοντο, χορηγῶν ἀποδεικνυμένων ἑκατέρῃ τῶν δαιμόνων δέκα ἀνδρῶν·· κακῶς δὲ ἠγόρευον οἱ χοροὶ ἄνδρα μὲν οὐδένα, τὰς δὲ ἐπιχωρίας γυναῖκας. ἦσαν δὲ καὶ τοῖσι Ἐπιδαυρίοισι αἱ αὐταὶ ἱροργίαι· εἰσὶ δέ σφι καὶ ἄρρητοι ἱροργίαι.

(**84**) κλεφθέντων δὲ τῶνδε τῶν ἀγαλμάτων οἱ Ἐπιδαύριοι τοῖσι Ἀθηναίοισι τὰ συνέθεντο οὐκ ἐπετέλεον. πέμψαντες δὲ οἱ Ἀθηναῖοι ἐμήνιον τοῖσι Ἐπιδαυρίοισι· οἱ δὲ ἀπέφαινον λόγῳ ὡς οὐκ ἀδικέοιεν· ὅσον μὲν γὰρ χρόνον εἶχον τὰ ἀγάλματα ἐν τῇ χώρῃ, ἐπιτελέειν τὰ συνέθεντο, ἐπεὶ δὲ ἐστερῆσθαι αὐτῶν, οὐ δίκαιον εἶναι ἀποφέρειν ἔτι, ἀλλὰ τοὺς ἔχοντας αὐτὰ Αἰγινήτας πρήσσεσθαι ἐκέλευον. (*2*) πρὸς ταῦτα οἱ Ἀθηναῖοι ἐς Αἴγιναν πέμψαντες ἀπαίτεον τὰ ἀγάλματα· οἱ δὲ Αἰγινῆται ἔφασαν σφίσι τε καὶ Ἀθηναίοισι εἶναι οὐδὲν πρῆγμα.

---

82. 3.   τε Ἀθηναίῃ Hude: Ἀθηναίῃ τε MSS.
         καρπὸν omitted A, deleted Hude.
83. 1.   οἱ Αἰγινῆται deleted Cobet.
83. 2.   ἐν κώμῃ inserted before τῇ Οἴῃ Powell.

no olives growing on any other territory than at Athens). (*3*) The Athenians said they would grant that on these terms, that every year they should bring offerings to Athena Polias and to Erechtheus. The Epidaurians agreed to these terms, obtained what they asked for, and made the images from these olives and set them up. Their land bore crops, and they performed to the Athenians what they had agreed.

(**83**) Still at this time and before, the Aeginetans had been doing the bidding of the Epidaurians in other respects, and they had crossed to Epidaurus to give and receive justice from one another. But after this they had built ships and, yielding to folly, had revolted against the Epidaurians. (*2*) In their dispute they were able to injure the Epidaurians, since they had mastery of the sea, and in particular they stole away these images of Damia and Auxesia, and conveyed them and set them up in their own land, in the interior, at a place called Oeë, which is about twenty stades from the city. (*3*) Having set them up in this land, they proceeded to propitiate them with sacrifices and ribald women's choruses, appointing ten men as chorus-leaders for each of the divinities. The choruses did not speak ill of any man, but of the local women. (The Epidaurians had the same sacred rites; and they also had secret rites.)

(**84**) When these images had been stolen, the Epidaurians did not continue to perform for the Athenians what they had agreed, and the Athenians sent and rebuked the Epidaurians. In reply they demonstrated that they were doing no wrong: for as long a time as they had the images in their land, they had performed what was agreed, but, since they had been deprived of them, it was not right that they should still send offerings, but they told the Athenans to exact them from the Aeginetans who had the statues. (*2*) In response to that the Athenians sent to Aegina and asked for the images back; but the Aeginetans said

(85) Ἀθηναῖοι μέν νυν λέγουσι μετὰ τὴν ἀπαίτησιν ἀποσταλῆναι τριήρεϊ μιῇ τῶν ἀστῶν †τούτους† οἳ πεμφθέντες ἀπὸ τοῦ κοινοῦ καὶ ἀπικόμενοι ἐς Αἴγιναν τὰ ἀγάλματα ταῦτα ὡς σφετέρων ξύλων ἐόντα ἐπειρῶντο ἐκ τῶν βάθρων ἐξανασπᾶν, ἵνα σφέα ἀνακομίσωνται. (2) οὐ δυναμένους δὲ τούτῳ τῷ τρόπῳ αὐτῶν κρατῆσαι, περιβαλόντας σχοινία ἕλκειν τὰ ἀγάλματα, καί σφι ἕλκουσι βροντήν τε καὶ ἅμα τῇ βροντῇ σεισμὸν ἐπιγενέσθαι· τοὺς δὲ τριηρίτας τοὺς ἕλκοντας ὑπὸ τούτων ἀλλοφρονῆσαι, παθόντας δὲ τοῦτο κτείνειν ἀλλήλους ἅτε πολεμίους, ἐς ὃ ἐκ πάντων ἕνα λειφθέντα ἀνακομισθῆναι αὐτὸν ἐς Φάληρον.

(86) Ἀθηναῖοι μὲν οὕτω γενέσθαι λέγουσι, Αἰγινῆται δὲ οὐ μιῇ νηὶ ἀπικέσθαι Ἀθηναίους (μίαν μὲν γὰρ καὶ ὀλίγῳ πλεῦνας μιῆς, καὶ εἰ σφίσι μὴ ἔτυχον ἐοῦσαι νέες, ἀπαμύνεσθαι ἂν εὐπετέως), ἀλλὰ πολλῇσι νηυσὶ ἐπιπλέειν σφίσι ἐπὶ τὴν χώρην, αὐτοὶ δέ σφι εἶξαι καὶ οὐ ναυμαχῆσαι. (2) οὐκ ἔχουσι δὲ τοῦτο διασημῆναι ἀτρεκέως, οὔτε εἰ ἥσσονες συγγινωσκόμενοι εἶναι τῇ ναυμαχίῃ κατὰ τοῦτο εἶξαν, οὔτε εἰ βουλόμενοι ποιῆσαι οἷόν τι καὶ ἐποίησαν. (3) Ἀθηναίους μέν νυν, ἐπείτε σφι οὐδεὶς ἐς μάχην κατίστατο, ἀποβάντας ἀπὸ τῶν νεῶν τραπέσθαι πρὸς τὰ ἀγάλματα, οὐ δυναμένους δὲ ἀνασπάσαι ἐκ τῶν βάθρων αὐτὰ οὕτω δὴ περιβαλομένους σχοινία ἕλκειν, ἐς οὗ ἑλκόμενα τὰ ἀγάλματα ἀμφότερα τὠυτὸ ποιῆσαι, ἐμοὶ μὲν οὐ πιστὰ λέγοντες, ἄλλῳ δὲ τεῷ· ἐς γούνατα γάρ σφι αὐτὰ πεσεῖν, καὶ τὸν ἀπὸ τούτου χρόνον διατελέειν οὕτω ἔχοντα. (4) Ἀθηναίους μὲν δὴ ταῦτα ποιέειν· σφέας δὲ Αἰγινῆται λέγουσι πυθομένους τοὺς Ἀθηναίους ὡς μέλλοιεν ἐπὶ σφέας στρατεύεσθαι, ἑτοίμους Ἀργείους ποιέεσθαι. τούς τε δὴ Ἀθηναίους ἀποβεβάναι ἐς τὴν Αἰγιναίην, καὶ ἥκειν βοηθέοντας σφίσι τοὺς Ἀργείους καὶ λαθεῖν τε ἐξ Ἐπιδαύρου διαβάντας ἐς τὴν νῆσον καὶ οὐ προακηκοόσι τοῖσι Ἀθηναίοισι ἐπιπεσεῖν ὑποταμομένους τὸ

85. 1. τούτους A: obelised Wilson, τουτέων other MSS, ὀλίγους Legrand, ὀλίγους <τινάς>, Wilson, _Herodotea_, 105, deleted Krüger, various more specific suggestions have been made.
πεμφθέντες: ἀποπεμφθέντες A.
85. 2. αὐτὸν: αὐτόθεν Wilson.
86. 4. perhaps delete τὸ or read τὸ ἐπὶ Wilson.

that they had no business with Athens. (**85**) The Athenians say that after asking that they dispatched some of their citizens in a single trireme, who were sent by the state. On reaching Aegina they asked for these images, as being made of their wood, and tried to uproot them from their bases in order to take them off. (*2*) Since they were unable to get control of them in that way, they fastened ropes around the images to drag them away, and as they were dragging them there occurred thunder and at the same time as the thunder an earthquake. The crew of the trireme, who were doing the dragging, were driven mad, and in that state they started to kill one another as enemies, until out of all of them there was only one left to convey himself back to Phalerum.

(**86**) That is what the Athenians say happened. But the Aeginetans say that the Athenians came not in a single ship (for, if they had sent just one or a few more than one, even if the Aeginetans had not had any ships they would easily have warded them off), but that they sailed against their land with a large number of ships, and they had given way to them and had not fought a naval battle. (*2*) They are not able to indicate with certainty whether they admitted that they were too weak to fight a naval battle and for that reason gave way, or they did that because they were intending to do what they actually did do. (*3*) The Athenians, they say, then, since nobody began a battle against them, disembarked from the ships and turned to the images, and since they were unable to uproot them from their bases they fastened ropes around them to drag them, until each of the images did the same thing: what they say is incredible to me, but somebody else may believe it. Each image fell on its knees, and throughout the time from then they have remained in that state. (*4*) That is what they say the Athenians did; and the Aeginetans say that they, on learning that the Athenians were going to campaign against them, made ready the Argives. The Athenians disembarked on Aeginetan territory, and the Argives were present to support the Aeginetans, having crossed undetected to the island from Epidaurus. They attacked the Athenians without warning

ἀπὸ τῶν νεῶν, ἅμα τε ἐν τούτῳ τὴν βροντήν τε γενέσθαι καὶ τὸν σεισμὸν αὐτοῖσι.

(87) λέγεται μέν νυν ὑπ᾽ Ἀργείων τε καὶ Αἰγινητέων τάδε, ὁμολογέεται δὲ καὶ ὑπ᾽ Ἀθηναίων ἕνα μοῦνον τὸν ἀποσωθέντα αὐτῶν ἐς τὴν Ἀττικὴν γενέσθαι· (2) πλὴν Ἀργεῖοι μὲν λέγουσι αὐτῶν τὸ Ἀττικὸν στρατόπεδον διαφθειράντων τὸν ἕνα τοῦτον περιγενέσθαι, Ἀθηναῖοι δὲ τοῦ δαιμονίου· περιγενέσθαι μέντοι οὐδὲ τοῦτον τὸν ἕνα, ἀλλ᾽ ἀπολέσθαι τρόπῳ τοιῷδε. κομισθεὶς ἄρα ἐς τὰς Ἀθήνας ἀπήγγελλε τὸ πάθος· πυθομένας δὲ τὰς γυναῖκας τῶν ἐπ᾽ Αἴγιναν στρατευσαμένων ἀνδρῶν, δεινόν τι ποιησαμένας κεῖνον μοῦνον ἐξ ἁπάντων σωθῆναι, πέριξ τὸν ἄνθρωπον τοῦτον λαβούσας καὶ κεντεύσας τῇσι περόνῃσι τῶν ἱματίων εἰρωτᾶν ἑκάστην αὐτέων ὅκου εἴη ὁ ἑωυτῆς ἀνήρ. (3) καὶ τοῦτον μὲν οὕτω διαφθαρῆναι, Ἀθηναίοισι δὲ ἔτι τοῦ πάθεος δεινότερόν τι δόξαι εἶναι τὸ τῶν γυναικῶν ἔργον. ἄλλῳ μὲν δὴ οὐκ ἔχειν ὅτεῳ ζημιώσωσι τὰς γυναῖκας, τὴν δὲ ἐσθῆτα μετέβαλον αὐτέων ἐς τὴν Ἰάδα· ἐφόρεον γὰρ δὴ πρὸ τοῦ αἱ τῶν Ἀθηναίων γυναῖκες ἐσθῆτα Δωρίδα, τῇ Κορινθίῃ παραπλησιωτάτην· μετέβαλον ὦν ἐς τὸν λίνεον κιθῶνα, ἵνα δὴ περόνῃσι μὴ χρέωνται. (88) ἔστι δὲ ἀληθέϊ λόγῳ χρεωμένοισι οὐκ Ἰὰς αὕτη ἡ ἐσθὴς τὸ παλαιὸν ἀλλὰ Κάειρα, ἐπεὶ ἥ γε Ἑλληνικὴ ἐσθὴς πᾶσα ἡ ἀρχαίη τῶν γυναικῶν ἡ αὐτὴ ἦν τὴν νῦν Δωρίδα καλέομεν. (2) †τοῖσι δὲ Ἀργείοισι καὶ τοῖσι Αἰγινήτῃσι† καὶ πρὸς ταῦτα ἔτι τόδε ποιῆσαι νόμον εἶναι παρὰ σφίσι ἑκατέροισι τὰς περόνας ἡμιολίας ποιέεσθαι τοῦ τότε κατεστεῶτος μέτρου, καὶ ἐς τὸ ἱρὸν τῶν θεῶν τουτέων περόνας μάλιστα ἀνατιθέναι τὰς γυναῖκας, Ἀττικὸν δὲ μήτε τι ἄλλο προσφέρειν πρὸς τὸ ἱρὸν μήτε κέραμον, ἀλλ᾽ ἐκ χυτρίδων ἐπιχωριέων νόμον τὸ λοιπὸν αὐτόθι εἶναι πίνειν. (3) Ἀργείων μέν νυν καὶ Αἰγινητέων αἱ γυναῖκες ἐκ [τε] τόσου κατ᾽ ἔριν τὴν Ἀθηναίων περόνας ἔτι καὶ ἐς ἐμὲ ἐφόρεον μέζονας ἢ πρὸ τοῦ.

---

88. 2.   τοῖσι δὲ Ἀργείοισι καὶ τοῖσι Αἰγινήτῃσι: obelised Hude, τοὺς δὲ Ἀργείους καὶ τοὺς Αἰγινήτας Hude _apparatus_, lacuna after Αἰγινήτῃσι and τούτοισι for ταῦτα Powell, other suggestions have been made.

88. 3.   τε deleted Eltz.

and cut them off from their ships; and at the same time as that the thunder and the earthquake happened to them.

(**87**) That, then, is what is said by the Argives and Aeginetans, and it is agreed by the Athenians too that just one of their men was saved and reached Attica – (*2*) except that the Argives say that it was when they had destroyed the Athenian force that this one man survived, but the Athenians attribute it to the divinity. In fact not even this one man survived, but he perished in the following kind of way. When he had been conveyed back to Athens he announced the disaster; and, when the wives of the men who had campaigned against Aegina learned of it, they took it very hard that that one man out of all had been saved, and they surrounded that person, stabbed him with the brooch pins from their cloaks, and each of them asked where her own husband was. (*3*) He was destroyed in that way; but the Athenians reckoned that the wives' deed was even worse than the disaster. They had no other way to punish the wives, but they changed their dress to the Ionian style: before this Athenian women had worn Dorian dress, very similar to the Corinthian; so they changed to the linen tunic, so that they should not use brooches. (**88**) To give a truthful account, this style of clothing was in the past not Ionian but Carian, since all the ancient Greek women's clothing was the same as that which we now call Dorian. (*2*) The Argives and Aeginetans in addition established this as a law, that among both of them they should make brooch pins half as long again as the then prevalent length, and that the women should particularly dedicate the brooches at the sanctuary of these gods, and that nothing else Athenian nor even pottery should be brought to the sanctuary, but the law was that in future they should drink there from local vessels. (*3*) So Argive and Aeginetan women, since that time, in contention against the Athenian women have continued to my time to wear brooches with longer pins than before then.

(**89**) τῆς δὲ ἔχθρης τῆς πρὸς Αἰγινήτας ἐξ Ἀθηναίων γενομένης ἀρχὴ κατὰ τὰ εἴρηται ἐγένετο. τότε δὲ Θηβαίων ἐπικαλεομένων προθύμως τῶν περὶ τὰ ἀγάλματα γενομένων ἀναμιμνησκόμενοι οἱ Αἰγινῆται ἐβοήθεον τοῖσι Βοιωτοῖσι. (*2*) Αἰγινῆταί τε δὴ ἐδηίουν τῆς Ἀττικῆς τὰ παραθαλάσσια, καὶ Ἀθηναίοισι ὁρμημένοισι ἐπ' Αἰγινήτας στρατεύεσθαι ἦλθε μαντήιον ἐκ Δελφῶν ἐπισχόντας ἀπὸ τοῦ Αἰγινητέων ἀδικίου τριήκοντα ἔτεα τῷ ἑνὶ καὶ τριηκοστῷ Αἰακῷ τέμενος ἀποδέξαντας ἄρχεσθαι τοῦ πρὸς Αἰγινήτας πολέμου, καί σφι χωρήσειν τὰ βούλονται· ἢν δὲ αὐτίκα ἐπιστρατεύωνται, πολλὰ μὲν σφέας ἐν τῷ μεταξὺ τοῦ χρόνου πείσεσθαι, πολλὰ δὲ καὶ ποιήσειν, τέλος μέντοι καταστρέψεσθαι. (*3*) ταῦτα ὡς ἀπενειχθέντα ἤκουσαν οἱ Ἀθηναῖοι, τῷ μὲν Αἰακῷ τέμενος ἀπέδεξαν τοῦτο τὸ νῦν ἐπὶ τῆς ἀγορῆς ἵδρυται, τριήκοντα δὲ ἔτεα οὐκ ἀνέσχοντο ἀκούσαντες ὅκως χρεὸν εἴη ἐπισχεῖν πεπονθότας ὑπ' Αἰγινητέων ἀνάρσια.

(**90**) ἐς τιμωρίην δὲ παρασκευαζομένοισι αὐτοῖσι ἐκ Λακεδαιμονίων πρῆγμα ἐγειρόμενον ἐμπόδιον ἐγένετο. πυθόμενοι γὰρ Λακεδαιμόνιοι τὰ ἐκ τῶν Ἀλκμεωνιδέων ἐς τὴν Πυθίην μεμηχανημένα καὶ τὰ ἐκ τῆς Πυθίης ἐπὶ σφέας τε καὶ τοὺς Πεισιστρατίδας, συμφορὴν ἐποιεῦντο διπλῆν, ὅτι τε ἄνδρας ξείνους σφίσι ἐόντας ἐξεληλάκεσαν ἐκ τῆς ἐκείνων, καὶ ὅτι ταῦτα ποιήσασι χάρις οὐδεμία ἐφαίνετο πρὸς Ἀθηναίων. (*2*) ἔτι τε πρὸς τούτοισι ἐνῆγον σφέας οἱ χρησμοὶ λέγοντες πολλά τε καὶ ἀνάρσια ἔσεσθαι αὐτοῖσι ἐξ Ἀθηναίων, τῶν πρότερον μὲν ἦσαν ἀδαέες, τότε δὲ Κλεομένεος κομίσαντος ἐς Σπάρτην ἐξέμαθον. ἐκτήσατο δὲ ὁ Κλεομένης ἐκ τῆς Ἀθηναίων ἀκροπόλιος τοὺς χρησμούς, τοὺς ἔκτηντο μὲν πρότερον οἱ Πεισιστρατίδαι, ἐξελαυνόμενοι δὲ ἔλιπον ἐν τῷ ἱρῷ, καταλειφθέντας δὲ ὁ Κλεομένης ἀνέλαβε.

(**91**) τότε δὲ ὡς ἀνέλαβον οἱ Λακεδαιμόνιοι τοὺς χρησμοὺς καὶ τοὺς Ἀθηναίους ὥρων αὐξομένους καὶ οὐδαμῶς ἑτοίμους ἐόντας πείθεσθαι σφίσι, νόῳ λαβόντες ὡς ἐλεύθερον μὲν ἐὸν τὸ γένος τὸ Ἀττικὸν ἰσόρροπον τῷ ἑωυτῶν ἂν γίνοιτο, κατεχόμενον δὲ ὑπὸ τυραννίδος ἀσθενὲς καὶ πειθαρχέεσθαι ἕτοιμον, μαθόντες δὲ τούτων

89, 1. κατὰ τὰ εἴρηται: τὰ deleted Struve.

(**89**) The origin of the Aeginetans' hostility to the Athenians came about as stated. On this occasion, when the Thebans invited them, the Aeginetans remembered passionately what had happened with regard to the images, and they went to support the Boeotians. (*2*) The Aeginetans proceeded to ravage the coastal parts of Attica, and when the Athenians were planning to campaign against the Aeginetans there came a prophecy from Delphi that, if they held off from wronging the Aeginetans for thirty years, and in the thirty-first year designated a precinct of Aeacus and began the war against the Aeginetans, things would go for them as they wanted; but, if they embarked on the campaign immediately, they would suffer much in the intervening time and also do much, but in the end would overcome them. (*3*) When this was brought back and the Athenians heard it, they dedicated to Aeacus this precinct which stands now in the agora, and they could not bear to hear that they must hold off for thirty years after the terrible things they had suffered from the Aeginetans.

(**90**) But when they were preparing for revenge a matter stirred up by the Spartans occurred as an impediment. For the Spartans learned what had been contrived by the Alcmaeonids with regard to the Pythia, and what had been done by the Pythia against them and the Pisistratids, and they considered it a double disaster, that they had driven men who were guest-friends of theirs out of their own land, and that no gratitude for their doing this was being shown on the part of the Athenians. (*2*) Moreover, in addition to this they were being urged on by oracles which said that many terrible things would come upon them from the Athenians, which they had not known of before but learned of when Cleomenes conveyed them to Sparta. Cleomenes had acquired the oracles from the Athenian acropolis: they had been acquired previously by the Pisistratids and left in the sanctuary when they were driven out, and Cleomenes had found them and taken them up.

(**91**) So now, when the Spartans took up the oracles, and saw the Athenians increasing and in no way ready to obey them, they took to heart that the Athenian race when free would be able to counterbalance their own, but when held down by tyranny it had been weak and

ἕκαστα μετεπέμποντο Ἱππίην τὸν Πεισιστράτου ἀπὸ Σιγείου τοῦ
ἐν Ἑλλησπόντῳ ἐς ὃ καταφεύγουσι οἱ Πεισιστρατίδαι. (2) ἐπείτε
δέ σφι Ἱππίης καλεόμενος ἧκε, μεταπεμψάμενοι καὶ τῶν ἄλλων
συμμάχων ἀγγέλους ἔλεγόν σφι Σπαρτιῆται τάδε· "ἄνδρες σύμμαχοι,
συγγινώσκομεν αὐτοῖσι ἡμῖν οὐ ποιήσασι ὀρθῶς· ἐπαρθέντες γὰρ
κιβδήλοισι μαντηίοισι ἄνδρας ξείνους ἐόντας ἡμῖν τὰ μάλιστα καὶ
ἀναδεκομένους ὑποχειρίας παρέξειν τὰς Ἀθήνας, τούτους ἐκ τῆς
πατρίδος ἐξηλάσαμεν, καὶ ἔπειτα ποιήσαντες ταῦτα δήμῳ ἀχαρίστῳ
παρεδώκαμεν τὴν πόλιν· ὃς ἐπείτε δι' ἡμέας ἐλευθερωθεὶς ἀνέκυψε,
ἡμέας μὲν καὶ τὸν βασιλέα ἡμέων περιυβρίσας ἐξέβαλε, δόξαν δὲ
φύσας αὐξάνεται, ὥστε ἐκμεμαθήκασι μάλιστα μὲν οἱ περίοικοι αὐτῶν
Βοιωτοὶ καὶ Χαλκιδέες, τάχα δέ τις καὶ ἄλλος ἐκμαθήσεται ἁμαρτών.
(3) ἐπείτε δὲ ἐκεῖνα ποιήσαντες ἡμάρτομεν, νῦν πειρησόμεθά σφεα
ἅμα ὑμῖν ἀκεόμενοι· αὐτοῦ γὰρ τούτου εἵνεκεν τόνδε τε Ἱππίην
μετεπεμψάμεθα καὶ ὑμέας ἀπὸ τῶν πολίων, ἵνα κοινῷ τε λόγῳ καὶ
κοινῷ στόλῳ ἐσαγαγόντες αὐτὸν ἐς τὰς Ἀθήνας ἀποδῶμεν τὰ καὶ
ἀπειλόμεθα."
    (92) οἱ μὲν ταῦτα ἔλεγον, τῶν δὲ συμμάχων τὸ πλῆθος οὐκ
ἐνεδέκετο τοὺς λόγους. οἱ μέν νυν ἄλλοι ἡσυχίην ἦγον, Κορίνθιος
δὲ Σωκλέης ἔλεξε τάδε· (α) "ἦ δὴ ὅ τε οὐρανὸς ἔνερθε ἔσται τῆς
γῆς καὶ ἡ γῆ μετέωρος ὑπὲρ τοῦ οὐρανοῦ, καὶ ἄνθρωποι νομὸν ἐν
θαλάσσῃ ἕξουσι καὶ ἰχθύες τὸν πρότερον ἄνθρωποι, ὅτε γε ὑμεῖς ὦ
Λακεδαιμόνιοι ἰσοκρατίας καταλύοντες τυραννίδας ἐς τὰς πόλις
κατάγειν παρασκευάζεσθε, τοῦ οὔτε ἀδικώτερόν ἐστι οὐδὲν κατ'
ἀνθρώπους οὔτε μιαιφονώτερον. (2) εἰ γὰρ δὴ τοῦτό γε δοκέει ὑμῖν
εἶναι χρηστὸν ὥστε τυραννεύεσθαι τὰς πόλις, αὐτοὶ πρῶτοι τύραννον
καταστησάμενοι παρὰ σφίσι αὐτοῖσι οὕτω καὶ τοῖσι ἄλλοισι δίζησθε
κατιστάναι· νῦν δὲ αὐτοὶ τυράννων ἄπειροι ἐόντες, καὶ φυλάσσοντες
τοῦτο δεινότατα ἐν τῇ Σπάρτῃ μὴ γενέσθαι, παραχρᾶσθε ἐς τοὺς

---

91. 1 ἐς ὃ καταφεύγουσι οἱ Πεισιστρατίδαι deleted Wesseling.
    σφεα Eltz: σφέας MSS.
    ἀκεόμενοι: ἀπικόμενοι τίσασθαι A.
92. *init.* Σωκλέης A (and Plut. *De Her. Mal.* 860 A, *P. Oxy.* vii 1012 fr. 9. 55):
    Σωσικλέης other MSS.

willing to be obedient. On learning this they sent for Hippias son of Pisistratus from Sigeum on the Hellespont, to which the Pisistratids had fled. (*2*) When Hippias came in response to their summons, the Spartiates sent for messengers from their other allies too, and said this to them: 'Men of the allies, we are conscious that we have not acted rightly. For buoyed up by counterfeit prophecies we have driven from their country men who were particular guest-friends of ours and who were undertaking to render Athens subject to us, and then having done that we have handed over the city to an ungrateful people, who since they have been freed through us have lifted up their heads, and have grievously insulted us and our king and driven us out. They have become proud and are increasing, as has been learned particularly by their neighbours the Boeotians and Chalcidians, and as anybody else will soon learn if he makes a mistake. (*3*) Since we were mistaken in doing that, we shall now try to put it right together with you. For it is for this reason that we have sent for this man Hippias and for you from the cities, so that by a joint discussion and a joint mission we can install him in Athens and give back what we took from him.'

(**92**) They said that; but the majority of the allies did not accept what they said. The others kept quiet, but the Corinthian Socles said this: (α) 'Indeed heaven will be below the earth and and earth up in the air above the heaven, and mankind will have a life in the sea and fish the life which mankind previously had, when you, Spartans, are prepared to overthrow equalities of power and restore tyrannies to the cities, something than which nothing is more unjust among mankind or more bloodthirsty. (*2*) For if it does seem to you to be a good thing that the cities should be under tyrants, then you should first establish a tyrant among yourselves and only after that seek to establish them for others. As it is now, you yourselves have no experience of tyrants and take the most urgent care that there should be no tyrants in Sparta, but

συμμάχους. εἰ δὲ αὐτῶν ἔμπειροι ἔατε κατά περ ἡμεῖς, εἴχετε ἂν περὶ
αὐτοῦ γνώμας ἀμείνονας συμβαλέσθαι ἤ περ νῦν.

(β) "Κορινθίοισι γὰρ ἦν πόλιος κατάστασις τοιήδε· ἦν ὀλιγαρχίη,
καὶ οἱ Βακχιάδαι καλεόμενοι ἔνεμον τὴν πόλιν, ἐδίδοσαν δὲ καὶ
ἤγοντο ἐξ ἀλλήλων. Ἀμφίονι δὲ ἐόντι τούτων τῶν ἀνδρῶν γίνεται
θυγάτηρ χωλή· οὔνομα δέ οἱ ἦν Λάβδα. ταύτην Βακχιαδέων γὰρ
οὐδεὶς ἤθελε γῆμαι, ἴσχει Ἠετίων ὁ Ἐχεκράτεος, δήμου μὲν ἐὼν ἐκ
Πέτρης, ἀτὰρ τὰ ἀνέκαθεν Λαπίθης τε καὶ Καινείδης. (2) ἐκ δέ οἱ
ταύτης τῆς γυναικὸς οὐδ᾽ ἐξ ἄλλης παῖδες ἐγίνοντο. ἐστάλη ὦν ἐς
Δελφοὺς περὶ γόνου. ἐσιόντα δὲ αὐτὸν ἰθέως ἡ Πυθίη προσαγορεύει
τοῖσιδε τοῖσι ἔπεσι·

> Ἠετίων, οὔτις σε τίει πολύτιτον ἐόντα.
> Λάβδα κύει, τέξει δ᾽ ὀλοοίτροχον· ἐν δὲ πεσεῖται
> ἀνδράσι μουνάρχοισι, δικαιώσει δὲ Κόρινθον.

(3) ταῦτα χρησθέντα τῷ Ἠετίωνι ἐξαγγέλλεταί κως τοῖσι Βακχιάδησι,
τοῖσι τὸ μὲν πρότερον γενόμενον χρηστήριον ἐς Κόρινθον ἦν ἄσημον,
φέρον τε ἐς τὠυτὸ καὶ τὸ τοῦ Ἠετίωνος καὶ λέγον ὧδε·

> αἰετὸς ἐν πέτρῃσι κύει, τέξει δὲ λέοντα
> καρτερὸν ὠμηστήν· πολλῶν δ᾽ ὑπὸ γούνατα λύσει.
> ταῦτά νυν εὖ φράζεσθε, Κορίνθιοι, οἳ περὶ καλήν
> Πειρήνην οἰκεῖτε καὶ ὀφρυόεντα Κόρινθον.

(γ) "τοῦτο μὲν δὴ τοῖσι Βακχιάδησι πρότερον γενόμενον ἦν
ἀτέκμαρτον· τότε δὲ τὸ Ἠετίωνι γενόμενον ὡς ἐπύθοντο, αὐτίκα καὶ
τὸ πρότερον συνῆκαν ἐὸν συνῳδὸν τῷ Ἠετίωνος. συνέντες δὲ καὶ
τοῦτο εἶχον ἐν ἡσυχίῃ, ἐθέλοντες τὸν μέλλοντα Ἠετίωνι γίνεσθαι
γόνον διαφθεῖραι. ὡς δ᾽ ἔτεκε ἡ γυνὴ τάχιστα, πέμπουσι σφέων αὐτῶν
δέκα ἐς τὸν δῆμον ἐν τῷ κατοίκητο ὁ Ἠετίων ἀποκτενέοντας τὸ
παιδίον. (2) ἀπικόμενοι δὲ οὗτοι ἐς τὴν Πέτρην καὶ παρελθόντες ἐς τὴν
αὐλὴν τὴν Ἠετίωνος αἴτεον τὸ παιδίον· ἡ δὲ Λάβδα εἰδυῖά τε οὐδὲν
τῶν εἵνεκα ἐκεῖνοι ἀπικοίατο, καὶ δοκέουσα σφέας φιλοφροσύνης
τοῦ πατρὸς εἵνεκα αἰτέειν, φέρουσα ἐνεχείρισε αὐτῶν ἑνί. τοῖσι δὲ

92. α. 2   εἰ δὲ αὐτῶν Weber: αὐτοὶ or αὐτοῦ MSS.
92. β. 1   οἱ Βακχιάδαι: οἱ or οἱ τότε Madvig, οὗτοι MSS.

you are careless of your allies. If you had experience of tyrants as we have, you would be able to offer better opinions about it than you can now.

(β) 'For the disposition of the Corinthians' city used to be like this. There was an oligarchy, and those called the Bacchiads administered the city, and they gave and received wives from one another. Amphion, who was one of those men, had a daughter who was lame; her name was Labda. None of the Bacchiads was willing to marry her, and she was taken by Eëtion son of Echecrates, a man from the village of Petra but by descent a Lapith and of the Caeneïds. (2) He had no children from this wife or any other; so he set out for Delphi about offspring. As soon as he entered, the Pythia addressed him in these words:

> Eëtion, nobody honours you though you are highly honourable.
> Labda is with child, and will give birth to a boulder. It will fall on to
> the men who rule monarchically, and bring justice to Corinth.

(3) This oracle to Eëtion was reported to the Bacchiads, to whom the previous oracle for Corinth was unintelligible. That bore on the same matter as Eëtion's oracle, and said this:

> An eagle in the rocks is with child, and will give birth to a lion,
> Mighty and ravening, which will loosen the knees of many.
> Think well about these things, Corinthians, who live
> About beautiful Pirene and beetling Corinth.

(γ) 'This oracle given to the Bacchiads previously had been insoluble; but then, when they learned of that given to Eëtion, they immediately understood that the previous one was concordant with that to Eëtion. Realising that also, they kept quiet, wishing to destroy the offspring that was going to be born to Eëtion. As soon as the woman gave birth, they sent ten of their own number to the village in which Eëtion lived to kill the child. (2) These men arrived at Petra, went into Eëtion's home and asked for the child. Labda, knowing nothing of the reason why they had come, and thinking that they were asking out of good will towards the father, brought the child and put him

ἄρα ἐβεβούλευτο κατ᾽ ὁδὸν τὸν πρῶτον αὐτῶν λαβόντα τὸ παιδίον προσουδίσαι. (*3*) ἐπεὶ ὦν ἔδωκε φέρουσα ἡ Λάβδα, τὸν λαβόντα τῶν ἀνδρῶν θείη τύχῃ προσεγέλασε τὸ παιδίον, καὶ τὸν φρασθέντα τοῦτο οἶκτός τις ἴσχει ἀποκτεῖναι, κατοικτείρας δὲ παραδιδοῖ τῷ δευτέρῳ, ὁ δὲ τῷ τρίτῳ. οὕτω δὴ διεξῆλθε διὰ πάντων τῶν δέκα παραδιδόμενον, οὐδενὸς βουλομένου διεργάσασθαι. (*4*) ἀποδόντες ὦν ὀπίσω τῇ τεκούσῃ τὸ παιδίον καὶ ἐξελθόντες ἔξω, ἑστεῶτες ἐπὶ τῶν θυρέων ἀλλήλων ἅπτοντο καταιτιώμενοι, καὶ μάλιστα τοῦ πρώτου λαβόντος, ὅτι οὐκ ἐποίησε κατὰ τὰ δεδογμένα, ἐς ὃ δή σφι χρόνου ἐγγινομένου ἔδοξε αὖτις παρελθόντας πάντας τοῦ φόνου μετίσχειν. (δ) ἔδει δὲ ἐκ τοῦ Ἠετίωνος γόνου Κορίνθῳ κακὰ ἀναβλαστεῖν. ἡ Λάβδα γὰρ πάντα ταῦτα ἤκουε ἑστεῶσα πρὸς αὐτῇσι τῇσι θύρῃσι· δείσασα δὲ μή σφι μεταδόξῃ καὶ τὸ δεύτερον λαβόντες τὸ παιδίον ἀποκτείνωσι, φέρουσα κατακρύπτει ἐς τὸ ἀφραστότατόν οἱ ἐφαίνετο εἶναι, ἐς κυψέλην, ἐπισταμένη ὡς εἰ ὑποστρέψαντες ἐς ζήτησιν ἀπικνεοίατο πάντα ἐρευνήσειν μέλλοιεν· τὰ δὴ καὶ ἐγίνετο. (*2*) ἐλθοῦσι δὲ καὶ διζημένοισι αὐτοῖσι ὡς οὐκ ἐφαίνετο, ἐδόκεε ἀπαλλάσσεσθαι καὶ λέγειν πρὸς τοὺς ἀποπέμψαντας ὡς πάντα ποιήσειαν τὰ ἐκεῖνοι ἐνετείλαντο. οἱ μὲν δὴ ἀπελθόντες ἔλεγον ταῦτα. (ε) Ἠετίωνι δὲ μετὰ ταῦτα ὁ παῖς ηὐξάνετο, καί οἱ διαφυγόντι τοῦτον τὸν κίνδυνον ἀπὸ τῆς κυψέλης ἐπωνυμίη Κύψελος [οὔνομα] ἐτέθη.

"ἀνδρωθέντι δὲ καὶ μαντευομένῳ Κυψέλῳ ἐγένετο ἀμφιδέξιον χρηστήριον ἐν Δελφοῖσι, τῷ πίσυνος γενόμενος ἐπεχείρησέ τε καὶ ἔσχε Κόρινθον. (*2*) ὁ δὲ χρησμὸς ὅδε ἦν·

> ὄλβιος οὗτος ἀνὴρ ὃς ἐμὸν δόμον ἐσκαταβαίνει,
> Κύψελος Ἠετίδης, βασιλεὺς κλειτοῖο Κορίνθου,
> αὐτὸς καὶ παῖδες, παίδων γε μὲν οὐκέτι παῖδες.

τὸ μὲν δὴ χρηστήριον τοῦτο ἦν, τυραννεύσας δὲ ὁ Κύψελος τοιοῦτος δή τις ἀνὴρ ἐγένετο· πολλοὺς μὲν Κορινθίων ἐδίωξε, πολλοὺς δὲ χρημάτων ἀπεστέρησε, πολλῷ δέ τι πλείστους τῆς ψυχῆς. (ζ) ἄρξαντος

---

92. γ. 2.   τὸ παιδίον προσουδίσαι A: τὸ παιδίον omitted other MSS.
92. ε. 1.   ἐπωνυμίη Κύψελος [οὔνομα] Powell: ἐπωνυμίην Κύψελος οὔνομα
MSS.

in the hands of one of them. Now they had planned on the way that whoever took the child first should dash it to the ground. (*3*) So, when Labda brought and gave the child, by divine chance the child smiled at the man who took him, and the man noticed this and was prevented by pity from killing him. In his pity he handed him to a second man, and he in turn to a third, and so he continued to be handed over to all of the ten, none of them being willing to dispose of him. (*4*) So they gave the child back to his mother and went outside, and standing by the doors they reproached and accused one another, and particularly the one who had taken him first, for not acting in accordance with their decision, until after some time had passed they decided to go in again and all to share in the killing. (δ) But evil for Corinth was bound to sprout from Eëtion's line. For Labda had stood right by the doors and had heard all this. Afraid that they would change their minds and the second time they would take the child and kill him, she took him and hid him in what seemed to her the most undetectable place, in a chest, knowing that if they turned and came back to search they would investigate everything. And that indeed happened. (*2*) When they came in and searched thoroughly and he was not to be seen, they decided to be gone and to say to those who had sent them that they had done everything which they had instructed. So they went back and said that. (ε) After this Eëtion's son grew up, and because he had escaped this danger as a result of the chest he was given the corresponding name Cypselus.

'When Cyspelus had become a man and sought a prophecy, he received a double-edged oracle at Delphi, and trusting in that he made his attempt and gained control of Corinth. (*2*) The oracle was this:

> Blessed is this man who goes down into my house,
> Cypselus son of Eëtion, king of renowned Corinth,
> He and his sons, but no longer the sons of his sons.

That was the oracle. When Cypselus had become tyrant he became this kind of man: many of the Corinthians he drove into exile, many he deprived of their property, and by far the greatest number he deprived of their breath. (ζ) He ruled for thirty years and wove his life well to

δὲ τούτου ἐπὶ τριήκοντα ἔτεα καὶ διαπλέξαντος τὸν βίον εὖ, διάδοχός
οἱ τῆς τυραννίδος ὁ παῖς Περίανδρος γίνεται.

"ὁ τοίνυν Περίανδρος κατ' ἀρχὰς μὲν ἦν ἠπιώτερος τοῦ πατρός,
ἐπείτε δὲ ὡμίλησε δι' ἀγγέλων Θρασυβούλῳ τῷ Μιλήτου τυράννῳ,
πολλῷ ἔτι ἐγένετο Κυψέλου μιαιφονώτερος. (2) πέμψας γὰρ παρὰ
Θρασύβουλον κήρυκα ἐπυνθάνετο ὅντινα ἂν τρόπον ἀσφαλέστατον
καταστησάμενος τῶν πρηγμάτων κάλλιστα τὴν πόλιν ἐπιτροπεύοι.
Θρασύβουλος δὲ τὸν ἐλθόντα παρὰ τοῦ Περιάνδρου ἐξῆγε ἔξω τοῦ
ἄστεος, ἐσβὰς δὲ ἐς ἄρουραν ἐσπαρμένην ἅμα τε διεξήιε τὸ λήιον
ἐπειρωτῶν τε καὶ ἀναποδίζων τὸν κήρυκα κατὰ τὴν ἀπὸ Κορίνθου
ἄπιξιν, καὶ ἐκόλουε αἰεὶ ὅκως τινὰ ἴδοι τῶν ἀσταχύων ὑπερέχοντα,
κολούων δὲ ἔρριπτε, ἐς ὃ τοῦ ληίου τὸ κάλλιστόν τε καὶ βαθύτατον
διέφθειρε τρόπῳ τοιούτῳ. (3) διεξελθὼν δὲ τὸ χωρίον καὶ ὑποθέμενος
ἔπος οὐδὲν ἀποπέμπει τὸν κήρυκα. νοστήσαντος δὲ τοῦ κήρυκος ἐς τὴν
Κόρινθον ἦν πρόθυμος πυνθάνεσθαι τὴν ὑποθήκην ὁ Περίανδρος· ὁ δὲ
οὐδέν οἱ ἔφη Θρασύβουλον ὑποθέσθαι, θωμάζειν τε αὐτοῦ παρ' οἷόν
μιν ἄνδρα ἀποπέμψειε, ὡς παραπλῆγά τε καὶ τῶν ἑωυτοῦ σινάμωρον,
ἀπηγεόμενος τά περ πρὸς Θρασυβούλου ὀπώπεε. (η) Περίανδρος
δὲ συνιεὶς τὸ ποιηθὲν καὶ νόῳ ἴσχων ὥς οἱ ὑπετίθετο Θρασύβουλος
τοὺς ὑπειρόχους τῶν ἀστῶν φονεύειν, ἐνθαῦτα δὴ πᾶσαν κακότητα
ἐξέφαινε ἐς τοὺς πολιήτας. ὅσα γὰρ Κύψελος ἀπέλιπε κτείνων τε καὶ
διώκων, Περίανδρός σφεα ἀπετέλεσε.

"μιῇ δὲ ἡμέρῃ ἀπέδυσε πάσας τὰς Κορινθίων γυναῖκας διὰ τὴν
ἑωυτοῦ γυναῖκα Μέλισσαν. (2) πέμψαντι γάρ οἱ ἐς Θεσπρωτοὺς ἐπ'
Ἀχέροντα ποταμὸν ἀγγέλους ἐπὶ τὸ νεκυομαντήιον παρακαταθήκης
πέρι ξεινικῆς οὔτε σημανέειν ἔφη ἡ Μέλισσα ἐπιφανεῖσα οὔτε κατερέειν
ἐν τῷ κέαται χώρῳ ἡ παρακαταθήκη· ῥιγοῦν τε γὰρ καὶ εἶναι γυμνή· τῶν
γάρ οἱ συγκατέθαψε ἱματίων ὄφελος εἶναι οὐδὲν οὐ κατακαυθέντων·
μαρτύριον δέ οἱ εἶναι ὡς ἀληθέα ταῦτα λέγει, ὅτι ἐπὶ ψυχρὸν τὸν ἱπνὸν
Περίανδρος τοὺς ἄρτους ἐπέβαλε. (3) ταῦτα δὲ ὡς ὀπίσω ἀπηγγέλθη τῷ
Περιάνδρῳ (πιστὸν γάρ οἱ ἦν τὸ συμβόλαιον ὃς νεκρῷ ἐούσῃ Μελίσσῃ

the end, and his son Periander succeeded him in the tyranny.

'Periander was at the beginning milder than his father, but when he had communicated through messengers with Thrasybulus the tyrant of Miletus he became much more bloodthirsty than Cypselus. (*2*) For he sent a herald to Thrasybulus to find out in what way he could most safely organise affairs and best take charge of the city. Thrasybulus took the man who had come from Periander outside the city, and going into a sown field he went through the standing grain, asking and questioning the herald about his coming from Corinth; and he repeatedly knocked off any of the ears which he saw standing above the rest, and after knocking them off he threw them away, until in this sort of way he had destroyed the best and tallest of the grain. (*3*) He went through the site without speaking any words, and sent the herald away. When the herald returned to Corinth Periander was eager to learn the advice. The herald said that Thrasybulus had not said anything to him, and he was amazed at what kind of man he had been sent off to, demented and destructive of his own property, and he expounded what he had seen of Thrasybulus. (η) But Periander understood what had been done, and took it to heart that Thrasybulus had advised him to slaughter those of the citizens who were above the others, and then he demonstrated every kind of evil towards the citizens: for whatever Cypselus had left undone in killing and exiling Periander completed.

'In a single day he stripped naked all the Corinthians' wives on account of his own wife Melissa. (*2*) For he sent messengers to the Thesprotians on the River Acheron, to the oracle of the dead, about something deposited by a guest-friend, and Melissa appeared and said she would not indicate or tell in what place the deposit was; for she was cold and naked; for the clothes which had been buried with her were no use as they had not been burned. As evidence that this was true, she said that Periander had put his loaves into a cold oven. (*3*) When this was reported back to Periander (who believed the sign, because he had had intercourse with Melissa after she was dead), immediately

ἐμίγη), ἰθέως δὴ μετὰ τὴν ἀγγελίην κήρυγμα ἐποιήσατο ἐς τὸ Ἥραιον ἐξιέναι πάσας τὰς Κορινθίων γυναῖκας. αἱ μὲν δὴ ὡς ἐς ὁρτὴν ἤισαν κόσμῳ τῷ καλλίστῳ χρεώμεναι, ὁ δ᾽ ὑποστήσας τοὺς δορυφόρους ἀπέδυσέ σφεας πάσας ὁμοίως, τάς τε ἐλευθέρας καὶ τὰς ἀμφιπόλους, συμφορήσας δὲ ἐς ὄρυγμα Μελίσσῃ ἐπευχόμενος κατέκαιε. (*4*) ταῦτα δέ οἱ ποιήσαντι καὶ τὸ δεύτερον πέμψαντι ἔφρασε τὸ εἴδωλον τὸ Μελίσσης ἐς τὸν κατέθηκε χῶρον τοῦ ξείνου τὴν παρακαταθήκην. τοιοῦτο μὲν ὑμῖν ἐστὶ ἡ τυραννίς, ὦ Λακεδαιμόνιοι, καὶ τοιούτων ἔργων.

(*5*) "ἡμέας δὲ τοὺς Κορινθίους τό τε αὐτίκα θῶμα μέγα εἶχε ὅτε ὑμέας εἴδομεν μεταπεμπομένους Ἱππίην, νῦν τε δὴ καὶ μεζόνως θωμάζομεν λέγοντας ταῦτα, ἐπιμαρτυρόμεθά τε ἐπικαλεόμενοι ὑμῖν θεοὺς τοὺς Ἑλληνίους μὴ κατιστάναι τυραννίδας ἐς τὰς πόλις. οὐκ ὦν παύσεσθε ἀλλὰ πειρήσεσθε παρὰ τὸ δίκαιον κατάγοντες Ἱππίην; ἴστε ὑμῖν Κορινθίους γε οὐ συναινέοντας."

(**93**) Σωκλέης μὲν ἀπὸ Κορίνθου πρεσβεύων ἔλεξε τάδε, Ἱππίης δὲ αὐτὸν ἀμείβετο τοὺς αὐτοὺς ἐπικαλέσας θεοὺς ἐκείνῳ, ἦ μὲν Κορινθίους μάλιστα πάντων ἐπιποθήσειν Πεισιστρατίδας, ὅταν σφι ἥκωσι ἡμέραι αἱ κύριαι ἀνιᾶσθαι ὑπ᾽ Ἀθηναίων. (*2*) Ἱππίης μὲν τούτοισι ἀμείψατο οἷα τοὺς χρησμοὺς ἀτρεκέστατα ἀνδρῶν ἐξεπιστάμενος· οἱ δὲ λοιποὶ τῶν συμμάχων τέως μὲν εἶχον ἐν ἡσυχίῃ σφέας αὐτούς, ἐπείτε δὲ Σωκλέος ἤκουσαν εἴπαντος ἐλευθέρως, ἅπας τις αὐτῶν φωνὴν ῥήξας αἱρέετο τοῦ Κορινθίου τὴν γνώμην, Λακεδαιμονίοισί τε ἐπεμαρτυρέοντο μὴ ποιεῖν μηδὲν νεώτερον περὶ πόλιν Ἑλλάδα.

(**94**) οὕτω μὲν τοῦτο ἐπαύσθη. Ἱππίῃ δὲ ἐνθεῦτεν ἀπελαυνομένῳ ἐδίδου μὲν Ἀμύντης ὁ Μακεδόνων βασιλεὺς Ἀνθεμοῦντα, ἐδίδοσαν δὲ Θεσσαλοὶ Ἰωλκόν. ὁ δὲ τούτων μὲν οὐδέτερα αἱρέετο, ἀνεχώρεε δὲ ὀπίσω ἐς Σίγειον, τὸ εἷλε Πεισίστρατος αἰχμῇ παρὰ Μυτιληναίων, κρατήσας δὲ αὐτοῦ κατέστησε τύραννον εἶναι παῖδα τὸν ἑωυτοῦ

---

92. η. 3. τὰ ἱμάτια inserted after συμφορήσας δὲ Stein.
92. η. 5. τό τε: τὸ τότε SV, τότε τε van Herwerden.
    οὐκ ὦν: οὐκ ὦν ἦν μὴ AC, οὔκων Legrand, ἢν ὦν μὴ Blaydes, perhaps νῦν ὦν ἦν μὴ Wilson *apparatus*.
93. 2. ἐλευθέρως, ἅπας: ἐλευθερῶσαι πᾶς A, ἐλευθερίως ἅπας Fitton Brown.
94. 1. τὸν ἑωυτοῦ: τὸν deleted Stein.

after the report he made a proclamation that all the Corinthians' wives were to go out to the Heraeum. They went as if to a festival, wearing their finest garb, but he had secreted the spear-bearers, and had them stripped all alike, free women and attendants, and their clothes collected into a pit and burned as he prayed to Melissa. (*4*) When he had done that he sent again and the ghost of Melissa told him in what place he had placed his guest-friend's deposit. This shows you what tyranny is like, Spartans, and this is what tyrants' deeds are like.

(*5*) 'We Corinthians were immediately seized with great surprise when we knew that you had sent for Hippias, and now we are even more surprised at hearing you say this; and we call to witness and invoke against you the gods of the Greeks that you should not install tyrannies in the cities. Will you not stop trying to reinstate Hippias in contravention of justice? Know that the Corinthians do not approve of your doing that.'

(**93**) That is what Socles as an envoy from Corinth said. Hippias responded to him, invoking the same gods as he had invoked, that indeed the Corinthians most of all would pine for the Pisistratids when the appointed days came round for them to be troubled by the Athenians. (*2*) Hippias gave them that response, as the man who had the clearest and most thorough knowledge of the oracles. The rest of the allies had first kept themselves in silence; but when they had heard Socles speaking freely every one of them burst into speech and adopted the opinion of the Corinthian, and adjured the Spartans not to take any drastic action concerning a Greek city.

(**94**) This matter was brought to an end in that way. When Hippias was driven away from there, Amyntas of Macedon offered him Anthemus, and Thessalians offered him Iolcus. He chose neither of those, but went back to Sigeum, which Pisistratus had taken by the spear from the Mytilenaeans, and when he had got the mastery of it

νόθον Ἡγησίστρατον, γεγονότα ἐξ Ἀργείης γυναικός, ὃς οὐκ ἀμαχητὶ εἶχε τὰ παρέλαβε παρὰ Πεισιστράτου. (*2*) ἐπολέμεον γὰρ ἔκ τε Ἀχιλληίου πόλιος ὁρμώμενοι καὶ Σιγείου ἐπὶ χρόνον συχνὸν Μυτιληναῖοί τε καὶ Ἀθηναῖοι, οἱ μὲν ἀπαιτέοντες τὴν χώρην, Ἀθηναῖοι δὲ οὔτε συγγινωσκόμενοι ἀποδεικνύντες τε λόγῳ οὐδὲν μᾶλλον Αἰολεῦσι μετεὸν τῆς Ἰλιάδος χώρης ἢ οὐ καὶ σφίσι καὶ τοῖσι ἄλλοισι, ὅσοι Ἑλλήνων συνεπρήξαντο Μενέλεῳ τὰς Ἑλένης ἁρπαγάς. (**95**) πολεμεόντων δὲ σφέων παντοῖα καὶ ἄλλα ἐγένετο ἐν τῇσι μάχῃσι, ἐν δὲ δὴ καὶ Ἀλκαῖος ὁ ποιητὴς συμβολῆς γενομένης καὶ νικώντων Ἀθηναίων αὐτὸς μὲν φεύγων ἐκφεύγει, τὰ δέ οἱ ὅπλα ἴσχουσι Ἀθηναῖοι, καί σφεα ἀνεκρέμασαν πρὸς τὸ Ἀθήναιον τὸ ἐν Σιγείῳ. (*2*) ταῦτα δὲ Ἀλκαῖος ἐν μέλεϊ ποιήσας ἐπιτιθεῖ ἐς Μυτιλήνην, ἐξαγγελλόμενος τὸ ἑωυτοῦ πάθος Μελανίππῳ ἀνδρὶ ἑταίρῳ. Μυτιληναίους δὲ καὶ Ἀθηναίους κατήλλαξε Περίανδρος ὁ Κυψέλου· τούτῳ γὰρ διαιτητῇ ἐπετράποντο· κατήλλαξε δὲ ὧδε, νέμεσθαι ἑκατέρους τὴν ἔχουσι. Σίγειον μέν νυν οὕτω ἐγένετο ὑπ' Ἀθηναίοισι.

(**96**) Ἱππίης δὲ ἐπείτε ἀπίκετο ἐκ τῆς Λακεδαίμονος ἐς τὴν Ἀσίην, πᾶν χρῆμα ἐκίνεε, διαβάλλων τε τοὺς Ἀθηναίους πρὸς τὸν Ἀρταφρένεα καὶ ποιέων ἅπαντα ὅκως αἱ Ἀθῆναι γενοίατο ὑπ' ἑωυτῷ τε καὶ Δαρείῳ. (*2*) Ἱππίης τε δὴ ταῦτα ἔπρησσε, καὶ οἱ Ἀθηναῖοι πυθόμενοι ταῦτα πέμπουσι ἐς Σάρδις ἀγγέλους, οὐκ ἐῶντες τοὺς Πέρσας πείθεσθαι Ἀθηναίων τοῖσι φυγάσι. ὁ δὲ Ἀρταφρένης ἐκέλευέ σφεας, εἰ βουλοίατο σόοι εἶναι, καταδέκεσθαι ὀπίσω Ἱππίην. οὐκ ὦν δὴ ἐνεδέκοντο τοὺς λόγους ἀποφερομένους οἱ Ἀθηναῖοι· οὐκ ἐνδεκομένοισι δέ σφι ἐδέδοκτο ἐκ τοῦ φανεροῦ τοῖσι Πέρσῃσι πολεμίους εἶναι.

(**97**) νομίζουσι δὲ ταῦτα καὶ διαβεβλημένοισι ἐς τοὺς Πέρσας, ἐν τούτῳ δὴ τῷ καιρῷ ὁ Μιλήσιος Ἀρισταγόρης, ὑπὸ Κλεομένεος τοῦ Λακεδαιμονίου ἐξελασθεὶς ἐκ τῆς Σπάρτης, ἀπίκετο ἐς Ἀθήνας· αὕτη γὰρ ἡ πόλις τῶν λοιπέων ἐδυνάστευε μέγιστον. ἐπελθὼν δὲ ἐπὶ τὸν δῆμον ὁ Ἀρισταγόρης ταὐτὰ ἔλεγε τὰ καὶ ἐν τῇ Σπάρτῃ περὶ τῶν ἀγαθῶν τῶν ἐν τῇ Ἀσίῃ καὶ τοῦ πολέμου τοῦ Περσικοῦ, ὡς οὔτε ἀσπίδα οὔτε δόρυ νομίζουσι εὐπετέες τε χειρωθῆναι εἴησαν. (*2*) ταῦτά τε δὴ ἔλεγε

had installed as tyrant his bastard son Hegesistratus, born from an Argive woman, and it was not without fighting that he held on to what he had taken over from Pisistratus. (*2*) For the Mytilenaeans and Athenians had made war for a long time, based on the cities of Achilleum and Sigeum respectively, the Mytilenaeans asking for the land back and the Athenians not granting their claim but arguing to demonstrate that the land of Ilium belonged no more to the Aeolians than to them and the other Greeks who had joined Menelaus in avenging the abduction of Helen. (**95**) During their war all kinds of things occurred in their battles, and in particular the poet Alcaeus, when there was an incident in which the Athenians were victorious, ran away and made his escape, but the Athenians gained possession of his arms and hung them up in the Athenaeum at Sigeum. (*2*) Alcaeus wrote of this in a poem, and sent it to Mytilene to report his misfortune to Melanippus, a companion of his. The Mytilenaeans and Athenians were reconciled by Periander the son of Cypselus, for they turned to him as an arbitrator: he reconciled them on these terms, that each should occupy what they possessed. In this way Sigeum came into the hands of the Athenians.

(**96**) When Hippias had gone from Sparta to Asia, he set everything in motion, maligning the Athenians to Artaphernes and doing everything to make Athens subject to himself and Darius. (*2*) When Hippias was doing that, the Athenians got to know of it and sent messengers to Sardis to forbid the Persians to let themselves be persuaded by the Athenian exiles. Artaphernes told them, if they wanted to be safe, to receive Hippias back. But the Athenians did not accept the message brought to them, and, not accepting it, they had decided to be open enemies of the Persians.

(**97**) When the Athenians were following that policy and had been maligned to the Persians, it was at this critical point that Aristagoras of Miletus, driven out of Sparta by Cleomenes the Spartan, came to Athens: for that city was the most preponderant of the others. Coming before the people, Aristagoras said the same as he had said in Sparta about the good things in Asia and Persian warfare, that they were accustomed to use neither shield nor spear and would be easy to

καὶ πρὸς τοῖσι τάδε, ὡς οἱ Μιλήσιοι τῶν Ἀθηναίων εἰσὶ ἄποικοι, καὶ οἰκός σφεας εἴη ῥύεσθαι δυναμένους μέγα. καὶ οὐδὲν ὅ τι οὐκ ὑπίσχετο οἷα κάρτα δεόμενος, ἐς ὃ ἀνέπεισέ σφεας. πολλοὺς γὰρ οἶκε εἶναι εὐπετέστερον διαβάλλειν ἢ ἕνα, εἰ Κλεομένεα μὲν τὸν Λακεδαιμόνιον μοῦνον οὐκ οἷός τε ἐγένετο διαβάλλειν, τρεῖς δὲ μυριάδας Ἀθηναίων ἐποίησε τοῦτο. (*3*) Ἀθηναῖοι μὲν δὴ ἀναπεισθέντες ἐψηφίσαντο εἴκοσι νέας ἀποστεῖλαι βοηθοὺς Ἴωσι, στρατηγὸν ἀποδέξαντες αὐτῶν εἶναι Μελάνθιον, ἄνδρα τῶν ἀστῶν ἐόντα τὰ πάντα δόκιμον· αὗται δὲ αἱ νέες ἀρχὴ κακῶν ἐγένοντο Ἕλλησί τε καὶ βαρβάροισι.

(**98**) Ἀρισταγόρης δέ, προπλώσας καὶ ἀπικόμενος ἐς τὴν Μίλητον, ἐξευρὼν βούλευμα ἀπ᾽ οὗ Ἴωσι μὲν οὐδεμία ἔμελλε ὠφελίη ἔσεσθαι, οὐδ᾽ ὦν οὐδὲ τούτου εἵνεκα ἐποίεε ἀλλ᾽ ὅκως βασιλέα Δαρεῖον λυπήσειε, ἔπεμψε ἐς τὴν Φρυγίην ἄνδρα ἐπὶ τοὺς Παίονας τοὺς ἀπὸ Στρυμόνος ποταμοῦ αἰχμαλώτους γενομένους ὑπὸ Μεγαβάζου, οἰκέοντας δὲ τῆς Φρυγίης χῶρόν τε καὶ κώμην ἐπ᾽ ἑωυτῶν, ὃς ἐπειδὴ ἀπίκετο ἐς τοὺς Παίονας, ἔλεγε τάδε· (*2*) "ἄνδρες Παίονες, ἔπεμψέ με Ἀρισταγόρης ὁ Μιλήτου τύραννος σωτηρίην ὑποθησόμενον ὑμῖν, ἤνπερ βούλησθε πείθεσθαι. νῦν γὰρ Ἰωνίη πᾶσα ἀπέστηκε ἀπὸ βασιλέος, καὶ ὑμῖν παρέχει σῴζεσθαι ἐπὶ τὴν ὑμετέρην αὐτῶν· μέχρι μὲν θαλάσσης αὐτοῖσι ὑμῖν, τὸ δὲ ἀπὸ τούτου ἡμῖν ἤδη μελήσει." (*3*) ταῦτα δὲ ἀκούσαντες οἱ Παίονες κάρτα τε ἀσπαστὸν ἐποιήσαντο καὶ ἀναλαβόντες παῖδας καὶ γυναῖκας ἀπεδίδρησκον ἐπὶ θάλασσαν· οἱ δέ τινες αὐτῶν καὶ κατέμειναν ἀρρωδήσαντες αὐτοῦ. ἐπείτε δὲ οἱ Παίονες ἀπίκοντο ἐπὶ θάλασσαν, ἐνθεῦτεν ἐς Χίον διέβησαν. (*4*) ἐόντων δὲ ἤδη ἐν Χίῳ, κατὰ πόδας ἐληλύθεε Περσέων ἵππος πολλὴ διώκουσα τοὺς Παίονας. ὡς δὲ οὐ κατέλαβον, ἐπηγγέλλοντο ἐς τὴν Χίον τοῖσι Παίοσι ὅκως ἂν ὀπίσω ἀπέλθοιεν. οἱ δὲ Παίονες τοὺς λόγους οὐκ ἐνεδέκοντο, ἀλλ᾽ ἐκ Χίου μὲν Χῖοι σφέας ἐς Λέσβον ἤγαγον, Λέσβιοι δὲ ἐς Δορίσκον ἐκόμισαν, ἐνθεῦτεν δὲ πεζῇ κομιζόμενοι ἀπίκοντο ἐς Παιονίην.

(**99**) Ἀρισταγόρης δέ, ἐπειδὴ οἵ τε Ἀθηναῖοι ἀπίκοντο εἴκοσι νηυσί, ἅμα ἀγόμενοι Ἐρετριέων πέντε τριήρεας, οἳ οὐ τὴν Ἀθηναίων χάριν ἐστρατεύοντο ἀλλὰ τὴν αὐτῶν Μιλησίων, ὀφειλόμενά σφι

overcome. (*2*) He said that, and in addition this, that the Milesians were colonists of the Athenians, and it was reasonable that since they were very powerful they should rescue them. There was nothing that he did not promise in begging desperately, until he persuaded them. It seems that it is easier to mislead many than one, if he was not able to mislead Cleomenes the Spartan on his own but did do this to thirty thousand Athenians. (*3*) So the Athenians were persuaded, and voted to send twenty ships to support the Ionians, appointing as their general Melanthius, a man among their citizens who was distinguished in every way. These ships were the beginning of evil for the Greeks and barbarians.

(**98**) Aristagoras sailed ahead, and when he reached Miletus he devised a plan from which no advantage was to come to the Ionians (and indeed he did not do it with that in view, but in order to trouble King Darius). He sent a man to Phrygia to the Paeonians who had been taken as prisoners from the River Strymon by Megabazus, and who were living by themselves in a place and village in Phrygia, and when he reached the Paeonians he said this: (*2*) 'Paeonian men, Aristagoras the tyrant of Miletus has sent me to offer salvation to you, if you are willing to be persuaded. For now the whole of Ionia has revolted against the King, and provides you with the opportunity to go to your own land for salvation. As far as the sea you yourselves must see to this, but after that we shall do so.' (*3*) On hearing this the Paeonians found it extremely welcome; and they took up their children and wives and ran away to the sea (but some of them were afraid and stayed behind). When the Paeonians had reached the sea, they crossed from there to Chios. (*4*) When they were already in Chios a large force of Persian cavalry came on their heels in pursuit of the Paeonians. Having failed to catch up with them, they sent a message to Chios to the Paeonians, that they should go back. The Paeonians did not accept the proposal; but from Chios the Chians took them to Lesbos, and the Lesbians conveyed them to Doriscus. From there they conveyed themselves on foot and reached Paeonia.

(**99**) As for Aristagoras, the Athenians arrived in their twenty ships, bringing also five triremes of the Eretrians, who came on the

ἀποδιδόντες (οἱ γὰρ δὴ Μιλήσιοι πρότερον τοῖσι Ἐρετριεῦσι τὸν πρὸς Χαλκιδέας πόλεμον συνδιήνεικαν, ὅτε περ καὶ Χαλκιδεῦσι ἀντία Ἐρετριέων καὶ Μιλησίων Σάμιοι ἐβοήθεον). οὗτοι ὦν ἐπείτε σφι ἀπίκοντο καὶ οἱ ἄλλοι σύμμαχοι παρῆσαν, ἐποιέετο στρατηίην ὁ Ἀρισταγόρης ἐς Σάρδις. (2) αὐτὸς μὲν δὴ οὐκ ἐστρατεύετο ἀλλ' ἔμενε ἐν Μιλήτῳ, στρατηγοὺς δὲ ἄλλους ἀπέδεξε Μιλησίων εἶναι, τὸν ἑωυτοῦ τε ἀδελφεὸν Χαροπῖνον καὶ τῶν ἄλλων ἀστῶν Ἑρμόφαντον.

(100) ἀπικόμενοι δὲ τῷ στόλῳ τούτῳ Ἴωνες ἐς Ἔφεσον πλοῖα μὲν κατέλιπον ἐν Κορησῷ τῆς Ἐφεσίης, αὐτοὶ δὲ ἀνέβαινον χειρὶ πολλῇ, ποιεύμενοι Ἐφεσίους ἡγεμόνας τῆς ὁδοῦ. πορευόμενοι δὲ παρὰ ποταμὸν Καΰστριον, ἐνθεῦτεν ἐπείτε ὑπερβάντες τὸν Τμῶλον ἀπίκοντο, αἱρέουσι Σάρδις οὐδενός σφι ἀντιωθέντος, αἱρέουσι δὲ χωρὶς τῆς ἀκροπόλιος τἆλλα πάντα· τὴν δὲ ἀκρόπολιν ἐρρύετο αὐτὸς Ἀρταφρένης ἔχων ἀνδρῶν δύναμιν οὐκ ὀλίγην. (101) τὸ δὲ μὴ λεηλατῆσαι ἑλόντάς σφεας τὴν πόλιν ἔσχε τόδε. ἦσαν ἐν τῆσι Σάρδισι οἰκίαι αἱ μὲν πλεῦνες καλάμιναι, ὅσαι δ' αὐτέων καὶ πλίνθιναι ἦσαν, καλάμου εἶχον τὰς ὀροφάς· τουτέων δὴ μίαν τῶν τις στρατιωτέων ὡς ἐνέπρησε, αὐτίκα ἀπ' οἰκίης ἐπ' οἰκίην ἰὸν τὸ πῦρ ἐπενέμετο τὸ ἄστυ πᾶν. (2) καιομένου δὲ τοῦ ἄστεος οἱ Λυδοί τε καὶ ὅσοι Περσέων ἐνῆσαν ἐν τῇ πόλι, ἀπολαμφθέντες πάντοθεν ὥστε τὰ περιέσχατα νεμομένου τοῦ πυρός, καὶ οὐκ ἔχοντες ἐξήλυσιν ἐκ τοῦ ἄστεος, συνέρρεον ἔς τε τὴν ἀγορὴν καὶ ἐπὶ τὸν Πακτωλὸν ποταμόν, ὅς σφι ψῆγμα χρυσοῦ καταφορέων ἐκ τοῦ Τμώλου διὰ μέσης τῆς ἀγορῆς ῥέει καὶ ἔπειτα ἐς τὸν Ἕρμον ποταμὸν ἐκδιδοῖ, ὁ δὲ ἐς θάλασσαν. ἐπὶ τοῦτον δὴ τὸν Πακτωλὸν καὶ ἐς τὴν ἀγορὴν ἀθροιζόμενοι οἵ τε Λυδοὶ καὶ οἱ Πέρσαι ἠναγκάζοντο ἀμύνεσθαι. (3) οἱ δὲ Ἴωνες ὁρέοντες τοὺς μὲν ἀμυνομένους τῶν πολεμίων τοὺς δὲ σὺν πλήθεϊ πολλῷ προσφερομένους, ἐξανεχώρησαν δείσαντες πρὸς τὸ ὄρος τὸν Τμῶλον καλεόμενον, ἐνθεῦτεν δὲ ὑπὸ νύκτα ἀπαλλάσσοντο ἐπὶ τὰς νέας.

(102) καὶ Σάρδιες μὲν ἐνεπρήσθησαν, ἐν δὲ αὐτῇσι καὶ ἱρὸν ἐπιχωρίης θεοῦ Κυβήβης, τὸ σκηπτόμενοι οἱ Πέρσαι ὕστερον ἀντενεπίμπρασαν τὰ ἐν Ἕλλησι ἱρά. τότε δὲ οἱ Πέρσαι οἱ ἐντὸς Ἅλυος

---

99. 2.   ἄλλων ἀστῶν: ἀστῶν ἄλλον Α.
100.   τῆς ὁδοῦ Α: omitted other MSS..

campaign to gratify not the Athenians but the Milesians themselves, to repay a debt to them (for earlier the Milesians had helped them in waging their war against the Chalcidians, when the Samians were giving support to the Chalcidians against the Eretrians and Milesians). When these had arrived and the other allies were present, Aristagoras made a campaign against Sardis. (*2*) He did not go on the campaign himself, but he stayed in Miletus and designated others as generals of the Milesians, his own brother Charopinus and Hermophantus of the other citizens.

(**100**) When the Ionians had arrived at Ephesus with this mission, they left their boats at Coresus in the territory of Ephesus and themselves went inland with a large force, using the Ephesians as guides. They travelled beside the River Caÿstrius, and from there when they had crossed Tmolus they arrived, and took Sardis without meeting any opposition. Apart from the acropolis they took everything else, but the acropolis Artaphernes himself defended with a substantial body of men. (**101**) But after they had captured the city they were prevented from looting it by this. Most of the houses in Sardis were of thatch, while some were of brick with thatched roofs. When one of the soldiers had set fire to one of these, the fire immediately spread from house to house and engulfed the whole city. (*2*) When the city was burning, the Lydians and as many Persians as were on the acropolis were cut off on every side so that, as the fire was feeding on the edges and they had no way of leaving the city, they flocked together into the agora and to the River Pactolus, which carries down their gold dust from Tmolus, flows through the middle of the agora and then debouches into the River Hermus, and that flows into the sea. The Lydians and the Persians crowded at this Pactolus and the agora, and were forced to defend themselves. (*3*) The Ionians saw some of the enemy defending themselves and others bearing down on them in large numbers; and they took fright, withdrew to the mountain called Tmolus, and from there by night departed to their ships.

(**102**) Sardis was burned, and in it the temple of the local god Cybebe, which the Persians later used as justification for their

ποταμοῦ νομοὺς ἔχοντες, προπυνθανόμενοι ταῦτα, συνηλίζοντο καὶ ἐβοήθεον τοῖσι Λυδοῖσι. (*2*) καὶ κως ἐν μὲν Σάρδισι οὐκέτι ἐόντας τοὺς Ἴωνας εὑρίσκουσι, ἑπόμενοι δὲ κατὰ στίβον αἱρέουσι αὐτοὺς ἐν Ἐφέσῳ. καὶ ἀντετάχθησαν μὲν οἱ Ἴωνες, συμβαλόντες δὲ πολλὸν ἐσσώθησαν. (*3*) καὶ πολλοὺς αὐτῶν οἱ Πέρσαι φονεύουσι ἄλλους τε ὀνομαστούς, ἐν δὲ δὴ καὶ Εὐαλκίδην στρατηγέοντα Ἐρετριέων, στεφανηφόρους τε ἀγῶνας ἀναραιρηκότα καὶ ὑπὸ Σιμωνίδεω τοῦ Κηίου πολλὰ αἰνεθέντα· οἳ δὲ αὐτῶν ἀπέφυγον τὴν μάχην, ἐσκεδάσθησαν ἀνὰ τὰς πόλιας.

(**103**) τότε μὲν δὴ οὕτω ἠγωνίσαντο. μετὰ δὲ Ἀθηναῖοι μὲν τὸ παράπαν ἀπολιπόντες τοὺς Ἴωνας, ἐπικαλεομένου σφέας πολλὰ δι' ἀγγέλων Ἀρισταγόρεω, οὐκ ἔφασαν τιμωρήσειν σφι. Ἴωνες δὲ τῆς Ἀθηναίων συμμαχίης στερηθέντες (οὕτω γάρ σφι ὑπῆρχε πεποιημένα ἐς Δαρεῖον) οὐδὲν δὴ ἧσσον τὸν πρὸς βασιλέα πόλεμον ἐσκευάζοντο. (*2*) πλώσαντες δὲ ἐς τὸν Ἑλλήσποντον Βυζάντιόν τε καὶ τὰς ἄλλας πόλιας πάσας τὰς ταύτῃ ὑπ' ἑωυτοῖσι ἐποιήσαντο, ἐκπλώσαντές τε ἔξω τὸν Ἑλλήσποντον Καρίης τὴν πολλὴν προσεκτήσαντο σφίσι σύμμαχον εἶναι· καὶ γὰρ τὴν Καῦνον, πρότερον οὐ βουλομένην συμμαχέειν, ὡς ἐνέπρησαν τὰς Σάρδις, τότε σφι καὶ αὕτη προσεγένετο. (**104**) Κύπριοι δὲ ἐθελονταί σφι πάντες προσεγένοντο πλὴν Ἀμαθουσίων· ἀπέστησαν γὰρ καὶ οὗτοι ὧδε ἀπὸ Μήδων. ἦν Ὀνήσιλος Γόργου μὲν τοῦ Σαλαμινίων βασιλέος ἀδελφεὸς νεώτερος, Χέρσιος δὲ τοῦ Σιρώμου τοῦ Εὐέλθοντος παῖς. (*2*) οὗτος ὡνὴρ πολλάκις μὲν καὶ πρότερον τὸν Γόργον παρηγορέετο ἀπίστασθαι ἀπὸ βασιλέος, τότε δέ, ὡς καὶ τοὺς Ἴωνας ἐπύθετο ἀπεστάναι, πάγχυ ἐπικείμενος ἐνῆγε. ὡς δὲ οὐκ ἔπειθε τὸν Γόργον, ἐνθαῦτά μιν φυλάξας ἐξελθόντα τὸ ἄστυ τὸ Σαλαμινίων ὁ Ὀνήσιλος ἅμα τοῖσι ἑωυτοῦ στασιώτῃσι ἀπεκλήισε τῶν πυλέων. (*3*) Γόργος μὲν δὴ στερηθεὶς τῆς πόλιος ἔφευγε ἐς Μήδους, Ὀνήσιλος δὲ ἦρχε Σαλαμῖνος καὶ ἀνέπειθε πάντας Κυπρίους συναπίστασθαι. τοὺς μὲν δὴ ἄλλους ἀνέπεισε, Ἀμαθουσίους δὲ οὐ βουλομένους οἱ πείθεσθαι ἐπολιόρκεε προσκατήμενος.

(**105**) Ὀνήσιλος μέν νυν ἐπολιόρκεε Ἀμαθοῦντα. βασιλέι δὲ

reciprocal burning of the temples in Greece. At this point the Persians who controlled provinces west of the River Halys had had advance information of this, and mustered and gave support to the Lydians. (*2*) And they found the Ionians no longer in Sardis, but followed in their tracks and caught them at Ephesus. The Ionians drew up against them, but when they joined battle they were badly defeated. (*3*) Many of them the Persians killed, including some notable men, and among them Eualcides the general of the Eretrians, who had been a victor in crown games and had been much praised by Simonides of Ceos. Some of the Ionians escaped from the battle and were scattered among the cities.

(**103**) So that conflict ended. Afterwards the Athenians altogether abandoned the Ionians, and although Aristagoras sent many appeals to them through messengers they refused to succour them. But the Ionians, though deprived of their Athenian alliance, on account of what they had done against Darius none the less prepared for the war against the King. (*2*) They sailed to the Hellespont and brought Byzantium and all the other cities there on to their side, and they sailed out from the Hellespont and gained most of Caria to be an ally of theirs. For even Caunus, which previously had not been willing to ally with them, did attach itself to them after Sardis had been burned; (**104**) and all the Cyprians voluntarily attached themselves to them, apart from those of Amathus, for these too revolted against the Medes in the following way. Onesilus was the younger brother of Gorgus the king of Salamis, being son of Chersis son of Siromus son of Euelthon. (*2*) This man had several times before incited Gorgus to revolt against the King, and then, when he learned that the Ionians had revolted, he urged him with all his insistence. When he failed to persuade Gorgus, then Onesilus watched for him to leave the city of Salamis, and together with his partisans he closed the gates. (*3*) Gorgus, deprived of his city, fled to the Medes; while Onesilus became ruler of Salamis and tried το persuade all the Cyprians to join in revolt. The others he succeeded in persuading; the people of Amathus, who were not willing to be persuaded, he settled down to besiege.

Δαρείῳ ὡς ἐξαγγέλθη Σάρδις ἁλούσας ἐμπεπρῆσθαι ὑπό τε Ἀθηναίων καὶ Ἰώνων, τὸν δὲ ἡγεμόνα γενέσθαι τῆς συλλογῆς ὥστε ταῦτα συνυφανθῆναι τὸν Μιλήσιον Ἀρισταγόρην, πρῶτα μὲν λέγεται αὐτόν, ὡς ἐπύθετο ταῦτα, Ἰώνων οὐδένα λόγον ποιησάμενον, εὖ εἰδότα ὡς οὗτοί γε οὐ καταπροΐξονται ἀποστάντες· εἰρέσθαι οἵτινες εἶεν οἱ Ἀθηναῖοι, μετὰ δὲ πυθόμενον αἰτῆσαι τὸ τόξον, λαβόντα δὲ καὶ ἐπιθέντα δὲ ὀϊστὸν ἄνω πρὸς τὸν οὐρανὸν ἀπεῖναι, καί μιν ἐς τὸν ἠέρα βάλλοντα εἰπεῖν· (*2*) "ὦ Ζεῦ, ἐκγενέσθαι μοι Ἀθηναίους τίσασθαι", εἴπαντα δὲ ταῦτα προστάξαι ἑνὶ τῶν θεραπόντων δείπνου προκειμένου αὐτῷ ἐς τρὶς ἑκάστοτε εἰπεῖν· "δέσποτα, μέμνεο τῶν Ἀθηναίων." (**106**) προστάξας δὲ ταῦτα εἶπε, καλέσας ἐς ὄψιν Ἱστιαῖον τὸν Μιλήσιον, τὸν [ὁ Δαρεῖος] κατεῖχε χρόνον ἤδη πολλόν· "πυνθάνομαι, Ἱστιαῖε, ἐπίτροπον τὸν σόν, τῷ σὺ Μίλητον ἐπέτρεψας, νεώτερα ἐς ἐμὲ πεποιηκέναι πρήγματα· ἄνδρας γάρ μοι ἐκ τῆς ἑτέρης ἠπείρου ἐπαγαγών, καὶ Ἴωνας σὺν αὐτοῖσι τοὺς δώσοντας ἐμοὶ δίκην τῶν ἐποίησαν, τούτους ἀναγνώσας ἅμα ἐκείνοισι ἕπεσθαι, Σαρδίων με ἀπεστέρησε. (*2*) νῦν ὦν κῶς τοι ταῦτα φαίνεται ἔχειν καλῶς; κῶς δὲ ἄνευ τῶν σῶν βουλευμάτων τοιοῦτόν τι ἐπρήχθη; ὅρα μὴ ἐξ ὑστέρης σεωυτὸν ἐν αἰτίῃ σχῇς." (*3*) εἶπε πρὸς ταῦτα Ἱστιαῖος· "βασιλεῦ, κοῖον ἐφθέγξαο ἔπος, ἐμὲ βουλεῦσαι πρῆγμα ἐκ τοῦ σοί τι ἢ μέγα ἢ σμικρὸν ἔμελλε λυπηρὸν ἀνασχήσειν; τί δ' ἂν ἐπιδιζήμενος ποιέοιμι ταῦτα, τεῦ δὲ ἐνδεὴς ἐών; τῷ πάρα μὲν πάντα ὅσα περ σοί, πάντων δὲ πρὸς σέο βουλευμάτων ἐπακούειν ἀξιοῦμαι. (*4*) ἀλλ' εἴπερ τι τοιοῦτον οἷον σὺ εἴρηκας πρήσσει ὁ ἐμὸς ἐπίτροπος, ἴσθι αὐτὸν ἐπ' ἑωυτοῦ βαλόμενον πεπρηχέναι. ἀρχὴν δὲ ἔγωγε οὐδὲ ἐνδέκομαι τὸν λόγον, ὅκως τι Μιλήσιοι καὶ ὁ ἐμὸς ἐπίτροπος νεώτερον πρήσσουσι περὶ πρήγματα τὰ σά. εἰ δ' ἄρα τι τοιοῦτο ποιεῦσι καὶ σὺ τὸ ἐὸν ἀκήκοας ὦ βασιλεῦ, μάθε οἷον πρῆγμα ἐργάσαο ἐμὲ ἀπὸ θαλάσσης ἀνάσπαστον ποιήσας. (*5*) Ἴωνες γὰρ οἴκασι ἐμεῦ ἐξ ὀφθαλμῶν σφι γενομένου ποιῆσαι τῶν πάλαι ἵμερον εἶχον· ἐμέο δ' ἂν ἐόντος ἐν Ἰωνίῃ οὐδεμία

---

106. 1.   ὁ Δαρεῖος deleted Wilson: τὸν ὁ Δαρεῖος κατεῖχε χρόνον ἤδη πολλόν deleted Stein.

106. 2.   τοιοῦτόν A: τούτων other MSS.

106. 4.   πεπρηχέναι: πεποιηκέναι A.

(**105**) Onesilus, then, was besieging Amathus. When it was announced to King Darius that Sardis had been captured and burned by the Athenians and Ionians, and that the leader of the assemblage through which this had been woven together was Aristagoras of Miletus, it is said that at first when he learned of this he took no account of the Ionians, knowing very well that they would not go unpunished for their revolt, but he asked who were the Athenians, and when he had learned he asked for his bow, took it and fitted an arrow and shot it to the heaven, and as he fired it into the air said, (*2*) 'Zeus, may it fall to me to be avenged on the Athenians'. When he had said that he instructed one of his attendants, when dinner was laid before him, to say three times on each occasion, 'Master, remember the Athenians'. (**106**) After giving that instruction, he called into his presence Histiaeus the Milesian, whom he had now been detaining for a long time, and said, 'I learn, Histiaeus, that your deputy, to whom you deputed Miletus, has taken drastic action against me: for he has brought in men from the other mainland, and Ionians with them (who will render justice to me for what they have done), and has induced the Ionians to follow them and has deprived me of Sardis. (*2*) Now, then, how can that seem good to you? And how can such a thing have been done without plans of yours? See that you are not later held to blame for this.' (*3*) Histiaeus said to that: 'King, what a saying you have uttered, that I should have planned an affair which would present any trouble to you, great or small! What should I be aiming for in doing that? What am I lacking? Everything is available to me as to you, and I have the right to hear of all your plans. (*4*) But if indeed the kind of thing you speak of is being done by my deputy, you must know that he has done this on his own initiative. Fundamentally, I do not accept what you say, that the Milesians and my deputy are taking drastic action with regard to your affairs. But if they are doing something of the kind, and what you have heard is fact, o King, you must realise what an affair you have brought about by uprooting me from the sea. (*5*) For the Ionians seem only when they were out of my

πόλις ὑπεκίνησε. νῦν ὦν ὡς τάχος ἄφες με πορευθῆναι ἐς Ἰωνίην, ἵνα τοι κεῖνά τε πάντα καταρτίσω ἐς τὠυτὸ καὶ τὸν Μιλήτου ἐπίτροπον τοῦτον τὸν ταῦτα μηχανησάμενον ἐγχειρίθετον παραδῶ. (6) ταῦτα δὲ κατὰ νόον τὸν σὸν ποιήσας, θεοὺς ἐπόμνυμι τοὺς βασιληίους μὴ μὲν πρότερον ἐκδύσασθαι τὸν ἔχων κιθῶνα καταβήσομαι ἐς Ἰωνίην, πρὶν ἄν τοι Σαρδὼ νῆσον τὴν μεγίστην δασμοφόρον ποιήσω." (107) Ἱστιαῖος μὲν λέγων ταῦτα διέβαλλε, Δαρεῖος δὲ ἐπείθετο καί μιν ἀπίει, ἐντειλάμενος, ἐπεὰν τὰ ὑπέσχετό οἱ ἐπιτελέα ποιήσῃ, παραγίνεσθαί οἱ ὀπίσω ἐς τὰ Σοῦσα.

(108) ἐν ᾧ δὲ ἡ ἀγγελίη τε περὶ τῶν Σαρδίων παρὰ βασιλέα ἀνήιε καὶ Δαρεῖος τὰ περὶ τὸ τόξον ποιήσας Ἱστιαίῳ ἐς λόγους ἦλθε καὶ Ἱστιαῖος μεμετιμένος ὑπὸ Δαρείου ἐκομίζετο ἐπὶ θάλασσαν, ἐν τούτῳ παντὶ τῷ χρόνῳ ἐγίνετο τάδε. πολιορκέοντι τῷ Σαλαμινίῳ Ὀνησίλῳ Ἀμαθουσίους ἐξαγγέλλεται νηυσὶ στρατιὴν πολλὴν ἄγοντα Περσικὴν Ἀρτύβιον ἄνδρα Πέρσην προσδόκιμον ἐς τὴν Κύπρον εἶναι. (2) πυθόμενος δὲ ταῦτα ὁ Ὀνήσιλος κήρυκας διέπεμπε ἐς τὴν Ἰωνίην ἐπικαλεύμενός σφεας, Ἴωνες δὲ οὐκ ἐς μακρὴν βουλευσάμενοι ἧκον πολλῷ στόλῳ. Ἴωνές τε δὴ παρῆσαν ἐς τὴν Κύπρον καὶ οἱ Πέρσαι νηυσὶ διαβάντες ἐκ τῆς Κιλικίης ἤισαν ἐπὶ τὴν Σαλαμῖνα πεζῇ· τῇσι δὲ νηυσὶ οἱ Φοίνικες περιέπλεον τὴν ἄκρην αἳ καλεῦνται Κληῖδες τῆς Κύπρου. (109) τούτου δὲ τοιούτου γινομένου ἔλεξαν οἱ τύραννοι τῆς Κύπρου, συγκαλέσαντες τῶν Ἰώνων τοὺς στρατηγούς· "ἄνδρες Ἴωνες, αἵρεσιν ὑμῖν δίδομεν ἡμεῖς οἱ Κύπριοι ὁκοτέροισι βούλεσθε προσφέρεσθαι, ἢ Πέρσῃσι ἢ Φοίνιξι. (2) εἰ μὲν γὰρ πεζῇ βούλεσθε ταχθέντες Περσέων διαπειρᾶσθαι, ὥρη ἂν εἴη ὑμῖν ἐκβάντας ἐκ τῶν νεῶν τάσσεσθαι πεζῇ, ἡμέας δὲ ἐς τὰς νέας ἐσβαίνειν τὰς ὑμετέρας Φοίνιξι ἀνταγωνιευμένους· εἰ δὲ Φοινίκων μᾶλλον βούλεσθε διαπειρᾶσθαι, ποιέειν χρεόν ἐστι ὑμέας, ὁκότερα ἂν δὴ τούτων ἕλησθε, ὅκως τὸ κατ' ὑμέας ἔσται ἥ τε Ἰωνίη καὶ ἡ Κύπρος ἐλευθέρη." (3) εἶπαν Ἴωνες πρὸς ταῦτα· "ἡμέας δὲ ἀπέπεμψε τὸ κοινὸν τῶν Ἰώνων φυλάξοντας τὴν θάλασσαν, ἀλλ' οὐκ ἵνα Κυπρίοισι τὰς νέας παραδόντες αὐτοὶ πεζῇ Πέρσῃσι προσφερώμεθα. ἡμεῖς μέν νυν ἐπ' οὗ ἐτάχθημεν, ταύτῃ πειρησόμεθα εἶναι χρηστοί· ὑμέας δὲ χρεόν ἐστι ἀναμνησθέντας οἷα

109. 1.   ἢ Πέρσῃσι ἢ Φοίνιξι A: omitted other MSS.

sight to have done what they long had a desire for; if I were in Ionia no city would have stirred. Now, as quickly as possible, release me to journey to Ionia, so that I can rectify everything to the same state it was in before, and hand over into your hands this deputy of Miletus who contrived these things. (*6*) I shall do this in accordance with your will, and I call on the royal gods to witness that I shall not take off this tunic which I am wearing when I go down to Ionia until I have made the largest island, Sardinia, tributary to you.' (**107**) Histiaeus in saying that was misleading, but Darius was persuaded and sent him away, instructing him to come back to him at Susa when he had accomplished what he had promised.

(**108**) While the message about Sardis was going up to the King, and Darius performed his act with the bow and engaged in conversation with Histiaeus, and Histiaeus was released by Darius and conveyed himself to the sea, in all that time the following happened. A report reached Onesilus of Salamis while he was besieging Amathus that Artybius, a distinguished Persian man, was expected by ship in Cyprus with a large Persian force. (*2*) On learning this Onesilus sent heralds to Ionia to call on them. The Ionians without spending long in deliberation came with a large mission. When the Ionians were present in Cyprus, the Persians crossed in ships from Cilicia and then went against Salamis on foot; and in the ships the Phoenicians sailed round the peninsula called the Keys of Cyprus. (**109**) When this had happened, the tyrants of Cyprus called together the Ionians' generals and said, 'Men of Ionia, we Cyprians give you the choice which you prefer to attack, the Persians or the Phoenicians. (*2*) If you wish to draw up on foot and make the attempt on the Persians, now would be the time for you to disembark from your ships and draw up on foot and for us to embark on your ships and contend against the Phoenicians. Or if you would rather make the attempt on the Phoenicians, you must act, whichever of these you choose, so that the freedom of Ionia and Cyprus depends on you.' (*3*) The Ionians said to that, 'We were sent by the common body of the Ionians to guard the sea, not to hand over our ships to the Cyprians and ourselves attack the Persians on foot.

ἐπάσχετε δουλεύοντες πρὸς τῶν Μήδων, γίνεσθαι ἄνδρας ἀγαθούς."
(110) Ἴωνες μὲν τούτοισι ἀμείψαντο· μετὰ δέ, ἡκόντων ἐς τὸ
πεδίον τὸ Σαλαμινίων τῶν Περσέων, διέτασσον οἱ βασιλέες τῶν
Κυπρίων τοὺς μὲν ἄλλους Κυπρίους κατὰ τοὺς ἄλλους στρατιώτας
ἀντιτάσσοντες, Σαλαμινίων δὲ καὶ Σολίων ἀπολέξαντες τὸ ἄριστον
ἀντέτασσον Πέρσῃσι· Ἀρτυβίῳ δὲ τῷ στρατηγῷ τῶν Περσέων
ἐθελοντὴς ἀντετάσσετο Ὀνήσιλος. (111) ἤλαυνε δὲ ἵππον ὁ Ἀρτύβιος
δεδιδαγμένον πρὸς ὁπλίτην ἵστασθαι ὀρθόν. πυθόμενος ὦν ταῦτα ὁ
Ὀνήσιλος, ἦν γάρ οἱ ὑπασπιστὴς γένος μὲν Κὰρ τὰ δὲ πολέμια κάρτα
δόκιμος καὶ ἄλλως λήματος πλέος, εἶπε πρὸς τοῦτον· (2) "πυνθάνομαι
τὸν Ἀρτυβίου ἵππον ἱστάμενον ὀρθὸν καὶ ποσὶ καὶ στόματι
κατεργάζεσθαι πρὸς τὸν ἂν προσενειχθῇ· σὺ ὦν βουλευσάμενος εἰπὲ
αὐτίκα ὁκότερον βούλεαι φυλάξας πλῆξαι, εἴτε τὸν ἵππον εἴτε αὐτὸν
Ἀρτύβιον." (3) εἶπε πρὸς ταῦτα ὁ ὁπάων αὐτοῦ· "ὦ βασιλεῦ, ἕτοιμος
μὲν ἐγώ εἰμι ποιέειν καὶ ἀμφότερα καὶ τὸ ἕτερον αὐτῶν, καὶ πάντως τὸ
ἂν σὺ ἐπιτάσσῃς· ὡς μέντοι ἔμοιγε δοκέει εἶναι τοῖσι σοῖσι πρήγμασι
προσφορώτερον, φράσω. (4) βασιλέα μὲν καὶ στρατηγὸν χρεὸν εἶναι
φημὶ βασιλέϊ τε καὶ στρατηγῷ προσφέρεσθαι· ἤν τε γὰρ κατέλῃς
ἄνδρα στρατηγόν, μέγα τοι γίνεται, καὶ δεύτερα, ἢν σὲ ἐκεῖνος, τὸ
μὴ γένοιτο, ὑπὸ ἀξιοχρέου καὶ ἀποθανεῖν ἡμίσεα συμφορή· ἡμέας δὲ
τοὺς ὑπηρέτας ἑτέροισί τε ὑπηρέτῃσι προσφέρεσθαι καὶ πρὸς ἵππον.
τοῦ σὺ τὰς μηχανὰς μηδὲν φοβηθῇς· ἐγὼ γάρ τοι ὑποδέκομαι μή μιν
ἀνδρὸς ἔτι γε μηδενὸς στήσεσθαι ἐναντίον."
(112) ταῦτα εἶπε, καὶ μεταυτίκα συνέμισγε τὰ στρατόπεδα πεζῇ
καὶ νηυσί. νηυσὶ μέν νυν Ἴωνες ἄκροι γενόμενοι ταύτην τὴν ἡμέρην
ὑπερεβάλοντο τοὺς Φοίνικας, καὶ τούτων Σάμιοι ἠρίστευσαν. πεζῇ
δέ, ὡς συνῆλθε τὰ στρατόπεδα, συμπεσόντα ἐμάχοντο. (2) κατὰ δὲ
τοὺς στρατηγοὺς ἀμφοτέρους τάδε ἐγίνετο· ὡς προσεφέρετο πρὸς
τὸν Ὀνήσιλον ὁ Ἀρτύβιος ἐπὶ τοῦ ἵππου κατήμενος, ὁ Ὀνήσιλος
κατὰ τὰ συνεθήκατο τῷ ὑπασπιστῇ παίει προσφερόμενον αὐτὸν τὸν
Ἀρτύβιον· ἐπιβαλόντος δὲ τοῦ ἵππου τοὺς πόδας ἐπὶ τὴν Ὀνησίλου
ἀσπίδα, ἐνθαῦτα ὁ Κὰρ δρεπάνῳ πλήξας ἀπαράσσει τοῦ ἵππου τοὺς

---

111. 3.   προσφορώτερον Macan (commentary): προφερέστερον MSS,
προσφερέστερον Stein.

We shall try to be valiant in the position assigned to us; and your duty is to remember what you have suffered as slaves under the Medes, and to be good men.'

(**110**) That was the Ionians' reply. Afterwards, when the Persians had come to the plain of Salamis, the kings of the Cyprians drew up the other Cyprians opposite the other soldiers, and picked out the best of the Salaminians and Solians to draw up opposite the Persians. Opposite Artybius the general of the Persians Onesilus volunteered to place himself. (**111**) Artybius rode a horse which had been taught to rear up opposite a hoplite. Onesilus learned of this, and, since he had an armour-bearer of Carian race, who was very distinguished in military matters and generally full of courage, he said to him, (*2*) 'I learn that Artybius' horse rears upright and with its hooves and mouth finishes off whomever it attacks. You then consider and tell me at once which you wish to watch out for and strike, the horse or Artybius himself.'(*3*) His retainer said to that, 'O king, I am ready to do both or either of them, and altogether to do whatever you command; but what seems to me to be more advantageous for your affairs I shall tell you. (*4*) I say that the king and general ought to attack the king and general (for if you kill a man who is a general it is a great achievement; and secondly, if he kills you – may it not happen – to have been killed by a worthy foe is only half the disaster); and we attendants ought to attack the other attendants and the horse. You must have no fear of the contrivances: I promise that it will no longer stand against any man.'

(**112**) So he spoke, and immediately afterwards the forces engaged, both on foot and with the ships. With their ships the Ionians excelled on that day and surpassed the Phoenicians, and of them the Samians performed best. On foot when the forces encountered they came to blows and proceeded to fight. (*2*) This is what happened with regard to the two generals. When Artybius, mounted on his horse, attacked Onesilus, Onesilus as he had agreed with his armour-bearer struck Artybius as he was attacking. When the horse brought its hooves

πόδας. Ἀρτύβιος μὲν δὴ ὁ στρατηγὸς τῶν Περσέων ὁμοῦ τῷ ἵππῳ πίπτει αὐτοῦ ταύτῃ. (113) μαχομένων δὲ καὶ τῶν ἄλλων, Στησήνωρ τύραννος ἐὼν Κουρίου προδιδοῖ ἔχων δύναμιν ἀνδρῶν περὶ ἑωυτὸν οὐ σμικρήν· οἱ δὲ Κουριέες οὗτοι λέγονται εἶναι Ἀργείων ἄποικοι. προδόντων δὲ τῶν Κουριέων αὐτίκα καὶ τὰ Σαλαμινίων πολεμιστήρια ἅρματα τὠυτὸ τοῖσι Κουριεῦσι ἐποίεε. γενομένων δὲ τούτων κατυπέρτεροι ἦσαν οἱ Πέρσαι τῶν Κυπρίων. (2) τετραμμένου δὲ τοῦ στρατοπέδου ἄλλοι τε ἔπεσον πολλοὶ καὶ δὴ καὶ Ὀνήσιλός τε ὁ Χέρσιος, ὅς περ τὴν Κυπρίων ἀπόστασιν ἔπρηξε, καὶ ὁ Σολίων βασιλεὺς Ἀριστόκυπρος ὁ Φιλοκύπρου, Φιλοκύπρου δὲ τούτου τὸν Σόλων ὁ Ἀθηναῖος ἀπικόμενος ἐς Κύπρον ἐν ἔπεσι αἴνεσε τυράννων μάλιστα. (114) Ὀνησίλου μέν νυν Ἀμαθούσιοι, ὅτι σφέας ἐπολιόρκησε, ἀποταμόντες τὴν κεφαλὴν ἐκόμισαν ἐς Ἀμαθοῦντα καί μιν ἀνεκρέμασαν ὑπὲρ τῶν πυλέων· κρεμαμένης δὲ τῆς κεφαλῆς καὶ ἤδη ἐούσης κοίλης, ἑσμὸς μελισσέων ἐσδὺς ἐς αὐτὴν κηρίων μιν ἐνέπλησε. (2) τούτου δὲ γενομένου τοιούτου, ἐχρέωντο γὰρ περὶ αὐτῆς οἱ Ἀμαθούσιοι, ἐμαντεύθη σφι τὴν μὲν κεφαλὴν κατελόντας θάψαι, Ὀνησίλῳ δὲ θύειν ὡς ἥρωι ἀνὰ πᾶν ἔτος, καί σφι ποιεῦσι ταῦτα ἄμεινον συνοίσεσθαι. (115) Ἀμαθούσιοι μέν νυν ἐποίευν ταῦτα καὶ τὸ μέχρι ἐμεῦ.

Ἴωνες δὲ οἱ ἐν Κύπρῳ ναυμαχήσαντες ἐπείτε ἔμαθον τὰ πρήγματα τὰ Ὀνησίλου διεφθαρμένα καὶ τὰς πόλις τῶν Κυπρίων πολιορκευμένας τὰς ἄλλας πλὴν Σαλαμῖνος, ταύτην δὲ Γόργῳ τῷ προτέρῳ βασιλέϊ τοὺς Σαλαμινίους παραδόντας, αὐτίκα μαθόντες οἱ Ἴωνες ταῦτα ἀπέπλωον ἐς τὴν Ἰωνίην. (2) τῶν δὲ ἐν Κύπρῳ πολίων ἀντέσχε χρόνον ἐπὶ πλεῖστον πολιορκευμένη Σόλοι, τὴν πέριξ ὑπορύσσοντες τὸ τεῖχος πέμπτῳ μηνὶ εἷλον οἱ Πέρσαι. (116) Κύπριοι μὲν δὴ ἐνιαυτὸν ἐλεύθεροι γενόμενοι αὖτις ἐκ νέης κατεδεδούλωντο.

Δαυρίσης δὲ ἔχων Δαρείου θυγατέρα καὶ Ὑμαίης τε καὶ Ὀτάνης, ἄλλοι Πέρσαι στρατηγοί, ἔχοντες καὶ οὗτοι Δαρείου θυγατέρας, ἐπιδιώξαντες τοὺς ἐς Σάρδις στρατευσαμένους Ἰώνων καὶ ἐσαράξαντές σφεας ἐς τὰς νέας, τῇ μάχῃ ὡς ἐπεκράτησαν, τὸ ἐνθεῦτεν

---

113. 1.   εὖ inserted after τῶν ἄλλων Gomperz.
116.   ἄλλοι Πέρσαι στρατηγοί deleted van Herwerden.

against Onesilus' shield, then the Carian struck with a sickle and cut off the horse's hooves. Artybius the Persians' general fell with his horse there in that way. (**113**) Among the others fighting Stesenor, tyrant of Curium, who had around him a substantial body of men, betrayed the cause (these Curians say that they are colonists of Argos). When the Curians betrayed, immediately the war chariots of the Salaminians too did the same as the Curians. And when this happened the Persians were superior to the Cyprians. (*2*) As their force was routed, many others fell, including Onesilus son of Chersis, who had brought about the revolt of the Cyprians, and the king of Soli Aristocyprus son of Philocyprus, that Philocyprus whom Solon the Athenian when he went to Cyprus praised most of the tyrants in his poetry. (**114**) The Amathusians, because he had besieged them, cut off Onesilus' head, conveyed it to Amathus and hung it above the gates. As the head was hanging, and was already hollow, a swarm of bees penetrated it and filled it with a honeycomb. (*2*) When this had happened, the Amathusians consulted an oracle about it, and their response was that they should take down the head and bury it, and sacrifice to Onesilus as a hero every year, and things would turn out better for them if they did that. (**115**) The Amathusians continued to do that even to my time.

The Ionians who had fought the naval battle in Cyprus understood that the plans of Onesilus were ruined, and that the other cities of the Cyprians were under siege, apart from Salamis, which the Salaminians handed over to their former king Gorgus. As soon as they understood this the Ionians sailed back to Ionia. (*2*) Of the cities in Cyprus the one which held out under siege for the longest time was Soli: the Persians took it in the fifth month by digging under the wall round it. (**116**) So the Cyprians after being free for a year were once more again enslaved.

Daurises, married to Darius' daughter, and Hymaeës and Otanes, other Persian generals who also were married to daughters of Darius, pursued those of the Ionians who had campaigned against Sardis and

ἐπιδιελόμενοι τὰς πόλις ἐπόρθεον. (**117**) Δαυρίσης μὲν τραπόμενος πρὸς τὰς ἐν Ἑλλησπόντῳ πόλις εἷλε μὲν Δάρδανον, εἷλε δὲ Ἄβυδόν τε καὶ Περκώτην καὶ Λάμψακον καὶ Παισόν. ταύτας μίαν ἐπ᾽ ἡμέρῃ ἑκάστῃ αἵρεε, ἀπὸ δὲ Παισοῦ ἐλαύνοντί οἱ ἐπὶ Πάριον πόλιν ἦλθε ἀγγελίη τοὺς Κᾶρας τὠυτὸ Ἴωσι φρονήσαντας ἀπεστάναι ἀπὸ Περσέων. ἀποστρέψας ὦν ἐκ τοῦ Ἑλλησπόντου ἤλαυνε τὸν στρατὸν ἐπὶ τὴν Καρίην.

(**118**) καί κως ταῦτα τοῖσι Καρσὶ ἐξαγγέλθη πρότερον ἢ τὸν Δαυρίσην ἀπικέσθαι· πυθόμενοι δὲ οἱ Κᾶρες συνελέγοντο ἐπὶ Λευκάς τε στήλας καλεομένας καὶ ποταμὸν Μαρσύην, ὃς ῥέων ἐκ τῆς Ἰδριάδος χώρης ἐς τὸν Μαίανδρον ἐκδιδοῖ. (*2*) συλλεχθέντων δὲ τῶν Καρῶν ἐνθαῦτα ἐγίνοντο βουλαὶ ἄλλαι τε πολλαὶ καὶ ἀρίστη γε δοκέουσα εἶναι ἐμοὶ Πιξωδάρου τοῦ Μαυσώλου ἀνδρὸς Κινδυέος, ὃς τοῦ Κιλίκων βασιλέος Συεννέσιος εἶχε θυγατέρα. τούτου τοῦ ἀνδρὸς ἡ γνώμη ἔφερε διαβάντας τὸν Μαίανδρον τοὺς Κᾶρας καὶ κατὰ νώτου ἔχοντας τὸν ποταμὸν οὕτω συμβάλλειν, ἵνα μὴ ἔχοντες ὀπίσω φεύγειν οἱ Κᾶρες αὐτοῦ τε μένειν ἀναγκαζόμενοι γινοίατο ἔτι ἀμείνονες τῆς φύσιος. (*3*) αὕτη μέν νυν οὐκ ἐνίκα ἡ γνώμη, ἀλλὰ τοῖσι Πέρσῃσι κατὰ νώτου γίνεσθαι τὸν Μαίανδρον μᾶλλον ἢ σφίσι, δηλαδὴ ἢν φυγὴ τῶν Περσέων γένηται καὶ ἐσσωθέωσι τῇ συμβολῇ, ὡς οὐκ ἀπονοστήσουσι ἐς τὸν ποταμὸν ἐσπίπτοντες. (**119**) μετὰ δὲ παρεόντων καὶ διαβάντων τὸν Μαίανδρον τῶν Περσέων ἐνθαῦτα ἐπὶ τῷ Μαρσύῃ ποταμῷ συνέβαλόν τε τοῖσι Πέρσῃσι οἱ Κᾶρες καὶ μάχην ἐμαχέσαντο ἰσχυρὴν καὶ ἐπὶ χρόνον πολλόν, τέλος δὲ ἐσσώθησαν διὰ πλῆθος. Περσέων μὲν δὴ ἔπεσον ἄνδρες ἐς δισχιλίους, Καρῶν δὲ ἐς μυρίους.

(*2*) ἐνθεῦτεν δὲ οἱ διαφυγόντες αὐτῶν κατειλήθησαν ἐς Λάβραυνδα ἐς Διὸς στρατίου ἱρόν, μέγα τε καὶ ἅγιον ἄλσος πλατανίστων. μοῦνοι δὲ τῶν ἡμεῖς ἴδμεν Κᾶρές εἰσι οἳ Διὶ στρατίῳ θυσίας ἀνάγουσι. κατειληθέντες δὲ ὦν οὗτοι ἐνθαῦτα ἐβουλεύοντο περὶ σωτηρίης, ὁκότερα ἢ παραδόντες σφέας αὐτοὺς Πέρσῃσι ἢ ἐκλιπόντες τὸ

---

117.   μίαν Powell: μὲν MSS.
118. 2.   ἡ inserted before Πιξωδάρου van Herwerden.

after defeating them in battle drove them pell-mell into their ships. Then dividing them among themselves they proceeded to capture the cities. (**117**) Daurises turned towards the cities on the Hellespont: he took Dardanus, and also took Abydus, Percote, Lampsacus and Paesus. These he took one on each day, and as he was proceeding from Paesus to the city of Parium a message reached him that the Carians in agreement with the Ionians had revolted against the Persians. He therefore turned away from the Hellespont and proceeded with his army against Caria.

(**118**) News of that reached the Carians before Daurises arrived. On learning this the Carians gathered at what are called the White Pillars and the River Marsyas, which flows from the Idrian land and debouches into the Maeander. (*2*) When the Carians were gathered there many other suggestions were made, and what seems to me to be the best was that of Pixodarus son of Mausolus, a man of Cindya who was married to the daughter of the Cilician king Syennesis. This man's opinion was that the Carians should cross the Maeander and fight with the river behind them, so that the Carians should not have the possibility of fleeing to their rear but should be compelled to remain there and should be even better than they naturally were. (*3*) That opinion did not prevail, but one that the Persians should have the Maeander behind them rather than themselves, so that if the Persians were put to flight and defeated in the encounter they should not be able to return home but fall into the river. (**119**) When the Persians were present and had crossed the Maeander, then at the River Marsyas the Carians attacked the Persians: they fought a hard battle for a long time, but in the end they were defeated by weight of numbers. There fell of the Persians about two thousand men and of the Carians about ten thousand.

(*2*) Then those of them who made their escape were trapped in the sanctuary of Zeus Stratius at Labraünda, in a large and sacred grove of plane trees. (Only the Carians of those whom we know perform sacrifices to Zeus Stratius.) So these men, trapped there, deliberated

παράπαν τὴν Ἀσίην ἄμεινον πρήξουσι. (**120**) βουλευομένοισι δέ σφι ταῦτα παραγίνονται βοηθέοντες Μιλήσιοί τε καὶ οἱ τούτων σύμμαχοι. ἐνθαῦτα δὲ τὰ μὲν πρότερον οἱ Κᾶρες ἐβουλεύοντο μετῆκαν, οἱ δὲ αὖτις πολεμέειν ἐξ ἀρχῆς ἀρτέοντο. καὶ ἐπιοῦσί τε τοῖσι Πέρσῃσι συμβάλλουσι καὶ μαχεσάμενοι ἐπὶ πλέον ἢ πρότερον ἑσσώθησαν· πεσόντων δὲ τῶν πάντων πολλῶν μάλιστα Μιλήσιοι ἐπλήγησαν. (**121**) μετὰ δὲ τοῦτο τὸ τρῶμα ἀνέλαβόν τε καὶ ἀνεμαχέσαντο οἱ Κᾶρες· πυθόμενοι γὰρ ὡς στρατεύεσθαι ὁρμέαται οἱ Πέρσαι ἐπὶ τὰς πόλις σφέων, ἐλόχησαν τὴν ἐν Πιδάσῳ ὁδόν, ἐς τὴν ἐμπεσόντες οἱ Πέρσαι νυκτὸς διεφθάρησαν καὶ αὐτοὶ καὶ οἱ στρατηγοὶ αὐτῶν Δαυρίσης καὶ Ἀμόργης καὶ Σισιμάκης· σὺν δέ σφι ἀπέθανε καὶ Μύρσος ὁ Γύγεω. τοῦ δὲ λόχου τούτου ἡγεμὼν ἦν Ἡρακλείδης Ἰβανώλλιος ἀνὴρ Μυλασεύς.

(**122**) οὗτοι μέν νυν τῶν Περσέων οὕτω διεφθάρησαν. Ὑμαίης δὲ καὶ αὐτὸς ἐὼν τῶν ἐπιδιωξάντων τοὺς ἐς Σάρδις στρατευσαμένους Ἰώνων, τραπόμενος ἐς τὸν Προποντίδα εἷλε Κίον τὴν Μυσίην. (**2**) ταύτην δὲ ἐξελών, ὡς ἐπύθετο τὸν Ἑλλήσποντον ἐκλελοιπέναι Δαυρίσην καὶ στρατεύεσθαι ἐπὶ Καρίης, καταλιπὼν τὴν Προποντίδα ἐπὶ τὸν Ἑλλήσποντον ἦγε τὸν στρατόν, καὶ εἷλε μὲν Αἰολέας πάντας ὅσοι τὴν Ἰλιάδα νέμονται, εἷλε δὲ Γέργιθας τοὺς ὑπολειφθέντας τῶν ἀρχαίων Τευκρῶν. αὐτός τε Ὑμαίης αἱρέων ταῦτα τὰ ἔθνεα νούσῳ τελευτᾷ ἐν τῇ Τρῳάδι. (**123**) οὗτος μὲν δὴ οὕτω ἐτελεύτησε, Ἀρταφρένης δὲ ὁ Σαρδίων ὕπαρχος καὶ Ὀτάνης ὁ τρίτος στρατηγὸς ἐτάχθησαν ἐπὶ τὴν Ἰωνίην καὶ τὴν προσεχέα Αἰολίδα στρατεύεσθαι. Ἰωνίης μέν νυν Κλαζομενὰς αἱρέουσι, Αἰολέων δὲ Κύμην.

(**124**) ἁλισκομενέων δὲ τῶν πολίων, ἦν γὰρ ὡς διέδεξε Ἀρισταγόρης ὁ Μιλήσιος ψυχὴν οὐκ ἄκρος, ὃς ταράξας τὴν Ἰωνίην καὶ ἐγκερασάμενος πρήγματα μεγάλα δρησμὸν ἐβούλευε ὀρέων ταῦτα· πρὸς δέ οἱ καὶ ἀδύνατα ἐφάνη βασιλέα Δαρεῖον ὑπερβαλέσθαι. (**2**) πρὸς ταῦτα δὴ ὦν συγκαλέσας τοὺς συστασιώτας ἐβουλεύετο,

---

119. 2.   ὁκότερα ἢ: ἢ deleted Cobet.
121.   Πιδάσῳ AB cf. *iota* in variants in other MSS: Πηδάσῳ H. Stephanus, ἐπὶ <Πη>δάσοισι Bean & Cook, which we could modify to .ἐπὶ <Πι>δάσοισι.
122. 2.   αὐτός τε Ὑμαίης: Ὑμαίης deleted Wilson.

about their salvation, whether they should hand themselves over to the Persians or would do better to leave Asia altogether. (**120**) While they were deliberating about this there arrived to support them the Milesians and their allies. Then the Carians abandoned their previous deliberation, and once again prepared to wage war. The Persians attacked, and they engaged and fought, but were defeated even more badly than before. Altogether many fell, and the Milesians suffered particularly badly. (**121**) But after that blow the Carians recovered and fought again. Learning that the Persians were planning to campaign against their cities, they set an ambush on the road in the land of Pidasus, into which the Persians fell at night: they were destroyed, including their generals Daurises, Amorges and Sisimaces; and with them died also Myrsus the son of Gyges. The leader of this contingent was Heraclides son of Ibanollis, a man of Mylasa.

(**122**) These Persians were destroyed in that way. Hymaeës, himself one of those who had pursued the Ionians who campaigned against Sardis, turned towards the Propontis and took Cius in Mysia. (*2*) After capturing that, when he learned that Daurises had left the Hellespont and was campaigning against Caria, he left the Propontis and led his army against the Hellespont, and he took all the Aeolians who occupy the land of Ilium, and took the people of Gergis, who are the survivors of the ancient Teucrians. After taking these peoples Hymaeës himself died of illness in the Troad. (**123**) That is how he died. Artaphernes the governor of Sardis and Otanes the third general were appointed to campaign against Ionia and neighbouring Aeolis. They took Clazomenae in Ionia and Cyme in Aeolis.

(**124**) When the cities had been captured, Aristagoras of Miletus was as he demonstrated not strong in spirit: after throwing Ionia into confusion and stirring up great trouble, on seeing this he planned to run away. In addition it seemed to him impossible to surpass King

λέγων ὡς ἄμεινον σφίσι εἴη κρησφύγετόν τι ὑπάρχον εἶναι, ἢν ἄρα ἐξωθέωνται ἐκ τῆς Μιλήτου, εἴτε δὴ ὦν ἐς Σαρδὼ ἐκ τοῦ τόπου τούτου ἄγοι ἐς ἀποικίην, εἴτε ἐς Μύρκινον τὴν Ἠδωνῶν, τὴν Ἱστιαῖος ἐτείχεε παρὰ Δαρείου δωρεὴν λαβών. ταῦτα ἐπειρώτα ὁ Ἀρισταγόρης. (125) Ἑκαταίου μέν νυν τοῦ Ἡγησάνδρου, ἀνδρὸς λογοποιοῦ, τουτέων μὲν ἐς οὐδετέρην στέλλειν ἔφερε ἡ γνώμη, ἐν Λέρῳ δὲ τῇ νήσῳ τεῖχος οἰκοδομησάμενον ἡσυχίην ἄγειν, ἢν ἐκπέσῃ ἐκ τῆς Μιλήτου· ἔπειτα δὲ ἐκ ταύτης ὁρμώμενον κατελεύσεσθαι ἐς τὴν Μίλητον. (126) ταῦτα μὲν δὴ Ἑκαταῖος συνεβούλευε, αὐτῷ δὲ Ἀρισταγόρῃ ἡ πλείστη γνώμη ἦν ἐς τὴν Μύρκινον ἀπάγειν. τὴν μὲν δὴ Μίλητον ἐπιτρέπει Πυθαγόρῃ ἀνδρὶ τῶν ἀστῶν δοκίμῳ, αὐτὸς δὲ παραλαβὼν πάντα τὸν βουλόμενον ἔπλεε ἐς τὴν Θρηίκην, καὶ ἔσχε τὴν χώρην ἐπ᾽ ἣν ἐστάλη. (2) ἐκ δὲ ταύτης ὁρμώμενος ἀπόλλυται ὑπὸ Θρηίκων αὐτός τε ὁ Ἀρισταγόρης καὶ ὁ στρατὸς αὐτοῦ, πόλιν περικατήμενος καὶ βουλομένων τῶν Θρηίκων ὑποσπόνδων ἐξιέναι.

126. 2.　　lacuna after ὑποσπόνδων ἐξιέναι Maas.

Darius. (*2*) In the light of this, then, he called together his partisans to deliberate, saying that it would be better for them to have some secure refuge available in case they were driven out of Miletus, whether he should lead them from this place to Sardinia for a colony, or to Myrcinus of the Edonians, which Histiaeus had fortified after receiving it as a gift from Darius. That was the question put by Aristagoras. (**125**) The proposal of Hecataeus son of Hegesandrus, a man who was a prose-writer, was that he should not set out for either, but should build a fort on the island of Leros and keep quiet if he were expelled from Miletus. Later he would be able to set out from there and return to Miletus. (**126**) That was the advice of Hecataeus, but to Aristagoras himself the strongest proposal was to lead a settlement to Myrcinus. Miletus he deputed to Pythagoras, a distinguished man among the citizens, and he himself taking everybody who was willing sailed to Thrace and occupied the land to which he had gone. (*2*) But when he set out from there Aristagoras and his army perished at the hands of the Thracians, besieging a city when the Thracians were willing to evacuate it under truce.

COMMENTARY

1–27. Persia's conquest of Thrace.

1. 1. Those of the Persians who were left in Europe by Darius: At the end of the Scythian expedition of *c.* 514: that expedition is narrated in IV. 1–144, with Darius' return to Asia in 143. 1 and Megabazus' being left in Europe in 143–4; it is not clear how we should dovetail with this the Scythian retaliatory raid which reached the Chersonese, mentioned in VI. 40 (where text and interpretation are problematic), but I should not rule out a raid, soon after Darius' withdrawal and not long-lasting, while Megabazus was active farther west. After devoting IV. 145–205 to Cyrene, Herodotus returns to his main narrative. Darius I (522–486) became King through the *coup* which followed the death of Cambyses (III. 61–87).

under the command of Megabazus: In IV. 143–4 he is one of Darius' most trusted commanders. On different bearers of this name see Burn, *Persia and the Greeks*, 335. His son Bubares will appear in 21. 2, and other possible sons are Oebares, satrap of Dascylium in 493 (VI. 33. 3), and Pherendates, commander of the Sarangae in 480 (VII. 67. 1). They may be related to Megabates the cousin of Darius (32), who was superseded as satrap of Dascylium in 478 (Thuc. I. 129. 1) and whose son Megabazus was one of Xerxes' four admirals in 480 (VII. 97).

first subdued the Perinthians, a Hellespontine community: Hornblower notes that κατεστρέψαντο here introduces the second, more recent and more continuous, part of Herodotus' history as in I. 6. 2 κατεστρέψατο of Croesus introduced the serious history of his first part. Perinthus (*Barrington Atlas* 52 B 3, *Inventory* 919–21 no. 678) was a colony of Samos; it was not on the Hellespont but on the European side of the Propontis, but the term 'Hellespont' could be extended to include the Propontis and the Bosporus, as it was when the tribute quota lists of Athens' Delian League were organised in regions (e.g. R. Meiggs, *The Athenian Empire* [Oxford UP, 1972], 543–47).

They had previously been treated harshly: 'Treat harshly' is a favourite expression of Herodotus (I. 114. 3 etc.). The story is not given

a historical context, and may simply have been invented for the sake of the pun in §§2–3.

1. 2. For the Paeonians from the Strymon: Even on the Strymon (Struma, east of Chalcidice) they would be a long way from Perinthus, and in fact they seem to have lived in the region of the Axius (Vardar, west of Chalcidice); they are likewise misplaced in 13. 2; but all Herodotus' details are consistent with his placing of them. In 12–15 Megabazus will deport them to Asia.

received an oracle from the God: The story perhaps envisages Apollo, to whom particularly though not uniquely paeans were sung, and his oracle at Delphi; or see VII. 111 for a Thracian oracle of Dionysus.

horse against horse: Possibly a horse race (C. Carey *ap.* Hornblower).

1. 3. won two of the contests: And were therefore overall winners.

began to sing a paean in joy … the point of the oracle: Celebration of victory was one of a number of occasions which could be marked by a paean (e.g. Hom. *Il.* XXII. 391–2); and here the invocation ἰὴ Παιάν is taken by the Paeonians to be 'calling out to them by name'.

2. 2. drove his force through Thrace: Westwards through coastal Thrace towards Macedon, as the narrative will show; coastal Thrace is specified in 10.

taming for the King: For the image see Brock, *Greek Political Imagery*, 108 with 127 n. 10. Hornblower notes that Herodotus uses this verb always of subjection to Persia; in IV. 118. 5 the Scythians use it of Darius. Substantially, though not verbally, this passage opens a ring which is closed at the end of 10 after Herodotus' account of the Thracians.

to subdue Thrace: Cobet's deletion of Θρηίκην καταστρέφεσθαι is perhaps an improvement rather than a correction.

3. 1. The Thracian people: For Herodotus' interest in places and peoples cf. Introduction, p. 5.

after the Indians: In III. 94. 2 the Indians are 'by far the most numerous of all men whom we know' – and this was a fair assessment in a sub-world which did not know China.

3. 2. If they were ruled by a single man … they would be impossible to fight against: Thucydides in his digression on Thrace (II. 96–7) says this of the Scythians, while judging that of the nations in Europe Thrace 'was the greatest in terms of the revenue it received and general prosperity,

though for strength in battle and the size of its army it fell a long way short of the Scythians' (97. 5–6). For Thrace under the Odrysian king Sitalces see IV. 80. 1–4, VII. 137. 3, and Thuc. II. 97. 1–98. 1 (remarking that Thrace was greatest under Sitalces' successor Seuthes).

4. 1. what the Getae who consider themselves immortal do I have already said: The Getae lived on the lower reaches of the Danube. Cf. IV. 93–4: they believe that people do not die but go to a deity called Salmoxis, and every fifth year they impale a man to send him as a messenger to Salmoxis.

The Trausi … for those who are born and who die among them they do this: In the second century the Trausi lived south of the Danube and to the east of Thasos: Livy XXXVIII. 41. 6–8 writes of their being defeated by the Romans under Cn. Manlius Vulso in 188.

4. 2. when one is born …. when one has died…: For the undesirability of human life cf. Artabanus' remark to Xerxes in VII. 46, and e.g. [Hesiod] fr. 377 Merkelbach and West, Theognis 425–8, Soph. *O.C.* 1225–8, Eur. fr. 449 *TrGF* (quoted by Strabo 520 / XI. 11. 8 in connection with peoples in the region of the Caucasus: R. Browning, *CR*² 11 [1961], 201–202, suggested that that was a quotation from Herodotus). Solon in speaking to Croesus in I. 32 focuses on the variability of life.

how many misfortunes he will have to endure: For ἀναπλῆσαι κακά cf. e.g. Hom. *Il.* XV. 132; and on Herodotus' use of Homeric expressions cf. Introduction, p. 27.

5. Those above the Crestonaeans: The Crestonaeans lived between the Axius and the Strymon, east of the Paeonians (Hammond, *History of Macedonia*, i. 179–82). 'Above' will mean inland, i.e. to the north.

Whichever one the judgment falls on and is honoured: It is not clear how the selection was made.

slaughtered at the tomb: Cf. the account of suttee among the Indians by Diod. Sic. XIX. 33–4. W. Heckel and J. C. Yardley, 'Roman Writers and the Indian Practice of Suttee', *Philologus* 125 (1981), 305–11, remark that accounts of the Indian practice are not based on this passage of Herodotus, as had often been claimed.

6. 1. they sell their children for export: For exporting slaves cf. VII. 156. 2; also Solon fr. 36. 8–15 West *ap. Ath. Pol.* 12. 4, M&L 32. 38–41.

they do mightily guard their wives: In order to ensure that the children are genuinely their own.

they buy their wives ... for large sums of money: Mentioned as a Thracian custom by Xen. *An.* VII. 2. 38.

6. 2. Being tattooed is judged noble: Cf. C. P. Jones, 'Stigma: Tattooing and Branding in Graeco-Roman Antiquity', *JRS* 77 (1987), 139–55 at 145.

To have leisure is judged finest ... Living from war and plundering is judged finest: Cf. II. 167, wondering where the Greeks learned to despise crafts and to esteem warfare; and Thuc. I. 5, noting that in primitive times and places raiding was not shameful. But for the Greeks farming one's own land was the most honourable kind of labour: e.g. Hes. *Op.*, Xen. *Oec.*

7. They worship only these gods: Ares, Dionysus and Artemis: The Greeks commonly identified other peoples' gods with those of their own who had similar characteristics; for Herodotus' practice cf. on Egypt II. 29, 42–4, 74, 83, and see Introduction, p. 19. For a connection between Ares and Thrace cf. Hom. *Od.* VIII. 362.

But their kings ... descended from Hermes: Cf. the descent of the Scythian kings from Heracles: IV. 8–10.

8. burials are like this: Cf. the lamentation, cremation and burial of, and games for, Patroclus in Hom. *Il.* XXIII.

for single combat: The expression, literally 'on account of single combat', is awkward, and Wilson suggests κατὰ λόγον <εὐδαιμονίης διὰ> μουνομαχίης, 'in proportion to wealth by single combat'.

9. 1. nobody can tell for certain ... the land appears to be uninhabited and boundless: Herodotus is uninformed and hesitant, stating what he can in indirect speech. He thought it possible that there was no sea bounding the Eurasian land mass on the north: IV. 36, 45. 1.

beyond the Ister: The Danube.

Sigynnae, who wear Median clothing: Ap. Rhod. *Argon.* IV. 319–22 mentions them with the Scythians; Strabo 520 / XI. 11. 8 locates them between the Caspian and the Caucasus, well to the east of Thrace. Herodotus is perhaps thinking of trousers.

9. 2. Their horses are shaggy all over their bodies … very fast when harnessed to chariots: Repeated by Strabo.

the Enetae in the Adriatic: In the region of, and giving their name to Venice. Cf. I. 196. 1; 'in the Adriatic' is perhaps stated to distinguish them from the Eneti of Paphlagonia (Hom. *Il.* II. 851–5).

9. 3. They say that they are colonists of the Medes: This would be more plausible if they were where Strabo puts them than if they were north of Thrace and abutting on the Adriatic.

anything might happen in the course of a long time: A striking way of not ruling out what Herodotus considers highly unlikely. Cf. Soph. *Phil.* 305–6; also I. 5. 4 (what was great is now small and *vice versa*; human prosperity never abides with the same people)

The Ligyes who live beyond Massalia call salesmen *sigynnai*, but the Cyprians … spears: The Ligyes are the Ligurians; and this is Herodotus' only mention of Massalia. Arist. *Poet.* 21. 1457 в 6 remarks on σίγυνον as a Cyprian word; Lycoph. *Alex.* 556–7 uses σίγυμνος in a Cyprian context to mean spear. The sentence appears as an afterthought to Herodotus' account of the Sigynnae, but it need not be suspected and deleted.

10. bees … it is impossible to penetrate farther: Herodotus does not rationalise the bees into the sting of cold, as in IV. 31 he rationalised Scythian feathers into snowflakes; Macan wondered if the 'bees' were gnats or mosquitoes.

these creatures seem to me to be intolerant of cold: In fact bees can live wherever there are flowering plants to supply them with pollen.

the regions under the Bear: Ursa Major (Bear or Waggon in Hom. *Il.* XVIII. 487; Great Bear or Plough in English) is one of the most northerly constellations, and the modern English 'Arctic' is derived from the Greek *arktos*.

That is what is said … Megabazus was making subject to the Persians: Herodotus closes a ring, substantially though not verbally, and continues the narrative from 2. 2.

11. 1. when he had crossed the Hellespont: On returning from his Scythian campaign (IV. 143. 1: διαβὰς here echoes δίεβη there).

Sardis: The capital of the former Lydian kingdom (I. 7. 2, etc.), and after the Persian conquest the capital of the satrapy of Lydia (I. 153. 3, III.

120. 1, etc.): *Barrington Atlas* 56 G 5. On his outward march Darius had gone via Calchedon and the Bosporus (IV. 85. 1 cf. 83. 1). Hornblower notes the chiastic structure of this section: Sardis – Hecataeus – Milesian – good service >< advice – Mytilenaean – Coes – Sardis.

Histiaeus the Milesian's good service: He was one of the Greek tyrants with Darius on his Scythian campaign: on his advice the response to the Scythians of the Greeks guarding Darius' Danube bridge was not to demolish the whole bridge and leave Darius stranded in Scythia but to demolish only a token part which could be repaired and to enable Darius to cross when he eventually reappeared. There was a cult of Hestia ('hearth') at Miletus (cf. *SIG*³ 57 = *Milet* i. iii 133. 12–13), and the name Histiaeus was common at Miletus and its colonies.

the advice of the Mytilenaean Coes: Not to demolish the Danube bridge when Darius advanced into Scythia but to leave it guarded so that he could use it on his return. Herodotus' account of that ends with Darius' telling Coes to claim a reward afterwards (IV. 97).

11. 2. being tyrant of Miletus: The Persians were controlling the Greek cities in their empire through vassal tyrants (IV. 137–8).

tyrant … tyranny … tyrant … tyrant: Herodotus often repeats different forms of the same word or family of words in this way.

Myrcinus of the Edones: See *Inventory* 862 no. 633. It was some way inland from the mouth of the Strymon (Struma) at Eïon, between the Chalcidic peninsula and Thasos; the site has not been identified, though a location north of Nine Ways/Amphipolis is given in *Barrington Atlas* 51 B 3; Thucydides writes of it as an Edonian city in 424 (IV. 107. 3, cf. 102. 2–3). For the sequel see 23–25. 1.

one of the people: Herodotus uses δημότης in the same sense elsewhere: II. 172. 2, 5.

tyrant of Mytilene: In IV. 97. 2 he was 'general of the Mytilenaeans'. For the sequel see 37–38. 1.

12. 1. saw something: A similar story is told of the Lydian king Alyattes and a Thracian woman by Nic. Dam. *FGrH* 90 F 71, and there is no point in asking which is 'the original' version of this floating story. See A. H. Griffiths, 'Behind the Lines: The Genesis of Stories in Herodotus', in *Homer, Tragedy and Beyond … P. E. Easterling* (London: Society for the Promotion of Hellenic Studies, 2001), 75–89, who studies this as

one of a number of stories in which an oriental king surveys his subjects parading before him, and suggests that this is one instance of a story in which elsewhere the purpose is to find a husband for the woman (as in *Genesis* 24). Cf. IV. 168. 2, where among the Libyans marriageable girls are displayed to the king.

instruct Megabazus ... from Europe to Asia: This opens a double ring, with a first closure in 14. 1 and a second in 17. 1. For the Paeonians see on 1. 2. The Persians were given to transplanting populations: cf. e.g. Darius' alleged plan to exchange the Phoenicians and the Ionians (VI. 3), and the transplanting of the Milesians after the Ionian Revolt (VI. 18–19) and of the Eretrians in 490 (VI. 101. 3, 119); III. 93. 2 refers to islands in the 'Red Sea' (in our terminology the Persian Gulf), where the King settled those known as the uprooted.

There were two Paeonian men: 'Beginnings of this kind are no doubt as old as the art of narrative itself': E. J. Kenney, *Apuleius, Cupid and Psyche* (Cambridge UP, 1990), 116, on Apul. *Met.* IV. 28. 1. From Herodotus he cites I. 6. 1.

tall and handsome sister: Cf. Phye in the story of Pisistratus' second seizure of power in Athens – from Paeania in Attica (I. 60. 4–5).

12. 2. take his seat in front of the Lydian capital: A Homeric ruler (e.g. Hom. *Od.* III. 404–12) or a Greek aristocrat (e.g. VI. 35. 2) would sit outside his house, and a greater ruler would sit outside his capital city (cf. Croesus outside Sardis, I. 78. 1).

Dressing their sister as well as they could: In I. 60. 4 Phye was dressed in armour. We next see the woman through Darius' eyes before he asks about her (cf. Introduction, p. 14).

with a jar on her head: Cf. Electra in Eur. *El.* 55–6. In *Genesis* 24. 15 Rebekah has a water jar on her shoulder.

spinning flax: Spinning was used to produce a twisted and stronger yarn, and was a regular occupation for Greek and other women (e.g. Hom. *Od.* II. 97–8).

12. 3. not characteristic ... of the peoples of Asia: Hornblower remarks that what was alien was the performance of the separate tasks at the same time, and that was alien to the Greeks too. For female workers in the Persian empire see Briant, *From Cyrus to Alexander*, 430–37 (engaged particularly in textile work).

13. 1. into his presence: Literally, into his sight.

13. 2. what people … what territory … what was their own wish:
Cf. 73. 2 (Artaphernes, about the Athenians); and (three questions, but
not the same three; '*Il.*' in Hornblower is a slip) Hom. *Od.* I. 170. They
answer in reverse order. In I. 153. 2 Cyrus asked who were the Spartans,
and in V. 105. 1 Darius will ask who are the Athenians. A. J. Woodman
reminds me that this kind of enquiry is parodied at the beginning of
A. E. Housman, 'Fragment of a Greek Tragedy', *The Bromsgrovian*
(1883), revised in *The Cornhill Magazine* 10 (1901), 443–45; Greek
'original' constructed and printed facing the *Cornhill* version by D. S.
Raven, *G&R*² 6 (1959), 14–19 = his *Poetastery and Pastiche* (Oxford:
Blackwell, 1966), 17–25.

they had come to give themselves up to him: If Darius was to make
them tyrants, then like the tyrants of the Greek cities of Asia they would
have to rule as vassals of his.

Paeonia was settled on the River Strymon: Literally, 'citied', which
will not have been true of the Paeonians in the sixth century; but cf. 15. 2–3,
and the reference to Thracian 'citizens' in 7. For their location cf. on 1. 2.

not far from the Hellespont: Cf. the story of the Paeonians and the
Perinthians in 1. 2–3. In fact the mouth of the Strymon is about 250 miles
(400 km), and the mouth of the Axius about 325 miles (520 km), from
the Hellespont in a straight line.

colonists of the Teucrians from Troy: Cf. Strabo VII fr. 38. For
Paeonians fighting for the Trojans see Hom. *Il.* II. 848–50, XVI. 287–8
(correctly locating the Paeonians on the Axius). VII. 20. 2 claims that
Mysians and Teucrians migrated from Asia to Europe before the Trojan
War; but it is in fact more likely that Mysians had migrated from Europe
to Asia (near the Propontis: as in Strabo 295 / VII. 3. 2, 586 / XII. 4.
8). The Teucrians were the Trojans, said to be descended from a hero
called Teucer (Teucrus); cf. the Teucrians of Gergis in 122. 2. The names
'Troy' (Τροία) and 'Ilium' were to some extent interchangeable, and for
Herodotus contrast 'Troy' here with 'Ilium' e.g. in I. 5. 1; but 'Troad'
remained standard for the whole region at the north-west corner of Asia
Minor (used by Herodotus in 26 and 122. 2), while 'Ilium' was the regular
name of the classical city (*Barrington Atlas* 56 C 2, *Inventory* 1009–10
no. 779: in 94. 2 and 122. 2 its territory is Ἰλιάς).

13. 3. for that indeed was precisely why they had done this: Herodotus'

explanation. Richards' πάντα for αὐτοῦ is attractive, but is perhaps not what Herodotus wrote.

14. 1. from their habitat: From their native land (a distinct sense of ἤθεα), but also, as noted by Hornblower, from their native customs.

14. 2. a horseman hurried: For Persian couriers cf. VII. 98.

the scroll: βύβλος and its diminutive βύβλιον refer to papyrus in particular and by extension to a document in any form. Cf. 58. 3.

15. 1. towards the sea … that way: It would indeed be natural for invaders of Herodotus' Paeonia to go to the mouth of the Strymon and strike inland from there.

15. 3. Siriopaeones: All of the peoples named seem to have lived around the Strymon, not around the Axius. For these cf. Siris in Paeonia, VIII. 115. 3. The *Barrington Atlas*, 51 B 2, places them in the lower Strymon valley, north of Lake Prasias (cf. below).

Paeoplae: Cf. VII. 113. 1, where they are mentioned with the Doberes (cf, 16. 1), to the north of Mount Pangaeum.

Lake Prasias: Generally identified with Tachinos (thus *Barrington Atlas* 51 B 3); but Hammond identified it with Butkova, farther upstream (*History of Macedonia*, i. 193–94: Kerkinitis in *Barrington Atlas* 50 D 2).

16. 1. But those around Mount Pangaeum … were not at first subjected by Megabazus: If this is correct, he passed through the peoples nearer to the coast to attack the Paeonians farther inland.

the Doberes, Agrianes and Odomantians: These words were deleted after ὄρος by Stein, transposed to where they are printed here by L. Weber, 'Lectiones Herodoteae', *BPW* 57 (1937), 219–24 at 220. The River Doberus flows from the west to enter the Strymon north of Lake Kerkinitis (*Barrington Atlas* 50 D 2); 49 E–F 1 places the Agrianians farther north (cf. Strabo VII fr. 36; but fr. 41 mentions Agrianians 'as far as Pangaeum'); 51 B 2 places the Odomantians farther south, on the north side of Lake Prasias. The Odomantians are mentioned in VII. 112 as near Mount Pangaeum, which is east of the Strymon near its mouth (*Barrington Atlas* 51 B–C 3).

in this way: Herodotus digresses to give an account of the lake-

dwellers, and does not return to write of the attempt to obliterate them. Understanding ὧδε with κατεικημένους ('those living in this way on the lake': cf. Macan, How and Wells) would lessen but not remove the problem.

In the middle of the lake: Hammond, *History of Macedonia*, i. 230–31, mentions evidence of pile-dwellers near the mouth of the Axius and farther west.

16. 2. a mountain ... Orbelus: To the east of the Strymon (*Barrington Atlas* 51 B 2).

16. 4. they feed on fish: Cf. Ath. VIII 345 E on cattle which were fed on fish at Mossynum in Thrace (Herodotus' Mossynoikoi, III. 94. 2, VII. 78), Plin. *H.N.* XI 281, from Theophtrastus (location not specified).

17. 1. seven Persian men: Numbered, yet not named, which Hornblower sees as helping to focalise the story through the Macedonians. Cf. the seven Persian conspirators after Cambyses' death (III. 70–71. 1) and the seven Chian conspirators before 479 (VIII. 132. 2); and on seven as a frequent number in Herodotus see Fehling, *Herodotus and His 'Sources'*, 216–17.

    to give earth and water: The standard symbols of submission to the Persian King (e.g. IV. 126; VI. 48. 2 with VII. 32, 133); in book V cf. 73. 2.

17. 2. Alexander: Alexander I, son of and successor to Amyntas, ruling from shortly after 500 to shortly before 450.

    a talent of silver every day: Probably exaggerated: this would be an enormous amount. For the mines of this region cf. VI. 46–7, Thuc. I. 100. 2–101.

    the mountain called Dysorum: 'Unseasonable', or if the *omega* is assimilated to *omicron* 'unpropitious mountain'. *Barrington Atlas* 50 D 2 places it north of Thessalonica, overlooking Lake Kerkinitis. Xerxes was to take the same inland route in 480 (VII. 124).

18. 1. When these Persians who had been sent reached Amyntas: Amyntas I, king at the end of the sixth century and the beginning of the fifth. This is presumably to be envisaged as happening at Aegeae, the old Macedonian capital to the west of the Thermaic Gulf (*Barrington Atlas* 50 B 4, *Inventory* 798–99 no. 529).

He gave these: Or the imperfect might mean only that he was willing to give these.

invited them to hospitality: What follows is a well-elaborated story; but how much or little truth is there behind the story? See especially E. Badian, 'Herodotus on Alexander I of Macedon: A Study in Some Subtle Silences', in Hornblower (ed.), *Greek Historiography*, 107–30, with citation of some earlier discussions. If Macedon did submit to Persia at this time, it slipped away in the 490s during the Ionian Revolt, and had to be reclaimed after it (VI. 44. 1). In 480–479 Alexander was on the Persian side, but was used as a go-between (VII. 173. 3, VIII. 136, 140–4), and afterwards claimed that in 479 he had benefited the Greeks (IX. 44–5). It is presumably true that Gygaea the sister of Alexander married Bubares the son of Megabazus, and probably true that Macedon paid money to the Persians (21. 2) – most probably in this period when Megabazus was campaigning in Thrace, from which Badian inferred that Macedon did submit to Persia at this time, but on its own initiative rather than in response to a Persian demand; but it can hardly be true that leading Persians were killed and the Persians were persuaded not to exact retribution. Badian argued that, since there was no record of a demand for submission, the messengers making the demand had to be invented and then to disappear without trace; but the marriage and the payment of tribute were known, and after the Persian Wars had to be presented with a suitable garnish.

18. 2–3. it is an institution among us Persians ... the institution among us is not that: For the Persian institution see M. Brosius, *Women in Ancient Persia, 559–331 BC* (Oxford UP, 1996), 94–97; that wives left when concubines remained (Heraclides of Cyme *FGrH* 689 F 2 *ap*. Ath. IV. 145 A–146 A, Plut. *Conj. Praec.* 140 B) was a Greek misunderstanding. For the Greek (and presumably Macedonian) custom of excluding women other than *hetairai* see e.g. Isae. III. *Pyrrhus* 14, [Dem.] LIX. *Neaera* 24, Theopomp. *FGrH* 115 F 204 *ap*. Ath. XII. 517 D–518 B (the Etruscans exceptional).

18. 3. since you are the masters: For the Persian King as master see Brock, *Greek Political Imagery*, 109.

18. 4. a distressing sight for their eyes: For the expression cf. Plut. *Alex*. 21. 10.

19. 1. remained calm: Cf. VIII. 16. 1, in a similar situation.

could not restrain himself: For the expression cf. Cleisthenes of Sicyon, VI. 129. 4.

19. 1–2. father … my boy: Hornblower remarks that they address each other like ordinary family members.

19. 1. everything that is appropriate for the foreigners: Cf. Proclus' *hypothesis* to the *Cypria*, §2, on Menelaus' instruction to Helen (Loeb *Greek Epic Fragments*, pp. 68–69).

19. 2. take drastic action: 'Newer' things are regularly in Greek undesirable novelties.

inflamed: This is Herodotus' only metaphorical use of the word.

20. 1. at your disposal: The solemn εὐπετείη, 'availability', is used only here by Herodotus.

20. 3. dressed in the women's clothes smooth-cheeked men: A floating story: cf. for instance the men who liberated Thebes from a pro-Spartan clique in 379, Xen. *Hell.* V. 4. 6, Plut. *Pel.* 11. 2–4; and in Herodotus I. 106. 2 (but without women or men posing as women).

20. 4. we lavish upon you: ἐπιδαψιλεύεσθαι is another solemn word used only here by Herodotus.

our own mothers and sisters: We might have expected daughters and sisters.

a Greek man: This prompts a digression in 22. Macan suggests that the Greekness or Greek sympathy of Alexander (cf. on 18. 1) is the point of the story.

governor: ὕπαρχος is Herodotus' term for a Persian satrap (provincial governor: cf. 25. 1, 27. 1), and is presumably used here together with the reference to the King to emphasise the submission which has been granted or promised; cf. 'since you are the masters', 18. 3.

21. 1. By this fate the Persians were destroyed: Cf. VII. 133. 1, on Athenian and Spartan reactions to Persian demands.

21. 2. Gygaea: An emendation in Just. *Epit.* VII. 4. 5 gives this name to a wife of Amyntas III, in the fourth century.

Bubares: Revealed in VII. 22. 2 to be a son of Megabazus. Their son was named Amyntas, and (Macedon being no longer available to the Persians) was given the revenues of 'Alabanda in Phrygia, a great city'

(perhaps Blaundus: S. Hornbower, *Mausolus* [Oxford UP, 1982], 218 with n. 2).

22. 1. these descendants of Perdiccas are Greeks: The digression is prompted by 'a Greek man' in 20. 4. As we see in Thuc. IV. 124. 1 cf. 125. 1, Macedonians could be considered intermediate between true Greeks and true barbarians.

   shall demonstrate in my later account: In VIII. 137–9 (but How and Wells, i. 15 n. 3, consider that to be 'a very meagre fulfilment' by contrast with some others).

   those who administer ... at Olympia: The *Hellanodikai* ('Greek judges'); but their appearance in A is probably an interpolated gloss.
22. 2. when Alexander wanted to compete: 'Wanted' fits the context better than the alternative 'chose'.

   not for barbarian competitors but for Greek: Cf. II. 160. 3.

   he was Argive: Cf. VIII. 137. 1: three brothers descended from Temenus of Argos were exiled and fled to Illyria; after an episode in which the youngest, Perdiccas, was revealed as a future king, they fled from there and eventually gained control of Macedon, and the subsequent kings of Macedon were descended from Perdiccas. That evidently is the claim made by the 'Argead' kings of Macedon in the fifth century (cf. Thuc. II. 99. 3, V. 80. 2). It has been accepted e.g. by Hammond, *History of Macedonia*, i. 432–34, but rejected, I think more persuasively, e.g. by E. N. Borza, *In the Shadow of Olympus: The Emergence of Macedon* (Princeton UP, 1990), 80–84. If an 'Argive' origin is to be accepted at all, we should perhaps think rather of Argos in Orestis (App. *Syr.* 333 cf. Strabo 326 / VII. 7. 7), in the mountains to the west of the heart of Macedon (*Barrington Atlas* 49 D 3).

   the foot race: The *stadion*, named after the track on which the race was held, and the length of the track (at Olympia, 192 m. or *c.* 210 yards). For the stade as a unit of measurement, cf. on 52. 1.

   came first equal: The meaning of the Greek is correctly explained by How and Wells. He does not appear in what is preserved of the Olympian victor lists (and is absent from L. Moretti, *Olympionikai: I vincitori negli antichi agoni olimpici* [*Mem. Acc. Naz. Linc.*[8] VIII (1957), ii = 53–198]): perhaps Alexander won, his opponents managed to have another man proclaimed, and the dead heat has been inferred from the divergent

claims. The occasion has often been dated 496 (e.g. M. Zahrnt, 'Herodot und die Makedonenkönige', in R. Rollinger *et al.* [eds], *Herodot und das Persische Weltreich / Herodotus and the Persian Empire* [Wiesbaden: Harrassowitz, 2011], 761–77 at 766–67), but Hornblower suspects that at about thirty-four Alexander would then be too old.

23. 1. Histiaeus ... Myrcinus: Cf. 11. 2. There follows another well developed story. It is presumably true that Histiaeus first went to Myrcinus but afterwards was summoned to Darius, and it is at least credible that this resulted from a warning by Megabazus. For the dialogue cf. Darius and Histiaeus in 106, after the sacking of Sardis at the beginning of the Ionian Revolt. Often in Herodotus and elsewhere a warning is not heeded when it ought to be (cf. Introduction, pp. 15–16): here the warning is heeded, but the involvement of Histiaeus in affairs will remain problematic.

gift ... as payment for guarding the bridge: Emendation is not necesssary.

he said this to Darius: On speeches in V–VI see L. Solmsen, *AJP* lxiv 1943, 194–207, suggesting that in the account of the Ionian Revolt speeches are used as a way of expressing judgments on what is reported. **23. 2. what a thing you have done:** Cf. VIII. 138. 1; and 'what a saying you have uttered' in 106. 3.

shipbuilding timber, many oars: I.e. timber which could be used for ships and for oars. ἴδη gave its name to Mount Ida in the Troad, another source of timber (Thuc. IV. 52. 3, Theophr. *Hist. Pl.* IV. 5. 5). For timber from Amphipolis, not far to the east of Macedon, see Thuc. IV. 108. 1.

silver mines: Cf. VI. 46–7, Thuc. I. 100. 2, 101. 3, on the gold and silver mines of Thasos and the adjacent mainland, again to the east of Macedon.

who will take him as their leader: On *prostates* see Brock, *Greek Political Imagery*, 140.

both by day and by night: Used by Greeks particularly in a Persian context: cf. Xerxes' letter to the Spartan Pausanias in Thuc. I. 129. 3.

24. 1. he could well foresee what was likely to happen: An instance of the *motif* of a prophecy's being fulfilled through an attempt to avoid fulfilment, as in the legend of Oedipus: for Histiaeus' implication in the 'domestic war' of the Ionian Revolt see 35. 2–36. 1, 106. 1–108. 1, VI. 1–5, 26–30.

not from words but from deeds: A favourite contrast of Thucydides (e.g. II. 65. 9 on the standing of Pericles in Athens) and other late-fifth-century Greeks, used several times by Herodotus.

24. 3. you had departed from my presence: The opposite of coming into the King's sight = presence, e.g. 13. 1.

24. 4. Susa: 'City of lilies', the former capital of Elam, 160 miles (250 km) north of the head of the Persian Gulf, and near the Tigris (*Barrington Atlas* 93 D 1): Darius built a palace there, and it was commonly regarded by the Greeks as the Persian capital (cf. 49. 7, 107).

my eating-companion: For the King's table-companions see Heraclides of Cyme, cited above on 18. 2–3. Herodotus uses *homotrapezos* ('together-table man') at III. 132. 1 and *homositos* ('together-eater') at VII. 119. 3; in Xen. *An.* I. 8. 25 *homotrapezos* seems to be a title. How far Histiaeus did become an honoured adviser, and how far he became a prisoner, has been much debated, but in Herodotus' account of his role in the Ionian Revolt he is presented as trusted by Darius.

25. 1. Artaphernes, his brother by the same father: Cf. 30. 5. In translating I use the more normal anglicised form; but 'Artaphrenes' is found in some manuscripts and in other texts, and is closer to the Persian form, so I print that in the Greek text.

governor of Sardis: I.e. of the Lydian province, of which Sardis was the capital.

Otanes as general of the men by the sea: In 26 he is successor to Megabazus, and his captures on the Asiatic mainland fall within the province of Hellespontine Phrygia, whose capital was near the Propontis at Dascylium (*Barrington Atlas* 52 C 4; cf. VI. 33. 3). See also 30. 5. In III. 90. 1, 127. 1, Herodotus mentions separately the Ionians, but they seem not to have formed a separate satrapy. This Otanes is not the advocate of democracy in the constitutional debate (III. 80); but he will reappear in connection with the Ionian Revolt (116, where we learn that he was married to a daughter of Darius; 123).

the royal judges: Cf. III. 31. 1–5, VII. 194. 1–2, where as here misconduct is envisaged or occurs.

and all his skin flayed: Powell, *Lexicon*, registers this as a special sense of ἀνθρωπηίη ('human'). Flaying was indeed used by the Persians as an extreme punishment (cf. R. Rollinger, 'Herodotus, Human Violence

and the Ancient Near East', in V. Karageorghis and I. Taifacos [eds], *The World of Herodotus* [Nicosia: A. G. Leventis Foundation, 2004], 121–50 at 141–42 with n. 40).

tanned: σπαδίξας is found only here, and perhaps means 'peeled off' or 'tanned'.

stretched: ἐντείνειν is normally used of stringing or drawing a bow (e.g. II. 173. 3).

in place of Sisamnes, whom he had killed and flayed: Deleted by Powell, but τὸν ἀποκτείνας ἀπέδειρε is the end of a hexameter and is more probably original.

26. became successor to Megabazus: Cf. on 25. 1.

He captured...: His briskness is reflected in a brisk narrative (cf. 117, and Introduction, p. 14).

Byzantium and Calchedon: On the European and Asiatic side respectively of the Bosporus: *Barrington Atlas* 53 A 2, B 3; *Inventory* 915–18 no. 674, 979–81 no. 743. Darius had gone to Scythia via the Bosporus (cf. on 11. 1) and a ruler of Byzantium had accompanied him (IV. 138. 1), so they must have revolted afterwards.

Antandrus: *Barrington Atlas* 56 D 2, *Inventory* 1064 no. 767.

Lamponium: Otherwise called Lamponeia. It too was in the Troad: *Barrington Atlas* 56 C 2, *Inventory* 1011 no. 783.

the Lesbians: For the island of Lesbos, near the coast of Asia Minor, whose principal city was Mytilene, see *Barrington Atlas* 56 B–D 3, *Inventory* 1018–32 nos 794–99. It was captured in time for Coes of Mytilene to be involved in Darius' Scythian campaign (cf. 11. 1).

Lemnos and Imbros: In the Aegean near the Hellespont: *Barrington Atlas* 56 A 1 and 51 F 4; *Inventory* 756–58 nos 502–503 (two cities, Myrina and Hephaestia) and 742–43 no. 483. Both were to be captured for Athens by Miltiades (Lemnos, VI. 137–40; Imbros, VI. 41. 3, 104. 1).

Pelasgians: A name given by the Greeks to a non-Greek people thought to have occupied various parts of Greece and the Aegean, including Athens (cf. 64. 2), in pre-classical times. For Pelasgians on Lemnos cf. IV. 145. 2, VI. 137–40, Thuc. IV. 109. 4.

27. 1. The Lemnians fought well: Powell's addition of the Imbrians is perhaps an improvement on rather than a correction of Herodotus' text.

Lycaretus: Cf. III. 143. 2, where expecting Maeandrius to die he has prisoners on Samos killed.

Maeandrius who had been king over Samos: Samos is one of the Aegean islands close to the coast of Asia Minor (*Barrington Atlas* 61 D 2, *Inventory* 1094–98 no. 864). For Maeandrius cf. III. 123, 142–9. He was secretary to Samos' tyrant Polycrates; and after Polycrates had been killed by the Persians he originally wanted to end the tyranny but in fact succeeded to it until he was driven out, fled to Sparta, but failed to persuade king Cleomenes to reinstate him.

27. 2. died – – – The reason: It seems clear that something is missing from the text as transmitted.

28–38. The Ionian Revolt (i)

28. a renewal of evil: The passage requires a resumption of evil, to be explained in what follows (ἀνανέωσις), rather than an easing of it (ἄνεσις). More adventurously, Griffiths suggests νέα Ἴωσι κακὰ ἦν ('there were new evils for the Ionians'), and Hornblower suggests ἀνὰ τὰς νήσους κακὰ ἦν ('there was evil throughout the islands, and evil began…').

evil began to come: Cf. in book V 97. 3; and Hom. *Il.* V. 62–3, XI. 604, *Od.* VIII. 81–2, Thuc. II. 12. 3. In 97. 3 the ships sent by Athens to take part in the Revolt are 'the beginning of evil for the Greeks and barbarians'.

for the second time: The Ionians were enslaved once by the Lydians and twice by the Persians (VI. 32 cf. I. 92. 1, 169. 2); but Herodotus' overall theme is the conflict between Greeks and Persians, and here he sets aside the Lydian conquest and begins the chain of evils with the original Persian conquest. He presents the Ionian Revolt as a disaster: cf. his comment on Aristagoras in 124. 1, that attributed to the Chians in VI. 3. 1, and on the end of the Revolt in VI. 32 (undermined by what he says of the settlement afterwards in VI. 42–3); also his comments on the approaches to Sparta and Athens and their responses, 50. 2, 97. 2.

from Naxos and Miletus: They were not implicated in the original Persian conquest, and indeed the Milesians claimed a special relationship with the Persians (I. 143. 1, 169. 2).

Naxos … first of the islands in prosperity Naxos is the largest of the islands in the southern Aegean (*Barrington Atlas* 61 A–B 3–4; *Inventory*

760–63 no. 507, with an account of its dedications at sanctuaries 763). Naxos was to be sacked and its population deported in 490 (VI. 95. 2–96).

Miletus ... its greatest height ... the glory of Ionia: *Barrington Atlas* 61 E 2, *Inventory* 1082–88 no. 854; it had a substantial plain (VI. 120. 1). Herodotus uses the verb ἀκμάζειν also of Sybaris in Italy, which later was destroyed by its rival Croton (VI. 127. 1). Miletus was to be sacked and its population deported at the end of the Ionian Revolt (VI. 18–20).

for two generations of men it had ailed: Herodotus often expresses periods of past time in terms of generations, which 'come with the story', and do not always imply the same length of time but can range from twenty-three to forty years (Rhodes, 'Herodotean Chronology Reconsidered', in *Herodotus and His World*, 58–72 at 67–68). There are references to dissension in Miletus in Plut. *Quaest. Graec.* 298 c–d, Ath. XII. 523 f–524 c. To write of a political condition in medical terms was common from Solon fr. 4. 17 West onwards: see Brock, *Greek Political Imagery*, 69–82, citing this passage at 69 with 77 n. 7. κακόν, ἀκμή and (but very rarely) καταρτ- are used by medical writers but are not peculiar to them.

the Parians rectified it: Paros is immediately to the west of Naxos: *Barrington Atlas* 61 A 3, *Inventory* 764–68 no. 509. It was often at war with Naxos in the archaic period; G. Reger in *Inventory* 765 dates this episode *c.* 525. Herodotus also uses καταρτιστήρ in connection with Mantinean involvement in Cyrene (IV. 161. 2).

29. 1. in a ... state of domestic ruin: Herodotus uses this verb also of Babylon after the Persian conquest (I. 196. 5) and of Athens when sacked in 480 (VIII. 142. 3, 144. 3).

the master of the plot: Macan saw this as a pointer to slave labour.

29. 2. assembly: Herodotus uses ἁλίη of assembly more often than ἐκκλησίη (also Persia, I. 125. 2; Thebes, V. 79. 2; Sparta, VII. 134. 2; but ἐκκλησίη only with reference to Samos, III. 142. 2); but at any rate in the hellenistic period Miletus called its assembly *ekklesia* (e.g. *Milet* I. iii 138, 143).

would take care of public property as they did of their own: Cf. Nicias in Thuc. VI. 9. 2. This is the earliest attested example of the comparison

of state and household: R. W. Brock, 'Political Imagery in Herodotus' in Karageorghis and Taifacos (above), 169–73 at 169–70; and his *Greek Political Imagery*, 25–42 ch. ii, citing this passage at 25, cf. 94.

30. 1. the bloated class: The 'fat'; cf. the recent English term 'fat cats'. Herodotus uses this term also of rich men in Chalcis (77. 2), Aegina (VI. 91. 1) and Sicilian Megara (VII. 156. 2).

the people: δῆμος can be used either of the whole (citizen) population and particularly of an assembly of it (e.g. I. 59. 4–5, but with reference to the rise of Pisistratus in Athens, V. 97. 1, VI. 104. 2) or, and by Herodotus more commonly, of the ordinary people in contrast to those in power.

30. 2. Aristagoras son of Molpagoras: At Miletus the Molpoi ('singers') were a religious group who were also politically important; and the name Molpagoras is peculiar to Miletus and places influenced by it. As the Ionian Revolt is presented as a disaster (cf. on 28), Aristagoras is unfavourably presented (cf. Introduction, pp. 16–17).

being both son-in-law and cousin of Histiaeus: Herodotus suggests that Aristagoras was the deputy of Histiaeus, who remained the 'true' tyrant (cf. 106. 1, 4, 5, using the same word as here, *epitropos*), but that was perhaps to make too regularly institutional the position of tyrant (and *epitropos* does not invariably denote a deputy: see 92. ζ. 2). Here making him merely a deputy contributes to his unfavourable presentation. In 35. 1, by contrast, Herodotus refers to his 'kingship of Miletus'; see also 37. 2, where he abdicates his tyranny, and after that abdication 49. 1, where Herodotus calls him tyrant, and 98. 2, where he calls himself tyrant. Probably Herodotus did not consciously ask himself what Aristagoras' formal position was, but in each context used formulations appropriate to that context.

guest-friends: A relationship based on reciprocity in giving support when needed. It was an upper-class phenomenon which gave men access to members of the upper class in other cities, and through them to those cities. See especially G. Herman, *Ritualised Friendship and the Greek City* (Cambridge UP, 1987).

30. 3. asked Aristagoras if … they could be restored: For one party to a civil dissension to invoke the help of an external power was very common in Greece: cf. e.g. the appeal by Isagoras of Athens to Cleomenes of Sparta against Cleisthenes (70. 1).

30. 4. cannot myself undertake: A rare and solemn word, used by Herodotus also when Artabanus says to Xerxes than no harbour is capable of accommodating the large Persian fleet (VII. 49. 2).

eight thousand shields: Eight thousand hoplites, heavy infantry. This seems an improbably high estimate for Naxos (How and Wells; cf. M. H. Hansen, *The Shotgun Method: The Demography of the Ancient Greek City-State Culture* (U. of Missouri P., 2006], 81–82).

long ships: Warships, as opposed to στρογγύλαι ('round') merchant ships (mentioned I. 163. 2).

30. 5. Artaphernes ... is a son of Hystaspes, and a brother of King Darius: For Darius as son of Hystaspes see I. 209. 2; for Artaphernes as brother of Darius cf. 25. 1.

rules over all the coastal people in Asia: How this relates to the position of Otanes in 25. 1 (παραθαλασσίων there, ἐπιθαλασσίων here) is unclear; but as noted above Otanes seems not to have excercised that command in Artaphernes' satrapy.

30. 6. none of these islands was yet under Darius: Persia's control at this stage seems to have been limited to islands close to the Asiatic mainland: Samos (III. 142–7, IV. 138. 2), Chios (IV. 138. 2), Lesbos (cf. on 26), Lemnos and Imbros (26–7). Hude was probably right to delete 'the Cyclades' as a gloss, in view of the way they are mentioned in 31. 2.

31. 1. not of a great size ... near to Ionia: Neither of those points is true. Herodotus presumably expected his audience to realise that and to think that Aristagoras misled Artaphernes.

slaves: Hornbower sees this as ambiguous between people who were already slaves and people who could be enslaved by the Persians.

31. 2. a great sum of money: Cf. the Naxians' offer in 30. 6.

we who are taking you there: Hornblower sees further ambiguity here, with ἄγοντας suggesting either guiding or leading in the sense of commanding.

Paros, Andros and the rest of what are called the Cyclades: For Paros cf. 28. Andros is the first of a string of islands continuing the line of Euboea to the south-east (*Barrington Atlas* 57 C 4, *Inventory* 736–7 no. 475). The Cyclades were the islands of the southern Aegean, so called because they encircled the sacred island of Delos (*Barrington Atlas* 57 D 4, *Inventory* 738–40 no. 478).

31. 3. Euboea: A long, narrow island, close to the east coast of mainland Greece (*Barrington Atlas* B–C 3; *Inventory* 643–63 nos 364–77).

no smaller than Cyprus: In fact Cyprus is almost three times the size of Euboea in area, and somewhat greater in its maximum length; but Herodotus' audience may have been less likely to realise this error. Cyprus had submitted to Persia at the time of Cambyses' campaign against Egypt (III. 19. 3, 91. 1).

very easy to capture: Though not as large as Aristagoras is made to suggest, Euboea with its several cities would have been much more difficult to capture than the separate islands of the Cyclades. In Herodotus, what a speaker says will be easy commonly turns out not to be easy.

The Persians' first venture beyond the straits into Europe took them into Thrace, and then first north across the Danube against the Scythians and next westwards towards Macedon. The question arises how soon they became seriously interested in the Aegean islands and mainland Greece. In III. 125. 1, 129–38, Herodotus told a novelistic story of Democedes, a doctor from Croton in southern Italy, who went with Polycrates of Samos to Sardis, cured Darius of a foot injury and then cured Darius' wife Atossa of a breast abscess. He wanted to return home, and so induced Atossa to incite Darius to attack Greece rather than Scythia. Darius kept to his Scythian plan, but sent a reconnaissance party with Democedes as guide to Greece and Italy. In Italy Democedes managed to escape, and the Persians were captured but eventually ransomed. Some later texts mention Democedes (see *Vorsokr.* 19), and it is credible that he did go to Sardis with Polycrates and became a doctor at the Persian court but eventually returned to Croton (cf. M. M. Austin, 'Greek Tyrants and the Persians, 546–479 BC', *CQ*² xl 1990, 289–306 at 299; and even the sceptical A. H. Griffiths, 'Democedes of Croton: A Greek Doctor at Darius' Court', *Achaemenid History* ii 1987, 37–51, is prepared to accept those basic details [p. 46]). Whether or not there is any truth in the story of Democedes' homeward journey, it is true that in Europe Darius first headed for Scythia.

By the time of this episode the Persians had received the ex-tyrant Hippias from Athens, and the Athenians had refused Artaphernes' order to take him back (cf. 65. 3, 91, 94. 1, 96); but apart from this foray against Naxos there is no further sign of Persian interest in the Aegean and Greece until after the Ionian Revolt, which had received support

from Athens and Eretria, when Darius sent heralds to demand the submission of the Greeks (VI. 48. 1–49. 1, probably to be dated not 491/0 where Herodotus mentions it but 493/2: W. G. Forrest, 'The Tradition of Hippias' Expulsion from Athens', *GRBS* x 1969, 277–86 at 285; Rhodes, in *Herodotus and His World*, 61–62).

31. 4. one hundred ships … two hundred: For Herodotus the conventional figure for a full Persian fleet is 600 ships (IV. 87. 1, VI. 9. 1, 95. 2), and the fleet which attacked Greece in 480 was just over 1,200 (VII. 89–95, 184. 1).

at the beginning of spring: If we calculate back from 490, this will be the spring of 499 (Rhodes, in *Herodotus and His World*, 60–62).

But the King too needs to join in approving this: How far the satraps needed to obtain the King's approval for action is uncertain (according to Diod. Sic. XV. 41. 5 they had very little freedom), but it is unlikely that Artaphernes could have mustered so large an expedition without support from the King.

32. 1. he was delighted: Hornbower notes that this is sinister, referring to delight which will be short-lived.

he prepared two hundred triremes: It appears from what follows that these were commandeered from the Greek cities. The trireme, with three banks of oars and a crew of *c.* 200, was replacing the simpler fifty-oared penteconter as the standard Greek warship in the years around 500 (see also on 85. 1).

Persians and the other allies: Herodotus forgets himself: the men enlisted for the campaign will have been Persian subjects rather than allies.

Megabates … of the Achaemenids … Darius: Megabates was perhaps the father of the Megabazus who is one of the commanders of the Persian fleet in VII. 97 (Burn, *Persia and the Greeks*, 335). Achaemenes as ancestor of the Persian Kings was stressed by Darius, and was perhaps invented in a genealogy designed to justify Darius' claim to the throne: cf. III. 75. 1–2, VII. 11. 2; and Darius' Behistun Inscription §§1–4 (e.g. Kuhrt, *The Persian Empire*, i. 141–58).

whose daughter was taken in marriage by Pausanias … tyrant of Greece: Herodotus goes beyond the end of his history in 479: for such a *prolepsis* to mention a future detail see Introduction, p. 14. Pausanias'

father Cleombrotus became king in 480 after the death of his brother Leonidas at Thermopylae; when Cleombrotus died in 480/79 his own son Pausanias became regent for Plistarchus, the presumably younger son of Leonidas, and so he commanded the Greeks' land forces in 479 (IX. 10). He then commanded the Greeks' naval forces in 478: cf. Thuc. I. 94. 1–95. 5, 128. 3–7, where it is alleged that Pausanias behaved arrogantly (Herodotus has a reference to that in VIII. 3. 2), was recalled and put on trial, then returned privately to the region of the Hellespont and wrote to Xerxes offering to rule Greece as a Persian vassal and to marry Xerxes' own daughter. That and the story told here by Herodotus are evidently variants on a rumour current at the time, and we cannot tell what truth lies behind the suspicions.

33. 1 ostensibly for the Hellespont, but when he was at Chios he kept his ships at Caucasa: See the smaller-scale map *Barrington Atlas* 57: Chios (first mentioned in I. 142. 4, 160. 3–161: *Inventory* 1064–69 no. 840; cf. on 30. 6) is well out of the way for a voyage from Miletus to Naxos. 56 B 5 tentatively places Caucasa in the north-west of the island ('SE' in Hornblower is a slip).

Herodotus gives us another vivid story, exemplifying as Hornblower remarks the clash of Greek and Persian cultures, of which we have to ask where fact ends and embroidery begins. It was presumably a publicly-known fact that the fleet went via Chios rather than directly to Naxos, and that the Naxians got to know of what was intended and were prepared when the attackers arrived. It may be true that Megabates and Anaxagoras quarrelled over Megabates' treatment of Scylax, but it is hard to believe that Anaxagoras addressed Megabates as he does in Herodotus' story or that Megabates deliberately undermined the campaign of which, as far as the Persians were concerned, he was the commander; and it is easy to suppose that, in spite of the feint to Chios and what Herodotus says in 34. 1, news of what the Naxian exiles had planned with Anaxagoras and the Persians had reached the party in control of Naxos.

33. 2. were not bound to be brought to ruin: For the expression cf. I. 8. 2, IV. 79. 1, V. 92. δ. 1, VI. 135. 3. The Naxians were brought to ruin in 490 (cf. on 28: for Hornblower's '**96** below' read VI. 96), and there is no need to think of the suppression of their later revolt against Athens.

Myndian ... Scylax: For Myndus in Caria see *Barrington Atlas* 61 E

3, *Inventory* 1129 no. 914. The word *skylax* means 'puppy'; the explorer Scylax was from nearby Caryanda (IV. 44. 1).

partitioning him: Stein suggested διέλκοντας ('dragging him through') and Powell διέχοντας ('thrusting him through'), but the manuscripts' text is not obviously wrong.

through a lower oar-port: The 'thalamian' oarports were the lowest and largest (Morrison, Coates and Rankov, *The Athenian Trireme*², 41, 131–32).

33. 4. obey me and sail wherever I order: Hornblower notes that Aristagoras had some justification in that he was paying for the campaign, 'but he goes preposterously further than that'.

34. 1. For the Naxians had no expectation at all: Necessary for the story, but see on 33. 1.

brought their things from the fields inside the wall: Except in the largest cities, while many citizens worked land in the countryside most of them actually lived in the city (cf. Hansen, in *Inventory* 74–79). Cf. at the beginning of the Peloponnesian War the Plataeans (Thuc. II. 5. 7), and the exceptional Athenians when they adopted a policy of abandoning the countryside to the invaders (Thuc. II. 13. 2, 14–16).

34. 3. built forts for the Naxian exiles: Cf. the oligarchs on Mount Istone in opposition to and attacking the democrats in the city, in Corcyra in the civil war of the 420s (Thuc. III. 85. 1, IV. 2. 3, 46. 1).

35. 1. he might be deprived of his kingship of Miletus: See on 30. 2, where Aristagoras was represented as deputy of the absent Histiaeus.

that the man with a tattooed head had arrived: What must have been a well-known story is introduced as well known, and then is explained. For other concealed messages cf. I. 123. 3–4 (where again the roads are guarded), VII. 239. 2–4 (where the same is implied).

35. 2. he chose to revolt: Herodotus represents the Ionian Revolt as brought about by Aristagoras and Histiaeus for personal reasons; but they could not have brought about the Revolt unless there was a wider body of dissatisfaction with Persian rule, and perhaps a feeling that the Persians were not invincible, on which they could build, and later in the narrative there are references to deliberation by the Ionians (cf. on 108. 2). See Introduction, p. 36. In VI. 3 Histiaeus claims (falsely, according

to Herodotus) that Darius was planning to move the Ionians to Phoenicia and the Phoenicians to Ionia, and it is possible that Histiaeus had heard that move planned or at least talked of and that the purpose of his message was to warn Aristagoras of that plan: for such transplantations cf. that of the Paeonians (12–15).

35. 3. as I have said before: Just a few lines before, not as elsewhere a cross reference to a different part of the work.

35. 4. he had great hope that … he would be released to go to the sea: This is consistent with Herodotus' view that Darius trusted Histiaeus (cf. on 24. 4); but he does not regard Histiaeus as happy in his position. On what Histiaeus actually hoped for, at this point and later, see Introduction, pp. 36–38. The verb μεθίστημι is often used of releasing prisoners (e.g. I. 24. 7).

36. 2. Hecataeus the prose-writer: He is given the same description in 125 and II. 143. 1 (and VI. 137. 1 refers to his *logoi*); otherwise Herodotus applies it only to Aesop, in II. 134. 3 – but prose-writing was after all a new art in Herodotus' time, and there will not have been many distinguished practitioners of it. Hecataeus wrote about geography and about the legends of Greek families; for Hecataeus and Herodotus see Introduction, p. 13. For the kind of advice which he gives, as a warner whose advice ought to be heeded but is not, cf. the options discussed in 124–6 (again involving Hecataeus), the advice of Bias or another to Croesus in I. 27, and the advice of Bias and Thales to the Ionians in I. 170, and see Introduction, pp. 15–16.

reviewing all the peoples whom Darius ruled and his power: Cf. Herodotus' catalogues in III. 89–96, VII. 61–80; also in book V 49, 52–4.

to see that they became masters of the sea: The narrative of the campaign against Naxos showed that for ships in the Aegean the Persians depended on their Greek subjects.

36. 3. he knew that the condition of Miletus was weak: Contrast what was said of Miletus' prosperity in 28, and Aristagoras' ability to fund the campaign against Naxos; but (as the course of the Ionian Revolt was to show) on land the Persians could when given time bring to bear much stronger forces than those deployed against them in any particular place.

the temple at Branchidae: About 10 miles (16 km) south of Miletus, in its territory and linked to it by a sacred way (I. 157. 3: see *Barrington*

Atlas 61 E 3, *Inventory* 1059, the latter classifying it as a non-*polis* settlement). The temple was dedicated to Apollo. The place was called Didyma: Herodotus uses that name in VI. 19. 2–3 (quoting a verse oracle and then repeating the name), Branchidae, the name of a priestly family controlling the sanctuary, regularly elsewhere (e.g. I. 46. 3, among the oracles tested by Croesus).

which Croesus the Lydian had dedicated: Cf. I. 92. 2 (but the oracle of the Branchidae did not pass Croesus' test).

the enemy would not be able to pillage them: At the end of the Ionian Revolt Miletus and the sanctuary were sacked, and the Milesians and the Branchidae were deported: the Milesians to the Persian Gulf (VI. 18–20), and the Branchidae to central Asia, where their alleged descendants were killed by the forces of Alexander the Great (Diod. Sic. XVII. *arg.* 2. 20, Curt. VII. 5. 28–35, Strabo 517–8 / XI. 11. 4, wrongly attributing the deportation to Xerxes).

36. 4. as I have indicated in the first of my accounts: In I. 92. 2 (cf. above); but this does not prove that the division into nine books was made by Herodotus himself (cf. Introduction, pp. 1–2).

That opinion did not prevail: νικᾶν is frequently used in this sense, from Homer (e.g. *Il.* I. 576, *Od.* X. 46) onwards. Herodotus uses the same expression in 118. 3.

to Myus: Originally on the coast, but by the time of Strabo, at the end of the first century BC and the beginning of the first AD, owing to the silting of the Maeander it was inland, upstream from Miletus (*Barrington Atlas* 61 E 2, *Inventory* 1088–89 no. 856; cf. Strabo 636 / XIV. 1. 10).

37. 1. Iatragoras: Presumably a Milesian; and Hornblower notes that the name though rare is attested in fifth-century Miletus (*Milet* I. iii 122. i. 107).

Olliatus son of Ibanollis of Mylasa: Caria was at the south-west corner of Asia Minor; the Carians were not Greeks, but their history was bound up with that of the eastern Greeks over a long period, and the eastern Greeks and the Carians influenced each other. Mylasa (*Barrington Atlas* 61 F 3, *Inventory* 1128–29 no. 913), inland from the Gulf of Iasus, was the capital of Caria. Before the fourth century the town was probably on the hill of Peçin Kale, to the south (J. M. Cook, 'Some Sites of the Milesian Territory', *BSA* lvi 1961, 90–101 at 98–101; G. E. Bean, *Turkey*

Beyond the Maeander [London: Murray, ²1989], 14, 30–32); Strabo 659 / XIV. 2. 23 mentions a harbour town at Physcus. Olliatus and his father Ibanollis have suitably Carian-looking names.

Histiaeus son of Tymnes of Termera: Termera, also in Caria, was at the west end of the peninsula on which Halicarnassus stood, and was one of the cities synoecised into Halicarnassus by Mausolus in the fourth century (*Barrington Atlas* 61 E 4, *Inventory* 1134–35 no. 937). Histiaeus was ruling again in 480 (VII. 98), and his son Tymnes is a rare ruler appearing in some of the Delian League's tribute quota lists (e.g. *IG* i³ 271. i. 84, with Termera entered separately at ii. 77).

Coes son of Erxandrus (to whom Darius had presented Mytilene): Cf. 11. 1–2. His father's name is not given there but was given in IV. 97. 2.

Aristagoras son of Heraclides of Cyme: Cyme was an Aeolian city, to the north (*Barrington Atlas* 56 D 4, *Inventory* 1043–45 no. 817). This Aristagoras was one of the tyrants at Darius' Danube bridge (IV. 138. 2).

contriving all that he could against Darius: For Aristagoras' 'contriving' cf. 30. 4; and for 'contriving all against' cf. 62. 2.

37. 2. he in theory laid aside his tyranny: This use of *logos* implies a contrast with deed or reality, *ergon* (cf. on 24. 1). In what follows, he expels tyrants elsewhere (37. 2–38. 2), goes to seek help from Sparta and Athens (38. 2, 49–51, where in 49. 1 Herodotus calls him tyrant of Miletus, 55, 65. 5, 97), invites the deported Paeonians to return home (98, in §2 calling himself tyrant of Miletus), appoints the commanders of the Milesians who attack Sardis (99), appeals to the Athenians not to withdraw (103. 1), and only after the Persians have begun to strike back considers withdrawal and does withdraw to Myrcinus, appointing an *epitropos* in his place (124–6). V. B. Gorman, *Miletos: The Ornament of Ionia* [U. of Michigan P., 2001], 140–41, suggests that after he resigned his tyranny he was appointed to a position of command by the Ionian *koinon* (for which see on 108. 1); but Herodotus clearly thinks on occasions of Aristagoras' remaining as ruler of Miletus. Nevertheless the claim that 'he in theory laid aside his tyranny', and then 'did the same for the rest of Ionia', is strange: so Griffiths *ap.* Hornblower suggests, instead of 'in theory', 'to the people'; and Wilson, 'at a meeting'.

creating legal equality for Miletus: Herodotus uses *isonomie* also of democracy in his Persian debate (III. 80. 6, 83. 1), and of Maeandrius'

attempt to resign his tyranny in Samos (III. 142. 3); cf. *isegorie* ('equality of speech': V. 78) and *isokratie* ('equality of power', V. 92. α. 1, said by the Corinthians) of Athens after the ending of the Pisistratid tyranny. There is a good case for thinking that these *iso-* words were used of free régimes in the years around 500, and that *demokratia* was a later coinage (e.g. K. A. Raaflaub, 'Equalities and Inequalities in Athenian Democracy' in J. Ober and C. Hedrick [eds], *Demokratia* [Princeton UP, 1996], 139–74, esp. 143–50); Thuc. III. 82. 8 in his discussion of *stasis* contrasts the slogans of *isonomia politike* on the democratic side and *aristokratia sophron* ('prudent') on the oligarchic; but in Thuc. III. 62. 3 the Thebans with reference to 480–479 contrast an *oligarchia isonomos* with the rule of a narrow clique, *dynasteia*.

38. 1. Coes … stoned him to death: Stoning by the populace was often the fate of men perceived as public enemies: in Herodotus cf. I. 166–7 (Phocaeans captured by Etruscans of Agylla after the battle of Alalia), IX. 4–5 (an Athenian who favoured granting an audience to Mardonius' emissary in 479), IX. 116–20 (the son of Artaÿctes – himself put to death by another means – who had looted the sanctuary of Protesilaus at Elaeus). See A. S. Pease, *TAPA* 38 (1907), 5–18, noting that stoning was not used by Greeks or Romans as a lawful punishment, as it was by the Persians and the Jews.

    but the Cymaeans … the others set theirs free: This suggests that the tyrants were not universally unpopular. We have to wait to learn what became of the deposed tyrants (cf. Introduction, pp. 14–15): the Persians' attempt later in the Ionian Revolt to use them to win back the cities was unsuccessful, but Herodotus suggests that the plan was mismanaged rather than rebuffed on principle (VI. 9–10); the Samians did eventually desert as their ex-tyrant Aeaces had advised (VI. 13. 2). In 492 tyrants were ruling again and were deposed again by Mardonius (VI. 43. 3) – unless, as Hornblower suggests, all Mardonius did was accept a *fait accompli*.

38. 2. told them: He was not in a position to issue orders to other cities, but κελεύειν is frequently less strong than that.

    he went as an emissary in a trireme to Sparta: His visit to Sparta and Athens will have been in 499/8 (Rhodes, in *Herodotus and His World*, 63).

39–54. Sparta.

For the articulation of this section see Introduction, p. 7, and the more detailed summary of book V on p. 44. The long digressions on Sparta and Athens serve to delay Herodotus' treatment of the actual outbreak of the Ionian Revolt, and to make it more effective when at last it occurs (cf. Introduction, p. 14).

39. 1. In Sparta Anaxandridas ... had died: This is presented as a sequel to the account of Sparta in the time of Croesus, in I. 65–8; cf. the comparable accounts of Athens in the time of Aristagoras (55–97) and in the time of Croesus (I. 59–64). This sentence is true of Sparta when Anaxagoras visited, but Herodotus backtracks to explain how Cleomenes became king.

Sparta had two kings, allegedly descended from twin descendants of Heracles, and in fact probably representing the amalgamation of two communities at an early stage in Sparta's history. They retained considerable powers, as commanders of Spartan armies and as *ex officio* members of the *gerousia* (on which cf. 40. 1). In the Agid line, whose genealogy Herodotus gives in VII. 204, Anaxandridas was king *c.* 560–520; for the Eurypontid line see on 75. 1, and the genealogy in VIII. 131. 2–3.

Cleomenes ... in accordance not with personal merit but with descent: Spartan kings always did succeed in accordance with descent, though there were some cases such as this where who had the strongest claim might be disputed. How Cleomenes became king is explained in what follows, with the allegation, sustained throughout the narrative, that he was lacking in personal merit but his rival Dorieus was well endowed with it (cf. Introduction, p. 16). Presumably this is how the two men were viewed by Herodotus' Spartan informants when he was making his enquiries. *Andragathie* is the quality of being an *aner agathos*, possessing such 'manly' virtues as being a good warrior and hunter.

Anaxandridas had as wife ... they had no sons: For similar trouble in Sparta's other royal line see VI. 61–9; and the story has Biblical parallels (Sarai and Hagar, *Genesis* 16, 20–21; Rachel and Leah, *Genesis* 29–30; Hannah and Peninnah, *I Samuel* 1). Marriage with his niece will have been a strategy to keep the property within the family (cf. S. J. Hodkinson, *Property and Wealth in Classical Sparta* [London: Duckworth for Swansea: Classical P. of Wales, 2000], 101–102).

39. 2. the ephors summoned him: While Sparta was unusual in its retention of two kings, it also had five officials elected annually from all the full citizens, the ephors ('overseers'), who counterbalanced the kings and had considerable executive power.

we cannot overlook: Etymologically appropriate to the ephors.

that the line of Eurysthenes should be obliterated: Herodotus' only other use of ἐξίτηλος is in I. *praef.*: he wrote his history 'so that the deeds of men should not be obliterated in the course of time'.

the Spartiates: The full citizens of Sparta (whereas 'Lacedaemonians' could, though it did not always, include the *perioikoi*, free men running their own communities but subordinate to the Spartiates in foreign policy, as well as the Spartiates).

40. 1. the ephors and the elders debated: Twenty-eight elders, men over sixty from a limited range of families, elected for what remained of their lives, with the two kings formed the *gerousia*, the council which had considerable direct power and which presented motions to the assembly of Spartiates. On the kings and the *gerousia* see VI. 56–9.

40. 2. he had two wives and maintained two households, a totally un-Spartiate practice: Literally, 'maintained two hearths'. D. M. MacDowell, *Spartan Law* (Edinburgh: Scottish Academic P., 1986), 82–88, notes that normally a Spartiate could have sexual relations with a second woman in order to produce children, but could not at the same time have two wives. Evidently in the case of a king needing an heir it was thought essential that the heir should be the son of the king and his wife.

41. 1. She revealed him to the Spartiates as king in waiting: Her duty was to bear an heir, and it had to be made public that she had done so. An *ephedros* is literally an athletic contestant waiting to compete against the winner of a previous bout (e.g. Pind. *Nem.* 4. 96).

41. 3. who had come in second, being the daughter of Prinetadas son of Demarmenus: Maas deleted the whole of this here, and inserted 'being the daughter of Prinetadas son of Demarmenus' after 'the previous wife' in §1, which would be logically more satisfying but is not necessarily what Herodotus wrote. This editor thinks of innumerable media reports in which 'thirty-year-old father of two' *vel sim.* is inserted in a sentence

to which the details have no relevance, when they have not been given earlier. Demarmenus was the name of the father of Chilon, who had a daughter who was to have married Leotychidas in the other royal house but who was preempted by Leotychidas' relative and predecessor as king, Demaratus (VI. 65. 2): Hornblower quotes an unpublished note by H. T Wade-Gery, which to ease generational problems postulates two men called Demarmenus in the same family.

42. 1. Cleomenes … was not of sound mind but was slightly mad: Cf. III. 25. 2 on the Persian Cambyses, IX. 55. 2 on the Spartan Amompharetus, each combining a negative and a positive and each using φρενήρης with the negative. Cleomenes' madness is reaffirmed at VI. 75. 1, and Herodotus' presentation of him, presumably based on the Spartan view of him when Herodotus made his enquiries, is consistently unfavourable. In fact he seems to have believed in a strong role for himself within Sparta, and to have been in trouble only towards the end of his reign (VI. 61–84).

Dorieus … in accordance with personal merit he would have the kingship: Dorieus is praised as Cleomenes is denigrated; for personal merit and the kingship cf. 39. 1 with commentary.

42. 2. he asked the Spartiates for a body of men: So he was not simply an indivdual departing in dudgeon, but led an expedition which had official approval. If Sybaris was destroyed in 510/09 (cf. on 44. 1), failure in the third year (42. 3) will put the beginning of this venture *c.* 513, some time after Cleomenes had succeeded to the throne. E. Will, *N. Clio* 7–9 (1955–57), 127–32, compares Miltiades' departure from Pisistratid Athens in VI. 35. 3.

though he did not ask the oracle at Delphi … or do any of the customary things: So we should not be surprised that his venture came to grief. Consultation of an oracle, commonly that at Delphi, before founding a colony was not an absolute requirement, but it was normal practice and omission of it could be invoked to explain a failure. On Herodotus and oracles see Introduction, pp. 19–21. In the Greek, χρηστηρίῳ χρησάμενος is alliterative.

they were guided by men of Thera: Thera, in the southern Aegean (*Barrington Atlas* 61 A 5, *Inventory* 782–84 no. 527), was believed to be a colony of Sparta, and had itself *c.* 638–630 sent the first Greek

colonists to Libya, who finally settled at Cyrene (*Barrington Atlas* 38 C 1, *Inventory* 1243–47 no. 1028). See IV. 145–58, to which Herodotus makes no cross reference here. Nenci notes that the involvement of Thera here does not mean that Cyrene was hostile to the project.

42. 3. On arrival in Libya he settled the finest site ... by the River Cinyps: Not where the Greek colonies were, but in western Libya near the later Lepcis Magna (*Barrington Atlas* 35 G 2, *Inventory* 1243 no. 1027). It is mentioned in IV. 175, 2, 198. 1; the fourth-century *periplous* known as Pseudo-Scylax mentions it as deserted (109: *GGM* i. 85).

by the Macian Libyans and the Carthaginians: The Macians are mentioned immediately before Cinyps at IV. 175. 1; *Barrington Atlas* 35 places them inland from Cinyps. The Phoenician colony of Carthage was about 350 miles (550 km) north-west of Cinyps (in a straight line, across the sea).

43. Eleon: Or Heleon (*Barrington Atlas* 55 E 4, *Inventory* 434 cf. 453 under no. 220 Tanagra): it was part of the *tetrakomia* forming part of rhe *polis* of Tanagra (Strabo 405 / IX. 2. 14).

the oracles of Laïus: Laïus was the legendary father of Oedipus, of nearby Thebes: there is no other mention of a collection of oracles associated with him, but this is not implausible and emendation to another name is not justified.

Heraclea in Sicily: Not in *Barrington Atlas*, but presumably in the north-west of the island (cf. on Eryx, below), *Inventory* 197–98 no. 21. Several Spartan colonies were called Heraclea, because of the Spartan kings' legendary descent from Heracles (cf. on 39. 1).

all the land of Eryx ... Heracles himself had gained it: Eryx was a mountain and a settlement of the Elymians, who claimed descent from the Trojans, in the far north-west of the island (*Barrington Atlas* 47 B 2, not in *Inventory*, Thuc. VI. 2. 3). In a foundation myth supporting Greek claims to the west of the island, Heracles was said to have defeated the local ruler Eryx (Diod. Sic. IV. 23. 1–3).

the Pythia: A woman appointed for life, who made the oracular pronouncements.

made his way past Italy: Ships travelling between Greece and Sicily normally kept close to the south of Italy rather than crossing the open sea.

44. 1. as the Sybarites say: Some Sybarites survived this defeat and there were later refoundations of the city (eventually as Thurii, where Herodotus is said to have ended his life: cf. Introduction, pp. 1–3), so there could have been Sybarites to tell the story when Herodotus was making his enquiries.

the Sybarites … were about to campaign against Croton: Sybaris (*Barrington Atlas* 46 D 2, *Inventory* 295–99 no. 70, where the city destroyed on this occasion is Sybaris I) and Croton (46 F 3, 266–70 no. 56) were both Achaean colonies of the late seventh century on the west side of the gulf between the 'toe' and the 'heel' of Italy. Croton was the home city of the doctor Democedes (cf. on 31. 3). Diod. Sic. XI. 90. 3 dates the destruction of Sybaris 510/09.

their king Telys: In the Crotoniate version he is tyrant (44. 2).

44. 2. The Sybarites say … but the Crotoniates say…: It suits Sybaris to ascribe its defeat to Spartan intervention, and it suits Croton to ascribe it to divine support.

Callias of the Iamidae, a seer from Elis: For this family cf. IX. 33–5, Pind. *Ol.* 6. 71–4.

45. 1. there is a precinct and temple by the dried-up Crathis … founded for Athena with the cult name Crathias: *Barrington Atlas* shows the river, named after a river in Achaea (I. 145).

45. 2. land set aside: ἐξαίρετος is used of what is set aside as a perquisite for somebody.

to my time: A favourite expression of Herodotus to indicate the continuation of something from the past: in book V cf. 77. 3, 88. 3, 115. 1; also 86. 3.

it is possible to go along with whichever one finds persuasive: On Herodotus' citing alternative versions in this way, and on his choosing or refusing to choose between them, see Introduction, p. 9–10.

46. 1. Thessalus, Paraebatas, Celeas and Euryleon: Hornblower notes that the names all have an equestrian/athletic flavour, appropriate to mobile and 'derailing' men liable to take action which upsets the course of events: cf. on this whole episode his *Thucydides and Pindar* (Oxford UP, 2004), 301–306.

the Phoenicians and Egestaeans: VII. 158. 2 mentions only the

Egestaeans in this connection; but refers to Phoenician *emporia* in the north-west of the island. It is credible that the Phoenicians should have opposed Dorieus in the region of Eryx. Egesta (Segesta in its own language but Egesta to the Greeks) was an Elymian settlement inland, south-east of Eryx (*Barrington Atlas* 47 B 3, not in *Inventory*).

only Euryleon survived this disaster: For the common *motif* of the sole survivor (e.g. *Hom. Hymn* 7. *Dionysus* 51–7) cf. 85. 2. In VI. 27. 2 there are two survivors in one instance, one in another.

46. 2. Minoa the colony of Selinus: Heraclea Minoa, on the south coast between Selinus and Acragas (*Barrington Atlas* 47 C 4, *Inventory* 196–97 no. 20; Hornblower p. 159 reverses the order of *Inventory*'s two Heracleas); after this episode it came under the control of Acragas. Selinus (47 B 3, *Inventory* 220–24 no. 44) was founded from the Sicilian Megara *c.* 628/7.

their ruler Peithagoras: Not mentioned elsewhere.

at the altar of Zeus Agoraios: Zeus of the agora, a common cult title of Zeus. Cf. the killing of Cylon's supporters in Athens (71).

47. 1. with his own trireme and his own force of men: The manuscripts' 'and his own expense of men' reads so strangely as to justify the emendation. The complex trireme with its large crew (cf. on 32. 1) was an expensive ship to build and to man, and only a very rich man could manage to do that: for Herodotus' other instance cf. Cleinias of Athens in VII. 17 (and Cleinias' great-grandson Alcibiades in Thuc. VI. 50. 1, 61. 6).

He was an Olympic victor: Perhaps in 520 (L. Moretti, *Olympionikai: I vincitori negli antichi agoni olimpici* [*Mem. Acc. Naz. Linc.*[8] viii (1957), ii = 53–198]). In the archaic period many of the competitors in the great games were prominent men in their cities: cf. in Herodotus Cylon of Athens (71. 1), Timesitheus of Delphi (72. 4 with Paus. VI. 8. 6), Eualcides of Eretria (102. 3), Damaratus of Sparta (VI. 70. 3), Cimon of Athens (VI. 103. 2), Callias of Athens (VI. 122. 1), Alcmaeon of Athens (VI. 125. 5), Cleisthenes of Sicyon (VI.126. 2), Phaÿllus of Croton (VIII. 47), Hieronymus of Andros (IX. 33. 2); also Alexander of Macedon (22).

the most handsome of the men of his time: Athletes (who competed naked: e.g. Thuc. I. 6. 5) were considered to embody human physical perfection (cf. e.g. Pind. *Ol.* 8. 17–19, 9. 94, 111); but we do not know the basis for Herodotus' saying this about Philippus. Another handsome

man in Herodotus is the Persian Tigranes (IX. 96. 2); Hornblower notes an athlete (a wrestler) who was not handsome (Pind. *Isthm.* 4. 53–5).

47. 2. he won: The verb is used of winning prizes in the games (Powell's sense I. 4 of φέρω).

at his tomb they founded a hero's shrine, and they sacrifice to propitiate him: On the heroisation of athletes see B. Currie, 'Euthymos of Locri: A Case Study in Heroization in the Classical Period' *JHS* 122 (2002), 24–44; *Pindar and the Cult of Heroes* (Oxford UP, 2005), 120–57. θύειν ('sacrifice') and cognates, and ἱλάσκεσθαι ('propitiate'), can be used either of a god (e.g. I. 50. 1) or of a hero. On heroes cf. Introduction, p. 19.

48. Cleomenes did not rule for a long time: This is palpably untrue: he was king by 519 (VI. 108 with Thuc. III. 68. 5), and we have seen that Dorieus began his travels *c.* 513 (cf. on 42. 2); and he remained king until shortly before 490 (VI. 49–93 with Rhodes, in *Herodotus and His World*, 60–62). Some have tried to ease the problem by emendation, here or elsewhere, but it is more likely that this untruth was part of the hostile account of Cleomenes which Herodotus heard in Sparta.

he died without a son: Stated more explicitly in VII. 205. 1 (cf. VI. 71. 2 on Leotychidas).

leaving a sole daughter, whose name was Gorgo: She will play an important part in this story below (51), and later as the wife of Leonidas (VII. 239. 4).

49. 1. So Aristagoras the tyrant of Miletus came to Sparta when Cleomenes was ruling: Herodotus resumes his main narrative, echoing the first sentence of this section (39. 1).

a bronze tablet on which the circuit of the whole earth was engraved: This must have been not just a list but some kind of map, perhaps showing the Royal Road, which Herodotus will describe in 52–4. The first Greek said to have drawn a map was Anaximander of Miletus, in the first half of the sixth century, followed by Hecataeus with a better map (*Vorsokr.* 12 A 6). For 'the circuit of the whole earth' cf. IV. 36. 2, likewise referring to maps.

49. 2. slaves instead of free: Cf. 28; and for the subjects of the Persian King as slaves see Brock, *Greek Political Imagery*, 108–10 with 127 n. 13.

in so far as you are the leaders of Greece: Cf. I. 69. 2, in Croesus' approach to Sparta in the middle of the century. 'Leaders of Greece' is an exaggeration, but Sparta was already the strongest state in the Peloponnese in the time of Croesus, and by the beginning of the fifth century had organised most of the Peloponnesian states under its leadership in what scholars call the Peloponnesian League (cf. 74. 1, 91. 2–94. 1).

49. 3. by the gods of the Greeks ... men of the same blood as you: The Greeks believed that Dorians and Ionians, together with Aeolians, were strands of a single Greek people (e.g. I. 6. 2, 56. 2), and Herodotus represents the Athenians when refusing to be won over by Mardonius in 479 as citing Greek identity (*to Hellenikon*), which involved being of the same blood and language, having common sanctuaries of and sacrifices to the gods, and having similar customs (VIII. 144. 2). In 97. 2 Aristagoras' ground for appealing to Athens is much more specific: that the Milesians are colonists of Athens.

Their mode of battle is like this: the bow and short sword: The Persians' infantry were not like Greek hoplites, and were not a match for Greek hoplites; but they had cavalry which the Greeks could not match.

wearing trousers, and peaked caps on their heads: Greeks considered the clothing of barbarians strange and fascinating (and, conversely, the sculptures at Persepolis depicting tribute-bearers show that the Persians were interested in the different costumes of their different subjects); but of course that was irrelevant to their capabilities in battle.

49. 4. embroidered clothing: As opposed to cheap, utilitarian clothing. In VI. 112. 3 the Athenians at Marathon are not put off by the sight of the Persians' embroidered clothing; in Aesch. *Ag.* 922–4 it is a sign of *hybris*. Cf. A. J. Woodman, *The Annals of Tacitus, Books 5 and 6* (Cambridge UP, 2017), 238, on Tac. *Ann.* VI. 34. 3.

49. 5. They live one in succession to another as I shall indicate: See conveniently *Barrington Atlas* small-scale map 3; and compare Herodotus' more detailed account of the Royal Road in 52–4.

Lydians: With their capital at Sardis, immediately inland from the coastal fringe of Asia Minor occupied by the Greek cities (cf. on 11. 1).

Phrygians: The dominant power in Asia Minor before the Lydians (cf. I. 35); their capital was at Gordium, 25 miles (40 km) north-east of Germa in map 3 B 2.

of all whom I know: 'Whom I know', here included in Aristagoras' speech, is a favourite expression of Herodotus: often 'the first known to us' (e.g. I. 5. 3 with B. Shimron, 'πρῶτος τῶν ἡμεῖς ἴδμεν', *Eranos* 71 (1973), 45–51. Cf. 119. 2, and Introduction, p. 6.

49. 6. the Cappadocians, whom we call Syrians: Cf. I. 72, where the same statement is made. Cappadocia was north of the Taurus range, inland from the corner where the coast turns from west–east to north–south. They are not here credited with any wealth, and in I. 71 they are said to be leather-clothed ruffians who have no wealth of any kind.

the Cilicians, reaching to this sea in which the island of Cyprus lies: They occupied the region at that corner, south of the Taurus. Cyprus is indeed near, and in 108. 2 the Persians set out from Cilicia to recover Cyprus when it had joined in the Ionian Revolt.

the Armenians: Armenia was north of the Taurus, east of Cappadocia.

the Matienians: They are not named on map 3, but map 89 places them south of the Matiane Limne in map 3 E 2.

49. 7. Cissia, in which by this River Choaspes here is Susa: Map 3 E 3, 93 D 1. For Cissia as the region in which Susa lies cf. III. 91. 4, and for the Choaspes as its river cf. I. 188. For Susa cf. 24. 4.

where … the treasuries with his money are: Cf. on 24. 4.

you could have the confidence to rival even Zeus for wealth: That would be the ultimate in *hybris*: cf. Hom. *Il.* V. 440–2, *Od.* IV. 78, Aesch. *Ag.* 922–4.

49. 8. the Messenians: Sparta's first expansion outside Laconia involved the conquest in the eighth and seventh centuries of Messenia, west of Laconia, in the south-west corner of the Peloponnese.

the Arcadians: North of Laconia, in the centre of the Peloponnese. In the first half of the sixth century Sparta failed to conquer it but was able to make it a subordinate ally: cf. I. 65–8, on Croesus' enquiries.

Argives: For Argos, in the north-east of the Peloponnese, see *Barrington Atlas* 58 D 2, *Inventory* 602–606 no. 347. In Greek legend, when the descendants of Heracles returned to the Peloponnese three branches of the family took Messenia, Argos and Sparta (Diod. Sic. IV. 57–8, Apollod. *Bibl.* II. 8 2–4). In the archaic and classical periods Argos was never willing to acknowledge Spartan superiority: Herodotus records conflicts between them in the 540s (I. 82) and in the 490s (VI. 76–3); in 480–479 Argos refused to join in the Greek resistance to Persia under Spartan leadership

(VII. 148–52, IX. 12); and Sparta had further conflicts with Messenians, Arcadians and Argives after the Persian Wars (IX. 35. 2).

49. 9. I shall delay my reply until the third day from now: Rationally, perhaps, so that he could consult other leading Spartans; narratologically, to provide for a build-up to the climax (Hornblower).

50. 1. the agreed place: Not Cleomenes' own house, since he goes there in 51. 1.

50. 2. had misled him well: διαβάλλειν can mean either 'malign' or as here, 'mislead'.

the journey inland was of three months: Herodotus will confirm the correctness of this (but for an individual traveller, not an army, which would take longer) in 52–4.

be gone from Sparta before sunset: Cf. the Argive ultimatum to Spartans in VII. 149. 1.

an acceptable account: Maas suggested εὐπρεπέα ('appropriate'). After the Persian Wars Sparta was notoriously reluctant to venture outside the Peloponnese (and cf. already IX. 6–10. 1, in 479); but it seems to have been somewhat less reluctant earlier (e.g. I. 69, the alliance with Croesus; I. 152. 1–153. 2, at the time of Persia's conquest of the Asiatic Greeks; III. 44–56, in the 520s).

51. 1. took a suppliant's branch: On supplication, the act not of claiming a right but of throwing oneself at the mercy of a god or of a human being in a superior position, see especially J. P. A. Gould, '*Hiketeia*', *JHS* 93 (1973), 74–103; F. S. Naiden, *Ancient Supplication* (Oxford UP, 2006). For an olive branch bound with wool as a sign of supplication cf. e.g. Aesch. *Supp.* 22, 191–2, Andoc. I. *Myst.* 110–6.

Cleomenes' daughter, whose name was Gorgo ... was eight or nine years old: Cf. 48.

51. 2. nodded his disagreement: Greeks nodded upwards to disagree and downwards to agree (as they still do): see LSJ ἀνανεύω, κατανεύω.

Father, the foreigner will corrupt you, if you don't go and leave him: J. A. Scott, *CP* 10 (1915), 331, suggests that using 'Father' rather than 'O father', is formal behaviour in the presence of a foreign visitor (whereas Plut. *Lacaen. Apophth.* 240 D has 'O father'). Earlier Cleomenes had been able to resist the attempt of Maeandrius of Samos to bribe him

(III. 148). The word translated 'corrupt' is διαφθείρω (a common usage, though this is the only instance of it in Herodotus): normally when used with a human object it means 'destroy' in the sense of 'kill'.

52. 1. The situation with regard to this road is as follows: Herodotus now supplies his own account of the Royal Road, to confirm the three months' journey of 50. 2. Presumably this information is derived ultimately from documents, though this does not necessarily mean that Herodotus himself obtained it from the documents (cf. Introduction, p. 12). See Kuhrt, *The Persian Empire*, ii. 730–41. The tablets from Persepolis show that this was one of a number of such roads in the Persian empire. How and Wells note various discussions of the route; for a road in Asia Minor see D. H. French, 'Pre- and Early-Roman Roads of Asia Minor: The Persian Royal Road', *Iran* 36 (1998), 15–43; for a papyrus commentary on 52–5 which compares this route with Cyrus' route in Xen. *An.* I see *POxy* lxv (1998) 4455.

    royal staging-posts and highest-quality inns: For one of these see A. Mousavi, 'The Discovery of an Achaemenid Way-Station at Deh-Bozan in the Asadabad Valley', *AMI* 22 (1989), 135–38, and Kuhrt, ii. 738.

    Stretching through Lydia and Phrygia … 94½ parasangs: For Herodotus a parasang was 30 stades (53, cf. II. 6. 3); but other writers give other equivalences. The Greek stade was itself variable (at Olympia it was 192 m. or *c.* 210 yards: cf. on 22. 2), and writers often give distances which were estimated rather than measured (cf. R. A. Bauslaugh, 'The Text of Thucydides IV. 8. 6 and the South Channel at Pylos', *JHS* 99 [1979], 1–6). How and Wells follow those who interpreted this as a route which ran via Gordium (cf. on 49. 5) and Ancyra, to the north of a salt desert.

52. 2. the River Halys, on which there are gates: Presumably at the bridge by which Croesus of Lydia had crossed (I. 75. 3). The road will have had to cross the Halys again, farther upstream.

52. 3. The border of Cilicia and Armenia … Euphrates: If it reached the Euphrates, Herodotus' Cilicia extended farther east than the region indicated in the note on 49. 6.

52. 4. first the Tigris; then the second and third named Zabatus: *Barrington Atlas* 91 E 1–2 has two rivers called Zabas, each flowing into the Tigris from the north-east.

52. 5. Gyndes, the river which Cyrus once divided into three hundred and sixty channels: This is the river now called Diyala, which in *Barrington Atlas* 91 F 4 is named 'Diabas'/Turnai, and again flows into the Tigris from the north-east. The four rivers are in Matiene rather than Armenia (whence Stein's transposition: see next note). For Cyrus cf. I. 189. 1–190. 1: he was punishing the river for the drowning of one of his horses.

When from this place Armenia you advance into the Matienian territory there are thirty-four staging-posts, and 137 parasangs: The insertion was made by de la Barre to save Herodotus' arithmetic; the whole sentence (with 'Armenia' deleted) was placed at the end of §3 by Stein.

52. 6. the River Choaspes … on which the city of Susa has been built: This seems to have been the Karkheh (*Barrington Atlas* 93 E 2); but the different accounts of different writers suggest that water courses towards the head of the Persian Gulf have changed more than once. The Choaspes mentioned in connection with Alexander the Great (e.g. Curt. VIII. 10. 22) was a different river, apparently a tributary of the Kabul River in Afghanistan (see A. B. Bosworth, *A Historical Commentary on Arrian's History of Alexander*, ii [Oxford UP, 1995], 155–57).

53. 1. and if a parasang is equivalent to 30 stades: Cf. on 52. 1.

what is called Memnon's Palace: Cf. VII. 151; this Memnon was a legendary Ethiopian ruler (cf. II. 106. 5).

54. 1. Ephesus: *Barrington Atlas* 61 E 2, *Inventory* 1070–73 no. 844. At the beginning of the Ionian Revolt the Ionians set out from Ephesus to attack Sardis (100). Smyrna (56 E 5, 1099–1101 no. 867; modern İzmir), from which the journey to Sardis would have been easier, seems to have been destroyed at the time of the Persian conquest and not refounded until the fourth century (see *Inventory*). Strabo 646 / XIV. 1. 37 goes further, and has Smyrna occupied 'in villages' from the Lydian conquest (cf. I. 16. 2) for four hundred years.

55–97. Athens.
For the articulation of this section see Introduction, p. 7, and the more detailed summary of book V on p. 44.

55. It had become free from tyrants in this way: This is presented as a sequel to the account of Athens in the time of Croesus (I. 59–64); cf. the comparable accounts of Sparta in the time of Aristagoras (49–54) and in the time of Croesus (I. 65–8). The ending of the tyranny is reported also by Thuc. I. 20. 2, VI. 54–9, *Ath. Pol.* 18–19. On the set of rings opened in this chapter see Introduction, pp. 29–30.

Hipparchus son of Pisistratus, brother of Hippias the tyrant: Like Thucydides after him (Thuc. I. 20. 2, VI. 55), Herodotus believed that Hippias was Pisistratus' eldest son and was 'the' tyrant after Pisistratus' death; but more was made of Hipparchus by Athenians who did not want to be grateful to Sparta and the Alcmaeonids for their liberation (cf. traces of this in VI. 109. 3, 123. 2). It is true that Hippias was the eldest son (see Davies, *APF* 445–48), but tyrant was not a formal office, and it is perhaps better to think of joint rule by Hippias and Hipparchus (thus *Ath. Pol.* 18. 1, though that text is badly confused on Pisistratus' sons).

though he had seen in his sleep a vision very similar to his disaster: ἐμφερής, whose superlative was restored here by Wyttenbach, is a favourite word of Herodotus. The dream is mentioned only by Herodotus, for whom dreams are experienced by barbarians and tyrants (W. V. Harris, *Dreams and Experience in Classical Antiquity* [Princeton UP, 2009], 146–47). It resembled his disaster in that he was assassinated and his assassins were themselves killed, and it was 'riddling' in that 'doing wrong' and 'paying the penalty' could be applied both to him and to the assassins.

Harmodius and Aristogeiton, whose family was descended from the Gephyraei: In what follows, this will be Herodotus' main interest in the episode. Hornblower suggests that Herodotus wanted to stress that both the Pisistratids (65. 3) and the assassins were immigrants.

the Athenians were for four years subject to tyranny no less than before but indeed more: Hipparchus was killed in 514/3, Hippias was expelled in 511/0. On the chronology of the tyranny see Rhodes, *The Athenian Constitution Written in the School of Aristotle* (Aris and Phillips Classical texts. Liverpool UP, 2017), 222–23, and more detailed studies cited there.

56. 1. the Panathenaea: In fact the four-yearly Great Panathenaea (Thuc. VI. 56. 2).

he seemed to see a large and handsome man ... speaking these riddling words: On dreams and on epiphanies (in this case Hipparchus dreams of an epiphany) cf. Introduction, pp. 19–20. For a dream of Hippias in 490 see VI. 107.

lion: Cf. the oracle to the Bacchiads (92. β. 3). When the lion is bidden to endure, this suggests that the image here is favourable; but Brock, *Greek Political Imagery*, 89–90, sees lion images as ambiguous.

No man who does wrong will avoid paying the penalty: By the same token, this might suggest that the wrongdoer is the killer of Hipparchus, not Hipparchus himself; but probably the ambiguity is intended (and in fact both Hipparchus and his killers 'paid a penalty').

56. 2. expounders of dreams: Cf. Hom. *Il.* I. 62–3.

dispatched the procession: In Thuc. I. 20. 2 Hipparchus marshalled the Panathenaic procession in the Leocoreum (in the Ceramicus or in the north-west of the agora, near the Ceramicus), in Thuc. VI. 57. 1–3 Hippias marshalled the procession in the Ceramicus and Hipparchus was in the Leocoreum, in *Ath. Pol.* 18. 3 Hippias was on the acropolis to receive the procession and Hipparchus marshalled the procession in the Leocoreum. Probably all that was reliably remembered was that Hipparchus was killed in the Leocoreum.

in the course of which he died: This is all that Herodotus says about the actual killing: if he intended to return to it after his digression on the Gephyraei, he forgot to do so.

57. 1. The Gephyraei, to whom the killers of Hipparchus belonged: This opens a small ring, which will be closed in 62. 1. On the Gaephyraei see Davies, *APF* 472–79.

originally from Eretria: In Euboea, facing the south-east of Boeotia (*Barrington Atlas* 55 F 4, *Inventory* 651–5 no. 370).

as I have discovered in my investigation: Herodotus uses ἀναπυνθάνομαι of his own enquiries only here. For Herodotus and his enquiries cf. Introduction, pp. 5, 9–13.

Phoenicians who came with Cadmus to the land now called Boeotia: The Greek legend was that Cadmus left Phoenicia to search for his sister Europa after she was abducted by Zeus, and while she went to Crete (cf. I. 2. 1) he went to the mainland and in response to a Delphic oracle founded Thebes. The various forms of the legendary

history of Thebes are conveniently discussed by R. J. Buck, *A History of Boeotia* (U. of Alberta P., 1979), 45–84; R. B. Edwards, *Kadmos the Phoenician: A Study in Greek Legends and the Mycenaean Age* (Amsterdam: Hakkert, 1979), 102–37, thinks a Phoenician settlement at Thebes in the bronze age 'at least plausible'. See also on the Gephyraei Davies, *APF* 472–73.

Tanagra: The nearest substantial Boeotian city to Eretria (*Barrington Atlas* 55 F 4, *Inventory* 453–54 no. 220). If we discount the Phoenician legend, it is credible that they should have moved from Eretria to Tanagra.

57. 2. after the Cadmeans had previously been expelled by the Argives: This refers to the legendary expulsion by the *epigonoi* (the sons of the Seven Against Thebes), who succeeded where their fathers had failed (Apollod. *Bibl.* III. 7. 2–4).

secondly these Gephyraei were expelled by the Boeotians: This is supposed to have been when the Boeotians arrived in Boeotia from Thessaly after the Trojan War (cf. Thuc. I. 12. 3).

on stated terms ... a few matters not worthy of mention: When the Plataeans were granted Athenian citizenship in 427 they were excluded from archonships and priesthoods in the first generation ([Dem.] LIX. *Neaera* 104–6). In the case of the Gephyraei, if the matters were 'not worthy of mention', they are more likely to have been 'few' than 'many' as in the manuscripts' text. For 'matters not worthy of mention' cf. R. H. Martin and A. J. Woodman, *Tacitus, Annals, Book IV* (Cambridge UP, 1989), on Tac. *Ann.* IV. 32. 1.

58. 1. brought ... writing, which did not previously exist among the Greeks: This digression is prompted by the alleged Phoenician origin of the Gephyraei, and if the subject was one of current debate that may help to explain why Herodotus chose to write about the Gephyraei rather than about the assassination of Hipparchus. We now know that, while there were scripts in bronze-age Greece (the Cretan Linear A, which has not yet been deciphered, and the mainland Linear B, which is now known to have been used for a form of Greek), their use ceased in the dark age (except apparently in Cyprus); and the Greek alphabet, which first appeared about the early eighth century, was based on the Phoenician script, but had symbols for vowels as well as consonants, whereas the Phoenician script had only consonants. See, for instance, L. H. Jeffery

rev. A. W. Johnston, *The Local Scripts of Archaic Greece* (Oxford UP, 1990), 1–42 with 425–28.

58. 2. while making slight changes in the letters: Particularly in the archaic period, different parts of Greece used different forms of the alphabet, both in the manner of writing individual letters and in the repertoire of letters which they used: see Jeffery *passim*.

calling them *phoinikeia*: ποινικήια ('lettering') is found in a text of *c.* 600–550 from Eltynia in Crete (*SEG* lx 986), and another Cretan text, of *c.* 500, appoints a man called Spensithius to be *poinikastas* ('letterer': *Nomima* i 22). An inscription from Teos about the second quarter of the fifth century uses *phoinikeia* and *phoinikographein* (O&R 102. B. 37–8, C. d. 19–21). Cf. Soph. fr. 514 *TrGF*.

58. 3. the Ionians have called scrolls skins: For βύβλος see on 14. 2.

when there was a shortage of papyrus … write on skins of that kind: For the Ionians see R. Pfeiffer, *History of Classical Scholarship from the Beginnings to the End of the Hellenistic Age* (Oxford UP, 1968–76), i. 19, 235–36. For fifth-century Aramaic documents from Egypt see G. R. Driver, *Aramaic Documents of the Fifth Century BC* (Oxford UP, 1957); cf. also Diod. Sic. II. 32. 4 (part of Ctesias *FGrH* 688 F 5).

59. I myself actually saw Cadmean letters: On Herodotus and inscriptions see S. R. West, 'Herodotus' Epigraphical Interests' *CQ*[2] 35 (1985), 278–305, on these inscriptions 289–95, though her suspicion that Herodotus did not see these inscriptions at all is excessive; also R. G. Osborne, 'Archaic Greek History', in *Brill's Companion*, 497–520 at 510–13; Rhodes, 'Documents and the Greek Historians', in J. Marincola (ed.), *A Companion to Greek and Roman Historiography* (Malden, Mass.: Blackwell, 2007), i. 56–66 at 56–58. What Herodotus meant by calling these inscriptions Cadmean is not obvious: perhaps, simply but wrongly, that they were actual documents of what we should call the legendary period, whereas to have been inscribed in the Greek alphabet they must in fact have been of the archaic period (thus How and Wells). For another early inscription from the same sanctuary see N. Papazarkadas, in Papazarkadas (ed.), *The Epigraphy and History of Boeotia: New Finds, New Prospects* (Leiden: Brill, 2014), 233–48, with M. Tentori Montalto, 'Some Notes on Croesus' Dedication to Amphiaraos at Thebes (*BE* 2015, n. 306)', *ZPE* 204 (2017), 1–9.

in the sanctuary of Apollo Ismenias at Thebes in Boeotia: With Boeotia specified to distinguish this from Egyptian Thebes, here and elsewhere. See *Barrington Atlas* 55 E 4, *Inventory* 454–57 no. 221. This sanctuary was on the Ismenion hill, south-east of the Cadmea (acropolis): A. Schachter, *Cults of Boiotia* (*BICS* Supp. 38, 1981–94), i. 77–85.

which in general are like those of the Ionians: Again it is not obvious what Herodotus meant. Boeotian and Ionian lettering were not markedly similar: Jeffery, 89–95, 325–45. Schachter, i. 82, thinks these could all have been real dedications of the archaic or early classical period.

this inscription: *Epigramma*, used also in VII. 228. 4 of inscriptions in elegiac couplets. This inscription is a hexameter: Herodotus specifies hexameters for those quoted in 60 and in 61. 1, as he does in I. 47. 2, 62. 4, VII. 220. 3, but he does not here.

Amphitryon dedicated me, †being† from the Teleboeans: The manuscripts' ἐὼν is unlikely, but it is not clear what the correct text would be. Amphitryon, the human father of Heracles, fought against the Teleboeans, living on islands off the north-west coast of Greece, because they had killed the brothers of his intended bride Alcmene (Apollod. *Bibl.* II. 4. 6–7).

This would be from the time of Laïus: Laïus the father of Oedipus was brother-in-law of Creon, who purified Amphitryon.

60. hexameter rhythm: See on 'inscription' in 59, above. The same expression is used in I. 47. 2, 62. 4.

Scaeus the boxer to you … this very fine treasure: This could be an authentic dedication of the archaic period, by 'another man with the same name'. Paus. VI. 13. 5 reports a dedication at Olympia by a boxer called Scaeus, from the fourth century.

Hippocoön's son: Scaeus son of Hippocoön helped his father to drive Tyndareus from Sparta, and they were killed there by Heracles (Apollod. *Bibl.* III. 10. 5). Thebes is not likely to have had even a spurious dedication attributed to that Scaeus.

61. 1. Leodamas as monarch … a very fine treasure: The use of 'monarch' suggests that this epigram like the first is one constructed to illustrate the legendary period.

61. 2. Laodamas son of Eteocles: And therefore grandson of Oedipus.

the Cadmeans were expelled and turned to the Encheleis: Cadmus supported the Encheleis against the Illyrians, to the north-west of Greece (Apollod. *Bibl.* III. 5. 4).

the Gephyraei were left behind … move to Athens: Cf. 57. 2.

They have sanctuaries … nothing to do with the rest of the Athenians: If the Gephyraei were from the beginning a *genos* in the technical sense, i.e. an extended family to which particular priesthoods were attached, modern scholarship would expect them to be involved in public cults rather than private cults of their own. Possibly they were not such a *genos* (though they were by the Roman period); or else something is wrong either with what Herodotus says or with modern expectations. See Parker, *Athenian Religion*, 288–89.

Demeter Achaea: The cult is attested in Boeotia, though not certainly at Tanagra: Schachter, i. 162–63, 169–71.

62. 1. Hipparchus' vision in his sleep … I have set out: This closes rings opened in 55 and in 57. 1 …

I still need to take up … how the Athenians were freed from tyrants: … and this reopens the large ring opened in 55. As Herodotus and Thucydides agreed, the killing of Hipparchus did not end the tyranny but made Hippias' rule harsher.

62. 2. he was becoming embittered … because of the death of Hipparchus: Reformulating what was said in 55. In narrating this episode Herodotus deploys a shifting focus: first on Athens and the Alcmaeonids (62. 2–3), then on the Spartans and their expeditions (63–4, cf. 90. 1), finally on the Pisistratids (65): cf. Introduction, p. 14.

The Alcmaeonids, an Athenian family who were exiled by the Pisistratids: The family first appeared in I. 61. 1–2, in connection with the rise of Pisistratus, 64. 3, on their exile after the final *coup*. VI. 121–4 alludes to this episode and says that the Alcmaeonids cannot have been guilty of treachery at Marathon, because they were conspicuously opposed to tyranny, and in exile throughout the time of the Pisistratid tyranny (after which VI. 125–31 has more on the family; V. 71. 2 will mention them in connection with the killing of Cylon's supporters). We now know from a fragment of the Athenian archon list that they were not in exile continuously from Pisistratus' final *coup* to the expulsion of Hippias, but Cleisthenes was archon in 525/4 (M&L 6. *c.* 3 = *IG* i³

1031. 18); presumably they went into exile again after the killing of Hipparchus.

when they fortified Leipsydrium above Paeonia: Cf. *Ath. Pol.* 19. 3. *Barrington Atlas* 59 B 2 places Leipsydrium close to the possible site of the deme Paeonidae, on the southern slope of Mount Parnes, and Holford-Strevens emends to that: there was no deme of Paeonia, the name given by the manuscripts here, but there was a deme of Paeania, on the eastern slope of Hymettus (59 C 3).

they took the contract from the Amphictyons to build the temple at Delphi: Cf. Isoc. XV. *Antid.* 232, Dem. XXI. *Midias* 144 with schol. (497 Dilts), *Ath. Pol.* 19. 4 (summarised by schol. Ar. *Lys.* 1150), Philoch. *FGrH* 328 F 115 (trans. Fornara 40). The previous temple was burned in 548/7 (Paus. X. 5. 3); Amasis of Egypt, who died in 526, made a contribution to the funds (Hdt. II. 180). The development of the story is traced by W. G. Forrest, 'The Tradition of Hippias' Expulsion from Athens', *GRBS* 10 (1969), 277–86: for Herodotus the Alcmaeonids had already done an expensive job and Delphi in gratitude (or because bribed by Alcmaeonids with good access: 63. 1) put pressure on the Spartans (Herodotus' manner of narration does not mean that the Alcmaeonids took the contract only at the point where the oracular pressure is mentioned); for Isocrates and Demosthenes the contract was made after Leipsydrium and provided the Alcmaeonids with the money for mercenaries; *Ath. Pol.* combined Herodotus' oracular pressure with misappropriation of the funds; Philochorus followed the version of Isocrates and Demosthenes but had the Alcmaeonids do an expensive job on the temple afterwards in gratitude. The sixth-century temple was in turn destroyed in 373/2 and had to be replaced: see R&O 45 with commentary.

For Delphi see *Barrington Atlas* 55 C–D 4, *Inventory* 412–16 no. 177. The Amphictyony (league of neighbours) was a body which shared with the *polis* of Delphi the administration of the sanctuary of Apollo (and also cared for the sanctuary of Demeter at Anthela near Thermopylae): its council, which had two regular meetings a year, comprised two *hieromnamones* ('sacred remembrancers') from each of the twelve *ethne* which made up the Amphictyony; the *ethne* were predominantly central Greek, but by the classical period there was also a Dorian *ethnos* (combining Doris in central Greece with the Dorians of the Peloponnese, the Spartans sometimes supplying the central Greek *hieromnamon*) and

an Ionian (with Athens supplying one of its two *hieromnamones*). See F. Lefèvre, *L' Amphictionie pyléo-delphique: Histoire et institutions* (BEFAR 298. Paris: De Boccard for École Française d' Athènes, 1998); P. Sánchez, *L'Amphictionie des Pyles et de Delphes: Recherches sur son rôle historique* (*Historia* Einz. 98, 2001).

63. 1. As the Spartans say: According to the manuscripts, as the Athenians say, and the allegation of bribery could have been made by Athenians opposed to the Alcmaeonids; but it is more likely that this was the story told by the Spartans to account for their doing what they later regretted doing (cf. 90. 1, 91. 2). On the story cf. VI. 123. 2.

these men ... induced the Pythia: In 66. 1, specifically Cleisthenes.

63. 2. Anchimolus the son of Aster: *Ath. Pol.* 19. 5 follows Herodotus on this episode. The name is Anchimolius in the manuscripts here; but *Ath. Pol.* gives it as Anchimolus. It is generally thought that Anchimolus is the correct form (e.g. *L.G.P.N.* iiiA *s.n.*; cf. *SEG* xi 667), in which case we must assume that Herodotus wrote 'Anchimolus', but the surviving manuscripts share a corruption absent from the version known to *Ath. Pol.* (thus Wilson, who emends to 'Anchimolus'). On this episode see L. J. Worley, *Hippeis: The Cavalry of Ancient Greece* (Boulder, Col.: Westview, 1994), 51–53, arguing that this was a rare occasion when cavalry successfully attacked a phalanx, because the phalanx was too weak.

63. 3. They sent these by sea in boats: The boats and the non-regal commander indicate that the Spartans thought a small force would suffice.

Phalerum: The beach there was used as Athens' harbour until the development of Piraeus in the early fifth century (both *Barrington Atlas* 59 B 3: see Thuc. I. 93. 3–7; cf. Herodotus' past tense in VI. 116).

for they had made an alliance with the Thessalians: Cf. Thessalus as the name of one of Pisistratus' sons (Thuc. I. 20. 2, VI. 55. 1, and the confused *Ath. Pol.* 17. 3–18. 2, with Davies, *A.P.F.* 445–50), and the support for Hippias in 94. 1.

the Thessalians took a common decision and sent them a thousand cavalry: For Thessaly in the 420s see Thuc. II. 22. 3 (which suggests decisions by individual cities rather than a common decision), IV. 78. 2–4 (where the mass of the Thessalians was pro-Athenian but rule by *dynasteiai* enabled Brasidas to take Spartan troops through Thessaly). 1,000 cavalry was a very large force.

their king Cineas, a man of Condaea: That is the likeliest correction of the manuscripts' Κονιαῖον: see *Barrington Atlas* 55 C 1, but the city is not securely attested until the hellenistic period and is not included in *Inventory.* 'King' is a word used of aristocratic Thessalians without denoting a formal position (B. Helly, *L' État thessalien* [Lyon: Maison de l' Orient Méditerranéen, 1995], 101–30). It used to be thought that at least in times of crisis Thessaly had a supreme official styled *tagos* (e.g. J. A. O. Larsen, *Greek Federal States: Their Institutions and History* [Oxford UP, 1968], 14–15); *tagoi* are attested in individual cities from an early date (*SEG* xxvii 183, Atrax; *IG* ix. ii 257 = O&R 118, Thetonium); but there may not have been a *tagos* of Thessaly as a whole before Jason of Pherae claimed that title in the fourth century. Earlier, if there was a principal official of Thessaly as a whole, his title seems to have been *archon, archos* or *tetrarchos* (Helly, 13–68). Helly, 103–104, 220–22, accepts 'of Condaea' here, and thinks Cineas was not *archon.*

63. 4. they cleared the plain of Phalerum and made it usable for horses: Cf. Arr. *Anab.* III. 8. 7, of the Persians before the battle of Gaugamela (again using ἱππασία, ἱππάσιμος).

in Attica at Alopece: South of the city and not far from Phalerum (*Barrington Atlas* 59 B 4). It was a deme to which Alcmaeonids belonged (D. M. Lewis, 'Cleisthenes and Attica', *Historia* 12 [1963], 22–40 at 23 = his *Selected Papers in Greek and Near Eastern History* [Cambridge UP, 1997], 77–98 at 78).

near the Heracleum in Cynosarges: Near the River Ilissus, in the deme Diomeia, due north of Alopece: it was a gymnasium with a cult of Heracles. See J. Travlos, *Pictorial Dictionary of Ancient Athens* (London: Thames and Hudson for German Archaeological Institute, 1971), 340–41.

64. 1. the king Cleomenes son of Anaxandridas: Repetition of the detail, supplied earlier (39. 1), adds to the seriousness of this more serious force. This episode belongs to 511/0 (cf. on 55); *Ath. Pol.* 19. 5–6 follows Herodotus' narrative, and also gives the date.

64. 2. The survivors departed for Thessaly as soon as they could: This suggests that not all the Thessalians may have been happy to support Athens against Sparta.

together with those of the Athenians who wanted to be free: It is not clear how many of the Athenians rallied to Cleomenes.

the Pelargic Wall: Here and elsewhere manuscripts vary between 'Pelargic' and 'Pelasgic'. It was believed that in the distant past the Pelasgians (cf. 26) came to Attica, built the acropolis wall (which was in fact built in the thirteenth century), and were allowed for a time to settle but later were expelled (Hecataeus *FGrH* 1 F 127 *ap.* VI. 137. 2). Probably at the north-west corner of the acropolis (e.g. R. J. Hopper, *The Acropolis* [London: Weidenfeld and Nicolson, 1971], 81 fig. 6 no. 12; J. McK. Camp, 'Water and the Pelargikon', in *Studies ... S. Dow* [*GRB*Mon. x 1984], 37–41) was a precinct called the *Pelargikon* (Thuc. II. 17. 1–2). Probably the precinct was called *Pelargikon* before the Pelasgians were invoked to explain anything (*pelargos* means 'stork', but the meaning of *Pelargikon* is unknown); later the Pelasgians were credited with the thirteenth-century wall and by assimilation it was called the Pelargic Wall; later still scribes who had heard of the Pelasgians corrupted *pelargikon* into *pelasgikon*. *Ath. Pol.* has 'Pelargic'; and here I print Πελαργικῷ though most manuscripts have Πελασγικῷ.

65. 1. they had not planned to mount a siege: Later the Athenians were reputed to be good at sieges as the Spartans were not (Thuc. I. 102. 2). Before the invention of various kinds of machinery to use in sieges, from the late fifth century onwards, a 'siege' was essentially a blockade; hence the importance for the besieged of being 'well provided with food and drink' (below).

well provided with food and drink: For water people on the acropolis probably had protected access to Travlos' Asclepieum spring and *klepsydra* immediately to the south and north-west respectively (Travlos, 52, 138, 323, with 61 fig. 71 no. 114 and 71 fig. 91 no. 133).

the children of the Pisistratids ... were captured: According to Thuc. VI. 55. 1 only Hippias of Pisistratus' sons was known to have had children.

65. 3. they left for Sigeum on the Scamander: In the Troad, just outside the Hellespont: *Barrington Atlas* 51 G 5 / 56 C 2, *Inventory* 1014 no. 791. On its history see 94–5.

They had ruled over the Athenians for thirty-six years: From Pisistratus' third and definitive *coup* in 546/5 to 511/0.

were themselves by descent Pylians and Neleïds: Cf. I. 147 on the Ionians of Asia Minor. The Athenians claimed, at least from the early sixth century (Solon fr. 4a West *ap. Ath. Pol.* 5. 2), to be the mother

city of the Ionians, on the grounds that men from elsewhere in Greece had taken refuge in Athens before setting out from there to Asia Minor (Thuc. I. 2. 6). Neleus was son of Poseidon and father of Homer's Nestor (e.g. Hom. *Od.* III. 79); and the legendary founder of Miletus was called Neleus (IX. 97; cf. Strabo 632–3 / XIV. 1. 3). Melanthus and Pisistratus were supposedly descended from different sons of Neleus.

Codrus and Melanthus ... kings of the Athenians: In Athenian legend, Melanthus, as a refugee from Pylos, killed the Boeotian Xanthus and supplanted Thymoetes, the last king of the orginal Erechtheïd dynasty. Melanthus was succeeded by his son Codrus, and (in what became the canonical version, but for a variant see *Ath. Pol.* 3. 3) Codrus' son Medon held the new office of archon for life (Hellanicus *FGrH* 323a F 23).

65. 4. Hippocrates ... Pisistratus son of Nestor: For Hippocrates as father of Pisistratus the tyrant see I, 59. 1–3; for Pisistratus as son of Nestor see e.g. Hom. *Od.* III. 36.

65. 5. In this way the Athenians were rid of tyrants: This closes the large ring opened in 55 and reopened in 62. 1.

they did or had done to them that is worthy of being set out: For 'did or had done to them' cf. Hom. *Od.* VIII. 490, and afterwards Arist. *Poet.* 8. 1451 в 11; cf. in Latin Fabius Pictor, reported in Cic. *Div.* I. 43. For 'worthy of being set out' cf. Herodotus' overall objective, of preserving 'what has been done by men', in particular 'great and wonderful deeds' (with Introduction, p. 5); and contrast the 'few matters not worthy of mention' in 57. 2.

before Ionia revolted ... ask them to give support: Reiterates the reason for this long digression on Athens, which began in 55.

66. 1. Athens had been great even before ... became greater: This will be explained in 74–96, after the account of Cleisthenes. 'Great even before' is hard to reconcile with the verdict on Athens under the tyranny in 78, 91. 1.

two men held preponderant positions: Herodotus normally uses δυναστεύειν of men in a powerful but not a formal ruling position in their city; cf. his use of it of Athens as a powerful city in 97. 1. On this episode *Ath. Pol.* 20. 1–3 follows Herodotus and 21 adds material from another source.

Cleisthenes ... persuaded the Pythia: Cf. 63. 1, where the persuasion

is attributed to the Alcmaeonids in general. Cleisthenes was son of the Megacles who figures in the story of Pisistratus' rise to power (I. 59. 3–61. 2); his descent from Cleisthenes of Sicyon will appear below.

Isagoras son of Teisandrus ... I am not able to report his descent: The name Teisandrus is found in the family of Miltiades, but in other families too, and 'much doubt attaches' to attempts to link Isagoras to that family (Davies, *APF* 296). *Ath. Pol.* 20. 1 describes him as 'a friend of the tyrants', but that is perhaps a too-simple inference from Cleisthenes' opposition to the tyranny, and 70. 1 here conflicts with it. See A. J. Woodman, *The Annals of Tacitus, Books 5 and 6* (Cambridge UP, 2017), 118, on Tac. *Ann.* VI. 7. 4: he follows Fehling, *Herodotus and His 'Sources'*, 102–103, 125–27, on statements of 'unsuccessful enquiry' as 'a literary device for enhancing an author's reliability'.

his kin sacrifice to Zeus Ikarios: Zeus Karios in the manuscripts; D. M. Lewis thought a Karios could be found in the deme Icarium (*IG* i³ 253), but more probably the deity there is Ikarios and I have suggested Ikarios here (*Historia* 12 [1963], 26 with n. 46, updated by Rhodes in Lewis's *Selected Papers in Greek and Near Eastern History* [Cambridge UP, 1997], 82). However, Hornblower defends Zeus Karios.

66. 2. getting the worse of it: This seems to be marked by the election of Isagoras as archon for 508/7 (*Ath. Pol.* 21. 1, Dion. Hal. *Ant. Rom.* I. 74. 6). Cleisthenes had already been archon, in 525/4 (cf. on 62. 2), but was presumably backing a rival candidate.

added the people to his following: Cf. 69. 2; and for the expression cf. III. 70. 2. Those familiar with Athens a century later will think of the upper-class associations known as *hetaireiai*, and *Ath. Pol.* rephrases this as 'defeated in the *hetaireiai*'; but it is very unlikely that such associations existed in the time of Cleisthenes, and unlikely that Herodotus supposed that they did.

he made the Athenians a people of ten tribes ... names from other heroes, local apart from Ajax: Tribal reorganisation is found in various Greek cities in the archaic period (for Sicyon cf. below, 68). For Athens, Attica was divided into three regions, City, Coast and Inland, ten tribes were constructed which each had one *trittys* ('third') in each of those regions, and each *trittys* comprised one or more local communities (demes, a special sense of *demos*). Cf. 69. 2; the main facts are given by *Ath. Pol.* 21. 2–4; this new organisation became the basis for the whole of

Athens' civic life; and it 'mixed up' in the same tribes men from different parts of Attica (*Ath. Pol.*), and gave the Athenians political institutions at local level as well as *polis* level. *Ath. Pol.* 21. 6 claims that Delphi had to choose the ten tribal heroes from a list of a hundred; but perhaps it was in fact asked to give its blessing to the ten. Ajax was associated with Salamis (cf. VIII. 64. 2), which both Athens and Megara had been claiming for a century, and which was finally awarded to Athens by Spartan arbitrators, probably at the end of the sixth century (cf. I. 59. 4, Plut. *Sol.* 8–10, 12. 5; M&L 14 = *IG* i³ 1; and R. J. Hopper, ' "Plain", "Shore" and "Hill" in Early Athens', *BSA* 56 [1961], 189–219 at 208–17); but it was always treated as a possession rather than as an integral part of Attica.

he got rid of the tribes named after Ion's sons, Geleon, Aegicores, Argades and Hoples: These tribes are attested in various Ionian cities. In legend, Ion was son of the Peloponnesian king Xuthus and Creusa, daughter of the Athenian king Erechtheus, and successfully defended Athens against an attack by Eleusis and the Thracians (cf. VIII. 44. 2, Thuc. II. 15. 1, Philoch. *FGrH* 328 F 13). In fact the old tribes were not abolished, but retained some religious functions (cf. Parker, *Athenian Religion*, 14).

67. 1. his maternal grandfather Cleisthenes the tyrant of Sicyon: For such a digression to the past for explanatory purposes (*analepsis*) see Introduction, p. 14. For the story of the marriage from which Cleisthenes was born see VI. 126–31. Cleisthenes ruled during about the first third of the sixth century; for Sicyon, north-west of Corinth on the Gulf of Corinth, see *Barrington Atlas* 58 D 2, *Inventory* 468–70 no. 228. It is hard to be sure how much truth lies behind the account given here. For a drastically revisionist treatment see S. Forsdyke, 'Peer-Polity Interaction', in N. Fisher and H. van Wees (eds), *Competition in the Ancient World* (Swansea: Classical P. of Wales, 2011), 147–74: she suggests that Cleisthenes was a figure to whom developments on various occasions were attached; the cult of Adrastus was not ended but adopted in the sixth century as Sicyon with other states claimed a connection with the Seven Against Thebes; Homeric performances were introduced in the sixth century (and that they were taken from Adtrastus is part of an anti-Cleisthenes tradition); the tribe names attributed to Cleisthenes were Sicyon's original names (derived from place names, Archelaoi being a

malicious corruption of Aegialeis, and the animal/obscene interpretation of the others coming from popular tradition), and Dorian names for three of them were adopted *c.* 510 when Sicyon claimed a Dorian identity (and when she believes the tyranny was ended).

For when Cleisthenes had fought a war against the Argives, ... for the most part Argives and Argos are sung of everywhere: Homer used 'Argives' and 'Argos' both to refer to the city of Argos and, along with other terms, to refer to the Greeks in general: Hom. *Il.* VI. 159, 66, gives the two senses in close proximity.

the reciters: Professional performers of the Homeric epics and other poetry.

there was and indeed is a hero's shrine of Adrastus son of Talaus: Adrastus was king of Argos and leader of the Seven Against Thebes, who sought to give the throne of Thebes to Polynices (Adrastus' son-in-law) rather than his brother Eteocles. The traveller Pausanias does not mention this in his account of Sicyon (II. 5. 6–11. 2), and at I. 43. 1 he says that Adrastus died and had a cult at Megara.

67. 2. He went to Delphi: Traditionally the First Sacred War for the control of Delphi was fought at the beginning of the sixth century, with Corinth (which had been influential at Delphi before) on the losing side and both Cleisthenes and the Athenian Alcmaeon (father of Megacles and grandfather of the Athenian Cleisthenes: in Herodotus, VI. 125) on the winning. Cleisthenes might have been provoked to join in the war by Delphi's rejection of his proposal (A. Griffin, *Sikyon* [Oxford UP, 1982], 52–54). The historicity of that war has been doubted by N. Robertson, 'The Myth of the First Sacred War', *CQ*² 28 (1978), 38–73, cf. most recently P. Londey, 'Making up Delphic History: The 1st Sacred War Revisited', *Chiron* 45 (2015), 221–38; defended, at least as 'a plausible hypothesis', by J. K. Davies, 'The Tradition about the First Sacred War', in Hornblower (ed.) *Greek Historiography*, 193–212.

Adrastus was a king of Sicyon but Cleisthenes was a stone-thrower: The response embodies the jingle *basileus* >< *leuster*. Adrastus is a former king of Sicyon in Hom. *Il.* II. 572, and Herodotus explains below how that came about; 'stone-thrower' is perhaps to be contrasted with a proper warrior.

Melanippus son of Astacus: Herodotus proceeds to explain. Melanippus was one of the Thebans who fought against the Seven.

the Thebans granted that: It is not clear what the Thebans had to grant; but, though Griffin, *Sikyon*, 50, writes, 'sent for the bones of Melanippos from Thebes', it is unlikely that they allowed the cult of Melanippus to be abolished in Thebes (what was considered to be his tomb was on the road from Thebes to Chalcis: Paus. IX. 18. 1) so that it could be instituted in Sicyon. In I. 68. 3–6 the bones of the hero Orestes are moved from Tegea to Sparta.

67. 3. right in the *prytaneion*: This presumably trumped the location of Adrastus in the agora (§1).

Melanippus … who had killed both his brother Mecisteus and his son-in-law Tydeus: In the fighting at the gates of Thebes. Adrastus' brother Mecisteus (Apollod. *Bibl.* I. 9. 13) was in some versions one of the Seven Against Thebes (Apollod. III. 6. 3 notes that some versions omitted Tydeus and Polynices but included Eteoclus and Mecisteus). Melanippus killed Tydeus, and Amphiaraus, a brother-in-law of Adrastus (or in some versions Tydeus himself), killed Melanippus; and the dying Tydeus was so vindictive that he swallowed Melanippus' brains (Apollod. III. 6. 8 and Pausanias have the Amphiaraus version).

67. 4. the land had belonged to Polybus … granted the rule to Adrastus: Adrastus had fled from Argos to his grandfather Polybus as a result of a family feud; he succeeded Polybus, as stated by Herodotus; but after a reconciliation he returned to be king in Argos (Menaechmus of Sicyon *FGrH* 131 F 10 *ap.* schol. Pind. *Nem.* 9. 30; Paus. II. 6. 6).

67. 5. with tragic choruses, honouring not Dionysus but Adrastus: If this is right, Sicyon had what Herodotus could call tragedy earlier than Athenian tragedy, which was performed at festivals of Dionysus, and whose creation by the addition of an individual actor to choral dithyrambs is attributed to Thespis perhaps in the 530s (Parian Marble *FGrH* 239 A 43; cf. on the development of tragedy Arist. *Poet.* 4. 1448 B 24–1449 A 31). Cleisthenes' giving the choruses to Dionysus suggests that there was already a perceived connection between *ur*-tragedy and Dionysus in the early sixth century.

68. 1. The tribes of the Dorians … he changed to other names: During the archaic period new tribes were created in various cities (e.g. Athens, 69; Corinth, Nic. Dam. *FGrH* 90 F 60. 2, Phot. π 168 Theodoridis, *Suda* π 225 Adler πάντα ὀκτώ); but Herodotus writes here simply of changes of name, for the three tribes found in various

Dorian states and a fourth, non-Dorian, tribe to which Cleisthenes himself belonged, and represents Cleisthenes as specifically anti-Argive rather than generally anti-Dorian. Macan wondered if there had been a restructuring which tied particular tribes to particular localities; and he and others have suggested that names which Herodotus saw as insulting may not have been seen that way in Sicyon at the time (for instance, L. H. Jeffery, *Archaic Greece: The City States c. 700–500 BC* [London: Benn, 1976], suggested that they were derived from place names: cf. Forsdyke, cited above). P. J. Bicknell, 'Herodotos 5. 68 and the Racial Policy of Kleisthenes of Sikyon' *GRBS* 23 (1982), 193–201, argued that to bring animals and tribe names into line we should not insert καὶ χοίρου but delete ἕτεροι δὲ Χοιρεᾶται, that Sicyon had just three tribes, and the fourth was added only when the original names were restored; but that is not an improvement on the normal reconstruction of the text. If there was a restructuring of the tribes, that is not directly attested and can only be inferred from changes made in other cities.

68. 2. after his death for sixty years: Cleisthenes perhaps died in the 560s (Griffin, *Sikyon*, 57); the ending of the tyranny can perhaps be dated *c.* 555/4 from *FGrH* 105 F 1 trans. Fornara 39. B (cf. Griffin, 45–47); and if that is right the old names were not restored immediately on the fall of the tyranny. 'Sixty years' perhaps means two generations of thirty years: Herodotus did not systematically use a standard length of generation (cf. Rhodes, in *Herodotus and His World*, 58–72 at 67–68), but cf. VII. 148. 4, and in book V 89. 2–3.

Hylleis, Pamphyloi and Dymanatai: Elsewhere the third tribe is regularly called Dymanes.

they attached a name from Adrastus' son ... Aegialeis: The word αἰγιαλός means 'beach'. There was an earlier Aegialus in legend, who was the first king of Sicyon and gave his name to the land (different versions Apollod. *Bibl.* II. 1. 1, Paus. II. 5. 6). According to Hdt. VII. 94 those who became the Ionians of Asia Minor, when they still lived in Achaea, on the north coast of the Peloponnese, were called *Pelasgoi Aegialeis* (cf. I. 56–8 on the Ionians as originally Pelasgian). If the earlier Aegialus had already been invented in the late sixth century, it is possible that the tribe name was derived from him and that Herodotus is mistaken.

69. 1. The Athenian Cleisthenes ... having his name from him: Closing the ring opened at 67. 1.

in his case looked down on the Ionians: A forced comparison, which seems to misunderstand Cleisthenes' purposes. As noted on 66. 2, he did not abolish the four Ionian tribes, but he created ten new tribes with a territorial basis, which served as the principal articulation of the citizen body for political and military purposes.

69. 2. previously he had spurned the Athenian people ... to his own side: Repeated from 66. 2. Bekker's πάντως is the simplest way to obtain sense from the manuscripts' πάντων.

he created ten phylarchs instead of four: Later the phylarchs were the commanders of tribal regiments of cavalry, parallel to the taxiarchs who commanded the tribal regiments of infantry (*Ath. Pol.* 61. 5 with 61. 3). Hornblower supposes Herodotus to mean the taxiarchs; I prefer the suspicion of How and Wells that he meant the formal heads of the tribes (*phylobasileis* for the Ionic tribes, e.g. *Ath. Pol.* 8. 3; the new tribes had a plurality of *epimeletai*, e.g. *IG* ii² 1138. 7–9, but their inscribed decrees do not state who presided at their meetings).

distributed the demes on a basis of ten: The demes were not mentioned in 66. 2, but see commentary there: they were the villages or other local communities which served as the smallest units in the new structure. There were 139 demes, if a few with 'upper' and 'lower' divisions are each counted as two (J. S. Traill, *The Political Organization of Attica* [*Hesperia* Supp. 14, 1975]), so Lolling's δέκαχα is to be preferred to the manuscripts' δέκα repeated from immediately before.

Having attached the people: Recapitulating 'added the people to his following' in 66. 2.

70. 1. Isagoras, getting the worse of it in turn: Balancing 'Cleisthenes, getting the worse of it' in 66. 2.

he invited Cleomenes the Spartan ... intercourse with Isagoras' wife): So Isagoras will not have been a 'friend of the tyrants' as in *Ath. Pol.* 20. 1 (cf. on 66. 1). Probably he represented Cleisthenes to Cleomenes as a budding tyrant and argued that there was no point in removing one tyrant to make way for another.

70. 2. calling them the accursed: This will be explained in 71.

71. 1. Cylon, an Olympic victor, who preened himself for tyranny:
For the standing of Olympic victors cf. 47. 1 with commentary. The verb
(cf. Ar. *Vesp.* 1317) means literally 'grow one's hair long'. It is used
by Herodotus in that sense except here (e.g. I. 82. 8), and Hornblower
wonders if it should be taken literally here too. On this episode cf. Thuc.
I. 126. 3–12, Plut. *Sol.* 12. 1–9 (*Ath. Pol.* 1, where the surviving text
begins, seems to have had the same account as Plutarch), schol. Ar. *Eq.*
445 (three accounts).

He attached to himself a following of his contemporaries: For
hetaireiai see on 66. 2. A man's *helikiotai* ('contemporaries') were men
with whom he would naturally associate. Thucydides and schol. Ar. §2
say that he was married to the daughter of Theagenes tyrant of Megara,
and that he consulted Delphi (and misinterpreted the response).

sat as a suppliant at the image: Of Athena: a suppliant to a god (cf.
on 51. 1) would go to the god's statue or altar.

71. 2. These men were removed ... liable to anything except death:
Herodotus slips from Cylon as an individual to 'these men', Cylon and his
supporters; and according to Thucydides and schol. Ar. §2 Cylon himself
escaped. The men were promised that their lives would be spared; in
Plutarch's version they attached a cord to the statue, and when that broke
their opponents felt free to kill them. Seizing the acropolis for a tyranny,
and killing suppliants after promising to spare their lives, could both
be represented as wicked; the episode had on-going repercussions, but
according to Plutarch a purification of Athens ascribed to Epimenides
the Cretan involved a curse on those judged responsible for the killing.
It is not clear what the standing of Alcmaeon the son of 'Megacles the
archon' was when he took part in the First Sacred War (cf. on 67. 2), but
Alcmaeon's son Megacles was active in Athens at the time of the rise of
Pisistratus (I. 59–61).

by the *prytaneis* of the *naukraroi* ... administered Athens:
Thucydides attributes responsibility equally emphatically, and
presumably in conscious disagreement with Herodotus, to 'the nine
archons, who at that time conducted most of the political business'.
Neither focuses directly on the Alcmaeonids, and only Plutarch explains
their involvement, by attributing responsibility to 'Megacles the archon'.
While it is clear that *naukrariai* and their officials the *naukraroi* were
important in early Athens (cf. *Ath. Pol.* 8. 3, 21. 5), it is likely that the

principal officials of the early state were the nine archons (as in *Ath. Pol.* 3).

This happened before the time of Pisistratus: Indeed, long before the time of Pisistratus – but this section began with the ending of the Pisistratid tyranny. Cylon's Olympic victory was in 640, according to Eusebius; the legislation of Draco on homicide, probably in part a reaction to this episode, was in 621/0 (Olympiad xxxix = 624/3–621/0 according to the chronographers, and a possible reading in Diod. Sic. IX. 17 yields that year); Cylon's attempted *coup* was in an Olympic year (Thucydides and schol. Ar. §2), so must have been in 636/5, 632/1, 628/7 or 624/3.

72. 1. seven hundred Athenian households: It is hard to believe that so many were contaminated by what had happened slightly over a century earlier, but 73. 1 and *Ath. Pol.* 20. 3 have the same number, so almost certainly it is what Herodotus wrote.

dissolve the council: That he should dissolve the Areopagus would be unthinkable, and Cleisthenes' council of five hundred did not yet exist: this must be the Solonian council of four hundred, whose existence has been doubted but unjustifiably (defended by P. Cloché, 'La Boulè d' Athènes en 508/507 avant J.-C.', *REG* 37 (1924), 1–26; but still doubted by C. Hignett, *A History of the Athenian Constitution* [Oxford UP, 1952], 92–96).

72. 2. The rest of the Athenians agreed among themselves and blockaded them: This is the basis for the argument of J. Ober for a spontaneous movement of the people rather than support by the people for one or more leaders: 'The Athenian Revolution of 508/7 BC: Violence, Authority and the Origins of Democracy', in C. Dougherty and L. Kurke (eds), *Cultural Politics in Archaic Greece* (Cambridge UP 1993), 215–32 = his *The Athenian Revolution* (Princeton UP, 1996), (32–)34–52. However, the people were supporting the council, and I think Ober extracts too much from Herodotus' words.

those of them who were Spartans departed from the land under a truce: It appears from 74. 1 that Isagoras himself was able to leave with the Spartans.

72. 3. The saying for Cleomenes was fulfilled: In a small-scale anticipation (*analepsis*) we are first told this, then told what the priestess said, and then told that Cleomenes was expelled.

he went into the shrine of the Goddess to address her: Cf. Agamemnon on returning to Argos in Aesch. *Ag.* 810–3.

the priestess rose up from her throne: The priestess of Athena Polias. As Hornblower notes, it will surely have been remembered who the priestess was, but mentioning her simply by title enhances her authority. The temple will perhaps be the 'old temple of Athena', on the 'Dörpfeld site' between the Parthenon and the Erechtheum, if that was built towards the end of the tyranny; but some have dated that temple after the overthrow of the tyranny (520s, W. B. Dinsmoor, 'The Hekatompedon on the Athenian Akropolis', *AJA*² 51 [1947], 109–51 at 112–18; last decade of century, W. A. P. Childs, 'The Date of the Old Temple of Athena on the Athenian Acropolis', in W. D. E. Coulson *et al.* [eds], *The Archaeology of Athens and Attica under the Democracy* [Oxford: Oxbow, 1994], 1–6).

it is not rightful for a Dorian ... I am not a Dorian but an Achaean: In VI. 81 Cleomenes will be forbidden to sacrifice at the temple of Hera in Argos as a 'foreigner' (*xeinos*). Here he is forbidden as a Dorian: cf. *IG* xii. v 225 = *LSCG* 110 (Paros, fifth century), which excludes Dorians and slaves from the rites of Kore there. There are signs that in the mid sixth century Sparta had, by appropriating the 'bones of Orestes' (I. 67–8), sought to be a leader of all the Peloponnesians (through what was to become the Peloponnesian League) rather than a Dorian conqueror of them (cf. W. G. Forrest, *A History of Sparta, 950–192 BC* [London: Duckworth, ²1980], 74–76), and that image of Sparta is here rejected. Cleomenes' reply can also be taken to mean, 'I am not [my brother] Dorieus'; and technically the Spartan kings could claim that as Heraclids they were not Dorians.

made his attempt: To take control of the acropolis, or to address the Goddess? Hornblower thinks the latter.

was driven out with the Spartans: And with Isagoras (74. 1), and a collection of oracles (90. 2). There is a comic account of this in Ar. *Lys.* 271–82.

imprisoned to put them to death: For the expression cf. III. 119. 2; also I. 109. 1.

Timesitheus the Delphian: Paus. VI. 8. 6 is justification for the emendation 'the Delphian', and mentions his statue at Olympia and his victories, and his condemnation for taking part when 'Isagoras seized the acropolis for tyranny'.

73. 1. they sent to Sardis, wanting to make an alliance with the Persians: At this stage Athens did not yet perceive the Persians as a threat, but was willing to invoke them when Sparta was hostile.

Artaphernes son of Hystaspes, the governor of Sardis: Cf. 25. 1. The formal introduction here adds weight to this first contact between Athens and Persia.

73. 2. asked who were these people ... who asked to become allies of the Persians: Cf. Darius' enquiry about the Paeonians, in 13. 2.

gave them this summary answer: Cf. Pind. *Ol.* 7. 68, *Pyth.* 3. 80.

If the Athenians will give King Darius earth and water ... he bids them be gone: For earth and water cf. 17. 1. As with Amyntas of Macedon, the Persians insist on formal subjection to them.

73. 3. The messengers on their own initiative ... they incurred great blame: Herodotus leaves unclear how far they went – whether they did actually make an act of submission which the Athenians afterwards repudiated, or they simply expressed willingness on the part of Athens but the Athenians were unwilling and no act of submission was made. E. Badian, 'Herodotus on Alexander I of Macedon: A Study in Some Subtle Silences', in Hornblower (ed.), *Greek Historiography*, 107–30 at 124–26, argued that the Athenians were encouraged to approach Persia by Alexander of Macedon, that there was an act of submission, and that Herodotus' failure to say more than that 'they incurred great blame' indicates that Athens did for a time formally become subject to Persia; and that (apart from the involvement of Alexander) is accepted by Hornblower – but I think that infers too much from 'they incurred great blame'.

74. 1. Cleomenes ... collected an army from the whole Peloponnese: This is the earliest indication that Sparta had organised its Peloponnesian allies in a League, through which they were bound to 'follow wherever the Spartans might lead' (formulation of Xen. *Hell.* II. 2. 20). See G. E. M. de Ste. Croix, *The Origins of the Peloponnesian War* (London: Duckworth, 1972), 101–24, 333–42; but probably there was less formalisation from the beginning and more responding to issues as they arose than he allowed. The date will be *c.* 506.

not stating the purpose ... to install Isagoras as tyrant: It is not clear whether he had a formal right to summon the allies without

explanation, or by force of personality simply did that, or this has been invented for the sake of the late-stage desertions to be mentioned below. Particularly in view of the coordinated expeditions of the Boeotians and Chalcidians, it must have been evident even if not directly stated that the expedition was aimed at Athens (How and Wells); but that the purpose was to make Isagoras tyrant may simply be an inference.

74. 2. invaded Eleusis: *Barrington Atlas* 59 B 2, the first part of Attica which an invader from the Peloponnese would reach. Cf. schol. Ar. *Lys.* 273.

the Boeotians ... captured Oenoë and Hysiae, the remotest demes of Attica: Oenoë, *Barrington Atlas* 59 A 2; both, 58 E 1. Oenoë, north-west of Eleusis, as one of the remotest demes of Attica is not a problem (cf. Thuc. II 18. 2; there was another Oenoë inland from Marathon, 59 C 2), but Hysiae is: it lay east of Plataea, on the north slope of Mount Cithaeron, and was never an Athenian deme, and even Eleutherae, between Hysiae and Oenoë, was reckoned as part of the territory of Plataea (*Hell. Oxy.* 19. 3 Chambers). However, in 519 Plataea had refused to join the Boeotian federation led by Thebes, and had made an alliance with Athens and probably had been given the kind of reciprocal citizenship rights which were later known as *isopoliteia* (VI. 108, Thuc. III. 55. 1–3, cf. for the date Thuc. III. 68. 5, which some have doubted but mistakenly). So from 519 until the destruction of Plataea in 427 the status of Plataea and its dependencies was anomalous, and Herodotus was not wholly unjustified in regarding Hysiae as part of Attica. A commemorative inscription from Thebes, almost certainly to be associated with this campaign, mentions not only Oenoë but Phyle (east of Oenoë: *Barrington Atlas* 59 B 2) and Eleusis (*SEG* lvi 521).

the Chalcidians attacked on the other side and ravaged sites in Attica: After the specificity with regard to the Boeotians, this is surprisingly unspecific; but it presumably refers to the north-east coast of Attica facing Euboea. Chalcis was at the centre of the mainland-facing coast of Euboea (*Barrington Atlas* 55 F 4, *Inventory* 647–49 no. 365).

though caught in a dilemma, planned to take account of the Boeotians and Chalcidians later: Hornblower writes of 'admiring words' and 'nonchalance'; but it is not surprising that the Athenians regarded the large army from the Peloponnese as the most serious threat.

75. 1. first the Corinthians ... and changed their minds and were gone:
The Corinthians regularly appear as the members of the Peloponnesian
League most willing to stand up to Sparta: cf. 92–3, and in connection
with the Peloponnesian War Thuc. I. 67–71, 119–24, V. 25. 1, 27–31.
Hornblower follows F. Schachermeyr in thinking that the true reason
for the collapse of the campaign was the news of Athens' submission to
Persia (cf. 73) and reluctance to risk Persian reprisals; but I doubt if the
mainland Greeks were worried about Persia as early as this.

**Demaratus son of Ariston, who was himself king of the Spartiates,
had joined in leading the force out from Sparta:** This is his first
appearance in Herodotus. He was king in the Eurypontid line, whose
genealogy Herodotus gives in VIII. 131. 2–3, and had perhaps been on the
throne since *c.* 515. If we accept the manuscripts' text of the genealogy,
which now seems correct, Demaratus' father and grandfather were kings
before him (his father, like Cleomenes' father, as recorded in 39–41, had
difficulty in producing an heir, and it was later claimed that Demaratus
was not his father's son), but before them the kingship had descended
in another line, which returned to favour when Demaratus, after another
dispute with Cleomenes had led to his deposition, was succeeded *c.* 491
by Leotychidas II (VI. 61–70).

had not previously been at odds with Cleomenes: But this was to
happen again: see previous note.

**75. 2. a law was enacted ... that it should not be permitted to both
kings to accompany an army:** I.e. that the two should not serve on
the same campaign: in 479 the regent Pausanias commanded the Greek
forces on land and the king Leotychidas commanded at sea (IX. 10. 1,
VIII. 131. 2). But Hornblower suggests that the rule was that the two
kings should not even serve on different campaigns at the same time,
and that in 479 though Pausanias went to Plataea the king for whom
he was regent did not. Aegina and Athens in turn refused to obey just
one king (VI. 50. 2, 73. 2; 86. 1); and what the Spartans say to Argos in
VII. 149. 2 seems to ignore the law. The decision reflects disapproval
of the undermining of the campaign, so presumably was prompted by
Cleomenes or a supporter of his. Another decision apparently taken at
the same time was that the allies should be consulted before a campaign
rather than simply summoned, but would then be bound by a majority
decision: contrast 91. 2, 93. 1–94. 1, with 74. 1.

one also of the Tyndarids was left behind: The Tyndarids were the Dioscuri, Castor and Pollux, and presumably statues of them were taken with the army. In Simonides' poem on the Plataea campaign the Spartans set out for Plataea with both Tyndarids and with Menelaus (fr. 11. 29–31 West²), and there Hornblower thinks the reference is not to statues but to a divine epiphany.

76. The first time was when they had founded Megara: This episode in the legendary period was 'for war': the Athenians claimed that Megara was once part of the kingdom of Athens, but in the time of Codrus the Peloponnesians captured it and refounded it as a Dorian city. In an alternative tradition Megara was founded from Boeotia. See Hellanicus *FGrH* 4 F 78, Strabo 392 / IX. 1. 6, Paus. I. 19. 4, 39. 4–6, Apollod. *Bibl.* III. 15. 1, 5–8; and Jacoby on Philoch. *FGrH* 328 F 107 (part of the passage from Strabo), Rhodes on the lost beginning of *Ath. Pol.*, §c.

the second and third ... to drive out the Pisistratids: The expeditions of Anchimolius (63. 2–4), and of Cleomenes in 511/0 (64–5). Cleomenes' expedition of 508/7 (70, 72), again 'for war', is omitted: he went 'without a large force' (72. 1), and the inclusion of this would have spoiled the symmetry.

77. 1. the Euripus: the strait between Euboea and the mainland, and especially the very narrow part of it, at Chalcis: *Barrington Atlas* 55 F 4.

they decided to make an attempt against the Boeotians before the Chalcidians: They had been intending to cross to Euboea, but on encountering the Boeotians on the mainland they not surprisingly decided to deal with them first.

77. 2. That very same day the Athenians crossed to Euboea and attacked the Chalcidians too: Fighting and winning two battles on the same day was a remarkable achievement.

left four thousand cleruchs on the land of the horse-rearers: Cleruchs ('allotment-holders') were Athenians who were given land in overseas terrritory but remained Athenian citizens: they benefited economically, whether they lived on the land or remained in Athens and had others work it for them, and when present on their land could act as an informal garrison to secure the loyalty of the community among which they lived. See P. A. Brunt, 'Athenian Settlements Abroad in the Fifth Century BC', in *Ancient*

Society and Institutions ... V. Ehrenberg (Oxford: Blackwell, 1966), 71–92
= his *Studies in Greek History and Thought* (Oxford UP, 1993), 112–34(–
36) at 87–89 = 132–34. In 490 these cleruchs returned to Athens and the
horse-rearers returned (VI. 100–2; Plut. *Per.* 23. 4).

**horse-rearers is what the bloated class of the Chalcidians are
called:** For 'the bloated class' cf. 30. 1. Arist. *Pol.* IV. 1289 в 36–40
mentions aristocracies of horsemen here, in neighbouring Eretria, and
in Magnesia on the Maeander and other places in Asia; cf. Arist. fr. 603
(Rose, 1867).

77. 3. they released them after setting a price of 2 minas: I.e. 200
drachmae (Hornblower's 1 mina = 200 drachmae is a slip). On the
ransoming of prisoners of war see W. K. Pritchett, *The Greek State at
War*, v (U. of California P., 1991), 245–97; rates paid varied, but VI. 79.
1 gives 2 minas as a standard rate among the Peloponnesians.

they still survived to my time: As Hornblower, stresses, Herodotus
does not explicitly say that he saw these himself (contrast 59), but it is
likely.

**hanging from the walls which had been scorched by fire by the
Medes:** In the sack of Athens in 480 (VIII. 53. 2). In 9. 3 'Medes'
means the Medes, but as here Herodotus and the Greeks generally often
used 'Medes' to refer to the Persians, who had overthrown the Median
kingdom in the middle of the sixth century (I. 107–30).

opposite the building which faces west: This is probably the 'old
temple of Athena', built in the late sixth century on a site between the
later Erechtheum and Parthenon (cf. on 72. 3); an earlier temple on the
site of the Parthenon was begun in the 480s and was still unfinished when
the Persians invaded. See e.g. Mee and Spawforth, 52–56.

77. 4. a bronze four-horse chariot ... the propylaea on the acropolis:
The elaborate building which now stands at the western entrance to
the acropolis was built between 437/6 and 432/1 (*IG* i³ 462–66, cf. 52
= O&R 144. *B.* 2–12): an earlier propylaea was built in the 480s and
destroyed by the Persians (Mee and Spawforth, 47–50). Paus. I. 28. 2
locates the chariot inside the propylaea of the 430s, near the statue of
Athena Promachos between the propylaea and the Erechtheum. Some
have found it hard to reconcile Herodotus' words with a location so far
beyond the propylaea: see M&L p. 29 (commentary on their 15, cited
below) for a suggestion that the chariot was twice moved; but if 'as

soon as you enter the propylaea on the acropolis' can be taken to mean 'as soon as you enter the acropolis through the propylaea' there is no problem (R. G. Osborne, in *Brill's Companion*, 497–520 at 511 n. 15). Powell deleted 'the propylaea' and Wilson deletes 'the acropolis', but the text need not be emended.

Inscribed on it is this: The chariot does not survive, but fragments of two versions of the inscription do (M&L 15 = *IG* i³ 501), the first (with lines 1 and 3 in the opposite order to Herodotus') presumably inscribed soon after the event and damaged by the Persians in 480, and the second (with the lines in Herodotus' order) perhaps set up after Athens' victory over Boeotia at Oenophyta *c*. 457. ἀχνυόεντι in the epigram (if that is right: see *apparatus*) will be derived from ἀχνύς ('pain').

Recently another inscription has been found (*SEG* lvi 521, cited in the commentary on 74. 2), in which the Thebans commemorate this episode in terms of their capturing Oenoe, Phyle and Eleusis, and of ransoming Chalcis.

Herodotus will have been conscious that in 447/6 Athens had again confronted enemies from the Peloponnese, Boeotia and Euboea (Thuc. I. 113. 1–115. 1).

78. The Athenians had increased, then: This resumes what was said at the beginning of 66. 1, and enlarges on it by contrasting Athens under the tyranny with Athens after the tyranny.

freedom of speech: See on 37. 2. In 92. α. 1 the Corinthians will use *isokratie* ('equality of power') as the alternative to tyranny.

when they were under tyrants were not superior in warfare … when rid of tyrants became by far the first: Cf. 91. 1; but contrast 66. 1, Thuc. VI. 54. 5. The achievement against the Boeotians and Chalcidians was remarkable (cf. on 77. 2), but Athens under the Pisistratids was not ineffective (capture of Sigeum, 94. 1; installation of Lygdamis in Naxos, purification of Delos, I. 64. 2), and after the liberation the appeal to Persia for support (73) does not point to confidence. Herodotus' emphasis is on liberated Athens, not on Athens as reformed by Cleisthenes: Wells, *Studies in Herodotus*, 153; Fornara, *Herodotus*, 48–50. It is not clear how far ahead 'by far the first' is looking.

labouring for a master: Cf. the remark of the Spartan Demaratus to Xerxes in VII. 104. 4.

79. 1. The Thebans after that sent to the God: I.e. to Apollo at Delphi. Above Herodotus wrote of 'the Boeotians'; but for the domination of Boeotia by Thebes see on 74. 2, and cf. 79. 2 on those 'nearest'.

take revenge: Cf. the Athenians in 77. 1.

bring the matter forward to the many-voiced: The assembly (cf. Hom. *Od.* II. 150), as below, but we do not need to follow Wilson in inserting ἀγορὴν to spell that out; here the word may be quoted from the oracle (How and Wells).

79. 2. held an assembly: Cf. on 29. 2. In later inscriptions decrees of Thebes and the other cities are normally formulated as resolutions of the *demos* (P. J. Rhodes with D. M. Lewis, *The Decrees of the Greek States* [Oxford UP, 1997], 113–25).

Tanagra, Coronea and Thespiae: For Tanagra cf. on 57. 1. Coronea was slightly north of west from Thebes, and at a greater distance than the other two (*Barrington Atlas* 55 D 4, *Inventory* 444–45 no. 210), and Thespiae slightly south of west from Thebes (*Barrington Atlas* 55 E 4, *Inventory* 457–58 no. 222). Men from Thespiae, unlike those from Thebes, are said to have fought willingly on the Greek side at Thermopylae (VII. 202, 222, 226. 1; for Thebes see on 80. 1).

80. 1. one of them eventually realised: For the *motif* of the one man or woman who understands cf. VI. 37. 2, VII. 239. 4; also VII. 142–3; but in IX. 33. 2–3 with 35 the one man Tisamenus is wrong and the Spartans are right. Hornblower adds parallels in other texts.

the daughters of Asopus were Thebe and Aegina ... we should ask the Aeginetans to be our avengers: For Thebe and Aegina as twin nymphs among the many daughters of Asopus cf. Pind. *Isthm.* 8. 16–18, Bacchyl. 9. 53–5; but later the complication was introduced that Thebe was daughter of a Boeotian Asopus and Aegina of a Peloponnesian Asopus (M. L. West, *The Hesiodic Catalogue of Women* [Oxford UP, 1985], 100; cf. *Barrington Atlas* 58 E 1, D 2).

Aegina was in the middle of the Saronic Gulf, on the north side of which Athens lay (*Barrington Atlas* 58 E–F 2, *Inventory* 620–22 no. 358; see also T. J. Figueira, *Aegina: Society and Politics* [New York: Arno, 1981]; *Excursions in Epichoric History*). This (79–89) is the first of a series of passages dealing with Athens and Aegina; see later VI. 48–50, 73, 85–93; VII. 144–5. The theme is important, because the war

with Aegina prompted Athens' building the large navy which was to be so important in 480–479 (VII. 144). Thebes and Aegina diverged then, with Thebes medising (VII. 222, 233) but Aegina being reconciled to Athens and resisting bravely (VII. 145, VIII. 86, 91–3). After the Persian Wars Aegina was forced into Athens' Delian League in the early 450s (Thuc. I. 105. 1–4, 108. 4); Athens' failure to grant it autonomy was one of Thucydides' proximate causes of the Peloponnesian War (Thuc. I. 67. 2, 139. 1, 140. 3); in 431 Athens expelled the inhabitants (VI. 91. 1, Thuc. II. 27), and in 424 it destroyed their refugee settlement in the Peloponnese (Thuc. IV. 56. 2–57, not mentioned by Herodotus).

80. 2. No other opinion was thought to seem better than this: Hornblower is perhaps unfair in judging the absence of positive delight as a reflection of the proverbial dullness of the Thebans (e.g. Pind. *Ol.* 6. 89–90).

were persuaded: Wilson's insertion makes sense of the manuscripts' divergence.

they would send them the sons of Aeacus: Presumably statues, as in 75. 2; in 81. 1 the Thebans in disappointment return them. Aeacus is credited with four sons – Telamon, Peleus, Menoetius, Phocus – and the expression could include remoter descendants, as in VIII. 64. 2 Telamon and his son Ajax are invoked from Salamis, and Aeacus and 'the other sons of Aeacus' are brought from Aegina. Here most probably Telamon and Peleus are meant.

81. 2. The Aeginetans were buoyed up by great prosperity: Cf. II. 168, III. 59, 131, IV. 152. 3 (and IX. 80. 3 has a discreditable story accounting for their wealth after the Persian Wars); and for Aegina's wealth as based on trade Arist. *Pol.* IV. 1291 в 24. 'Buoying up' (ἐπαίρειν) in Herodotus tends to be used of the pride which comes before a fall (cf. their 'folly' in 83. 1): for another instance in book V see 91. 2.

mindful of their ancient enmity towards the Athenians: 'Already incurred' in 82. 1, but Herodotus gives no further indication of when. T. J. Figueira, 'Aiginetan Independence', *CJ* 79 1983/4, 8–29, revised in his *Excursions in Epichoric History*, 9–33, suggests that Aegina was dependent on Argos in the first half of the seventh century, on Epidaurus in the second half, and had asserted its independence by the end of the century. In 'Herodotus on the Early Hostilities between Aigina and

Athens', *AJP* 106 (1985), 49–74, revised in *Excursions*, 35–60, he explores the different versions of the story and considers what truth may lie behind them.

they began to wage a war without heralds: A truceless war, in which heralds did not travel between the two sides: A. Andrewes, 'Athens and Aegina, 510–480 BC', *BSA* 37 (1936/7), 1–7 at 2. Herodotus implies that this episode and the episodes narrated in book VI all occurred before the battle of Marathon in 490. Many scholars have redated some or all of the events to the 480s (see Hornblower, who like me is not persuaded by them), but a good case was made by N. G. L. Hammond for accepting Herodotus' implication ('Studies in Greek Chronology of the Sixth and Fifth Centuries BC', *Historia* 4 [1955], 371–411 at 406–11 = his *Collected Studies* [Amsterdam: Hakkert, 1993–2001], i. 355–95 at 390–95); for a way to ease his tight timetable for the late 490s see Rhodes, in *Herodotus and His World*, 58–72 at 60–62. This episode will have begun *c.* 505 (cf. on 74. 1).

81. 3. long ships: Cf. 30. 4.

Phalerum and many other demes along the rest of the coast: For Phalerum see on 63. 3.

82. 1. The territory of the Epidaurians was bearing them no crops: For such a digression to the past for explanatory purposes (*analepsis*) see Introduction, p. 14. For Epidaurus, on the south coast of the Saronic Gulf, see *Barrington Atlas* 58 E 2, *Inventory* 606–608 no. 348. It was previously mentioned in passing in I. 146. 1, and in connection with the Cypselid tyranny at Corinth in III. 50–2. Hornblower notes that Athens, Aegina, Epidaurus and Argos were all members of the Calaurean Amphictyony, centred on Calaurea, an island with a sanctuary of Poseidon south-east of Epidaurus towards the tip of the Argolid (Strabo 374 / VIII. 6. 14; see *Barrington Atlas* 58 E–F 2, *Inventory* 622–23 no. 360), and this may help to explain the interactions and the cults recounted here. It is hard to determine in this story where authentic memory ends and enbroidery begins. For crop failure and an oracle cf. IV. 150–8, where Thera experiences a failure from its first receiving an oracle until it at last complies. For a discussion of this episode and Herodotus' treatment of it see J. H. Haubold, in Irwin and Greenwood (eds), *Reading Herodotus*, 226–44.

Damia and Auxesia: On these deities which were locally important but outside the repertoire of Greek myths see Parker, *On Greek Religion*, 72. The etymology and significance of Damia are unknown, but Auxesia presumably denotes agricultural 'increase'. They are attested epigraphically on Aegina in *IG* iv. ii² 787 (late fifth century) as Mnia and Auzesie, and at Epidaurus e.g. in *IG* iv. i² 410 (AD) as Mnia and Auxesia.

things would turn out better: Those who consulted an oracle often asked whether things would turn out better if they did *A* or *B*: e.g. εἰ λῶιον καὶ ἄμεινόν ἐστι … ('if it is more desirable and better…', R&O 58 = *IG* ii³ 292. 24–5): Herodotus uses the same formulation as here in connection with oracles in 114. 2 and IV. 15. 3.

82. 2. of bronze or of stone … cultivated olive wood: Oracles were often asked to choose between two options (e.g. R&O 58 = *IG* ii³ 292. 23–30, from Athens in 352/1); for the rejection of both cf. e.g. Hom. *Il.* I. 62–7, 93–100. In the Aeginetan inscription cited above the statue of Mnia is not of olive but of cypress.

theirs were the most sacred olives: For sacred olives at Athens see VIII. 55, Lys. VII. *Olive Stump, Ath. Pol.* 60.

82. 3. every year they should bring offerings to Athena Polias and to Erechtheus: With whom the olives were associated (VIII. 55). Athena Polias was Athena as patron deity of Athens; Erechtheus was a legendary early king of Athens and/or ancestor of all the Athenians, born from Earth after Poseidon had failed to rape Athena; and they were worshipped together on the acropolis (Hom. *Il.* II. 546–51, *Od.* VII. 80–1, with Parker, *Athenian Religion*, 19–20). For such regular offerings cf. in legend the Athenian offerings to Minos of Crete (Plut. *Thes.* 15–19), and in fifth-century practice those required by Athens at first from the Ionians and eventually from all members of the Delian League (*IG* i³ 14 = O&R 121. 2–5, 46 = 142. 15–17, 71 = 153. 55–7, 34 = 154. 41–3; in 78 = 141. 12–36 members are commanded and other Greeks are invited to send offerings to Eleusis).

83. 1. had been doing the bidding of the Epidaurians … to give and receive justice from one another: Aegina may have been subject to Epidaurus for a time in the seventh century; and Herodotus believed it to have been colonised from Epidaurus (VIII. 46. 1). In the fifth century Athens had some lawsuits transferred from allied courts to Athenian

courts ([Xen.] *Ath. Pol.* 16–18, cf. *IG* i³ 14. 26–9 = O&R 121. 26–9, 40 = 131. 70–6, Antiph. V. *Herodes* 47).

yielding to folly: For what happened to Aegina at the hands of Athens in the fifth century see on 80. 1; but *sub specie aeternitatis* a century and a half of independence and prosperity was no mean achievement.

83. 2. since they had mastery of the sea: Herodotus uses this expression elsewhere only of Minos in the legendary period and Polycrates of Samos as the first 'of the Greeks whom we know / of what is called the human generation' (III. 122. 2). Sea power was an important element in Thucydides' sketch of the development of power in the Greek world (beginning with Minos again, and ending with Aegina and Athens: Thuc. I. 4–5. 1, 7–8, 13–15. 1). Eventually lists of 'thalassocrats' were compiled (see Diod. Sic. VII. fr. 11, with W. G. Forrest, 'Two Chronographic Notes', *CQ*² 19 [1969], 95–110 at 95–106, where Aegina is the last, perhaps from 489 to 479).

at a place called Oeë ... twenty stades from the city: Not yet located; but the city was near the north-west corner of the island.

83. 3. with sacrifices and ribald women's choruses: Similar to the rites practised at Epidaurus, as stated below. Ribald women's choruses would have been appropriate to Auxesia as a fertility goddess comparable to Demeter (cf. the Thesmophoria at Athens: R. C. T. Parker, *Polytheism and Society at Athens* [Oxford UP, 2005], 270–83).

appointing ten men as chorus-leaders for each of the divinities: Chorus-leaders, in the literal meaning of the word, not as at Athens men performing the liturgy of training and paying for the chorus (as in Antiph. VI. *Chorus Member*). Men as leaders of women's choruses were not uncommon.

The choruses did not speak ill of any man, but of the local women: Emphatic, and perhaps implying that one might expect otherwise: cf. Parker, *On Greek Religion*, 207 with n. 131.

and they also: Probably the Epidaurians, but Parker, *On Greek Religion*, expresses uncertainty.

84. 2. the Aeginetans said that they had no business with Athens: The beginning of the hostility: the Aeginetans, having stolen the statues, do not accept that with them they have taken over the Epidaurians' obligation to Athens.

85. 1. The Athenians say: Herodotus now gives rival accounts (cf. Introduction, pp. 9–11). The Athenians claim that they sent a modest deputation, and no Aeginetan response is mentioned but they encountered divine resistance; the Aeginetans claim that the Athenians sent a substantial expedition, they themselves invoked the help of Argos, and the divine resistance coincided with a battle. The version attributed to the Athenians is intelligible, but would suggest to a pious reader that the Athenians were in the wrong (Hornblower on 87. 2); that attributed to the Aeginetans is the more creditable to them; it is agreed between the two that only one Athenian returned home.

they dispatched some of their citizens in a single trireme: The manuscripts' τούτους/τουτέων cannot be right, and Wilson's τινας ('some') is more likely than any of the more specific suggestions which have been offered.

How seriously should we take 'in a single trireme'? Large Greek fleets of triremes probably did not yet exist as early as the beginning of the sixth century (cf. on 32. 1), but some individual triremes may have done: see Thuc. I. 13. 2–3 (Corinthian triremes) with Morrison, Coates and Rankov, *The Athenian Trireme*², 36–40, and the more sceptical H. T. Wallinga, *Ships and Sea-Power before the Great Persian War* (Leiden: Brill, 1993), 103–29. But Herodotus may have used the word without worrying about that question.

85. 1–2. to uproot them from their bases … to drag them away: Graphic details to give substance to the story that the statues resisted all attempts to remove them.

85. 2. there occurred thunder and at the same time as the thunder an earthquake: Thunder and earthquakes were in any case alarming as natural phenomena, and might also be seen as messages from the gods: cf. in Herodotus III. 86. 2, IV. 28. 3, 94. 4, VI. 98. 3, VII. 10. ε, 42. 2, 129. 4, VIII. 12, 64; and in Thucydides esp. I. 23. 3, 101. 2 with III. 54. 5, II. 8. 3, III. 89, V. 45. 4, 50. 5, VI. 70. 2, 95. 1, VII. 79. 3, VIII. 6. 5.

The crew of the trireme … were driven mad, and … started to kill one another as enemies: In this version the goddesses protected themselves; cf. the salvation of Delphi in 480 (VIII. 37–9), and the salvation of a statue of Hera (Ath. XV. 672 B–E). For killing one another cf. the earthborn men when attacked by the Argonauts, and the Spartoi at Thebes (Ap. Rhod. *Argon.* III. 1373–6; Apollod. *Bibl.* III. 4. 1).

there was only one left: Cf. on 46. 1.

86. 2. They are not able to indicate with certainty ... they were intending to do what they actually did do: Here we have an unresolved alternative within the Aeginetan version, and Herodotus heightens the tension by not yet telling us 'what they actually did do'.

86. 3. what they say is incredible to me, but somebody else may believe it: Cf. Introduction, pp. 6, 9; Figueira sees this as an allusion to Herodotus' informants rather than to the credulous among his readers (*AJP* 106 (1985), 55 = *Excursions*, 40). For Herodotus' expressions of disbelief in stories of the gods' involvement in the mortal world cf. e.g. I. 182. 1, IV. 5. 1, VI. 105, and the less sceptical VI. 117. 2, VIII. 38–39. 1; and E. Baragwanath and M. de Bakker, in Baragwanath and de Bakker (eds), *Myth, Truth and Narrative in Herodotus* (Oxford UP, 2012), 13 with n. 49. Hornblower remarks that Herodotus seems to find 'heroic' battle epiphanies easier to credit than outright suspensions of the laws of nature.

Each image fell on its knees ... they have remained in that state: Presumably, whatever the reason, the statues which existed in Herodotus' time were kneeling; Hornblower cites some preserved instances of kneeling statues, and suggests that this aetiology and that of the change in costume (87. 3, below) may explain the inclusion of this long excursus. But in II. 131. 2–3 Herodotus rejects an aetiology of handless statues, remarking that the hands had simply broken off.

86. 4. made ready the Argives: Herodotus has said nothing hitherto to prepare us for their intervention.

87. 2. the Argives say ... but the Athenians attribute it…: In accordance with the two versions of the story given above.

they surrounded that person ... stabbed him ... and each of them asked…: Powell, *Lexicon*, classifies this use of ἄνθρωπος as resumptive (3. a); but more probably there is a sense of pity (LSJ 5). For this kind of action by women cf. the 'Lemnian deeds' of VI. 138. 4 and the stoning of Lycides' wife and children in IX. 5. 3. The bringer of bad news was regarded as a *pharmakos* (scapegoat) to be punished: M. Gras, in *Du Châtiment dans la cité* (Rome: École Française de Rome, 1984), 75–89 at 80.

87. 3. They had no other way to punish the wives: A strange remark; but the point of the story is to explain a supposed change from garments with pins to garments without.

they changed their dress to the Ionian style … they changed to the linen tunic: From a pinned *peplos* to an unpinned *chiton*. In fact in the classical period the unpinned *chiton* ('tunic': *kithon* in the manuscripts here) became a regular garment for women, often worn as an undergarment with a *peplos* or *himation* over it (H. Granger-Taylor, 'Dress', *OCD*⁴ 478–79). Thuc. I. 6. 3 writes of a change which started among Athenian men from the elaborate Ionian linen *chiton* to the simpler Dorian woollen *chiton*, which Hornblower suggests is a response to this passage.

88. 1. this style of clothing was in the past not Ionian but Carian: For Caria and the Carians, at the south-west corner of Asia Minor, see on 37. 1. See I. 171. 2–5, and Thuc. I. 4, 8. 1, for the Greeks' belief that earlier the Carians had occupied the Aegean islands.

all the ancient Greek women's clothing was the same as that which we now call Dorian: Contrast Thucydides' view, cited above, that Dorian clothing was simpler than Ionian.

88. 2. they should make brooch pins half as long again as the then prevalent length: Emphasising their brooches when the Athenians abandoned them – but the alleged longer pins seem not to be authentic (P. Jacobsthal, *Greek Pins and Their Connexions with Europe and Asia* [Oxford UP, 1956], 90–91). Cf. short hair for men in Argos and long in Sparta, I. 82. 7–8.

the women should particularly dedicate the brooches at the sanctuary of these gods: Cf. *IG* iv. ii² 787. 10–14: there is at any rate some current practice behind the story.

nothing else Athenian nor even pottery should be brought to the sanctuary: Unverifiable, since it applied only to the sanctuary, which has not been found.

89. 1. The origin of the Aeginetans' hostility to the Athenians came about as stated: Herodotus closes the ring opened in 82. 1, and resumes the narrative of what happened from *c*. 505.

89. 2. The Aeginetans proceeded to ravage the coastal parts of Attica: Cf. 81. 3.

there came a prophecy from Delphi: Presumably in response to an Athenian enquiry. Hornblower plausibly suggests that the first part of the response was to the original enquiry, and the second was to a supplementary enquiry about what would happen if the Athenians did not wait thirty years (cf. VII. 140–3, on the Athenians' consultation of Delphi before the Persian invasion of 480).

if they held off from wronging the Aeginetans for thirty years: Probably one generation (cf. 68. 2).

89. 3. they dedicated to Aeacus this precinct which stands now in the agora: A building of *c.* 500 near the west end of the south side (beginning of fifth century, H. A. Thompson and R. E. Wycherley, *The Athenian Agora*, xiv. *The Agora of Athens* [Princeton: ASCSA, 1972], 62–65; sixth century, J. McK. Camp, II, *The Athenian Agora: Site Guide* [Princeton: ASCSA, ⁵2010], 170–71), previously thought to be the *eliaia*, was identified as this by R. S. Stroud in publishing *SEG* xlvii 96 = R&O 26 (*The Athenian Grain-Tax Law of 374/3 BC* [*Hesperia* Supp. 29, 1998], 85–104).

they could not bear to hear that they must hold off for thirty years: So we are not entitled to count back from Athens' eventual defeat of Aegina in the early 450s and date this to the early 480s (cf. on 80. 1, 81. 2).

90. 1. a matter stirred up by the Spartans occurred as an impediment: With this Herodotus leaves the story of Athens and Aegina, to be resumed at VI. 49. Aeginetan raids on Attica may have continued, but presumably there was no significant Athenian retaliation at this point.

the Spartans learned ... with regard to the Pythia: Cf. 62. 2–63. 1.

they had driven men who were guest-friends of theirs out of their own land: Cf. 63. 2.

no gratitude for their doing this was being shown on the part of the Athenians: Not directly stated before, but cf. 70–6.

90. 2. urged on by oracles ... Cleomenes had found them and taken them up: Not mentioned at 72. For the Pisistratids' interest in oracles and the like (but not at Delphi) cf. 56, 93. 2 (Hippias' knowledge of oracles), and I. 59. 1–2, 62. 4–63. 1, 64. 2, VI. 107. 1–108. 1, VII. 6. 3–5.

91. 1. saw the Athenians increasing and in no way ready to obey them: Cf. 78 (increasing), 90. 1 (ungrateful).

when free … but when held down by tyranny…: Cf. 66. 1 (with a different emphasis), and again 78.

they sent for Hippias son of Pisistratus from Sigeum … to which the Pisistratids had fled: Cf. 65. 3. This episode is to be dated *c.* 504 (cf. on 81. 2).

91. 2. sent for messengers from their other allies too: Neither Cleomenes nor any other individual Spartan is mentioned here (though it was Cleomenes who had obtained the oracles: 90. 2). This passage, 91. 3, and the outcome in 93. 2–94. 1, show that since the aborted campaign of *c.* 506 (74–6) there had been a change from Sparta's simply summoning its allies to a campaign to its consulting them in advance of proposed action. Some, including G. E. M. de Ste. Croix, *Athenian Democratic Origins and Other Essays* (Oxford UP, 2004), 421–38 at 424, Hornblower on 91. 1, attribute the change to men other than Cleomenes; but both this change and the rule that the two kings should not campaign together (75. 2) reflect a desire to prevent the kind of collapse that had occurred in that earlier campaign, and I am inclined to see Cleomenes' influence here too (cf. W. G. Forrest, *A History of Sparta, 950–192 BC* [London: Duckworth, [2]1980], 89).

buoyed up: Cf. 81. 2.

men who were particular guest-friends … an ungrateful people…: Repeated from 90. 1.

have grievously insulted: Cf. 74. 1.

driven us out: Cf. 72. 2–3.

They have become proud and are increasing: Cf. 91. 1.

as has been learned particularly by their neighbours the Boeotians and Chalcidians: Cf. 77.

we can install him in Athens and give back what we took from him: This proposal casts doubt on the Spartans' claim to have been always opposed in principle to tyranny (Thuc. I. 18. 1, *FGrH* 105 F 1 trans. Fornara 39. B, Plut. *De Her. Mal.* 859 c–d).

92. *init.* the majority of the allies did not accept … the Corinthian Socles said this: For the contrast cf. VII. 10. *init.*, in a Persian context; Thuc. V. 27. 2, again the Peloponnesians and again Corinth as the exception. For Corinth as the member of the Peloponnesian League most likely to express disagreement with Sparta cf. 75. 1 with commentary. In the 430s we find Corinth not restraining Sparta but urging a reluctant

Sparta to action against Athens (Thuc. I. 67–88, 119–24); for the change, to be linked with the rise of Athens and the decline of Aegina, cf. on 93. 1. Socles (Σωκλέης, better attested in the manuscripts, or Σωσικλέης) is a reasonably common name in Corinth and other parts of the Peloponnese, but this bearer of it is not otherwise known.

This is the longest speech in Herodotus; most nearly comparable is VI. 86 (the Spartan king Leotychidas to the Athenians). It opposes the Spartan plan to reinstate Hippias as tyrant in Athens by warning the Spartans who have not experienced tyranny what tyranny is like. Hornblower sees it as a 'historical hinge', the last opportunity to 'put a stop to the growth of self-confident democratic Athens', though the breach between Sparta and Athens did not occur until the end of the 460s (Thuc. I. 102), and notes as precedents for this 'story-telling speech' Hom. *Il.* IX. 524–605 and passages in epinician poetry such as Pind. *Pyth.* 1. 92–8, *Pyth.* 2. 21–52. This is one of a series of passages devoted to the Cypselid tyranny in Corinth (cf. I. 14. 2, 20, 23–4, III. 48–53, V. 95. 2, VI. 128. 2); in this part of Herodotus' history it complements the end of the Pisistratid tyranny (55–65) and the Sicyonian tyranny (67–8), and the inclusion in this story of Miletus (92. ζ. 1–η. 1) reminds us that this is part of a long digression on the visit of Aristagoras of Miletus to Sparta and Athens.

Among discussions of this speech see V. J. Gray, 'Herodotus and Images of Tyranny: The Tyrants of Corinth', *AJP* 117 (1996), 361–89; J. L. Moles, in Irwin and Greenwood (eds), *Reading Herodotus*, 245–68; R. F. Buxton, 'Instructive Irony in Herodotus: The Socles Scene', *GRBS* 52 (2012), 559–86.

92. α. 1. heaven will be below the earth and and earth up in the air above the heaven: Dion. Hal. VI. 95. 2 quotes from a treaty, 'Let there be peace between the Romans and all the Latin cities as long as the heavens and the earth shall remain where they are'; and for the abuse of a similar clause see Hdt. IV. 201. 2–3.

equalities of power: Herodotus uses *isokratie* only here; for *iso*-words at the end of the sixth century cf. on 37. 2.

something than which nothing is more unjust among mankind or more bloodthirsty: Very forcefully expressed: the Thebans in Thuc. III. 62. 3 describe their narrow oligarchy in 480 as 'most directly opposed to laws and the greatest restraint'.

92. α. 2. you yourselves have no experience of tyrants: Cf. Thuc. I. 18. 1, and on Sparta's *eunomie* Hdt. I. 65. 2–66. 1.

92. β. 1. the disposition of the Corinthians' city: For *katastasis* cf. *Ath. Pol.* 42. 1.

There was an oligarchy, and those called the Bacchiads administered the city: The principal later sources on the Cypselid tyranny and the Bacchiad dynastic oligarchy which preceded it are Diod. Sic. VII. 9 and Nic. Dam. *FGrH* 90 FF 57–60, both derived from Ephorus; for a modern treatment see J. B. Salmon, *Wealthy Corinth* (Oxford UP, 1984), 55–74, 187–230.

they gave and received wives from one another: For the formulation (normally with *ekdidonai*) cf. II. 47. 1, Thuc. VIII. 21. Control of Corinth rested within an extended family: Diod. Sic. VII. 9. 4–6 writes of a series of kings descended from Bacchis, followed for ninety years by the appointment of an annual *prytanis* from their number.

Amphion ... had a daughter who was lame ... None of the Bacchiads was willing to marry her: In the story of the rise of Cypselus there is a large amount of legendary material. The lameness explains why Labda was a marginal Bacchiad who took a non-Bacchiad husband; and the name Labda was said to be a reflection of her deformity (*Etym. Magn.* 199. 23–31 βλαισός). ταύτην Βακχιαδέων γὰρ οὐδεὶς ἤθελε γῆμαι is a hexameter (cf. 92. η. 3), and Ogden, 57, wonders if Herodotus was using a verse source.

Eëtion son of Echecrates, a man from the village of Petra but by descent a Lapith and of the Caeneïds: No Petra is known in the territory of Corinth; *Barrington Atlas* 50 B 4 has a Petra in the far north of Thessaly; *Inventory* has no Petra in mainland Greece. Powell insisted that the meaning is 'a man of the people from Petra' (J. E. Powell, 'Notes on Herodotus – II', *CQ* 29 [1935], 159, against e.g. Macan, How and Wells); but γ. 1–2 confirms the alternative interpretation. The Lapiths were considered to be a pre-Greek people from Thessaly, and Eëtion was perhaps from a leading family of Larisa (M. Sordi, *La lega tessala fino ad Alessandro Magno* [Rome: Istituto Italiano per la Storia Antica, 1958], 26 n. 2); Caeneus was a woman who was changed into a man and whose skin was made impenetrable; when the part-human Centaurs became drunken at the wedding feast of the Lapith Pirithous they used pine trunks to hammer him into the ground (Pind. *Thren.* 6 Snell and Maehler; Ap. Rhod. *Argon.* I. 57–64; Ov. *Met.* XII. 171–535).

92. β. 2. about offspring: Cf. 82. 1 for an enquiry about (agricultural) fertility.

   As soon as he entered: Without waiting for him to make his enquiry; cf. I. 65. 2, to the Spartan Lycurgus.

   Eëtion, nobody honours you though you are highly honourable: An alliterative pun.

a boulder: A pun on Petra. The word is used again, without a pun, in VIII. 52. 2. On the image here, representing a depersonalised natural force, see Brock, *Greek Political Imagery*, 89. Falling stones from Acrocorinth will have been familiar: G. Roux, *REA* 65 (1963), 279–89 at 281–82 (in an article, followed by Nenci, which argues that a *kypsele* was a beehive and the 'chest' is a misinterpretation introduced by Pausanias).

   the men who rule monarchically: For *monarchos* as a pejorative term cf. Thgn. 51–2, Solon fr. 9. 3–4 West.

   bring justice to Corinth: If the Bacchiads are seen unfavourably, the man who will supplant them can be seen favourably.

92. β. 3. An eagle in the rocks: The name Eëtion was (wrongly) considered cognate with αἰετός ('eagle'); and 'in the rocks' is again a pun on Petra.

   a lion: Cf. the lion in Hipparchus' nocturnal vision (56. 1). This lion will be an enemy not only to the Bacchiads but in Herodotus' view of Cypselus to the Corinthians in general. See V. J. Gray, 'Herodotus and Images of Tyranny: The Tyrants of Corinth', *AJP* 117 (1996), 361–89 at 372–76, who regards both the boulder in the first oracle and the lion here as hostile; Brock, *Greek Political Imagery*, 89–90, who sees the lion as intentionally ambiguous.

   loosen the knees: I.e. kill (cf. Hom. *Il.* XI. 579, XIII. 360).

   Pirene: There was a fountain of that name in the agora, and another on Acrocorinth, the first wrongly believed to have been fed from the second (Strabo 379 / VIII. 6. 21: see Mee and Spawforth, 154–55, 159). In Pind. *Ol.* XIII. 61 Corinth is 'city of Pirene'.

   beetling Corinth: In Acrocorinth Corinth had an exceptionally high acropolis.

92. γ. 1. wishing to destroy the offpsring that was going to be born to Eëtion: The *motif* of trying but failing to kill the child of whom an oracular warning is given is a common one: cf. in Herodotus I. 107–13 (Cyrus of Persia); in Greek legend Oedipus (e.g. Soph. *O.T.* 711–22) and Paris (e.g. Euripides' *Alexander*: Loeb Euripides, *Dramatic Fragments*,

i, pp. 33–75); in the Roman world Romulus and Remus (e.g. Dion. Hal. *Ant. Rom.* I. 79. 1–11); in the Judaeo-Christian world Moses (*Exodus*, 1. 13–2. 10) and Jesus (*Matthew*, 2. 1–18). Herodotus gives us here a story elaborated with circumstantial details.

ten of their own number: Hornblower explains the number in terms of recitation and counting the men on the fingers (cf. VI. 63. 2).

92. γ. 2. thinking that they were asking out of good will towards the father: Cf. Hom. *Il.* IX. 256 with 312–3, where likewise apparent good will turns out not to be so.

92. γ. 3. by divine chance: Cf. III. 139. 3.

In his pity he handed him to a second man ... to all of the ten: In I. 109–12 Cyrus is handed from Harpagus to herdsman to wife.

92. δ. 1. evil for Corinth was bound to sprout: For what 'is bound' to happen cf. 33. 2 with commentary; for 'sprout' cf. III. 62. 4.

in a chest: For *kypsele* as chest cf. Paus. V. 17. 5 (what was said to be that very chest, dedicated at Olympia).

92. ε. 1. he was given the corresponding name Cypselus: In fact the name is derived from a bird: some kind of martin (Hornblower). In Nic. Dam. *FGrH* 90 F 57. 2–3 Eëtion took him away from Corinth, first to Olympia and afterwards to Celonae.

gained control of Corinth: For this use of ἔχω cf. VI. 36. 1. On Cypselus' seizure of power Herodotus gives no details. In 90 F 57. 4–6 Cypselus consulted Delphi, returned to Corinth, became polemarch and made himself popular through leniency to men who were fined; he became a demagogue, built up a body of supporters, killed the current *basileus* Patroclides or Hippoclides and was appointed *basileus* in his place.

92. ε. 2. He and his sons, but no longer the sons of his sons: Herodotus deals with Cyspelus' son Periander below, but does not recount the end of the dynasty. In III. 49–53 he has a story in which Periander had two sons and wanted to be succeeded by the younger, Lycophron: there was friction between them; Lycophron was banished to Corcyra; in the end Periander proposed that Lycophron should succeed him in Corinth and he should go to Corcyra, but to prevent that the Corcyraeans killed Lycophron. According to 90 F 60. 1 Periander was succeeded by his nephew Cypselus (called Psammetichus in 90 F 59. 4) but after a short time the tyranny was overthrown.

When Cypselus had become tyrant … by far the greatest number he deprived of their breath: In 90 F 57. 7–8 Cypselus was a mild and popular ruler; but Herodotus' Socles needs to paint an unfavourable picture of the tyranny.

92. ζ. 1. He ruled for thirty years: Arist. *Pol.* V. 1315 B 22–6 gives Cypselus 30 years + Periander 40½ (emended from 44) + 'Psammitichus' 3 = 73½; 90 F 57. 8 gives Cypselus 30 years. Diod. Sic. VII. 9. 3 dates Cypselus' *coup* 657/6, and Sosicrates (*ap.* Diog. Laert. I. 95) probably dated Periander's death 586/5. From time to time much lower dates have been proposed for this episode and other episodes in archaic Greek history but have not gained general acceptance; in this case an Athenian archon called Cypselus in 597/6 (M&L 6. *a*. 2 = *IG* i³ 1031. 7) is plausibly explained as a grandson of the Cypselus who founded the Corinthian tyranny and as confirming that the chronographers' dates are approximately correct.

wove his life well to the end: I.e. he died a natural death. In IV. 205. 1 Pheretime of Cyrene 'did not weave her life well to the end' but died a gruesome death.

Periander was at the beginning milder than his father, but became much more bloodthirsty than Cypselus: 'Much more bloodthirsty' echoes 92. α. 1. Periander is presented as cruel in other passages in Herodotus; and in 90 F 58 after the mild Cypselus of F 57 he is cruel without a mild beginning; cf. also Diog. Laert. I. 94–100. He was included among the Seven Wise Men of sixth-century Greece (cf. Diog. Laert. I. 97–9), but was excluded from some versions (including the earliest to survive, Pl. *Prt.* 343 A 1–5: cf. Diod. Sic. IX. 7).

when he had communicated through messengers with Thrasybulus the tyrant of Miletus: Thrasybulus was tyrant of Miletus when *c.* 600 at the end of a twelve-year war he achieved a special relationship between the Lydian kingdom and Miletus (I. 17–22); in I. 20 Periander was a particular *xeinos* of Thrasybulus, and gave him information which helped him towards that.

92. ζ. 2. he sent a herald to Thrasybulus to find out in what way he could … best take charge of the city: In Arist. *Pol.* III. 1284 A 26–33, V. 1311 A 20–2, Periander gives the advice to a messenger from Thasybulus. But this is a floating story, told also of Tarquinius Superbus of Rome and his son Sextus at Gabii (Livy I. 54. 5–8). For another non-verbal communication see 35. 3.

he repeatedly knocked off any of the ears which he saw standing above the rest: In VII. 10. ε Artabanus warns Xerxes that 'the god knocks off everything that stands above the rest'. On this image of the tyrant see Brock, *Greek Political Imagery*, 90 with 101 n. 62.

92. ζ. 3. destructive: Herodotus uses the cognate verb at I. 152. 3, VIII. 35. 1.

92. η. 1. he demonstrated every kind of evil: Cf. III. 158. 1 (with δόλον rather than κακότητα).

whatever Cypselus had left undone in killing and exiling: ε. 2 attributed to Cypselus exile, deprivation of property and killing: Hornblower suggests that deprivation of property is dealt with now in the story of the wives which follows.

on account of his own wife Melissa: Melissa was daughter of Procles tyrant of Epidaurus, and Periander had killed her: III. 50.

92. η. 2. to the Thesprotians on the River Acheron, to the oracle of the dead: At Ephyra in Epirus (*Barrington Atlas* 54 C 3, *Inventory* 345 no. 96), this was one of the four principal oracles of the dead; but the building once thought to have been that of the oracle (e.g. Mee and Spawforth, 382–84) now seems not to have been that (see Ogden, cited below, and *Inventory*). Paus. I. 17. 5 thought that the mention of the Acheron and Cocytus in Hom. *Od.* X. 513–5 before Odysseus' visit to the underworld was a reflection of this. On this oracle see D. Ogden, *Greek and Roman Necromancy* (Princeton UP, 2001), 17–21, 43–60 (on this story, 54–60).

about something deposited by a guest-friend: There is no obvious reason why this enquiry should have been directed to an oracle of the dead, and it may be that a desire to appease the ghost of Melissa has been lost from the story (E. Eidinow, *Oracles, Curses and Risk among the Ancient Greeks* [Oxford UP, 2007], 262 n. 60).

she was cold and naked; for the clothes … had not been burned: I.e. her clothes should have been burned with her body so that they would go to the underworld with her.

Periander had put his loaves into a cold oven: This is not relevant to her being cold and naked, but confirms her authenticity as Melissa by alluding to the necrophilia which is to be mentioned below.

92. η. 3. all the Corinthians' wives were to go out to the Heraeum: Hera was the goddess of marriage. Corinth's best-known Heraeum was

(conveniently for Periander) at a distance from the city, at the tip of the peninsula of Perachora, which projects into the Gulf of Corinth to the north (*Barrington Atlas* 58 D 1; Mee and Spawforth, 168–71) – but Macan and How and Wells supposed that the sanctuary of Hera Bounaea on Acrocorinth (Paus. II. 4. 7) is meant.

had them stripped all alike: In the presence of the bodyguards, shockingly deprived of their *aidos* (cf. I. 8. 3).

attendants: I.e. slaves.

into a pit and burned as he prayed to Melissa: The Greek is an almost complete hexameter (cf. 92. β. 1), and Ogden, 57, wonders if Herodotus was using a verse source.

92. η. 4. This shows you what tyranny is like: Socles returns with a bump to the point of the Cypselid narrative.

92. η. 5. We Corinthians were seized with great surprise: This repeats more simply and directly what was said in α. 1.

hearing you say this: What they said in 91. 2–3.

we call to witness and invoke against you the gods of the Greeks: Cf. Aristagoras of Miletus to Cleomenes of Sparta in 49. 3.

Know that the Corinthians do not approve of your doing that: Cf. Hom. *Il.* IV. 29, XVI. 443 (both Hera to Zeus), XXII. 181 (Athena to Zeus).

93. 1. Socles as an envoy from Corinth: In 91. 2 the Spartans had summoned 'messengers'.

invoking the same gods as he had invoked: Cf. 92. η. 5.

the Corinthians most of all would pine for the Pisistratids: Herodotus uses the compound ἐπιποθέω only here; but he uses the simple verb and noun a few times, and cf. Hom. *Il.* I. 240–1 (the Greeks at Troy will long for Achilles).

when the appointed days came round for them to be troubled by the Athenians: We cannot tell when Herodotus wrote this. However, friction was to break out already in 480 at the battle of Salamis (VIII. 94); *c.* 460 Corinth was Athens' first opponent in the First Peloponnesian War (Thuc. I. 103. 4, 105–6); and Corinth plays a leading role in Thucydides' narrative of the events leading up to the Peloponnesian War of 431 (Thuc. I. 24–88, 119–25). While the Corinthians succeeded in putting a stop to Sparta's plan to reinstate Hippias, Hippias' counter-warning failed to deter them (cf. Introduction, pp. 15–16).

93. 2. the man who had the clearest and most thorough knowledge of the oracles: Cf. 90. 2.

The rest of the allies had first kept themselves in silence: Cf. 92. *init.*

speaking freely: Speaking as a free man, i.e. using *isegorie* (cf. 78 with commentary on 37. 2); and also speaking in favour of freedom for Athens now.

burst into speech: Cf. I. 85. 4 (Croesus' hitherto dumb son), II. 2. 3 (the first intelligible utterance of boys never exposed to human voices).

not to take any drastic action concerning a Greek city: For 'drastic action' cf. 19. 2. 'Greek city' echoes 'the gods of the Greeks' in 92. η. 5, and foreshadows the need for Greek unity against the Persians when they invaded.

94. 1. This matter was brought to an end in that way: I.e. the Spartans bowed to the oppposition and abandoned their plan.

Amyntas of Macedon offered him Anthemus: In the northern part of Chalcidice (*Barrington Atlas* 50 D 4, *Inventory* 824–25 no. 562, arguing that originally it was a district and the town did not emerge until the fourth century). For Amyntas cf. 17–19; his connection with the Pisistratids may be due to their interest in Rhaecelus, to the west of Anthemus (How and Wells: see *Ath. Pol.* 15. 2; *Barrington Atlas* 50 C 4, not in *Inventory*).

Thessalians offered him Iolcus: Hornblower wonders whether the lack of the definite article means that the offer came simply from one group of Thessalians. Iolcus was on the north of the Gulf of Pagasae (*Barrington Atlas* 55 D 2, *Inventory* 719 no. 449); it is 'well-built' in Hom. *Il.* II. 712–3, and 'famous' as the place from which the Argonauts set out in Pind. *Pyth.* 4. 77, but was overshadowed by Pagasae in the classical period. For the Pisistratids' Thessalian connection see 63–4 with commentary.

went back to Sigeum: Cf. 65. 3, 91. 1.

which Pisistratus had taken by the spear from the Mytilenaeans … what he had taken over from Pisistratus: Herodotus has not given this information before: Hornblower sees the placing of the information here as inserting a further pause before Aristagoras finally arrives at Athens.

had installed as tyrant his bastard son Hegesistratus, born from an Argive woman: Pisistratus had three sons by his (unknown) Athenian

wife, Hippias, Hipparchus and Thessalus, and two by Timonassa of Argos, Iophon and Hegesistratus (Thuc. VI. 55. 1–2 cf. I. 20. 2; *Ath. Pol.* 17. 3 cf. Plut. *Cat. Mai.* 24. 8 wrongly supposed Thessalus to be an alternative name for Hegesistratus: see Davies, *APF* 445–50). As the son of a non-Athenian mother Hegesistratus would have been a bastard under Pericles' citizenship law of 451/0 (*Ath. Pol.* 26. 4), and Herodotus has wrongly applied that rule to this earlier period.

94. 2. For the Mytilenaeans and Athenians had made war for a long time: Herodotus backtracks, to report a war which began before 600 and was concluded when Hegesistratus reconquered Sigeum for Athens. On the chronology see especially D. L. Page, *Sappho and Alcaeus* (Oxford UP, 1955), 152–61.

Achilleum: On the Aegean coast south of Sigeum (*Barrington Atlas* 56 C 2, *Inventory* 1003–1004 no. 766). Sigeum was originally founded from Mytilene, and the Mytilenaeans used Achilleum after Sigeum was first captured by Athens ('the Mytilenaeans asking for the land back').

the land of Ilium belonged no more to the Aeolians ... the abduction of Helen: The Aeolian strand of the Greek people, from Boeotia and Thessaly, had settled on Lesbos and expanded on to the adjacent mainland. The Athenians appealed to the legend of the Trojan War, with an argument which did not support their own particular claim but may have been a rejoinder to a claim by the Mytilenaeans that they had a particular right to land in the Troad (Hornblower); for a more positive Athenian claim see Aesch. *Eum.* 397–402.

95. 1. the poet Alcaeus ... ran away and made his escape: Strabo 599–600 / XIII. 1. 38–9 says that the Athenians sent Phrynon, an Olympic victor of 636, to take possession of Sigeum; he notes Alcaeus' flight; and adds that Pittacus of Mytilene eventually killed the Athenian Phrynon, an event which Eusebius dated 607/6. Cf. also Diog. Laert. I. 74. Plut. *De Her. Mal.* 858 A–B complains that Herodotus mentions the flight of Alcaeus but not the heroic deed of Pittacus. For the duplication φεύγων ἐκφεύγει cf. IV. 23. 5.

but the Athenians gained possession of his arms: For the *motif* of abandoning one's shield, in order to escape more easily, which is not deployed uniformly in tone and *persona*, cf. Archil. fr. 5 West, Anac. fr. 381(b) *PMG*; and see J. M. Smith, 'Horace, *Odes*, 2. 7, and the Literary

Tradition of *Rhipsaspia'*, *AJP* 136 (2015), 243–80 (on Alcaeus, esp. 251–55).

hung them up in the Athenaeum at Sigeum: This is mentioned in fr. Z 105(b) *PLF* (from Strabo).

95. 2. Alcaeus wrote of this in a poem ... to Melanippus: See Page, *Sappho and Alcaeus*, 153, 300. Melanippus is addressed also in fr. B 6 *PLF.*

reconciled by Periander the son of Cypselus: Periander ruled *c.* 627–586 (cf. on 92. ζ. 1). After that Sigeum was regained by Mytilene, and Pisistratus had to reconquer it (94. 1).

each should occupy what they possessed: I.e. that the *status quo* should be preserved. Another possible basis for a settlement was that conquests made after a specified date should be returned (as in the Thirty Years' Peace of 446/5 and the Peace of Nicias of 421 between Athens and Sparta: Thuc. I. 115. 1, V. 18. 5–8); and a fourth-century formulation which provided opportunities for dispute was ἔχειν τὰ ἑαυτῶν, that each side should possess what belonged to it by right (see Rhodes, in P. de Souza and J. France [eds], *War and Peace in Ancient and Medieval History* [Cambridge UP, 2008], 6–27 at 24–27).

96. 1. When Hippias had gone from Sparta to Asia ... to make Athens subject to himself and Darius: Cf. the ambitions (for all of Greece) of the Spartan Pausanias in 32. As Athens had been happy to turn to Persia when Sparta was hostile, though it rejected Persia's demand for earth and water (73), Hippias was happy to turn to Persia when the possibility of reinstatement in Athens by Sparta had collapsed.

maligning: This is echoed in 97. 1, and διαβάλλειν is used twice more, to mean 'mislead' (as in 50. 2), in 97. 2.

Artaphernes: Satrap of Sardis (cf. 25. 1).

96. 2. the Athenians got to know of it and sent messengers to Sardis: It does not follow from this that the Athenians had become subject to Persia (believed by Hornblower; but see on 73. 3). Cf. the Spartans' message to Cyrus after his conquest of Lydia (I. 152. 3).

they had decided to be open enemies of the Persians: Whatever may have happened at the time of the earlier Athenian deputation, this marks a further stage in the developing hostility between Athens and Persia.

97. 1. it was at this critical point that Aristagoras of Miletus ... came to Athens: This at last picks up the narrative of the outbreak of the Ionian Revolt from 55 and 65. 5, and recapitulates also Aristagoras' visit to Sparta from (39–)49–51(–54).

for that city was the most preponderant of the others: On Athens' greatness cf. 66. 1, 78; and compare the judgment on Sparta and Athens in the time of Croesus (I. 56. 2).

Coming before the people: Hornblower notes that Herodotus says nothing about his approaching the council before the assembly, and suspects that Herodotus like Thucydides by omitting the council deliberately 'exaggerates Athenian impetuosity' (on Thucydides see Hornblower, 'Thucydides and the Athenian *Boule* (Council of Five Hindred)', in L. G. Mitchell and L. Rubinstein [eds], *Greek History and Epigraphy: Essays in Honour of P. J. Rhodes* [Swansea: Classical P. of Wales, 2009], 251–64, cf. his *A Commentary on Thucydides*, iii [Oxford UP, 2008], 23–31). However, it does not seem to me that any explanation is needed when Herodotus or Thucydides omits to mention the council in cases where the final decision rested with the assembly: '*cela va sans dire*' (Macan).

the good things in Asia: Cf. 49. 4–8.

Persian warfare ... would be easy to overcome: Cf. 49. 3–4.

97. 2. the Milesians were colonists of the Athenians ... they should rescue them: Cf. I. 143–6, and see on 65. 3. To the Spartans Aristagoras could claim only that as Greeks the Milesians were 'men of the same blood' (49. 3).

it is easier to mislead many than one ... thirty thousand Athenians: C. B. R. Pelling, in Irwin and Greenwood (eds), *Reading Herodotus*, 179–201 at 183–84, notes that he did not say anything false but led them to make an unwise decision. The quip should not be taken as a serious condemnation of Athenian democracy.

Cleomenes the Spartan on his own: In 51 Cleomenes had to be stiffened by his daughter Gorgo.

thirty thousand Athenians: Cf. VIII. 65. 1. R. Meiggs, 'A Note on the Population of Attica', CR^2 14 (1964), 2–3, used these and other texts to suggest that 30,000 may have been the number of citizens enrolled after Cleisthenes' reform.

97. 3. voted to send twenty ships to support the Ionians: A serious contribution, if they had fifty ships in all in the late 490s (VI. 89).

Melanthius ... distinguished in every way: Son of Phalanthus, if three *ostraka* of the early fifth century were used to vote against the same man (E. Vanderpool, in *Commemorative Studies ... T. L.Shear* [*Hesperia* Supp. 8, 1949], 394–412 at 400; S. Brenne, *Ostrakismos und Prominenz in Athen* [*Tyche* Supp. 3, 2001], 230–31), but no more is known about him.

These ships were the beginning of evil for the Greeks and barbarians: Cf. 28 with commentary. There the evil was for the Ionians; now the involvement of Athens and Eretria begins the story of evil for the Greeks and barbarians which was to culminate in 480–479. Plut. *De Her. Mal.* 861 A–D took exception to this judgment.

98–126. The Ionian Revolt (ii)
98. 1. Aristagoras sailed ahead: After the long digression surrounding Aristagoras' visits to Sparta (39–54) and Athens (55–97) Herodotus returns to the main narrative of the Ionian Revolt.

a plan from which no advantage ... to trouble King Darius: This further problem for the Persians in Asia Minor may in fact have benefited the Ionians somewhat; but the comment forms one more element in Herodotus' denunciation of the Ionians and their revolt.

He sent a man to Phrygia to the Paeonians ... by Megabazus: Cf. 14–15; and for Phrygia see 49. 5 with commentary.
98. 2. Aristagoras the tyrant of Miletus: For Aristagoras' position in Miletus see on 30. 2.
98. 3. Chios: Cf. on 30.6, 33. 1.
98. 4. Lesbos: Cf. on 26, 30. 6.

Doriscus: Near the mouth of the Hebrus, which flows into the Aegean north of the Chersonese (*Barrington Atlas* 51 G 3, *Inventory* p. 871 as a non-*polis* settlement). It features in 480 as a place where supplies were laid up for Xerxes' force (VII. 25. 2), and where he reviewed his force (VII. 58. 3–108. 1; location described 59. 1, which alleges that there had been a Persian garrison there ever since the Scythian expedition).

99. 1. the Athenians arrived in their twenty ships, bringing also five triremes of the Eretrians: The fact that the Athenians are credited with 'ships' but the Eretrians with 'triremes' suggests that the Athenian ships were not triremes (J. S. Morrison, J. F. Coates and N. B. Rankov, *The*

Athenian Trireme [Cambridge UP, ²2000], 42); and we cannot be sure of the one trireme in 85. 1 (see commentary). For triremes see on 32. 1; for Eretria see on 57. 1.

to gratify not the Athenians: Though in view of recent hostility between Athens and Chalcis (74–7) relations between Athens and Chalcis' neighbour and rival Eretria are likely to have been good.

the Milesians had helped them … when the Samians were giving support to the Chalcidians against the Eretrians and Milesians: This refers to the much-discussed Lelantine War, named after the Lelantine Plain between Chalcis and Etretria (*Barrington Atlas* 55 F 4), a war which according to Thuc. I. 15. 3 involved 'the rest of the Greeks' on one side or the other. It is probably to be dated to the late eighth century, and will not have been a unified war, but several local conflicts about the same time will have fitted into a coherent pattern of friendships and enmities. See J. Boardman, in *CAH²* III. i. 760–63; and for Samos cf. on 27. 1.

Aristagoras made a campaign against Sardis: For Sardis cf. on 11. 1, 25. 1. This campaign was perhaps in 498 (Rhodes, in *Herodotus and His World*, 71).

99. 2. He did not go on the campaign himself … designated others as generals of the Milesians: He continues to be regarded as in some sense in charge after his resignation of the tyranny. Hornblower suggests that he was appointing commanders of the whole force, who happened to be Milesians, by virtue of a position conferred on him by the Ionians (following V. B. Gorman: cf. on 37. 2). His not going on the campaign (though in VII. 8. β. 3 Xerxes states that he did go) can be regarded as a sign of cowardice: see E. Baragwanath, *Motivation and Narrative in Herodotus* (Oxford UP, 2008), 169 n. 20; and cf. 124. 1.

100. at Ephesus … at Coresus in the territory of Ephesus: For Ephesus as the starting-point for the march to Sardis see on 54. 1. *Barrington Atlas* 61 E 2 has only a Mount Koressos, inland from Ephesus; *Inventory* p. 1000 has Coresus as a non-*polis* settlement; it is shown to have been a harbour by Xen. *Hell.* I. 2. 7–10, *Hell. Oxy.* 1. 1 Chambers.

using the Ephesians as guides: Taking not the main road (cf. 54) but mountain paths, to surprise the enemy (How and Wells).

beside the River Caÿstrius: Cf. the simile of birds in the water

meadows in Hom. *Il.* II. 459–65 (with the same -ius form of the name). This is the river which reached the sea at Ephesus.

from there when they had crossed Tmolus they arrived: Tmolus (cf. I. 84. 3) is the mountain range running inland from Smyrna, to the north of the Caÿster valley, and Sardis was on its north flank. On the site of Sardis see G. E. Bean, *Aegean Turkey: An Archaeological Guide* (London: Benn, 1966), 259–71.

101. 1. engulfed the whole city: The earliest use of the verb in this sense (in the active it means 'allot', 'distribute'). Hornblower suggests that this use may have originated as a medical term, and notes that there is no sign that anything was amiss with Sardis when Histiaeus arrived there in VI. 1. 1.

101. 2. the River Pactolus ... debouches into the River Hermus: See *Barrington Atlas* 56: the Hermus reaches the sea north of Smyrna, on the south side of the peninsula at whose tip lay Phocaea. What is said here adds to what was said in I. 93. 1.

101. 3. the mountain called Tmolus: It is not clear why Herodotus uses 'the mountain called' of Tmolus only now.

102. 1. the temple of the local god Cybebe: This Cybebe was perhaps at first distinct from the Phrygian Cybele, the Great Mother. L. E. Roller, *In Search of God the Mother: The Cult of Anatolian Cybele* (U. of California P., 1999), esp. 44–53, 128–31, discusses the cult in Sardis and cites physical remains. But the most prominent surviving temple is of Artemis, who at Sardis was not identified with Cybebe (Bean, 265–68).

used as justification for their reciprocal burning of the temples in Greece: Cf. VI. 101. 3, also VII. 8. β. 3, 11. 2; but the Persians did not sack Delos (VI. 97) or Delphi (VIII. 36–9). After that in turn the Greeks and Macedonians used the burning of temples in Greece (and particularly in Athens) as justification for acts against the Persians: Polyb. II. 6. 13, cf. e.g. Arr. *Anab.* III. 18. 12.

provinces west of the River Halys: For the Halys as marking the eastern frontier of Phrygia cf. 52. 2. In the middle of the sixth century Croesus of Lydia had crossed the Halys at the beginning of his campaign against the Persians (I. 75).

102. 2. when they joined battle they were badly defeated: Plut. *De Her. Mal.* 861 C–D objects that no such defeat was mentioned by Charon of Lampsacus (= *FGrH* 262 F 10), but that is not sufficient reason to doubt the defeat. This narrative is continued in 116.

102. 3. Eualcides the general of the Eretrians: Not otherwise known.

    a victor in crown games: The crown games, victors at which were given a crown of foliage (cf. VIII. 26), were the Olympian, Pythian (at Delphi), Isthmian and Nemean. *Inventory* no. 370 at p. 654 overlooks Eualcides in stating that 'Only one Eretrian citizen is attested as victor in the Olympic Games … and none in any of the other major Panhellenic games'.

    had been much praised by Simonides of Ceos: This passage appears as Simonides fr. 518 in *PMG*, but Eualcides is not mentioned in any other surviving fragment.

103. 1. Afterwards the Athenians altogether abandoned the Ionians: Herodotus does not give a reason, and we can only guess. Dissatisfaction with the conduct of that campaign and/or prospects for further campaigns is one possibility. Some (e.g. Burn, *Persia and the Greeks*, 201) have inferred a change of policy in Athens from the election as archon for 496/5 of Hipparchus (Dion. Hal. *Ant. Rom.* VI. 1. 1), probably the Hipparchus son of Charmus who was to be ostracised in 488/7 (*Ath. Pol.* 22. 4) and perhaps a grandson of Hippias (Davies, *APF* 451–2). Or indeed, since our knowledge of Athens at this time is patchy, there may have been some other reason, of which no indication survives.

    It is possible that the Eretrians did not withdraw at the same time. Plut. *De Her. Mal.* 861 B–C (citing Lysanias of Mallus *FGrH* 426 F 1) protests that the Eretrians went out to meet the approaching Persian fleet, won a naval victory over the Cyprians, returned to the Aegean, attacked Sardis and thus succeeded in raising the Persian siege of Miletus. If there is any truth in that, it is seriously garbled: the war in Cyprus (104, 108–16) was not before but after the attack on Sardis, and the Cyprians were not on the Persian side but in revolt against them; and there is no reason to think that the Persians were besieging Miletus at this early stage. However, it may be true that the Eretrians did go to Cyprus with the Ionians (cf. Burn, *Persia and the Greeks*, 199–200, though he suggested an earlier campaign there, not mentioned by Herodotus).

103. 2. They sailed to the Hellespont … and they sailed out from the Hellespont…: I.e. they went both north and south.

Caria: Cf. on 37. 1, 88. 1.

Caunus: On the coast in the east of Caria (*Barrington Atlas* 65 A 4, *Inventory* 1120–21 no. 898). Herodotus in mentioning their capture by the Persians after the capture of Lydia distinguishes Caunus both from the Carians to their west and from the Lycians to their east, and reports that its people claimed to have originated in Crete (I. 171. 1, 172).

104. 1. and all the Cyprians voluntarily attached themselves to them: For Persia's acquisition of Cyprus in the time of Cambyses cf. on 31. 3. Cyprus acted as a bridge between the Greek world and the near-eastern world, and over a long period (as still today) its population was a mixture of people who were or perceived themselves as Greek and people who were or perceived themselves as non-Greek. The campaign in Cyprus probably occupied 497 and 496.

Amathus: On the south coast (*Barrington Atlas* 72 C 3, *Inventory* 1225 no. 1012).

the Medes: For the use of 'Medes' to denote the Persians cf. 77. 3 with commentary.

Onesilus … of Salamis, being son of Chersis son of Siromus son of Euelthon: Salamis was the largest city of Cyprus, on the east coast south of the north-eastern 'pan handle' (*Barrington Atlas* 72 D 2, *Inventory* 1229 no. 1020). The dynasty claimed to be descended from the legendary Teucer, who founded Cyprian Salamis when exiled from the Salamis in the Saronic Gulf (cf. Pind. *Nem.* 4. 46–8). While the name Siromus, given by the MSS, is attested in Cyprus, *L.G.P.N.* i. 147, 174, preferred the also-attested Eiromus. Euelthon was mentioned in IV. 162. 3–5 as involved with Cyrene and as dedicating at Delphi. For another brother see VIII. 11. 2.

105. 1. When it was announced to King Darius that Sardis had been captured and burned: Herodotus digresses from his narrative of the war in Cyprus, to which he will return in 108. 1.

he asked who were the Athenians: Cf. 13. 2, 73. 2.

he asked for his bow, took it and fitted an arrow and shot it to the heaven: While among the Greeks archers like other light-armed troops

were esteemed less than hoplites, the Persians valued archery as a skill (cf. I. 136. 2, Strabo 525 / XI. 13. 9), and for the King as an archer cf. e.g. III. 21. 3, 30. 1; depictions such as that of the Behistun Inscription which show the King carrying a bow (e.g. Kuhrt, *The Persian Empire*, i. 150 fig. 5.3; and see Briant, *From Cyrus to Alexander*, 210–16); and the important status of the King's bow-bearer (Darius' tomb: Kuhrt, ii. 500–501 fig. 11.14 with notes).

105. 2. Zeus: If the story were true, Darius would have prayed to Ahuramazda: Herodotus without qualms substitutes the supreme Greek god.

may it fall to me to be avenged on the Athenians: In 77. 1 the Athenians wanted revenge on the Chalcidians and Boeotians; in 79. 1. the Thebans consulted Delphi when wanting revenge on the Athenians. Editors have noted this use of the infinitive in prayers to Zeus in Hom. *Il.* II. 412–7, VII. 179–80, *Od.* XVII. 354–5, and Hornblower comments, 'Dareios knew his Homer!'

he instructed one of his attendants ... to say ... 'Master, remember the Athenians': Herodotus mentions this in VI. 94. 1 before the Marathon campaign of 490.

106. 1. he called into his presence Histiaeus the Milesian, whom he had now been detaining for a long time: 'Darius' in the relative clause is awkward, and is probably with Wilson to be deleted as an intrusion, but Stein's further deletion is unnecessary. For 'into his presence' cf. 13. 1, and for the opposite see 106. 5; Histiaeus' detention was mentioned in 23–5, 30. 2–3 (where §2 uses the same verb), 35. 2–36. 1; it was a known fact that Histiaeus did leave the Persian court and return to Ionia, but how much truth beyond that there is in this account is unclear.

your deputy, to whom you deputed Miletus: For the status of Aristagoras when he succeeded Histiaeus cf. 30. 2 with commentary.

from the other mainland: I.e. from Europe. Cf. IV. 118. 1, where the Scythians learn that Darius after overrunning everything on 'the other mainland' has bridged the Bosporus and crossed to 'this mainland'. Herodotus saw the clash between Greeks and Persians as a clash between Europe and Asia (I. 4. 4, 209. 1, IV. 89. 1, 143. 1, VII. 54. 2), while noting that some people divided the world into Europe, Asia and Libya (II. 16, IV. 36. 2–42. 2).

who will render justice to me for what they have done: Restating in different words what was said in 105. 1.

has deprived me of Sardis: Exaggerated: see on 101. 1.

106. 3. what a saying you have uttered: Cf. VII. 103. 1; also I. 8. 3, and 'what a thing you have done' in 23. 2. This is a Homeric expression (e.g. Hom. *Il.* XVI. 440).

great or small: 'The clever Greek adopts elaborate and stylised "orientalising" courtesies' (Hornblower, comparing 'both by day and by night' in 23. 2).

106. 4. uprooting me from the sea: Histiaeus left the sea to go to Myrcinus by his own choice (11. 2), and Darius uprooted him from Myrcinus when prompted by Artabazus (23–4).

106. 5. when they were out of my sight: The opposite of 'into my presence' (106. 1): cf. 24. 3.

106. 6. I shall not take off this tunic … until…: Cf. the vivid promises of Tissaphernes in Thuc. VIII. 81. 3, Cyrus the younger in Xen. *Hell.* I. 5. 3. In VII. 120 Xerxes first unfastens his belt at Abdera when fleeing from Athens in 480.

the largest island, Sardinia: At the time of the Persian conquest Bias of Priene had proposed that the Ionians should migrate *en masse* to Sardinia (I. 170. 2: 'the largest of all the islands'); when Aristagoras left Miletus he was to consider Sardinia as one of the places to go to (124); but in fact no Greek colonies there are known. At VI. 2. 1 Herodotus remarks on Histiaeus' failure to keep this promise. Hornblower notes that Sardinia has a slightly longer coastline than Sicily (both are larger than Corsica, mentioned in I. 165–7, and Cyprus), and that its mention here is perhaps prompted by the similarity of the name to Sardis.

107. Darius was persuaded and sent him away: Whatever Histiaeus himself intended, and whatever others thought his intentions to be, in Herodotus' account, after this conversation Histiaeus consistently is trusted by Darius: cf. commentary on 24. 4, and VI. 30.

Susa: Cf. 24. 4.

108. 1. While the message about Sardis … in all that time…: This will be 498–497, with the end of the Cyprian campaign, to be narrated below, in 496.

released: Cf. 35. 4.

A report reached Onesilus of Salamis ... that Artybius ... was expected by ship in   Cyprus with a large Persian force: Herodotus returns to the main narrative, from which he digressed at the beginning of 105.

108. 2. The Ionians without spending long in deliberation: This is Herodotus' first indication that decisions were made not just by Aristagoras but by the Ionian *koinon*: cf. 109. 3, VI. 7.

the Persians crossed in ships from Cilicia: Cf. on 49. 6.

in the ships the Phoenicians sailed round the peninsula called the Keys of Cyprus: The Phoenicians provided the Persians with their main navy in the eastern Mediterranean: VII. 89. 1, 96. 1; cf. I. 143. 1. The Keys of Cyprus were in the far north-east, at the tip of the pan handle: Strabo 682 / XIV. 6. 3 gives the name to a group of off-shore islands, and *Barrington Atlas* 72 F 1 gives it both to the peninsula and to the islands. Presumably the Phoenicians sailed to Salamis (cf. 112. 1).

109. 1. we Cyprians give you the choice which you prefer to attack: This is polite to those who have come to support the Cyprians, but surprising: we should not expect the Ionians who have come as a naval force, and they do not choose, to hand over their ships to the Cyprians and themselves to fight on land. When the Greeks appealed to Gelon of Syracuse to support them against the Persians' invasion of 480, he said he would do so if allowed to command either at sea or on land (VII. 160. 2).

109. 3. what you have suffered as slaves: Responds to the Cyprians' 'freedom of Ionia and Cyprus' in §2.

110. the plain of Salamis: There is a large plain in the south-east of the island: see *Barrington Atlas* 72.

Solians: Soli was on the north coast of the island, towards the west end (*Barrington Atlas* 72 B 2, *Inventory* 1229–30 no. 1021).

111. 1. Artybius rode a horse which had been taught to rear up opposite a hoplite: Cf. for Greek hoplites 30. 4 and for Persian cavalry 49. 3. This episode echoes the legend of Myrtilus, the charioteer who for his master Pelops sabotaged the chariot of Oenomaus (e.g. Pind. *Ol.* 1); and the dialogue slows down the narrative (cf. Introduction, p. 14).

an armour-bearer of Carian race: Not named, and in §4 he declares himself to be a nonentity. Hornblower remarks that Caria was not cavalry country (*aphippos*, Xen. *Hell.* III. 4. 12); but the Carians had experienced Persian cavalry, and what this man does is act on foot against a Persian horse. Herodotus uses *hypaspistes* (literally, 'man under a shield') only in this episode: in the Macedonian army of Alexander the Great the *hypaspistai* were an élite body among the infantry (e.g. Arr. *Anab.* II. 4. 3). Darius had a faithful groom when he seized the Persian throne (III. 85–7).

112. 1. both on foot and with the ships: As in the battle of the Eurymedon *c.* 469 (Thuc. I. 100. 1) and the battle near Cyprian Salamis *c.* 450 (Thuc. I. 112. 4), both of which will have been known to Herodotus when he wrote (Macan).

    the Ionians excelled on that day ... and of them the Samians performed best: Contrast the battle of Lade in 49<u>5</u>/4, where the Samians would desert and the Ionians would be defeated (VI. 11–17). For 'performed best' cf. the Aeginetans after the battle of Salamis (VIII. 93. 1): Hornblower wonders whether there was a formal award after the battle.

112. 2. with a sickle: A weapon characteristic of the Lycians and Carians (VII. 92–3).

    cut off the horse's hooves: The fore hooves (Macan).

113. 1. Stesenor, tyrant of Curium: Curium was on the south coast, west of Amathus (*Barrington Atlas* 72 B 3, *Inventory* 1227 no. 1016). A Stasanor from Soli was a commander under Alexander the Great (Diod. Sic. XVII. 81. 3, XVIII. 3. 3); Macan notes that the traitor is a 'tyrant' but Onesilus (cf. 104. 1) and Aristocyprus of Soli (113. 2) are 'kings'. C. Gallavotti, *Kadmos* 16 (1977), 160–63, restored Stasanor as patronymic in an inscription of Curium, but that restoration is doubted by T. B. Mitford, *The Inscriptions of Kourion* (Philadelphia: American Philosophical Society, 1971), 377–82 no. 218.

    these Curians say that they are colonists of Argos: Argos (see on 49. 8) was not much involved in the colonising activity of the archaic period, but this is an early claim, and in *IG* iv 583 (shortly after 331) Argive ancestry was claimed for a Cyprian Nicocreon.

the war chariots of the Salaminians: See P. A. L. Greenhalgh, *Early Greek Warfare: Horsemen and Chariots in thw Homeric and Archaic Ages* (Cambridge UP, 1973), esp. 17–18: war chariots were 'heroic property' in Homer and Geometric art, but they had no place in Greek warfare after the end of the Mycenaean period except in Cyprus, where they survived in proximity to oriental chariot-using peoples.

113. 2. Onesilus son of Chersis, who had brought about the revolt of the Cyprians: This was stated in 104, and it is a little surprising to find the details repeated here, so soon afterwards.

the king of Soli Aristocyprus son of Philocyprus: For Soli cf. on 110; the names point to a sense of Greek Cyprian solidarity.

whom Solon the Athenian ... praised most of the tyrants in his poetry: Cf. Solon fr. 19 West, quoting this passage, the *Life of Aratus* and Plut. *Sol.* 26. 2–4 (the last including six lines of a poem, which mention Soli and address its ruler as *anasson*, 'lording'); we may guess that Solon like Plutarch, if he used any other term, will have labelled him 'king' rather than 'tyrant'. On Herodotus and poets see Introduction, p. 13.

114. 1. The Amathusians, because he had besieged them: Cf. 104. 3–105. 1, 108. 1.

114. 1–2. As the head was hanging ... they should take down the head and bury it, and sacrifice to Onesilus as a hero every year: The decapitation seemed shocking to Herodotus (cf. that of Histiaeus, VI. 30. 1); the subsequent heroisation was intended to assuage Onesilus' hostility (cf. Parker, *On Greek Religion*, 117). For another herosiation cf. 47. 2.

a swarm of bees penetrated it and filled it with a honeycomb: Bees were sometimes perceived positively (cf. Theoc. *Id.* 7. 78–9); but in Plut. *Cleom.* 39, when a snake kept birds off the body of Sparta's hellenistic king Cleomenes III, his heroisation was prevented when it was pointed out that bees appeared in dead cattle. See N. Horsfall, *Virgil, Aeneid 7: A Commentary* (*Mnemosyne* Supp. 198, 1999), 87–88, on Virg. *Aen.* VII. 64–70, remarking that bees are not automatically a good or a bad omen.

consulted an oracle: We are not told which.

things would turn out better: Cf. 82. 1.

115. 1. even to my time: Cf. on 45. 2.

the other cities of the Cyprians were under siege: This takes us beyond what Herodotus has said hitherto. An inscription cited by How and Wells, which records a siege of inland Idalium (*Barrington Atlas* 72 C 2, *Inventory* 1225–26 no. 1013) by Medes and Citians, is now dated later (*IChS* 217); but the Persian siege mound at Paphos has been excavated (F. G. Maier, *RDAC* 1967, 30–49 at 39–42, 1968, 86–93 at 86–88, 1969, 33–42 at 33–34).

Salamis, which the Salaminians handed over to their former king Gorgus: Cf. 104. Since Gorgus was pro-Persian his reinstatement amounted to submission to the Persians; he was still ruling in 480 (VII. 98).

digging under the wall round it: Cf. the Persian siege of Barca in Libya (IV. 200).

116. Daurises ... and Hymaeës and Otanes ... married to daughters of Darius: This episode is the only appearance of the first two, both of whom died at the end of it; for Otanes see 25–8, but we hear no more of him after this episode. The Achaemenids were polygamous and were remarkably philoprogenitive, and there was a very large pool of men born in or married into the royal family who could be given positions by the King (D. M. Lewis, *Sparta and Persia* [Leiden: Brill for U. of Cincinnati, 1977], 23–24).

pursued those of the Ionians ... drove them pell-mell into their ships: This continues the Ionian narrative from 102.

117. Dardanus ... Abydus, Percote, Lampsacus and Paesus: Dardanus was at the south-west end of the Hellespont (*Barrington Atlas* 51 G 4, *Inventory* 1006–7 no. 774), Abydus north of Dardanus (51 G 4, 1002–3 no. 765), Percote north-east of Abydus (51 H 4, 1013 no. 788), Lampsacus north-east of Percote (51 H 4, 986–88 no. 748) and Paesus north-east of Lampsacus (51 H 4, 990–91 no. 755). Some at least of these were Milesian colonies.

These he took one on each day: The distances between the cities are very short. The briskness of this narrative matches the briskness of his achievement (cf. 26, and Introduction, p. 14).

Parium: East of Paesus (*Barrington Atlas* 52 A 4, *Inventory* 991–92 no. 756).

the Carians ... had revolted against the Persians: For the Carians see on 37. 1, 88. 1.

118. 1. what are called the White Pillars and the River Marsyas, which flows from the Idrian land and debouches into the Maeander: The river flows from the south into the Maeander (*Barrington Atlas* 61 F 2–G 2–3). The White Pillars have not been located with certainty, but one possibility is Gerga (61 G 2; not in *Inventory*). The region of Idrias was on the upper Marsyas (61 G 3); see *Inventory* 1119 no. 892 for a city Idrias or Edrias (not marked in *Barrington Atlas*).

118. 2. When the Carians were gathered there: There was a Carian *koinon*, centred on Mylasa (cf. on 37. 1): see S. Hornblower, *Mausolus* (Oxford UP, 1982), 55–62.

Pixodarus son of Mausolus, a man of Cindya: The names recur among the fourth-century satraps of Caria, when it had become a province of the Persian empire separated from Lydia; they were presumably descended from or otherwise related to these men, and Hornblower, *Mausolus*, 48, suggests that the family claimed a hereditary 'kingship' over Caria. Here, however, Herodotus credits him simply with one suggestion among several; for unsuccessful advisers cf. on 36. 2. Cindya was between Mylasa and Halicarnassus (*Barrington Atlas* 61 F 3, *Inventory* 1122–23 no. 902).

the Cilician king Syennesis: For Cilicia cf. on 49. 6. This family, again continuing to the fourth century, seems to have occupied a similar position in Cilicia to the family of Pixodarus in Caria. Hornblower offers a possible family tree, making the Syennesis of I. 74. 3 grandfather of the Syennesis here and in VII. 98 (cf. Aesch. *Pers.* 326–7).

fight with the river behind them ... not have the possibility of fleeing to their rear: An incentive to fight valiantly, but a problem if they were defeated. Cf. Cyrus' campaign against the Massagetae (I. 205–7); also the manoeuvres before the battle of Plataea in 479 (IX. 36–37. 1).

118. 3. That opinion did not prevail: For the expression cf. 36. 4.

119. 1. at the River Marsyas the Carians attacked the Persians: Not at or near the White Pillars, but presumably near the junction of the Marsyas and the Maeander (How and Wells).

There fell of the Persians about two thousand men and of the

Carians about ten thousand: The numbers, at least of the Carians, must be greatly exaggerated.

119. 2. the sanctuary of Zeus Stratius at Labraünda: North of Mylasa, in the mountains south of the Maeander and west of the Marsyas, and linked to Mylasa by a sacred way (*Barrington Atlas* 61 F 3, not in *Inventory*; sacred way Strabo 659 / XIV. 2. 23). See G. E. Bean, *Turkey Beyond the Maeander* (London: Murray, ²1989), 38–47.

Only the Carians of those whom we know perform sacrifices to Zeus Stratius: I.e. Zeus of armies. On this cult at Labraünda see A. Laumonier, *Les Cultes indigènes en Carie* (BEFAR 188. Paris: De Boccard, 1958), 45–101; the same epithet is attested also in northern Asia Minor (Laumonier, 61–62). For 'whom we know' cf. 49. 5.

would do better to leave Asia altogether: For migration to the west cf. Aristagoras in 124. 2; also I. 164–7 (the Phocaeans after the Persian conquest). VI. 22–3 (the Samians after the battle of Lade), VIII. 62. 2 (Themistocles' threat in 480).

120. the Milesians and their allies: probably no great significance should be seen in Herodotus' writing this rather than 'the Ionians': Milesian casualties will be stressed below.

The Persians attacked ... defeated even more badly than before: There is no indication of where this battle was fought.

121. they set an ambush on the road in the land of Pidasa: The MSS have Pid- here but Ped- in I. 175–176. 1, VI. 20 (but Hornblower favours Pid- there), VIII. 104–105. 1; and Pidasa, on Mount Grion between Mylasa and Miletus (*Barrington Atlas* 61 F 3, *Inventory* 1131–32 no. 925) makes more sense in this context than Pedasa near Halicarnassus (61 E 3, 1131 no. 923). In either case the toponym is regularly neuter plural: *Inventory* does not record this passage or the singular form used here under either Pedasa or Pidasa. It may be that the form used here means 'the land of Pidasa', as in my translation; or G. E. Bean and J. M. Cook, 'The Halicarnassus Peninsula', *BSA* 50 (1955), 85–171 at 150 n. 272, suggested ἐπὶ <Πη>δάσοισι, which we could modify to ἐπὶ <Πι>δάσοισι.

Daurises, Amorges and Sisimaces: For Daurises cf. 116–118. 1. An Amorges, bastard son of Pissuthnes satrap of Lydia, was prominent

at the end of the fifth century (e.g. Thuc. VIII. 5. 5); Sisimaces is the Ziššamakka of the Persepolis fortification tablets (D. M. Lewis, 'Persians in Herodotus', in *The Greek Historians* ... *A. E. Raubitschek* [Stanford: ANMA Libri, 1985], 101–17 at 113 = his *Selected Papers in Greek and Near Eastern History* [Cambridge UP, 1997], 345–61 at 356).

Myrsus the son of Gyges: Left unexplained by Herodotus, but presumably from the Lydian royal family: cf. Candaules son of Myrsus, the last of the Heraclidae (I. 7. 4), and Gyges, the first of the Mermnadae (I. 8. 1). The Myrsus of III. 122. 1 will be the same man or a relative.

Heraclides son of Ibanollis, a man of Mylasa: Olliatus son of Ibanollis of Mylasa, one of the tyrants deposed at the beginning of the Ionian Revolt (37. 1), was probably a brother; but Olliatus collaborated with the Persians while Heraclides opposed them. The contemporary explorer Scylax of Caryanda (cf. IV. 44) wrote about Heraclides (*FGrH* 709 T 1).

122. 1. Hymaeës ... took Cius in Mysia: After disposing of Daurises, the first of the three commanders mentioned in 116, Herodotus turns to the second. Cius (*Barrington Atlas* 52 E 4, *Inventory* 982–83 no. 745) was said to be another colony of Miletus.

122. 2. all the Aeolians who occupy the land of Ilium: For the Aeolians and for their claim to the land around Troy cf. 94. 2.

the people of Gergis, who are the survivors of the ancient Teucrians: Cf. VII. 43. 2. The city was inland, east of Troy (*Barrington Atlas* 56 D 2, *Inventory* 1008 no. 777). For the Teucrians cf. 13. 2; whatever the truth of the claim, Gergis was evidently a non-Greek city.

Hymaeës died of illness in the Troad: Cf. the Persian Mazares in I. 161, the Spartan Aristodemus in VI. 52. 2, Artachaeës the Persian in VII. 117. 1.

123. Artaphernes the governor of Sardis and Otanes the third general were appointed: For Artaphernes cf. 25. 1 and his subsequent appearances in the narrative. If even he was 'appointed', the orders must have come from Darius.

Clazomenae in Ionia and Cyme in Aeolis: Clazomenae (*Barrington Atlas* 56 D 5, *Inventory* 1076–77 no. 847) was listed among the Ionian cities in I. 142. 3, and appeared at I. 16. 2, II. 178. 2, and cf. I. 51; for Cyme cf. 37. 1.

124. 1. When the cities had been captured: Persia's recovery of the cities, in parallel to the campaign in Cyprus (cf. on 104. 1), probably occupied 497 and 496. We can date Aristagoras' time at Myrcinus to 496/5 from Thuc. IV. 102. 2–3, schol. Aeschin. II. *Embassy* 31 (67a Dilts: emend to obtain 465/4 as the date of the Athenian disaster); Herodotus is probably alluding to the Athenian disaster in IX. 75.

after throwing Ionia into confusion and stirring up great trouble: A very forthright denunciation, but it is consistent with Herodotus' view of the Ionian Revolt as a disaster (cf. 28 with commentary), and in his narrative Herodotus has presented the Revolt as simply the work of Aristagoras, incited by Histiaeus (see particularly 30, 35–6).

he planned to run away: For the expression cf. VIII. 4. 1, 18, 75. 2, 97. 1, 100. 1.

it seemed to him impossible to surpass King Darius: The Persians did not keep large armies in the provinces, so a revolt could get off to a promising start, but in time they could bring in irresistible forces to quell a revolt.

124. 2. he called together his partisans to deliberate: Cf. Aristagoras in 36. 1 (where the simple *stasiotai* is used; this compound is used in 70. 2).

some secure refuge: Cf. VIII. 51. 2, IX. 15. 2, 96. 3, using κρησφύγετον always of a fortified stronghold.

to Sardinia for a colony: In 106. 6 Histiaeus proposed to conquer Sardinia for Darius. For flight to the west cf. on 119. 2.

to Myrcinus of the Edonians … a gift from Darius: Cf. 11 (Histiaeus asked Darius for Myrcinus), 23. 1–25. 1 (Megabazus induced Darius to take Histiaeus to Susa). We are not told what happened to Myrcinus after Histiaeus left it; but, whereas going to Sardinia would amount to 'running away', going to Myrcinus might be seen as going to a place from which Aristagoras could watch developments and perhaps build up a position from which he could later negotiate (cf. Hecataeus' advice with regard to Leros, in 125).

125. Hecataeus son of Hegesandrus, a man who was a prose-writer: Cf. 36. 2, where he advises against embarking on the Ionian Revolt, and is given the same description but not his patronymic; also II. 143. 1. VI. 137. 1 repeats the patronymic and refers to his *logoi*.

build a fort on the island of Leros … set out from there and return to Miletus: South-west of Miletus, and about 35 miles (56 km) from it (*Barrington Atlas* 51 D 3, *Inventory* 758 no. 504). It is said to have been a Milesian colony, and was being occupied by settlers or dissidents from Miletus in 454/3 (*IG* i³ 269. vi. 19–20, the first of the tribute quota lists of Athens' Delian League). This is a variation on the *motif* of the warner who ought to be heeded but is not (cf. Introduction, pp. 15–16).

126. 1. Miletus he deputed to Pythagoras: The name is fairly common, and we know nothing else about this man. To the end Aristagoras remained in some sense in charge of Miletus (cf. on 37. 2); 'depute' and the cognate noun were used of Histiaeus' appointment of him (30. 2, 106. 1, 4, 5).

taking everybody who was willing: This was not just the flight of a cowardly individual, but was akin to the (re)founding of a colony.

126. 2. when he set out from there Aristagoras and his army perished at the hands of the Thracians: Cf. Thuc. IV. 102. 2, stating that Aristagoras 'when he was in flight from King Darius' had tried to colonise Nine Ways/Amphipolis (*Barrington Atlas* 51 B 3, *Inventory* 819–20 no. 553) but was driven out by the Edonians (for Myrcinus as an Edonian city see on 11. 2).

besieging a city when the Thracians were willing to evacuate it under truce: The lack of detail is frustrating (the city may have been Nine Ways: Macan), and Maas suspected a lacuna. Whether or not that is right, there is no major break between the end of book V and the beginning of book VI, which starts with the typical rounding-off sentence, 'Aristagoras who had caused the revolt of Ionia died in that way' and then picks up the story of Histiaeus from 106–7 (VI. 1. 1). On the division of Herodotus' history into books see Introduction, pp. 1–2.

INDEX

This index is not exhaustive: in particular, it omits some persons, places and subjects mentioned only in a context in which there are other names or words for which readers are more likely to search. References are to pages, mostly in the Introduction and translation; references to the Commentary are sometimes added to guide readers to discussions of a subject or to references which could not be inferred from the translation. In some cases a principal reference is given first, in bold type.